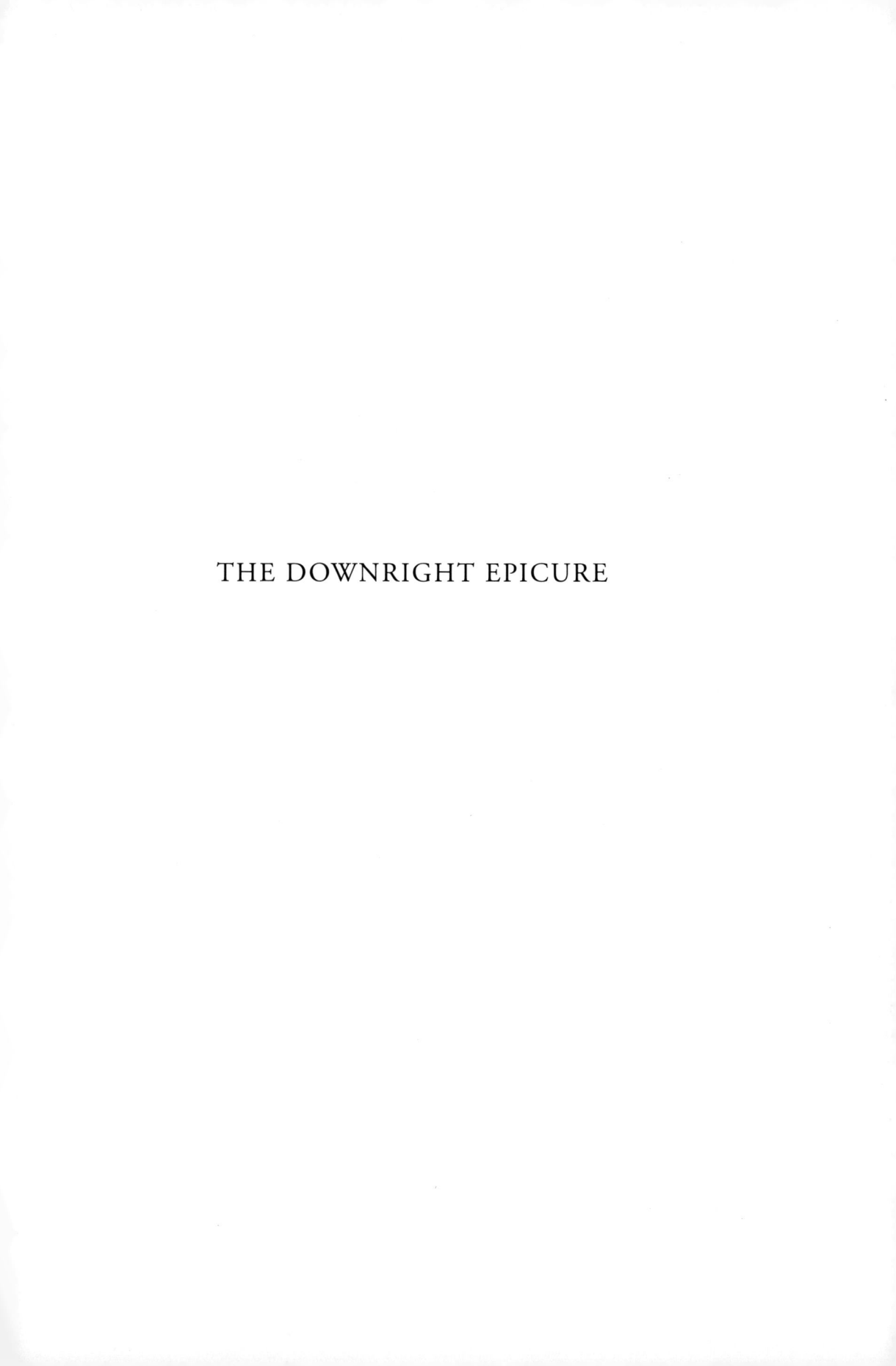

THE DOWNRIGHT EPICURE

BUNYARD'S FRUIT TREES

Three Excellent Apples

SANSPAREIL   EDWARD VII.   ROSS NONPAREIL

Write for our Illustrated Catalogue of Fruits, full of valuable information.

GEORGE BUNYARD & Co., Ltd.,
Royal Nurseries, MAIDSTONE.

Frontispiece. 'Bunyard's Fruit Trees'. This advertisement appeared as the back cover of *The Garden*, LXXXV, no. 2583, Saturday, 21 May 1921. The same plate had appeared as Coloured Plate no. 1437 (Hudson & Kearns, Ltd., London, S. E.), 'Three Good Apples', the apples provided by and discussed by George Bunyard in *The Garden*, LXXV, no. 2084, Saturday, 28 October 1911, pp. 523–4.

The
DOWNRIGHT EPICURE

Essays on
EDWARD ASHDOWN BUNYARD
(1878–1939)

edited by

EDWARD WILSON

The down-right Epicure plac'd heav'n in sense
And scornd pretence.

Henry Vaughan, 'The World', *Silex Scintillans*, I, 1650

PROSPECT BOOKS
2007

First published in Great Britain in 2007 by Prospect Books,
Allaleigh House, Blackawton, Totnes, Devon TQ9 7DL.

© 2007 Edward Wilson and the named contributors.

The editor and the several authors, Edward Wilson and those named in the table of contents, assert their right to be identified as editor and authors of this work in accordance with the Copyright, Designs & Patents Act 1988.

No part of this publication may be reproduced, stored in a retrieval system, or transmitted in any form or by any means, electronic, mechanical, photocopying, recording or otherwise, without the prior permission of the copyright holders.

BRITISH LIBRARY CATALOGUING IN PUBLICATION DATA:
A catalogue entry of this book is available from the British Library.

Typeset and designed by Tom Jaine.

ISBN 1-903018-48-x; 978-1-903018-48-4

Printed and bound in Great Britain by the Cromwell Press, Trowbridge, Wiltshire.

Contents

Illustrations	7
Notes on Contributors	8
Acknowledgements	9
Preface	11
Amuse-Gueule *Arnd Kerkhecker*	15

CHAPTER ONE
Edward Ashdown Bunyard: A Biographical Essay — 17
Edward Wilson

CHAPTER TWO
Edward Bunyard and Literature — 75
Edward Wilson

CHAPTER THREE
Edward Bunyard and Norman Douglas — 109
Edward Wilson

CHAPTER FOUR
Bunyard on Xenia — 157
Simon Hiscock

CHAPTER FIVE
Bunyard and the Saintsbury Club — 169
Alan Bell

CHAPTER SIX
The Epicurean Context of Edward Bunyard 175
Richard Sharp

CHAPTER SEVEN
Edward Bunyard the Epicurean Nurseryman 189
Joan Morgan

CHAPTER EIGHT
Edward Bunyard the Pomologist 231
Joan Morgan

CHAPTER NINE
Edward Bunyard the Rosarian 271
Joan Morgan

CHAPTER TEN
Edward Bunyard the Committee Man 305
Joan Morgan

The Apple War 343
U. A. Fanthorpe

Bibliography of the Publications of Edward Ashdown Bunyard 345
Edward Wilson

Bibliography of Articles and Obituaries on
    Edward Ashdown Bunyard 381
Edward Wilson

APPENDIX
Edward Bunyard: In Memoriam 385
Maurice Healy

Index 389

Illustrations

'Bunyard's Fruit Trees', advertisement on the back cover of
The Garden, LXXXV, no. 2583, Saturday, 21 May 1921.　　*Frontispiece*

Figure 1. 'Mr. Edward A. Bunyard', *The Journal of Horticulture
and Home Farmer*, 1910.　　16

Figure 2. The Bunyard Family at Oakwood Lodge, Ide Hill,
Sevenoaks, *c.* 1898.　　29

Figure 3. 'Mr. Edward A. Bunyard', *The Gardeners' Magazine*, 1912.　　30

Figure 4. 'Edward A. Bunyard, F.L.S.', *The Journal of
Pomology and Horticultural Science*, 1940.　　30

Figure 5. The cover of the first issue of *The New Flora and Silva*,
published by Dulau, listing 'The Anatomy of Dessert' by EAB.　　74

Figure 6. Page 109 of the second issue of *The New Flora and Silva*
displaying the second extract from *The Anatomy of Dessert*.　　74

Figure 7. Detail of the dustwrapper of *The Anatomy of Dessert*,
as issued by Dulau in 1929.　　108

Figure 8. The dustwrapper of *The Anatomy of Dessert*,
as published in America in 1934.　　108

Notes on Contributors

ALAN BELL, a member of the Saintsbury Club, is a former Librarian of Rhodes House, University of Oxford, and of the London Library. In retirement he continues research and writing on nineteenth-century English literature.

U.A. FANTHORPE was awarded the Queen's Gold Medal for Poetry in 2003, and was appointed a C.B.E. in 2001.

SIMON HISCOCK is Reader in Botany in the School of Biological Sciences, University of Bristol, and Director of the University of Bristol Botanic Garden. He was formerly a Senior Research Fellow at Worcester College, Oxford.

ARND KERKHECKER was Fellow and Tutor in Classics at Worcester College, Oxford, from 1995–2003, and is now Ordinarius für Klassische Philologie at the University of Berne, Switzerland.

JOAN MORGAN is the author, with Alison Richards, of *A Paradise out of a Common Field* (1990), and *The Book of Apples* (1993; revised edition, *The New Book of Apples*, 2002) She is at present working on a book about pears. She is closely associated with the Defra National Fruit Collections at Brogdale, Kent. She is vice-chairman of the Royal Horticultural Society Fruit and Vegetable Committee and Chairman of the RHS Fruit Trials Sub-Committee.

RICHARD SHARP is an ecclesiastical historian. From 1995–2002 he was a Senior Research Fellow and, latterly, Garden Master, at Worcester College, Oxford. He now lives in Northumberland and has recently become Honorary Secretary of the Literary and Philosophical Society of Newcastle.

EDWARD WILSON is Fellow and Tutor in Medieval English Literature at Worcester College, Oxford, where he is also the Garden Master.

Acknowledgements

Specific debts in the making of this book are acknowledged as they occur. None the less, I should like to express particular gratitude to: Mr Ian Jackson, of Berkeley, California, who combines in his knowledge the panoptic and the microscopic; Miss Katharine Bunyard, niece of Edward Bunyard and daughter of his brother Norman, who readily answered my queries; Mrs Freda Cox of the Mediterranean Garden Society and Dr Wilhelm Meusburger, organizer of the Norman Douglas Symposia at Bregenz, whose requests for papers concentrated the mind wonderfully; and Ms U. A. Fanthorpe who generously allowed the re-publication of her poem 'The Apple War' first published in her collection *Queueing for the Sun* (2003).

Two libraries have been exceptional in their welcome and helpfulness – Dr Brent Elliott and the Lindley Library of the Royal Horticultural Society, and Mr Theo Dunnet of the Radcliffe Science Library, Oxford.

Ms Sara Smith not only typed my contributions with exemplary accuracy, but made adopted suggestions and caught infelicities and errors.

I have attempted, not always successfully, to trace the holders of copyright material. I am indebted to The Society of Authors as the Literary Representative of the Estate of Norman Douglas for permission to publish letters of Norman Douglas to EAB, and to the following in whose keeping they are preserved: the Vorarlberger Landesbibliothek, Bregenz, Austria; the National Library of Scotland; the Department of Special Collections, Charles E. Young Research Library, the University of California, Los Angeles; Professor Arthur S. Wensinger of Higganum, Connecticut, U.S.A.; the Beinecke Rare Book and Manuscript Library, Yale University; the Henry W. and Albert A. Berg Collection of English and American Literature, the New York Public Library. An extract from a letter of Vita Sackville-West is published courtesy of the Lilly Library, Indiana University, Bloomington, Indiana; the correspondence between Ian Parsons and EAB, now in the Chatto & Windus Archive at Reading University, copyright of which is in the author's estate, is reproduced by permission of the Random House Group. The International Wine and Food Society gave permission to reprint

Maurice Healy's obituary of EAB; Mrs Alyson Price, Archivist of the Harold Acton Library, the British Institute of Florence, kindly told me of Bunyard's letter to Edward Hutton and sent me a Xerox of it; Ms Claudia Wolfers, Artistic Trustee of the Estate of John Nash, gave permission for quotation of extracts from the letters of John Nash now in the Hyman Kreitman Research Centre, Tate Britain.

E. W.

Preface

Who knows whether the best of men be known? or whether there be not more remarkable persons forgot, than any that stand remembered in the known account of time?

Sir Thomas Browne, *Urne-Burial*, 1658, chapter v.

On 19 October 1939 Edward Bunyard died by his own hand. He had been, with his brother, Norman, in charge of one of the world's great nurseries; one of England's finest students and growers of old varieties of apples and roses; an inimitably distinctive writer on food and wine; and a great friend of the writer, Norman Douglas. Within a year of his death his roses (and later his apples), his outstanding horticultural library (save for those volumes purchased by the Lindley Library of the Royal Horticultural Society), were, like his ashes, scattered we know not where. It was not just one life over, but a whole world that vanished under the dark skies of the Second World War. Humphrey John Denham (1893–1970), who wrote under the name Humphrey John, already sensed in the 1930s that the old world of discrimination before commerce was slipping away, and he associated that *ancien régime* with Edward Bunyard. In his *The Skeptical Gardener Or Potterer's End*, published in 1940 but its 'Author's Apology' is dated August 1939, he wrote:

> Disheartened by the lack of bouquet in the modern apples of commerce, which seemed to have only half the fragrance of the fruit of my boyhood, and fired by the tales of old men and the sound of forgotten names, I started off to make a 'stamp collection' of obsolescent names, selected solely by the one qualification of remarkable flavour. Many of them are still on the market in this country: Messrs Bunyard's catalogue, for instance, lives neatly up to Mr E. A. Bunyard's *Anatomy of Dessert*. (p. 192)

Yet though Bunyard partly slipped into that oblivion which was once one of the sequelae of suicide, he has none the less left some 'footprints on the sands of time'. In 1944 the novelist Louis Golding (1895–1958), a contributor to *Wine and Food*, and André Simon (1877–1970), President of the Wine and Food Society and editor of *Wine and Food*, edited *We Shall Eat and Drink Again: A Wine & Food Anthology*, and reprinted EAB's 'The Wine List' from *Wine and Food* (Winter 1936); Silvio Martini, *Geschichte der Pomologie in Europa* (Bern, 1988) included Bunyard, and of course he was discussed in Joan Morgan and Alison Richards, *The Book of Apples* (1993; revd. edn. 2002), Joan Morgan also writing Bunyard's entry in the *Oxford Dictionary of National Biography* (2004); Bunyard's *A Handbook of Hardy Fruits* was reprinted in one volume by Picton Publishing in 1994; the couturier Sir Hardy Amies (1909–2003) wrote to *Country Life* to assert that old roses had been reintroduced into cultivation 'by Edward Bunyard in a book produced by – guess who – COUNTRY LIFE in 1936' (22 May 1997, 95); *The Anatomy of Dessert*, in both the 1929 and 1933 editions is still cited: by Richard Girling in 'Paradise lost', a fine article on old varieties of apple (*Sunday Times Magazine*, 17 August 1997); by Rowley Leigh in an article on apricots (*Sunday Telegraph Magazine*, 8 August 1999); in *Waitrose Food Illustrated* (September 2000) s.v. Marjorie's Seedling Plums, and still cited on the Web in 2005; by the Duchess of Devonshire in her *Counting My Chickens ... And Other Home Thoughts* (2001) where s.v. 'Best Gardening Books' in an extensive praise of the *Anatomy* she acutely observes, 'There is no question of anything so vulgar as selling the delectable produce to people who might not appreciate their finer points' (130); by Robert Palter in his magnificent and beautifully produced *The Duchess of Malfi's Apricots, and Other Literary Fruits* (2002); by Tim Longville in his 'Snippets' in *Hortus* (no. 67, Autumn 2003); by Christopher Lloyd (1921–2006), doyen of garden writers, who in his 'Essential Reading' included the *Anatomy* as 'a gem' (*The Guardian Weekend*, 29 May 2004); and by Richard Mabey's autobiography, *Nature Cure* (2005) which quotes (p. 204) 'the 1930s fruit gourmet Edward Bunyard' and his comment in the *Anatomy* on the gooseberry as a fruit for 'ambulant consumption'. Graham Stuart Thomas (1909–2003) discussing Maud Messel's work in preserving old garden roses at Nymans, Handcross, in Sussex, wrote discreetly and justly of EAB's role: 'Edward A. Bunyard, of the then famous nursery at Maidstone, had been helping her before his untimely death and had indeed produced a delightful book about them. Sadly I never met him but he was not only a good nurseryman but erudite about shrubs and plants in general, as his highly informative articles in *The New Flora and Silva* in the 1930s will prove' (Graham Stuart Thomas, *Recollections of Great Gardeners*, 2003).

Not forgotten but, in the view of the authors of this volume, insufficiently remembered for his work as a nurseryman, a worker in the new field of genetics, an epicure, a contributor to the clubbable pleasures of life, and in all matters a writer of distinction. To his 'Author's Apology' for *The Skeptical Gardener* Humphrey John added a 'Postscript', dated January 1940, in which he said that with the outbreak of War he had been told to revise what he had written about his garden, but he concluded 'I would ask leave to leave these pages untouched, to show what it was under happier skies'. *The Downright Epicure* has a similar purpose. In *Gardening Illustrated* (15 November 1930, 738) Bunyard had mused that for a memorial he would choose not the 'gloomy Cypress' but 'an avenue of Japanese Cherries'. I doubt that it was ever planted; this book will have to serve.

E. W.
Worcester College, Oxford,
15 September, 2006.

Amuse-gueule

quomodo vivendum? bene. quid bene? tale roganti
    Bunyardus cecinit poma roseta nuces.[1]

What is the good life? Let
Who with this question grapples
Consider Bunyard's books
On roses, nuts, and apples.

ARND KERKHECKER

---

[1] The lines are an imitation of the epitaph Vergil is said to have composed for himself on his deathbed:

    Mantua me genuit, Calabri rapuere, tenet nunc
        Parthenope. cecini pascua rura duces.

(Mantua bore me, Calabria snatched me away, now Naples holds me. I sang of pastures, farms, and heroes.) [E. W.]

Figure 1. 'Mr. Edward A. Bunyard'. This photograph appeared in *The Journal of Horticulture and Home Farmer*, 3rd series, LXI, no. 3238, 20 October 1910, p. 370.

CHAPTER ONE

Edward Ashdown Bunyard: a Biographical Essay

EDWARD WILSON

> When I am buried, all my thoughts and acts
> Will be reduced to lists of dates and facts,
> And long before this wandering flesh is rotten
> The dates which made me will be all forgotten;
> And none will know the gleam there used to be
> About the feast-days freshly kept by me,
> But men will call the golden hour of bliss
> "About this time," or "shortly after this."
>
> John Masefield, 'Biography',
Philip the King and Other Poems (London, 1914)

One date in Edward Bunyard's life, and on which we can be precise, can still be recognized by us as a 'golden hour', a feast day kept by the whole family: the centenary of the founding of the firm of Bunyard by James Bunyard on 16 September 1796. A Centenary Show was held at the Corn Exchange in Maidstone on Tuesday and Wednesday 15 and 16 September 1896, and the celebration began shortly after one o'clock on Tuesday, 15 September with the playing of the National Anthem by the Bijou Orchestra, after which George Bunyard, the head of the firm, entertained the judges and officials, editors of horticultural magazines, friends and gardeners, at a luncheon in the Mechanics' Hall. After George Bunyard had proposed 'The Health of the Queen, Prince and Princess of Wales and the Royal Family', a toast he said he thought particularly appropriate as he was the holder of the Royal Warrant, the speeches began.[1] One element in George Bunyard's address was charged with significance for both him and his seventeen year-old son Edward, and which the *Gardeners' Magazine* reported thus:

> He felt he could not say all that it was in his heart to say, … Mr. Bunyard concluded by stating that his son had that day come into the business, as the first of the fourth generation of Bunyards.
> (XXXIX, no. 2238, 19 September 1896, p. 648)

In addition to the luncheon for some 60 to 70 guests (*Journal of Horticulture*, XXXIII (3rd series), no. 2503, 17 September 1896, p. 268), there was a magnificent exhibition, both competitive and non-competitive, in the Corn Exchange of fruit, vegetables and flowers. What impressed all correspondents who described the Show was the Fruit Trophy Car, for all the world like a Roman triumphal cart or Renaissance *trionfo*, designed to instruct, delight, honour and celebrate. Its iconic significance merits quotation of the fullest account of it in the *Kent Messenger* (19 September 1896, p. 6):

> The principal attraction was undoubtedly a reproduction of the "Fruit trophy car," which was placed in the centre of the Corn Exchange, and which formed a conspicuous feature in the Lord Mayor's show of 1893. The car, which was shown by permission of the Worshipful Court and Company of Fruiterers, was designed by Mr. Bunyard, and carried out by Messrs. Wallis and Sons, and Mr. Martin, of Middle-row, assisted by the staff of the Nurseries. The sides of the car were hidden beneath red, green and white cloth with silver fringe. Upon one side was inscribed "God giveth the increase [a translation of the second motto of the Fruiterers' Company,

---

[1] *Kent Messenger*, 19 September 1896, p. 6. Other accounts of the Centenary Show which I have consulted are: *The Gardeners' Magazine*, XXXIX, no. 2238, 19 September 1896, pp. 647–8; *Journal of Horticulture*, XXXIII (3rd series), no. 2503, 17 September 1896, pp. 267–8; *The Garden*, L, no. 1296, 19 September 1896, pp. 238–9; *The Gardeners' Chronicle*, XX (3rd series), no. 508, 19 September 1896, p. 343.

Deus dat incrementum]," and on the other "Britain can grow her own fruit." Surmounting the trophy were the words "Ye Fruiterers' Companie," and in an oblique position numerous baskets of the choicest apples and pears were displayed to great advantage on either side of the car. As a conspicuous centre piece were large bunches of luscious black grapes, peaches, etc., and from the summit to the four corners two lines of apples, separated by tomatoes, were carried with pleasing effect. The light woodwork above the car was neatly treated, whilst the names of the four principal fruit-growing counties – Kent, Devon, Hereford, Somerset – were prominently displayed. Other fruits, etc., were introduced to fill up the minor positions, and the whole combined produced a trophy which must be seen in order to fully appreciate its beauty and artistic arrangements. Around the car Messrs. Bunyard exhibited a large assortment of apples and pears. A collection of geraniums of various colours evoked much admiration, and amongst the numerous varieties shown was a new zonal geranium. Handsome liliums, maidenhair ferns, and other plants were advantageously displayed in this group. A third exhibit in the centre of the hall was that of hardy flowers, shrubs and plants, with grapes, apples and pears growing in pots. The gladiolus, asters and roses were of pretty hues, and the new giant violets, "Princess de Galles," were universally admired.

The Garden gives details of the varieties of fruit in the car:

> … some of the very best fruits ever staged; the base was built up of pyramids of the best kinds of fruit, the centre Pears and Apples, the ends Peaches, Grapes, Figs. The whole was relieved with small plants of various kinds, the Pernettyas and various berried plants being most effective. The whole was festooned with Grapes and wreathed with small fruits in variety. Mention must be made of the grand dishes of fruit, the Pears most noticeable being Dr. Jules Guyot, Beurré Mortillet, Doyenné Boussoch, Clapp's Favourite, and Pitmaston Duchess. Apples made a grand show and were superb as regards colour. Duchess of Oldenburg, Duchess, Cox's Orange, Ribston, and other dessert kinds were very fine, and the cooking varieties were extra large and in great quantities, many of them seedlings not in commerce. At each end of the trophy were large collections of plants from the firm, with a fine group of fruit trees in pots, the colour of the fruit being noticeable.

> We have seldom seen such Mère de Ménage, Emperor Alexander and Cox's Pomona Apples as seen on pot trees here. Cordon Pears, a fine collection of small Fig trees in 10-inch pots, excellent pot Vines (Hamburgh and Foster's Seedling), with baskets of small fruits were also included.
> (L, no. 1296, 19 September 1896, pp. 238–9)

In this setting of such sumptuous magnificence did EAB hear his father (1841–1919) extolled. He had entered the family firm on 5 September 1855, eventually easing out his father, Thomas (c. 1804–80), and, after a period of partnership with his brother Tom which did not go well, he 'was obliged to make him bankrupt' in 1880 – though these details, which are from George Bunyard's *The History of the Bunyard Firm from 1796 to 1911* (published privately, Maidstone, 1911),[2] naturally did not make it to the speeches. However, he cleared all debts, expanded the acreage from 20 to 100 (*Journal of Horticulture*, 17 September 1896, p. 268), and as he himself put it in his *History*:

> Once free, fortune seemed to smile on my efforts, and in 1880, I was placed on the Fruit Committee of the Royal Horticultural Society … In 1883, I was one of the chiefs at the Apple Conference at Chiswick … I was Chairman of the Edinburgh Fruit Conference in 1886. The first edition of "Fruit Farming for Profit" was printed in 1881 … The Fruiterers' Company, later on, 1896, honoured me by presenting me with the Freedom of the City of London, for the active part I took in the Great Fruit Show, held in the Guildhall, London [in 1890]. A Certificate was presented to me in the Mansion House by Baroness Burdett-Coutts, 1891 … (pp. 22–3)

---

[2] The only surviving copy of this work which I know of is in The Centre for Kentish Studies, Sessions House, Maidstone (shelf mark U1945, Z1/1; a photostat of this is U1945, Z1/2). The printed dedication reads: 'I dedicate this private [underlined in ink twice] family history to my eight children. George Bunyard, V.M.H. Maidstone, February, 1911.' On the last page (32) it is signed 'George Bunyard', and the same hand has inscribed the front with the name of one of his daughters, 'Janet Bunyard'.

A BIOGRAPHICAL ESSAY

At the Centenary Show the young Edward heard John Wright, acting-editor of the *Journal of Horticulture*, proposing 'The Health of the Chairman', say that:

> Mr. Bunyard, jun., was to join the firm that day, and he heartily wished them a long period of prosperity. It was Mr. Bunyard's attention to business that had made him what he was, and he had done very much for the fruit industry of this country (applause). He bore an honoured name, which was known far beyond the confines of this land, because he was at the head of one of the largest and most important fruit-growing tree establishments in the world (applause). (*Kent Messenger*, 19 September 1896, p. 6)

Nor would Edward think that he was the son of a man resting on his laurels: the acreage continued to expand, and other books and other honours (such as the Victoria Medal of Honour in 1897 and the Mastership of the Fruiterers' Company in 1906) were to follow.

On this splendid and overwhelming occasion the concerts, which were part of the celebration, must have been a steadying and calming contribution. According to the *Kent Messenger*:

> The concerts took place in the Concert Hall, where the platform had been prettily decorated for the occasion. In the afternoon and evening of each day the Bijou Orchestra, conducted by Mr. J. C. Lomas, A.C.V., discoursed a capital selection of music, which included solos for the piccolo, viola, cornet, trombone, and clarinet. Mr. Dennis Lamb's Choral Class was present each evening and rendered some attractive vocal music. Mr. D. Lamb officiated as conductor, and Mr. F. Gilbert Lamb as accompanist. Besides a number of part songs by the Class, Mrs. F.S. Spender, Miss Haywood, Miss and Messrs. Lamb delighted the audiences with their quartettes, trios, and songs, which were heartily applauded and much appreciated.

Both George and Edward Bunyard were keen amateur musicians. In a portrait of George Bunyard the *Journal of Horticulture* records that for 40 years he was a 'bass singer in Maidstone Church choirs and choral societies' (LX, 3rd series, no. 3205, 3 March 1910, p. 198), and it is improbable that Edward's enthusiasm for music had not begun to show itself by the age of seventeen.

A biographical sketch of him in the *Gardeners' Magazine* says that:

> His chief hobby is music, and he acts as accompanist to the Maidstone Choral Union. Of this society he has been secretary since its institution in 1903, and it is in no small measure due to his skill that the society won the championship for Kentish societies, and in 1909 won the "Daily Telegraph" shield at the South London Musical Festival. (LV, no. 3036, 6 January 1912, p. 2)

Thus was Edward Bunyard inducted into the firm in its centenary year, along with, we may add, the commercial introduction of the Allington Pippin apple.[3] At the time, the occasion must indeed have seemed, in Masefield's words, 'gated by golden moments' ('Biography'). When 43 years later, haunted by the bankruptcy from which his father had saved the firm, he put a revolver to his temple, it must rather have appeared a scene from which the visionary gleam had fled, its bright hope now mocked by a dark despair, a reproof for the *dégringolade* he felt he had brought about.

Understanding how this fall had happened should probably involve not just a consideration of Edward Bunyard's own life, but an examination of what looks almost a genetic disposition to bankruptcy and financial mismanagement; indeed, as EAB delivered a paper at the Third International Conference on Genetics in 1906, the idea of failure, in Philip Larkin's words on a shied apple core

> spreading back up the arm
> Earlier and earlier, the unraised hand calm,
> The apple unbitten in the palm,
>
> ('As Bad as a Mile')

---

[3] This apple, a cross between Cox's Orange and King of the Pippins, was first raised by W. & J. Brown of Stamford as South Lincoln Beauty, and it received a Royal Horticultural Society First Class Certificate on 13 November 1894 (see *Journal of the Royal Horticultural Society*, XVII (1894–5), pp. clxvi–clxvii); George Bunyard, in his 'New Fruits of Recent Introduction' read at the Second Annual Great Exhibition of, and Conference on, British-Grown Fruit at the Crystal Palace in September 1895, said that as there were already several Lincoln Pippins, it had been re-named the Allington Pippin (see *JRHS*, XIX (1895–6), 257–69, p. 258).

is a notion which is perhaps not anachronistic even in Bunyard's own categories of thought. Certainly in his ancestry there is what appears an astonishing number of instances of financial incompetence and an inability to handle money in a prudent, competent, and business-like way. Though the evidence comes from George Bunyard's *History* of the firm (see n. 2), a private account written from his perspective only, it is hard to believe that there can be other than a factual basis for much of what is asserted.[4]

The founder of the firm, James Bunyard (d. 1844), had, besides two daughters, three sons: James (the eldest), Thomas (George Bunyard's father; Edward's grandfather), and Charles. Of James, George writes:

> James (Uncle Jim) ran through seven thousand pounds in cash, gifts and loans, from Grandfather, and then became a drag on Father till he died under my care, (*History*, p. 9)

and of Charles:

> Charles was a handsome, dressy man, he was quite domineering in his manner, and having married money with his wife (Miss Bodman), kept a carriage and pair in London, and did the swagger, but unfortunately lived beyond his means, and committing forgery (at that time a hanging offence, I believe), bolted – no one knew where – and was never heard of again. (p.8)

James Bunyard's second son, Thomas, though neither a wastrel nor a flamboyant crook, simply lacked energy and crisp financial control:

---

[4] The anonymous [but presumably by EAB] 4-page pamphlet, *The House of Bunyard 1796–1919* (no place or date stated), published on 'the lamented death of our late principal, Mr. George Bunyard', being addressed to 'our customers' is naturally much blander and less frank than GB's *History*; for the location of copies see the Bibliography, s.v. *Pamphlets*. Also worth consulting is the well-illustrated 3-part article by Alan Major, 'The Bunyards of Kent', Part One, *Bygone Kent*, XII no. 3 (March 1991), 176–81; Part Two, ibid., XII no. 4 (April 1991), 228–32; Part Three, ibid., XII no. 5 (May 1991), 275–80; it has a few slips.

Looking back, I can now see that it was more owing to the energy, hard work, and household economy practised by my Mother, than to Father's exertions, that we boys owe what education we had; and her saving ways tided Father over a very difficult time, which as a child I did not fully recognise until I came into the business at 14 years old in 1855. Father was what may be called a worthy man, with no failings, honorable and respected, but he wanted that gift of leading and foresight so needful in our business, and contracted the habit of trusting those about him in both the selling and buying, more than any master should. His health inclined him more to retirement and taking things easy than to any sustained effort in a business direction. (p. 11)

George (born 5 February 1841) had four brothers: Thomas (Tom), the eldest; John Butler (Jack); Frederick; and Harry. Though George had entered the firm in 1855, Tom 'unfortunately did not get on with his parents, and ructions were frequent, so that he had to take work away' (p. 16). He remained keen as the eldest son to come into the family business, 'but again his want of tact, and readiness to make a row, prevented this, and so he returned to London [where he was with various seed and florist firms, p. 13] until 1863' (p. 17), when 'Father took Tom and myself into partnership, under the name of Thos. Bunyard & Sons' (p. 17), Tom working land at Ashford and George at Maidstone. Though at first things went well, 'Father had ceased to take any garden papers or periodicals; thus we fell behind the times. (p. 17) … After a few years Father was unable to do much, and would not second our endeavours; so that I drew up an agreement whereby he retired, and Tom and I jointly agreed to pay him £150 a year, and to continue this to Mother and sister Mary Ann for their joint lives' (p. 18). Then, however, Tom had a very serious illness, and George:

> had to go to and fro to manage for him, and found the Ashford books kept in a very slipshod way, and he was much annoyed at my setting them right, but we got on pretty comfortably, except [a significant 'except'] that Tom never carried out any agreement as to territory, paying for goods, or the up-keep of Father, always quoting as a grievance that I had the "Homestall" [i.e. Maidstone whereas Tom had new territory at Ashford]. His wife was extravagant and trouble began to brew. To extend Tom's trade at Ashford

we bought fifteen acres at Willesborough. I raised other loans for Tom; but even then matters did not equalise. (p. 18)

At this point the youngest brother Harry's financial folly dealt a terrible blow. He had borrowed a large sum from a George Smeed, of Sittingbourne, who had 'egged him on and discounted his paper at 2½ %, till he got him in a hole, and then made it 10%' (p. 19). George and the other brothers were involved financially in trying to sort matters out, but the crash came in 1879–80, 'and in consequence of Harry's failure the old firm had to go into liquidation, pulling down Jack in London, and crippling Fred [a bookseller, stationer, and printer], but he managed to get through; Harry, like a coward, "bunked" to Spain' (p. 19).

George behaved generously to Tom:

I gave Tom the Ashford business with the book debts and stock as his portion, free from debt, and, had he then lived within his income, all would have been well; alas! he did not do so, and, after several years of bother and help, I was obliged to make him bankrupt. (p. 20)

None the less, as is often the way, Tom and his family were resentful, and considered that George had 'behaved shabbily', a charge that he vigorously denied:

Well, after lending him no end of cash and supplying stock at half-price, he [Tom] actually sent a lot of trees to be sold in Maidstone Market under my nose, contrary to our agreement. This decided me; even then I paid for his furniture to be sent to St. Leonard's, where his wife took a swell boarding house [echoes of the scorn for his Uncle Charles who 'did the swagger'], and even then I helped him at times. Can you wonder then that I refused to allow his family to be friendly with mine or me; and I could recite many other hard facts to justify my conduct.[5] (p. 21)

---

[5] Thomas Bunyard's bankruptcy was listed in *The Times*, 3 February 1892, p. 10 col. f: Thomas Bunyard, Ashford and Willesborough, Kent, nurseryman. *The Gardeners' Chronicle*, under the headline 'Golden Wedding of Mr. and Mrs. Thomas Bunyard', is wonderfully unaware of all this, recalling that 'Many of our readers will remember the

Being a fourth generation of Bunyard was in many respects a *damnosa hereditas*. James (junior) was a wastrel, Charles and his nephew Harry each fled from financial disgrace, and both Thomas senior and Tom junior were without any business acumen or regimen. That Edward Bunyard should have died bankrupt, his suicide being the extremest form of Charles's 'bolting' and Harry's 'bunking', is not surprising. The surprise is that his father should have been such a hard-working, ambitious, successful, and necessarily ruthless nurseryman who recovered from a £12,000 loss (*History*, p. 22) to establish a large, prosperous, and world-famous firm; interestingly, when Thomas Bunyard took George and Tom into the Company it became Thos. Bunyard & Sons (see above), as it had earlier been James Bunyard & Son, but even when George died, and the firm was run by Edward and Norman Bunyard, it remained (as it did until its close in the 1960s) George Bunyard and Co. Yet Hamlet's words hover in the mind, that 'virtue cannot so inoculate [appropriately, in the old horticultural sense of 'engraft'] our old stock, but we shall relish of it'. Edward Bunyard achieved much as a nurseryman and grower of fruit and roses, pomologist, antiquarian bibliophile, and writer on gastronomic subjects, but Fred Stoker's elegiac words in his obituary have a sombre and sable significance when seen as part of a ruinous inheritance from his great-uncles James and Charles, his grandfather Thomas, and his uncles Tom and Harry:

> he never struck me as bearing the insignia of a business man. His cheerful equanimity, breadth of vision and mellow wisdom spoke rather of the scholar than the trader; his gentle tact and conversational range indicated contact with literature rather than with balance-sheets.
>
> (*Proceedings of the Linnean Society of London*, 152nd session (1939–40), Part 4 (1940), p. 362)[6]

---

pleasantly written and instructive articles on nursery management [*sic*] and propagation contributed to these columns some years ago by Mr. THOMAS BUNYARD, over the nom de plume "Experience"' [*sic*], and recording that 'Mr. THOMAS BUNYARD many years ago was in partnership with his brother, Mr. GEORGE BUNYARD, of the Royal Nurseries, Maidstone, and since those days has filled several appointments with other firms' (LV, no. 1434, 20 June 1914, pp. 440–1).

[6] Bunyard presented a copy of his *The Epicure's Companion* (1937) to Fred Stoker, and it is now in the Lindley Library of the Royal Horticultural Society (Case 641.5; Shelf

Thus freighted, the journey to this sad catastrophe had begun on 14 December 1878 when Edward Ashdown Bunyard was born at 74 King Street, Maidstone. His second name was from his mother, Katharine Sophia Ashdown, daughter of Charles Ashdown, a paper-maker of Mereworth in Kent. She had married, aged 22, George Bunyard, then 32, nurseryman of Maidstone, on 3 June 1873. George's father, Thomas, was more grandly described on the marriage certificate as 'Gentleman', suggesting a certain social aspiration and bearing out the son's belief that his father was not cut out for 'trade' (though in fairness it should be remembered that George had probably eased his father out of the firm by 1873, and so he was no longer an active nurseryman; see above). Indeed, even the business-like George thought it worth recording in his *History* that his mother 'was a Butler and a direct descendant of Rollo, the uncle of William the Conqueror, as our family tree shows' (pp. 10–11; the family tree is in The Centre for Kentish Studies, Sessions House, Maidstone; shelfmark U1945, Z3).

There were ten children, though two boys died in infancy:

1. George Pierson (30 March 1874 – 25 January 1883).
2. Lorna Frances (20 August 1876 – 27 May 1963).
3. Katharine Mary (4 November 1877 – 24 March 1963).
4. Edward Ashdown (14 December 1878 – 19 October 1939).
5. Norman Philip (29 September 1880 – 5 February 1883).
6. Janet (11 July 1882 – 29 June 1958).
7. Richard Geoffrey (19 August 1883 – 6 June 1973).
8. Frances Lucy Butler (15 August 1884 – 22 September 1982).
9. George Norman (21 October 1886 – 9 February 1969).
10. Marguerite Eveline (11 July 1890 – 14 May 1959).

George Pierson died first on 25 January 1883, aged 8, from bronchitis and measles which he had suffered for 13 and 12 days respectively (Death Certificate); Norman Philip died a little later on 5 February 1883 from

---

Bun); Stoker's obituary of Bunyard justifies the inscription: 'To F. Stoker / Scriptor sapiens / E A Bunyard'. There is an admiring review of *The Epicure's Companion* by F.S., who must be Fred Stoker (*c.* 1879–1943), in *The Gardeners' Chronicle*, CII (3rd series), no. 2657, 27 November 1937, pp. 397–8.

whooping cough, capillary bronchitis, and exhaustion (Death Certificate). Though in September 1896 Edward had been 'the first of the fourth generation of Bunyards', he had not been born the eldest boy.

Of his childhood we know nothing except that the *Kent Messenger* in its report of his death says that 'he was educated privately, as he was a delicate boy' (21 October 1939, p. 4). His books show him as prodigiously well-read (see below the chapter 'Edward Bunyard and Literature'), and this literary predilection must have begun in childhood. No university education followed for, as we have seen, he entered the family firm in 1896 at the age of 17.

In a wireless broadcast entitled 'Novelties from the Kitchen Garden' in the 'In Your Garden' series of the Radio Gardener, C. H. Middleton, Sunday 2 April, 1939, 2.00 – 2.20 p.m., Bunyard told Middleton that 'I suppose I can date my first adventures among vegetables to the year 1900 when I went to live in France. My hosts were an old couple and Marie the cook. All cooks were called Marie in France at that time'.[7] He must have been 21 when he went, but how long he spent there is not recorded; *The Gardeners' Chronicle* obituary says, 'As a young man, Mr. Bunyard spent some time in France, where he studied French nursery practice and became a fluent speaker of the French language' (CVI (3rd series), no. 2757, 28 October 1939, p. 274). His knowledge of France, its horticulture, food, and wine, was profound. His last article in *Wine and Food*, 'A Few Meals in France', begins:

> 'Come and stay here,' said my friend B [Basil Leng: see my 'Edward Bunyard by the Mediterranean', *The Mediterranean Garden*, no. 38, October 2004, 5–14, pp. 8–10; and also later in this chapter], who lives on the Cap d'Antibes, 'the roses are out and the orange blossom, too.' Who could resist such an invitation? – and I knew that the nightingales would also be singing.' (VI.23, Autumn 1939, p. 223)

---

[7] Copy of a typescript supplied by the British Broadcasting Corporation, Written Archives Centre, Caversham Park, Reading; the last Bunyardian humorous sentence was omitted from the version printed in *The Listener*, XXI, no. 534, 6 April 1939, p. 749. For other surviving texts of broadcasts involving Bunyard see the Bibliography of his publications at the end of this book.

Figure 2. The Bunyard Family at Oakwood Lodge, Ide Hill, Sevenoaks, *c.* 1898. Back row, left to right: Janet (1882–1958), George (1841–1919), Katharine (1851–1939), Geoffrey (1883–1973), Katharine (1877–1963), Edward (1878–1939). Front row, left to right: Frances (1884–1982), Norman (1886–1969), Marguerite (1890–1959), Lorna (1876–1963). *(Photograph courtesy of Miss Katharine Bunyard, daughter of Norman Bunyard.)*

Figure 3. 'Mr. Edward A. Bunyard'. This photograph appeared in *The Gardeners' Magazine*, LV, no. 3036, 6 January 1912, p. 1

Figure 4. 'Edward A. Bunyard, F.L.S.' This photograph is reproduced from one which appeared in *The Journal of Pomology and Horticultural Science*, XVII, no. 4, January 1940, facing p. 294. However, it had appeared earlier in *Amateur Gardening*, XLIX, no. 2513, 2 July 1932, p. 188.

And so he is off, to an *al fresco* luncheon at the bottom of the garden at 'one of the show places behind Cannes' –

> With the tongues of many nations, we chattered our way down the hill, past crystal swimming pools, cypresses lifting their dark exclamation marks in telling corners, roses, azaleas and all the profusion of Riviera spring around us (p. 224) –

and then on over the days to Collobrières, Menton, St-Tropez, the hills near Grasse, and finally Paris at his 'favourite hotel' where:

> there was a great find, a Pontet-Canet '24 at 20 francs a bottle. I could not bear to think that it might be drunk by some Philistine, so I dined there for the few days of my visit. How well it showed up an excellent Matelote d'Anguilles [eels stewed in a wine sauce], which Ambrose Heath [a writer on gastronomic matters] calls 'a dish in a million'. I agree – provisionally. (p. 229)

The visit to France in 1900 was the beginning of extensive European travel. The *Gardeners' Chronicle* obituary already quoted says that Bunyard 'also studied and spoke German' (ibid., p. 274), and an article on the Himalaya Berry in the same journal indicates that he had been to Germany by at least the age of 33: 'When in Germany in the autumn of 1912…' (LXIV (3rd series), no. 1665, 23 November 1918, p. 205). A letter (23 March 1935) from the writer Norman Douglas to EAB (see below the chapter 'Edward Bunyard and Norman Douglas', Letter C.1) indicates that though Douglas did not care to visit the Germany of the 1930s, Bunyard, when in pursuit of seeds, was not deterred: 'I don't know Trier or Erfurt. Don't think I should care about Germany any more, seeds or no seeds'.

Though his travels also included Switzerland and Luxemburg (*The Garden*, LXXXIV, no. 2556, 13 November 1920, p. 561), the west Pyrenees (*Gardeners' Chronicle*, XC, no. 2324, 11 July 1931, p. 36), and even South Africa (see *Gardeners' Chronicle*, Bibliography, nos. 49 and 52; ' … On a recent visit to South Africa…', *Gardening Illustrated*, LII, no. 2668, 26 April 1930, p. 267; cf. ibid., LIII, no. 2712, 28 February 1931, p. 128), Bunyard's other great love besides France was Italy. This had begun with an admiration for the writings of Norman Douglas, then living in Florence, and a first visit took place in 1922; one outcome was the article 'Some Early Italian Gardening Books' which:

> presents the fruits of a hurried search in Italian bookshops and street barrows, a pursuit, it may be said, demanding some patience and an entire disregard for dust. (*Journ. of the Royal Hort. Soc*, XLVIII (1923), p. 177)

As my later chapter shows, the friendship with Douglas developed and deepened, and lasted through the 1930s; inter alia, it led to a visit to Capri by Bunyard, armed with a letter of introduction from Douglas to its mayor, Edwin Cerio (see the chapter on Bunyard and Norman Douglas, Letter G.8). Another motive for Italian travel was of course plants. Thus Graham Stuart Thomas writes of the rose Brunonii, 'La Mortola', that it 'was brought by E. A. Bunyard from the famous garden whose name it bears'.[8]

Of course, the pursuit of old books had begun long before the Italian visit of 1922. Already the brief biography of Edward Bunyard in the *Journal of Horticulture* of 1910 had noted that 'one of his several hobbies is the collecting of old books dealing with fruit culture' (LXI (3rd series), no. 3238, 20 October 1910, 369–70, p. 369), and his two early articles in the *Journal of the Royal Horticultural Society* of October and December 1911, listing illustrations of apples and pears, draw extensively on English and European books of the eighteenth and nineteenth centuries. By 1927 the *Gardeners' Chronicle* is declaring in 'An Afternoon with a Pomologist' that:

---

[8] G. S. Thomas, *Climbing Roses Old and New* (London, 1983 edn.), p. 33. On the great garden of La Mortola, the creation of the Hanbury family in the 19th century, on the Italian Riviera, see C. Quest-Ritson, *The English Garden Abroad* (London, 1992), pp. 63–75. Cf. also Thomas, ibid., s.v. 'Filipes': 'Western China. Introduced in 1908. Though seldom seen in gardens this species should take a high place. The only form that I have grown or seen is one secured, probably from the Roseraie de l'Haÿ, by the late E. A. Bunyard, but so far I have found no record of it in his writings. A plant was purchased from him by Mrs Muir about 1938, and still grows strongly at Kiftsgate Court' (p. 34).

> He has made his home in the midst of some four hundred acres of fruit trees at Allington, and formed a library of books on fruit and fruit-growing, the equal of which is not be found elsewhere', (anon., LXXXII (3rd series), no. 2124, 10 September 1927, 213–14, p. 213)

and a long final paragraph lists a number of the volumes, including an Italian treatise published in 1590, and ends:

> he has collected – and still collects – everything which might serve to illustrate the history of fruit-cultivation in particular and gardening in general. (p. 214)

But books for Bunyard were not mere bibliographical items; his 'entire disregard for dust' in Italian bookshops and barrows reveals the ardour of the bibliophile. Indeed, in his love of fruit, roses, wine and literature, one informed the other. There is something of Goldsmith's Mr Hardcastle – 'I love every thing that's old: old friends, old times, old manners, old books, old wine' – when he writes in his essay, 'The Winter Dessert':

> One secret only can I reveal. A fireside chair, a Blenheim Apple, slightly warmed, and in the other hand a volume of Fielding, whose mellow wisdom and acid sap find in the Apple their perfect counterpoise. (*Wine and Food*, I.4 (1934), 26–9, p. 29)

Not only was Bunyard early collecting old horticultural works, but he soon began what was to be a remarkably productive life as a writer of books and articles on matters horticultural and, later, gastronomic. His father, George, published, as well as a number of articles, several horticultural books, though with nothing like the range nor in the number of his son.[9] EAB's first published appearance, however, was as a photographer.

---

[9] George Bunyard's books are: *Fruit Farming for Profit* … (Maidstone and London, 1881; there were also later editions); *Modern Fruit Culture … Being a Reprint of the Cultural Articles from George Bunyard & Co.'s Catalogues* … (Maidstone, 1892; most articles, though not all, are by G. B.); *England's National Flower* (Maidstone and London, [?1904]); George Bunyard and Owen Thomas, *The Fruit Garden* (London

When he was 25 there came out his father's *England's National Flower* [the rose] (Maidstone and London; n.d. but the Bodleian Library's copy is date-stamped '4.2.1904'), the photographs being, as the Introduction acknowledges, 'by my son, Mr. EDWARD ASHDOWN BUNYARD', and they are of considerable subtlety and beauty. The unsigned review in the *Gardeners' Chronicle* states: 'Photographic illustrations are given, which show how very beautiful Roses are when lightly arranged in vases and not throttled in the regulation boxes' (XXXV (3rd series), no. 892, 30 January 1904, p. 67). However, when in 1936 EAB published his own work on roses, *Old Garden Roses*, scholarly, substantial, and magisterial where his father's had been, designedly, a slighter (26pp.) though charming work, the photographs were taken by a Maidstone photographer, the improbably named Sweatman Hedgeland.[10]

There was indeed an artistic strain in the family. In George Bunyard and Owen Thomas, *The Fruit Garden* (London and New York, 1904), gratitude is expressed in the plural for the 'outline drawings of fruits to members of Mr. George Bunyard's family' (p. vi). However, it was Frances L. B. Bunyard, described on her Death Certificate – she was 98 – as 'Art Teacher (Retired)', who was the acknowledged artist.[11] She did the drawings for her father's *Handbook of Hardy Trees and Shrubs* (Maidstone, 1908), and was involved in

---

and New York, 1904); *Handbook of Hardy Trees and Shrubs* … (Maidstone, 1908); *Apples and Pears* (London and Edinburgh, [1911]). The British Library once held the only copies I know of 4 pamphlets, but they were destroyed in World War II: *Cherries: How and Where to Plant and Sell*, 15pp., (London, 1895); *Gooseberries and Currants for Garden and Market*, 15pp., (London, 1895); Edward Bartrum and George Bunyard, *Raspberries for Garden, Field, and Market* …, 16pp., (London, 1897); Edward Bartrum and George Bunyard, *Strawberries for Garden, Field, and Market*, 16pp., (London, 1897).

[10] I owe this identification to Dr Joan Morgan. Hedgeland's business in the Broadway was close to Bunyard's shop.

[11] In the Lindley Library of the Royal Horticultural Society, London, are her watercolours of 53 varieties of cherry; the dates, on some of them only, are 1926 and 1928; the Library also holds a watercolour of 'Abnormal Pear (second crop)' dated October 1911. In the Library of East Malling Research (information courtesy of Ms. Sarah Loat, former Librarian of East Malling Research) are watercolours of various fruits: 3 of cherry, 24 of pear, 21 of apples, 33 of plum, 4 of fig, and 1 of peach; such

several of her brother Edward's publications (see the Bibliography of EAB's publications at the end of this volume for full references): (i) an article on red currants in the *Gardeners' Chronicle* (1917); (ii) an article on cherries in *The Garden* (1921); (iii) an article on fruit trees in the *Journ. of the Royal Hort. Soc.* (1922); (iv) the drawings and end-paper design, and probably the water-colour of a rose on the dust-jacket of *Old Garden Roses* (1936); (v) the drawings and possibly the dustwrapper of *The Epicure's Companion* (1937); (vi) an article on wild roses in *Country Life* (1938).

EAB's first written (as distinct from photographic) publication was his paper 'On Xenia' ('A supposed direct action or influence of foreign pollen upon the seed or fruit which is pollinated': *OED*), delivered, when he was 27, on 1 August 1906 at the Third International Conference on Genetics, and published in the *Report* of the Conference, edited by W. Wilks, for the Royal Horticultural Society, in 1907. Though both Edward and George Bunyard were invited guests (*Report*, pp. 22–3), only Edward gave a paper; it is remarkable that someone who was educated at home, and entered the family firm at the age of 17, should have been sufficiently learned and known in the field of Mendelism to be invited to deliver a paper at an international conference.[12] The *Gardeners' Chronicle* in the early years of the twentieth century records a number of scientific papers which EAB gave to the Horticultural Club in London (see Bibliography of EAB's publications, s.v. 'Reports of Papers delivered to the Horticultural Club').[13]

---

dates as they bear range from 1925–30; 4 of the watercolours appeared in N. B. Bagenal, *Fruit Growing: Modern Cultural Methods* (London and Melbourne, 1939; revd. edn. 1945).

[12] For the general background to Mendelism and the development of genetics see C. Tudge, *In Mendel's Footnotes* ... (London, 2000); see also Simon Hiscock's chapter below on Bunyard's paper on xenia. For secondary citation of Bunyard's genetics work see A. D. Darbishire, *Breeding and the Mendelian Discovery* (London, 1911), p. 131; C. M. Woodworth, 'Inheritance of Cotyledon, Seed-Coat, Hilum and Pubescence Colors in Soy-Beans', *Genetics*, VI (1921), 487–553, p. 504.

[13] The Horticultural Club (still in existence) was founded by the Rev. Henry Honywood D'Ombrain (1818–1905) in 1876 (see M. Hadfield, *Gardening in Britain* (London, 1960), p. 335). I am indebted for this reference, and for knowledge of Bunyard's 1909 paper to the Club, to Dr Vicky Graham of the Wisley Laboratory Library.

On 29 October 1901 he was elected a Fellow of the Royal Horticultural Society (*JRHS*, XXVI (1901–2), p. ccix), and it was in the March 1910 issue of the *JRHS* that his first major article, 'The Physiology of Pruning', appeared (XXXV (1909–10), pp. 330–4); his father had published 'Root Pruning of Fruit-Trees' in the same journal (XV (1892–3), pp. 211–17). By one of those accidents that sometimes lend a kind of fortuitous symmetry to lives abruptly ended, one of his posthumous articles, 'Simple Pruning for Beginners', was in the same area and appeared in the November 1939 issue of the same journal (LXIV (1939), pp. 511–16). The other article published after his death, 'Rose Hunting in 1939', in *The New Flora and Silva* (November 1939), seems a ghostly echo of his photographic contribution to his father's *England's National Flower* (?1904). Over his life Bunyard published some five books, and around 400 articles, reviews, and letters (excluding 31 letters to *The Times*) in various journals and on topics horticultural and, after *The Anatomy of Dessert* (1929), gastronomic. In addition, there were wireless broadcasts, though only four scripts (1937–9) are known (see s.v. Bibliography at the end of this volume).

We have seen how Frances Bunyard was involved as an artist in some of both her father's and EAB's books, and two of Edward's other sisters also played a part in his *The Epicure's Companion* (1937). Lorna, described on her Death Certificate as a retired health visitor, co-edited this book and made many major contributions, writing the sections on Soups; Fish; Meat and Poultry; Sausages; Fungi as Food; Sauces; Macaroni, Pâté, Pasta; Pastry and Pies; Breads; Buns and Cakes; Soft Drinks; Kitchen Fitments; and the Kitchen Bookshelf; she wrote, like her brother, not just in practical terms but with a remarkably rich range of historical, geographical, and literary reference. In their whole cast of mind Edward and Lorna Bunyard were clearly extraordinarily at one. I have also come across L. Yarde Bunyard, *Modern Salads* (1938), a 14-page pamphlet published by the Royal Horticultural Society, and I am grateful to her niece, Miss Katharine Bunyard (daughter of George Norman Bunyard) for confirming that this is indeed Lorna Bunyard (though I have not traced the other publications to which she refers): 'She adopted the name "Yarde" and used this in her many publications for the Women's Institute & RHS. …My family never knew why she used Yarde' (letter of 9 August 2003).

EAB's sister, Marguerite Eveline, the youngest of the Bunyard children, described on her Death Certificate as 'Doctor's Secretary Agricultural Research Station (Retired)',[14] besides contributing Spices (again, profoundly historical: 'We began with romance and we conclude with reality. This is the trend of history') and 'A Dinner in India' (a personal reminiscence) to *The Epicure's Companion*, also shared his interest in the problems of the colour description of flowers, and published several articles on the topic (see Bibliography, s.v. *The Gardeners' Chronicle*, no. 19).

Not all EAB's siblings have left records of any direct or persistent involvement with either the firm or with his interests and publications. His brother, Richard Geoffrey, emigrated to Canada where he was an architect (*Kent Messenger*, 21 October 1939, p. 4), and died at North Saanich, Vancouver Island (British Columbia Archives); according to their Death Certificates his sister Katharine Mary was a retired secretary, and Janet a retired masseuse. However, (George) Norman Bunyard, the youngest of the three brothers to survive to adulthood, eight years younger than Edward and three than Richard, was to share the running of the nursery with him. In 1903 the firm became a limited company, though the whole of the capital was still held by the family (*The House of Bunyard 1796–1919* [see n. 4], p. 4); and in 1908, when EAB was approaching 30, the *Journal of Horticulture* noted: 'Mr. George Bunyard has the assistance of his two sons [ignoring Richard], the elder of whom, Mr. Edward Bunyard, is now a partner in the company. Mr. Edward bids fair to emulate his father's achievements as an accomplished pomologist' ('D.', 'Messrs. Geo. Bunyard & Co., Ltd., Maidstone', LVII (3rd series), no. 3135, 29 October 1908, 436–7, p. 437). Two years later the same journal records: 'Now that Mr. George Bunyard, V.M.H., is upon the borders of his seventieth year a considerable part of the business conduct of the firm of George Bunyard and Co., Ltd., Maidstone, devolves upon the elder of his two sons' ('Leaders in the Fruit World. Mr. E. A. Bunyard', *JH*, LXI (3rd series), no. 3238, 20 October 1910, 369–70, p. 369). By 1915 the *JH* is recording that both Edward and Norman are directors of the Company and with defined separate responsibilities:

---

[14] Ms. Sarah Loat, former Librarian of East Malling Research, has told me that they have records of M. E. Bunyard working at the East Malling Research Station (as it then was) from 1944 to 1955, though the records do not state in what capacity.

The company is purely a family arrangement in which Mr. George Bunyard retains the chairmanship and has the assistance of his two sons – Edward A. Bunyard and G. Norman Bunyard – as directors. Of these the first named entered the firm in 1896, and makes the Allington nurseries his headquarters, while the latter presides at the home nurseries, the seed and bulb warehouses, and the offices. …

The special object of the present visit was to see the fruits, shrubs, and trees at Allington under the wing of Mr. Edward A. Bunyard, but the time was found for a glance round the divided charges of Mr. G. Norman Bunyard at home. Here are the houses containing the general collections of flowering and foliage plants. The bedding plants, of which immense numbers are grown, also find accommodation. The younger of the brothers has made a special study of alpine and aquatic as well as of hardy herbaceous plants, of which the collections are remarkably complete, especially when it is borne in mind that not a few people throughout the land think that Bunyards do nothing but fruit. If a comparison of the bulk of the older brother's charge were made with that of the younger brother the former would win in a canter, but number for number the latter would make a good race of it. …

More interesting, if not more profitable from a business point of view, Mr. Edward Bunyard has travelled widely in Europe to find and bring home the best of the shrubs and trees that the continental nurseries afford, and he has drawn stock from all the principal distributing nurseries of the civilised world. (anon., 'Famous Nurseries. Bunyards of Maidstone.', *JH*, LXX (3rd series), no. 1809, 25 February 1915, 141–3, pp. 141, 143)

Does the antithesis between interest and profit in the last paragraph sound what in hindsight might appear a faint tocsin? It will get louder as the years advance.

Shortly before the outbreak of the First World War, public recognition of the scientific side of his work came with his admission on 4 June 1914 as a Fellow of the Linnean Society (proposed 19 February 1914; elected 19 March 1914: *Proc. of the Linnean Soc.*, 126th session (1913–14), pp. 11, 12, 68; his brother Norman was elected a Fellow on 14 December 1922 and admitted on 18 January 1923, but his 'withdrawal' was reported on 28 May 1931, 143rd session (1930–31), p. 107). Though I can trace only one paper, 'On the Origin of the Garden Red Currant', delivered to the Society on 4 May 1916 (see Bibliography, s.v. *Proc. of the Linn. Soc.*), he played a considerable part in its administration, first being elected to the Council on 22 May 1924, and being thrice elected as one of the Auditors for the Council (2 April 1925, 15 April 1926, 7 April 1927). Though he retired as a Councillor on 24 May 1927, he was still on the Society's Library Committee at his death (*Proc. of the Linn. Soc.*, 152nd session (1939–40), p. 362).

We have seen that EAB was educated privately because he was 'a delicate boy', and this in itself would account for why he did not serve in the First World War. However, according to Alan Major (see n. 4 above), his brother Norman had served in the Territorials from 1905–12, and fought in the war with the 10th Royal West Kent Regiment in France, Belgium, and Italy, and, having been a victim of mustard gas, was demobilized in 1919 with the rank of Captain (*art. cit.*, p. 279). Though Major's belief that he joined the Nursery only in 1919 (for the health reason of an outdoor life as a mustard gas victim) is not borne out by the *Journal of Horticulture* which has him on site and a Director in 1915 (see quotation above), his statement that Edward 'spent little time on the affairs of the nursery business from 1919 … responsibility for this task being taken over by [Norman] and whose work was a considerable contribution towards the continuing success of G. Bunyard & Co.' (p. 279)[15] bears out once again Fred Stoker's words (see above) on Edward being a scholar rather than a trader, and the *Journal of Horticulture*'s reference to his pursuit of interest before profit. Throughout the war he published steadily on horticultural topics, often with a scholarly and historical emphasis; only two articles register the great conflict: an article by 'A.E.B.' (which is probably a misprint for 'E.A.B.') on increasing the supply of vegetables in *The Garden* of 13 February 1915, and a lecture read on 11 April 1917, on increasing the home fruit supply, in the *JRHS* for May 1918.

---

[15] *The House of Bunyard* (see n. 4) also states that Norman Bunyard 'released from Army service, now resumes his position as Director' (p. 4). On NB's later role in the firm, and particularly his focus on irises, see, e.g. 'Nursery Notes. Irises at Maidstone', *The Gardeners' Chronicle*, LXXVII, no. 2008, 20 June 1925, p. 438; 'Nursery Notes. Messrs. Geo. Bunyard & Co. Ltd.', ibid., XCIX, no. 2583, 27 June 1936, p. 423; and G. L. Pilkington's obituary in *The Iris Year Book* (1969), p. 103.

The year 1919 saw not only the return of his brother Norman to the firm, but the death of their father, aged 77, at Mereworth on 22 January from asthma and influenza (Death Certificate), one of the many who fell to the Influenza Epidemic at the time. In 1915 the *Journal of Horticulture* had said: 'The "soul" of Bunyards is as it has been for the last hundred years, and we hope that it will endure for another century' (LXX, no. 1809, 25 February 1915, p. 141). The nursery as George Bunyard knew it was to survive his death for a mere twenty years. His grave, below a yew tree, is in front of the west wall of the churchyard of St. Lawrence, Mereworth; the inscription, including the words 'And this mortal must put on immortality' (I. Corinthians xv. 53) is now barely legible.

The end of that year saw the appearance of the first issue of the *Journal of Pomology* (the Bodleian Library's copy is date-stamped 21 November 1919), founded by EAB and edited by him until July 1924. His own articles are all in the first three volumes, though he also published a few reviews in it thereafter; he was on its Publication Committee at his death. About this time, there is a sense of an efflorescence of energy, an enrichment of his life in terms both scholarly and personal. In 1920, in his forty-second year, there appeared *A Handbook of Hardy Fruits ... Apples and Pears*; the second volume on other fruits came out in 1925. His friendship with the writer Norman Douglas (see my later chapter) began with his visit to Italy to see him in 1922, and was to last his lifetime. In January 1923 the Royal Horticultural Society announced the administration of a scheme for 'The Testing of Varieties of Hardy Fruit for Commercial Purposes': under the chairmanship of the geneticist, William Bateson (1861–1926), there was a committee of ten – five representatives from the Ministry of Agriculture and five from the RHS, of whom EAB was one (*JRHS*, XLVIII (1923), 65–7, p. 66). At the Annual General Meeting of the RHS, on 13 February 1923, he was elected to the Society's Council (*JRHS*, XLIX (1924), ii), and became Chairman of the Fruit and Vegetable Committee in 1929 (*JRHS*, LV (1930), cxxi ff.) – both positions previously long held by his father.

By the 1920s the *Gardeners' Chronicle* declared that 'Mr. Edward A. Bunyard has made fruit his hobby as well as business, and no one would dispute that he is the foremost pomologist in this country to-day' (anon., 'An Afternoon with a Pomologist', LXXXII, no. 2124, 10 September 1927, 213–14, p. 213). As always with Bunyard, there is the Janus-faced quality:

certainly he knew his Mendelian genetics and he was a nurseryman, and yet he was also a connoisseur with a scholar's disinterestedness – profit was not put before pleasure, or the balance sheet before botanical curiosity. The *Gardeners' Chronicle* expresses this well:

> Of course, the most serious side of the business is the raising and selling of large quantities of all kinds of fruit trees, but Mr. Bunyard likes to embark on what he facetiously terms "joy rides" from which no profit is derived, but much pleasure. For example, he has collected as many varieties of Gooseberries as he can secure with a view to classifying them and discovering if any of them are synonymous, whilst in another part of the nursery he has planted over two hundred varieties of Pears obtained from all over Europe, the United States of America, and elsewhere, to see whether any of them are of value in this country. ... Not much of merit has, so far, appeared amongst his Pear collection, but he has obtained what he considers a most valuable variety in Admiral Gervais ... Mr. Bunyard was careful to point out that none of these varieties will be sent out by his firm until its merits have been thoroughly proved.[16] (ibid., p. 213)

Similarly, Collingwood Ingram has drawn attention to EAB's role in obtaining two unusual varieties of ornamental cherry: (i) the Yingtao or Chinese Fruiting Cherry: this had been introduced into this country in 1819 by Samuel Brooks who then owned a nursery on Newington Green, London, but it subsequently disappeared from Western cultivation. It was then re-introduced simultaneously by Ingram who in the spring of 1922 obtained two specimens from Japan, and by Bunyard who obtained grafts from America in the winter of 1922–3; in May 1927 Bunyard exhibited its fruit, which had been ripened indoors, at the Chelsea Flower Show;[17]

---

[16] Interestingly for a somewhat conservative man, EAB's term 'joy rides' was something of a modernism (and originally an American term), *joy-rider* being first recorded in *OED²* in 1908; it meant 'pleasure trip' with none of today's connotations of irresponsibility and even illegality; see J. Aitchison, *Language Joyriding* (Oxford, 1994), pp. 23–9.

[17] See C. Ingram, 'The Yingtao or Chinese Fruiting Cherry', *Journal of the Royal Horticultural Society*, LXVIII (1943), 307–9; C. Ingram, *Ornamental Cherries* (London, 1948), 122. The *Gardeners' Chronicle* in describing Bunyard's exhibition of the tree at

(ii) *Prunus cerasus,* var. *Bunyardii*: in 1924 EAB presented this tree to the Royal Botanic Garden, Edinburgh, saying that it had come from Persia; though Ingram observes that 'in view of the fact that Edward Bunyard was pre-eminently a pomologist, it is not unlikely that he received it as a fruiting variety', the fact that EAB presented the only known specimen to a Botanic Garden makes it look like another of his 'joy rides'.[18]

A discriminatingly phrased instance of what became a pervasive preference of beauty before pelf can be seen in his article 'Fruit Blossom in Kent', where, reflecting his musical interests (see above), he constructs a 'floral symphony' in four movements through the blossom season. It is worth quoting a whole paragraph for its unworldly praise of loveliness and its dismissal of commerce:

> Our final movement has more colour and no less majesty, as it introduces the apple with its elusive shades of pink, apt to be seen against a blue sky, and for preference in an old orchard of gnarled and distorted trees, of which there are still a few in Kent. For apples let us, therefore, avoid the orchard of the successful commercial grower, on the brick earth or limestone soils as a rule, and pass through to the poorer clays of the Weald, where venerable trees may still be found, all worthy to be cursed as fruit producers, but to the artistic eye a cause of thankfulness and joy. (*Country Life*, LV, no. 1425, 26 April 1924, 659–60, p. 659)

Chelsea in 1927 gives a different source for it, though its non-commercial nature as a fruit tree is evident: 'It was discovered by the late F. N. Meyer in 1907 near Tangsi, Chekiang Province ... Mr. Meyer sent grafts to Messrs. Bunyard from which they raised the first trees in this country. ... Mr. E. A. Bunyard informs us that the tree is quite self-fertile, and fruits quite well *where one tree only is grown*' (my italics; *GC*, LXXXI, no. 2109, 28 May 1927, 383–4).

[18] Ingram, *Ornamental Cherries*, 85. Miss Leonie Paterson, Archives Librarian of the Royal Botanic Garden, Edinburgh has kindly informed me (letter of 5 August 2004) that on 29 March 1924, Messrs. G. Bunyard & Co. Ltd. presented a number of plants from Persia: 'Apricot Bitter Kernel, Cherry Blabitu [later referred to as Prunus cerasus var. Bunyardii, though now I believe it has been amalgamated into Prunus vulgaris], Almond Hard-shell, Almond Thin-shell, Almond Pistachio, Plum Gurjeh'. Miss Paterson tells me that apparently the firm also made other gifts of seeds.

On occasion artistic flair might well properly serve commercial ends, as in the display of apples at the Chelsea Show of 1929. *Gardening Illustrated*'s caption to its dramatic photograph of Bunyard's apples brings out the surprising modernism of EAB's debt to cubism, whilst we may also see it as the lineal descendant of the visual awareness evident in his photographs for his father's *England's National Flower* (?1904; see above):

> a distinct breakaway from the basket or dish method, and the whole scheme is evidently influenced by the cubist movement. Vast cubes of black tower one above the other rather in the manner of New York's skyscrapers, and the fruit is piled on these without baskets or dishes. The gold and red of the Apples show admirably on such sombre backgrounds, and the whole represents an attempt to break away from the stereotyped methods of showing fruit. (F.A.H., 'Comments on the Chelsea Show', LI, no. 2621, 1 June 1929, 383; the photograph appeared again in the issue of 28 December 1929, 866.)

The devotion to the unusual, the interesting, and the epicurean was noble, but as Joan Morgan and Alison Richards have commented: 'For all it helped to keep the tradition of apple connoisseurship alive in sympathetic circles, Bunyard's evangelism could not arrest the slide away from diversity as commercial growers sought the holy grail of a few "perfect" market apples.'[19] Even his bold Chelsea display of 1929 provoked the admiring *Gardening Illustrated* to the humorous, but none the less ominous, comment on the cubist towers: 'Some people are saying that this arrangement is Mr. Bunyard's allusive way of announcing the issue by his firm next year of the square Apple, which has been so long demanded by the packing trade' (ibid., 383). In personal terms, his eventual bankruptcy must derive in part from his 'joy rides' where profit was not served; as the medieval proverb had it, 'Un jour viendra qui tout paiera'.

Though an article in *The New Flora and Silva*, 'The Anatomy of Dessert: I. The Cherry Succession', appeared in October 1928, heralding *The Anatomy of Dessert* in 1929, in which it was reprinted as the chapter on 'Cherries',

---

[19] J. Morgan and A. Richards, *The New Book of Apples* (London, 2002), p. 100. See also Dr Morgan's chapter 7 below.

EAB's greatness as a writer on food and wine must have been a long time a-ripening. Gourmets, like wine, are laid down and need time to mature. But prior to 1928 there are only two references to his epicurean appreciation: first, a mention of Carrie, the cook of his childhood days:

> Carrie was our cook, a very dark, akimbo sort of woman, with a tender heart for an admirer of her skill. A hot potato out of the saucepan before they went to the dining-room, or fresh jam-tart – tantalising thing – too hot to eat, too good to wait for. Such was Carrie, bless her! (*The Epicure's Companion*, 1937, p. 155)

In gastronomy as in horticulture 'the Child is father of the Man'. The second indication of a honed gourmet's palate is that in a letter to EAB of 22 August 1924 Norman Douglas writes that 'The *Anatomy of Dessert* is excellent' (see my chapter on 'Edward Bunyard and Norman Douglas', Letter A7, n. 5), and thus the book must have been in existence in some form five years before its publication.

The *Anatomy* was a limited edition of 1000 copies, signed by the author, and was published by Dulau of Bond Street, booksellers specializing in botanical books who also published the journal *The New Flora and Silva* in which two of the chapters first appeared. Its frontispiece, printed in green (and again in red on the dustwrapper), was by John Nash (1893–1977).[20] He describes the project in an undated letter to Dora Carrington:

> I have just finished a block for a Book called the Anatomy of Dessert – bisected apples, a melon gashed open, bananas protruding from their skins & half peeled apples also etc Fun with the fruit shapes![21]

Nash's engraving was used to draw attention to the book in leading literary journals of the day: J. C. Squire's *The London Mercury* (XX, no. 120,

---

[20] For details see J. Lewis, *John Nash: The Painter as Illustrator* (Loxhill, Godalming, 1978), pp. 125, 131; C. Colvin, *John Nash: Book Designs* (Colchester, 1986), pp. 31–2, no. 1.16; J. Greenwood, *The Wood-Engravings of John Nash* (Liverpool, 1987), p. 113.

[21] John Nash Archive, Hyman Kreitman Research Centre, Tate Britain, TGA 8910.13.2.109, end of letter.

October 1929, 587); and Desmond MacCarthy's *Life and Letters* (III, no. 18, November 1929, inside back cover). The periodicals in which reviews appeared reflected its appeal not only to gardeners but also to a wider constituency of connoisseurship. In the horticultural journals there was an anonymous review in *JRHS* LV (1930), 160–1, and one by Sir William Lawrence (1870–1934), Treasurer of the Royal Horticultural Society 1924–8, in the *Gardeners' Chronicle*, LXXXVI, no. 2235, 26 October 1929, 329; interestingly, Sir William drew attention to a quality of Bunyard which keeps recurring: a man who was not at ease in a commercial age:

> Like Rolla [*vid.* Alfred de Musset, 'Rolla' (1833), I: 'Je suis venu trop tard dans un monde trop vieux'], Mr. E. A. Bunyard, whose book *The Anatomy of Dessert* I have just read with pleasure and with profit, was born too late into a world too old. Canning, chemicals and cold storage have combined with mass-production and marketing boards to produce a uniformly low standard of food, or, in Mr. Bunyard's words, "The Jonathan Apple and Jamaican Banana level" [p. v].

In journals of a non-specialist nature one may cite: George Forrester Scott (1864–1937), who published under the names John Halsham and John Halstead, and whose interests were gardening, classical literature, cricket, the country, brickwork [*sic*], and whose Sunday afternoons were devoted to the *Divina Commedia* in Bunyardian fashion 'in his beloved and worn Venetian edition of 1568' (*Times* obituary, 16 April 1937, p. 16; cf. also the *TLS* files), in the *Times Literary Supplement*, 17 October 1929, 807 (the review was published anonymously); E. V. Lucas (1868–1938), a prolific journalist, essayist, and author, in the *Sunday Times*, 3 November 1929, 14; G. C. Taylor (1901–62), gardening editor of *Country Life* and gardening correspondent of the *Observer*, and author of horticultural works, in *Country Life*, 2 November 1929, l (i.e. 50). It is worth drawing attention to a delightful review, 'The Compleat Carpophilist' (i.e. fruit-lover), by Martin Armstrong (1882–1974), novelist, poet, short-story writer, literary journalist, and *bon vivant* (like EAB, he was a member of the Saintsbury Club, and EAB would anthologize his poems on wine in *The Epicure's Companion*), in the *Saturday Review*, CXLVIII, no. 3868, 14 December 1929, 717–18; thus a brief extract:

Mr. Bunyard's book, though written in prose, is of the essence of poetry, and like all good poetry it is highly practical. He knows each variety of each fruit and calls it by its name, and he describes lovingly and accurately its flavour, texture and appearance, its excellences and shortcomings, and tells when it should be gathered and when, on a subtle expected change in its appearance, it is ready for eating. (717)

The association with John Nash, begun with the *Anatomy*, continued. In 1931 Bunyard's began the annual issue of a catalogue, 'Vegetables for Epicures', for 'those who prefer dining to exhibiting' (1931 preface); it was welcomed by a letter from 'East Sussex' in *Gardening Illustrated* (LIII, no. 2709, 7 February 1931, 83), stating that 'Messrs. Bunyard, of Maidstone, strike a new note in their little List, just issued, entitled "Vegetables for Epicures"'. All the catalogues save those for 1933, 1934, and 1938, are preserved in the Lindley Library of the Royal Horticultural Society, and each, apart from 1931, has a guest preface by a gastronomic writer: 1932 – Marcel Boulestin (1878–1943), restaurateur, author, and the first television chef; 1935 – Lady Alice M. Martineau (1865–1956), author of gardening and cookery books; 1936 – Dr H. E. Durham 'whose enterprise and skill in the garden and kitchen places him in the front rank of our apostles of Good Living' (Introduction), and presumably the author of *Notes on the Medical History of Cider, Past and Present* (Cambridge, 1929; copy in the British Library); 1937 – Rosine Rosat (probably a humorous pseudonym for Bunyard: see below in this chapter re *Old Garden Roses*); 1939 – André Simon (1877–1970), inter alia, President of the Wine and Food Society. Clare Colvin (see n. 20) reproduces (p. 91, no. 3.8) John Nash's line drawing for the fourth edition of the catalogue, 1934, showing: 'a hod full of bursting pea-pods, new carrots, marrow and parsley; more carrots, onions, baby turnips and a large cabbage complete the traditional summer medley of vegetables' (a copy must be in the John Nash Archive, now at Tate Britain, but is not currently retrievable). In 1963 Nash sent preliminary material to Studio and Vista Books, London, for some kind of autobiography (see SVBooks's reply of 19 July 1963; John Nash Archive, TGA 8910.3.1.4); in these unpublished notes is an account of his relationship with Bunyard:

In [the year is left blank, but probably 1929] I became acquainted with E A Bunyard for whose book the Anatomy of Dessert I did a cover design & was asked by him to serve on a ['the' written above] Committee of the RHS that criticised & made awards to the flower paintings sent in to the Society's Shows. [The award was the Grenfell Medal, instituted in 1919; though Frances Bunyard several times (e.g. 1932, 1934, 1935) won the Silver Grenfell Medal for paintings of fruit or flowers, less good fortune attended Nash on apparently the one occasion he entered:] ... [I] sent in 8 paintings of plants over which I lavished considerable effort ['care' written above]. I was awarded a Bronze Grenfel [*sic*] medal for – as the citation went – my flower studies & felt properly put in my place! [see *JRHS*, LX (1935), clxxviii] The War terminated these pleasant occasions but before that I visited Bunyard at his bungalow in the middle of the orchards at Allington. His was a very comfortable bachelor existence carried on with due regard to the science of living. His collection of books on Pomology & other fruits was remarkable. On the morning after the night of my arrival he went out early & returned very gloomily with a branch of cherry on which the fruit then as big as large peas were blackened by frost. It was a ['the' written above] disastrous late frost of May 17th 193 [the final number is omitted, but it must be '5': *The Times* of Saturday 18 May 1935, 14 d, has a number of reports, the first headed 'A Return to Winter/Frost and Snow/Extensive Damage to Crops', and the second headed 'In the Orchards/Fruit Crops Almost Ruined' begins with south-west Kent] & all the fruit crops suffered, while young ash & oak growth hung black & limp on the trees. (John Nash Archive, Tate Britain, TGA 8910.3.1.4, pp. 8–9)

In that fruit is, after all, grown for eating, we could regard all EAB's writing as gastronomic, but the turn taken in his publications from the late 1920s shows his epicurean interests becoming overt and specialized: in addition to the *Anatomy* (1929) and its two chapters which appeared first in *The New Flora and Silva* (1928–9), there was 'The Gourmet's Fruit Garden' (*Country Life*, 19 October 1929). He must indeed for some time have been establishing an acknowledged gastronomic expertise: André Simon records him as a guest at a luncheon on 15 October 1929 at the Connaught Rooms which sought to explore Saint-Pinot wines from Champagne and Burgundy; other guests were Sir Herbert Jackson, Sir George Chadwick, and Stephen Tallents, all from the Empire Marketing Board, together with Sir Gerald Du Maurier (1873–1934; the actor-manager); Maurice Healy (1887–1943; barrister; he was to write EAB's obituary in *Wine and Food*); Compton Mackenzie (1883–1972; novelist, journalist, and memoirist); J. C. Squire (1884–1958; literary journalist and anthologist); A. J. A. Symons (1900–41; bibliophile, authority on literature of the 1890s, and now best remembered for his *The Quest for Corvo*, 1934); and Michael Sadleir (1888–1957; bibliographer and novelist, his best-remembered novel being *Fanny by Gaslight*, 1940).[22] This was a brave new world of gastronomic, social, and literary sensibility in which EAB clearly moved at ease and at will. And who but Bunyard would bring these spheres together in an advertisement in *The New Flora and Silva* (VII.ii, January 1935, vii) for the 1935 edition of 'Vegetables for Epicures' where he quotes a couplet from an untitled work (mis-ascribed to Thos. King), William King (1663–1712), *The Art of Cookery, In Imitation of Horace's Art of Poetry* (London, 1708):

> The foods we eat, by various juice control
> The narrowness or largeness of our soul. (141–2)

1931 saw the first dinner of the Saintsbury Club,[23] founded to honour that doyen of the wine cellar, Professor George Saintsbury, on 23 October; the menu included 'Pommes d'Allington' and 'Noix à la glace', the apples and walnuts being a present from Bunyard. The choice of Allingtons was a good one, not just because of the taste, but because its commercial introduction had been in 1896, the centenary year of Bunyards when EAB had entered the firm; now it had appeared on the first menu of the Saintsbury Club. Records of the Club are incomplete, but the surviving ones show that Bunyard attended dinners on 23 April 1935; 23 April 1936; 23 October 1936; 21 April 1937; 19 October 1937; 27 April 1938; and

---

[22] See A. L. Simon, *Tables of Content: Leaves from My Diary* (London, 1933), 42–3; and his *By Request: An Autobiography* (London, 1957), 68–9.

[23] Simon, *Tables of Content*, 142–4; *By Request*, 80–5; see also 'The Cellarer' [i.e. André Simon], *The Saintsbury Club: A Scrap Book* (first printed privately 1943; the edition published in 140 copies by the Rare Wine Co., Sonoma, California, 1993, has additional material). On Bunyard as a clubman see Alan Bell's chapter below.

26 October 1938;[24] he must also have almost certainly been at the third Dinner on 24 October 1932 as 'Les Ribstons d'Allington' were on the menu (*Saintsbury Club: Scrap Book* (see n. 23), p. 47). He was clearly coming into professional association with André Simon, one of the founders of the Club and its Cellarer; he became a regular contributor to Simon's *Wine and Food*, the journal of the Wine and Food Society, from its first issue in 1934, and the Winter 1938 issue records him for the first time as a member of the Society's Advisory Council.[25] On 23 February 1933 Simon records him as the Guest of the Day at the Wine Trade Club luncheon at which he spoke on 'the selling of wine – at the consumer's point of view' (Simon, *Tables of Content* (see n. 22), pp. 240–1).

However, 1933 was more significant for the second edition of the *Anatomy*, now published 'With a Few Notes on Wine' by Chatto and Windus who republished it in their Phoenix Library of Food and Drink in 1936, the year which also saw Bunyard's essay, 'Gardening for Epicures' in Miles Hadfield's *The Gardener's Companion*. Again, reviews of the second edition of the *Anatomy* were in both horticultural journals and in ones of a wider cultural interest. Thus H. S. Redgrove, a chemist, states in the *Gardeners' Chronicle*, XCIV, no. 2428, 8 July 1933, that 'It is a volume which everyone who grows, sells or eats fruits, and, indeed, everyone who loves good living and good literature, should secure, not only for the valuable information it contains but also for the sheer joy of reading it' (28); and the

---

[24] I am indebted to Mr Merlin Holland for copies of the seating plans of the Saintsbury Club dinners. The Club dines twice a year, in April and October, but extant seating plans only begin with the April 1935 dinner.

[25] Given Bunyard's pursuit of connoisseurship at the expense of profit in fruit and roses, it is worth recording the opinion of Julian Symons (brother of A. J. A. Symons, Secretary of the Wine and Food Society) in his *A. J. A. Symons: His Life and Speculations* (London, 1950) that the articles in *Wine and Food* increasingly 'were written, more and more, not merely for a minority, but for a very small minority of the membership, conscious of its own gastronomic culture; the recondite nature of many of the subjects, and the tone of airy superiority in which they were treated must have frightened away more prospective members than it attracted. Lunches and dinners gradually became fewer, better, and – more costly' (pp. 157–8). Though EAB's articles should escape these strictures, one notes the unworldly ethos in which he moved.

anonymous reviewer in *The Listener*, IX, no. 229, 31 May 1933, declares that 'this book is eminent, a little peak of wisdom, disgraceful to the flats of ignorance about it. No wife can become perfect without it.' (883)

If we may trace the sophisticated gourmet back to the taste for the potatoes and jam-tarts of Carrie, the cook of his childhood, then perhaps the genealogy of Bunyard the rosarian goes back at least to 1904 and the photographs he took for his father's *England's National Flower*. He published on old varieties of rose in *The New Flora and Silva* from 1929, in *The Rose Annual of the National Rose Society* from 1930, in *Gardening Illustrated* from 1932, in *Country Life* from 1934, as well as in *The Countryman* in 1934 and in *JRHS* in 1938. Of course, Bunyard's great publication on roses was his book published by *Country Life*: *Old Garden Roses* (London, 1936). Of this Graham Stuart Thomas wrote:

> And then E. A. Bunyard turned his rare ability to the old roses, and the result, charming, readable, and erudite, *Old Garden Roses*, appeared in 1936. As far as I know this was the first book for over a hundred years which owed its inception to a deep-seated love for all the old roses. His life was prematurely ended, otherwise he would undoubtedly have corrected the several inaccuracies which are to be found in his book, but he gave new zest to the cause of old roses, and collected many varieties together. We of this generation owe much to his guidance.[26]

The Hon. Robert James (1873–1960) declared in the *JRHS*, LXII (1937), 190–4, that Bunyard had 'written beautifully and with charm of expression. He has command of his own language as well as knowledge of his subject (190), and 'Oriflamme', in *Gardening Illustrated*, LVIII, no. 3016, 26 December 1936, 754, reported that 'A close study of Mr. Bunyard's book has given your reviewer, as it will others, so much pleasure that frequently he lost himself in its pages'.

Bunyard's own copy is in the Lindley Library of the Royal Horticultural Society (Case: 930; Shelf: ROS; No.: Bun), with a label that it was 'From the Library of EDWARD ASHDOWN BUNYARD Purchased in 1940 out of the REGINALD CORY BEQUEST'. Bunyard had had it rebound in red

---

[26] *The Old Shrub Roses*, revd. edn. (London, 1979), p. 38.

leather, with gilt top-edges, and the title in gilt on the spine. At the back are two letters of appreciation: one, 6 May 1937, from Mrs Frederick Love Keays of Great Neck, Long Island, and the other from Vita Nicolson (Vita Sackville-West, 1892–1962). It is dated 12th January 1937, from Sissinghurst Castle, Kent, and is about two typed pages in length. Four paragraphs are detailed points which need not be quoted, but the opening is worth citation:

> Dear Mr. Bunyard,
> I must really write and tell you with what intense enjoyment I have been reading your book on roses. I have read every word of it and made careful notes at the end. It had the effect of driving me to look at the Wilton Diptych [on which EAB had written, pp. 49–50] in the National Gallery, and has also had the effect of giving me fresh ideas for the garden here. In other words, I want to plant a long rose hedge and also some roses under an overhanging tree. I wonder if you could possibly spare the time to come over here one day and give me your advice. Any day except January 21st. 22nd. and 23rd or February 8th and 9th would suit me.

Bunyard did spare the time. On 20 January 1937 VS-W wrote from Sissinghurst to her husband, Harold Nicolson, in terms which show she was aware that Bunyard was a gourmet as well as a rosarian:

> My darling Hadjikins,
> I've spent a lovely orgiaical day with Mr. Bunyard, ordering roses recklessly. He came to luncheon, and knowing that he was very epicurean in his tastes I gave him a delicious luncheon: Indian corn on the cob to start with, then woodcock sitting on a croûton with paté de foie gras and a necklace of truffles round it, and Clos Vougeot 1911 to drink – and Chateau Yquem to finish up with – all of which he greatly appreciated. Then when he was well-fed and well-wined (I also gave him one of Richard's cigars!) we went out and talked about roses for the rest of the afternoon.[27]

---

[27] This letter is now in Sackville-West, V. mss. collection, Manuscripts Department, The Lilly Library, Indiana University, Bloomington, Indiana. On Bunyard and Sissinghurst see J. Brown, *Vita's Other World: A Gardening Biography of V. Sackville-West* (London, 1985), 131; J. Brown, *Sissinghurst: Portrait of a Garden* (London, 1990), 31 ('[EAB] ... a visitor who amused her'), 72, 110 (Harold Nicolson ordered 20 musk roses from EAB).

So far as I am aware, no reviewer or correspondent commented on a sly Bunyardian piece of humour: the creation of an improbable pseudonym. The Appendix 'The Rose in the Still Room' is ascribed to 'Rosine Rosat'; when we learn from the *Oxford English Dictionary* (which Bunyard must have consulted in its multi-volume version) that *rosine* = 'rose', sb., is recorded once, 1500–20, in Dunbar, and that *rosat*, adj. and sb., is recorded between 1579 and 1674 as a form of *roset*, adj., = 'distilled from roses', recorded between 1398 and 1657 (Rosine Rosat talks about 'a rose vinegar "Roset"', p. 151), then failure to find the author Rosine Rosat is no mystery. This dark lady also figures in the 1937 edition of the annual catalogue 'Vegetables for Epicures' as the author of the prefatory 'Recipes and Reflexions'. Though humorous *noms de plume* were loved by gardening writers of the 1920s and '30s (e.g. Anne Amateur, Aytch Pea, White Lady, Smilax, Sub Rosa, Blackthorn, Ladybird, Ladye of the Flowers, Hortulanus, and see 'Ruslin Lieves' below), Rosine Rosat's 'Reflexions' have an edged wit which is EAB's signature: '[of cabbage:] Prolonged cooking reduces an otherwise honest personality to an insurgent of lamentable power … [of peas:] Plain boiling water for these when young. And not too much of that. Their preparation demands the absorbed attention which moderns accord to the young. … Older peas, and if it be not heresy, the first peas of all, which have been a little hardened by adversity, may be simmered with butter, onion and lettuce leaf. Who does not prefer a woman of the world, whose sophistication is an added charm, to the "old girl" whose aggressive maturity knows no ameliorative disguise? But youth should arrive unadorned' (copy in the Lindley Library of the RHS).

Behind *Old Garden Roses* were not only the Bunyard Nurseries which raised 400 varieties of rose, but a colloquy over the years with other great rose growers, both in England and Europe. Thus in his 'Some Rose Memories of 1937' in *The New Flora and Silva* (1938) Bunyard recalls staying with Major Lawrence Johnston (1871–1958) near Menton, and visiting Captain George Warre's garden at Roquebrune (Mrs Norah Warre, 1880–1979, continued gardening there into the 1970s after Captain Warre's death in 1957), and the Hanbury garden of La Mortola, near Ventimiglia; in England he visited Nymans in Sussex, owned by Col. Leonard Messel (1873–1953) who with his gardener, James Comber (c. 1866–1953), raised a great collection of old roses; the Hon. Robert James (1873–1960) who was assembling an 'enchanted Rose garden' at St. Nicholas, Richmond, Yorkshire; and the Hon. David Bowes Lyon (1902–61) at St. Paul's Walden Bury, Hitchin, as well as the institutional gardens of the National Rose Society Trial Ground; Kew; and Wisley. He mentions saving several varieties from the collection of roses of the late Miss Ellen Willmott (1858–1934) who bankrupted herself gardening at Warley Place, Essex, as well as at her properties on the Riviera (cf. also *Old Garden Roses*, p. 77). In his article on rose hunting in 1939 in the same journal, he again begins on the Riviera, staying with his friend, Basil Leng (1898–1979, on whom see below and fn. 35), visiting the garden of Mrs Andrea (about whom I have discovered nothing) at Peymeinade, as well as many of the Riviera and Parisian nurseries.[28] It was from La Mortola, according to Graham Stuart Thomas, that Bunyard obtained the 'particularly fine form' of *Rosa brunonii*, 'La Mortola', and Thomas secured it from Kiftsgate Court in Gloucestershire where Mrs Heather Muir had planted it, and introduced it under the name 'La Mortola'; Mrs Muir had also obtained the *Rosa filipes* 'Kiftsgate' from Bunyard who in turn had probably secured it from the Roseraie de l'Haÿ, near Châtenay-Malabry, Paris, which he visited at the end of his 1939 tour.[29]

Yet all the time the development of these newer interests in gastronomy and rose-culture was taking place, articles, notes, reviews, and letters on fruit of all kinds and on the bibliography of matters horticultural continued to appear. Official recognition of his gifts also grew. We have already noted that he was on the Council of the Linnean Society from 1924–7, and he remained on its Library Committee until his death. He had joined the Council of the Royal Horticultural Society in 1923 (*JRHS*, XLIX (1924), ii), and became a member of four of its standing committees, and chairman of two: the Fruit and Vegetable Committee in 1929, following in his father's

---

[28] Most of the biographical details of the gardeners mentioned in this paragraph can be found in: R. Desmond, *Dictionary of British and Irish Horticulturalists* … (London, 1994); G. S. Thomas, *Recollections of Great Gardeners* (London, 2003); C. Quest-Ritson, *The English Garden Abroad* (London, 1992); V. Russell, *Gardens of the Riviera* (London, 1993).

[29] G. S. Thomas, *Climbing Roses Old and New*, revd. edn. (London, 1983), 33, 34.

path, and the Library Committee in 1925.[30] He was involved with E. A. Bowles (1865–1954) in the appointment of W. T. Stearn (1911–2001) as Librarian of the Lindley Library in 1932.[31] Notable recognition came in 1934 when he was awarded the Veitch Memorial Gold Medal 'for his contributions to pomology'.[32] At some point he was elected a Member of the Royal Societies Club; founded in 1894, it was 'for the association in Membership of Fellows and Members of the principal Learned Societies, Universities, and Institutions of the United Kingdom, India, and the Colonies; Academicians and Associates of the Academies, together with persons distinguished in Literature, Science, and Art, with the object of affording facilities for social intercourse and re-union, while furthering the objects and interests of the Learned Societies' (*Royal Societies Club*, London, 1914, 11; copy in the Bodleian Library, Oxford). Though Bunyard did not appear in the membership list of 1914, that list does give an idea of the Club's scope and eminence: it included A. C. Benson, Louis Blériot, Lord Curzon, Sir Edward Elgar, Sir Arthur Evans, Lord Halsbury, Thomas Hardy, Lord Kitchener, Nansen of the Antarctic (Captain Scott had been a Member), Ivan Pavlov, and Theodore Roosevelt; obviously not all were of this stature but the Society was no mean company. This 1914 list is the only one I know, and, grimly, we only know of Bunyard's membership because it was in its premises, at 63 St. James's Street, London, that he shot himself on 19 October 1939.

There is evidence, too, 'about this time', of a more popular recognition. Beginning in 1930, the weekly *Gardening Illustrated* ran a series of poems by 'Poeticus' under the title 'Potted Plantsmen'; the second of these biographical sketches was Bunyard (LII, no. 2671, 17 May 1930, 316):

---

[30] F. Stoker's obituary of EAB, *Proceedings of the Linnean Society of London*, 152nd session (1939–40), 362; J. Morgan and A. Richards, op. cit. n. 19, 100; B. Elliott, 'The gastronomic works of Edward Ashdown Bunyard', *The Garden* (as the *JRHS* is now called) CXVI (1991), 320–1, p. 321; *JRHS*, LV (1930), cxxi ff.

[31] M. Allan, *E. A. Bowles & His Garden at Myddelton House [1865–1954]* (London, 1973), 189–90.

[32] H. R. Fletcher, *The Story of the Royal Horticultural Society 1804–1968* (London, 1969), 518.

A BIOGRAPHICAL ESSAY

E. A. BUNYARD, F.L.S.,
Pomologist, Author, and principal of
G. Bunyard and Co., of Maidstone.

> His initials "E.A.B."
> Mean a lot to you and me
> When they come below a "Fruit" dissertation.
> He marks, and learns, and grows
> Before his scholarly pen flows.
> What he writes about, he knows
> And no man better in his generation.

Four years later, the same journal had an article by Ruslin Lieves (*sic*), 'Round the World in an Hour: A Christmas Broadcast' (LVI, no. 2910, 22 December 1934, 747–8). In this imaginary broadcast there is a charming vignette of EAB and his brother, Norman, engrossed in the library at Allington:

> We then trespass upon Edward A. Bunyard and G. Norman Bunyard taking their ease in the former's library at Allington. "E.A." is probably deep either in the very earliest or the very latest treatise on pomology, or he is writing one himself, and "G.N." is amusing himself with a few rhizomes under his new microscope, the present of the Iris Society, inscribed "From his admirers in grateful recognition of his work for the advancement of Iris cultivation and towards stopping the rot." (p. 747)

Scripts survive from 1937–9 of four wireless broadcasts in which EAB took part (see Bibliography for details).

In 1936 Miles Hadfield edited *The Gardener's Companion*, one of a series of *Companions* published by Dent, including *The Motorist's Companion* (1936), *The Golfer's Companion* (1937), and, of course, Bunyard's *The Epicure's Companion* (1937). There were five contributors to Hadfield, EAB's essay being a chapter on 'Gardening for Epicures', a *tour de force* in 24 pages on vegetables, herbs, and fruit: practical, deeply informed, humorous, epigrammatic, and full of literary and contemporary allusion. So we move from Petronius to the Marx brothers:

Those followers of Calvin who have tried to charge the epicure with the grosser indulgences of the gourmand cannot reach us in the garden. Trimalchio and all his crew would be sadly deflated here. No moral reprobation falls upon us as we compare the texture and flavour of our fruits and vegetables and decide to grow only the best. ... (p. 13)

The family of Cucurbitaceae are the Marx brothers of the vegetable garden, protean in their disguises and surprises, not for all tastes, it may be, but it would be unfair to judge them by their worst jokes. (p. 18)

As Edward Cahen said in his review of the book on EAB's contribution: 'a dissertation on vegetables and fruits packed full of good sense and fun as well. Alas! only 24 pages, but what pages!' (*Gardening Illustrated*, LVIII, no. 3008, 31 October 1936, 645)

'Shortly after this', in 1937, EAB had two gastronomic essays in the short-lived journal *Night and Day*. Other contributors to this weekly included Rose Macaulay, V. S. Pritchett, William Empson, Elizabeth Bowen, Graham Greene, Anthony Powell, Evelyn Waugh, Osbert Lancaster, John Betjeman, Hugh Casson, Pamela Hansford Johnson, Cyril Connolly, T. F. Powys, Stevie Smith, Christopher Isherwood, Alistair Cooke, James Thurber, Henry Miller ... once again, one reflects, no mean company.

However, 1937 was more significant in that it saw the publication of Bunyard's latest book, *The Epicure's Companion*. I have noted earlier in this chapter what a family production this was, with the editorial labour shared between Edward and Lorna, and between them they contributed almost all the articles; the illustrations were by Frances Bunyard, and their sister Marguerite also wrote two brief pieces. There were only six other essayists. EAB was the author of 'Oysters, Vegetables, Herbs, Strange Meats, Game, Foie Gras, Salads, Apple Pie, Cheese, Dessert, Oranges and Lemons, the Ceriman and the Grapefruit, the Banana, the Art of Drinking, the Wine List, a Table of Vintage Years, the Handling and Storage of Wine, the Lineage of Brandy, Rum, Gin, Cyder, Ale and Beer, On Wine-Merchants' Catalogues, Tea, Coffee, and Restaurant Technique'. There was also 'An Epicure's Anthology' chosen by Edward and Lorna Bunyard. EAB did indeed have in gastronomic matters 'the largest and most comprehensive soul'. It is small wonder that he became a member of the Advisory Council of the Wine and Food Society in 1938.

The reviews were admiring. The anonymous reviewer of *Night and Day* (though there are preceding reviews by Evelyn Waugh, I think this one, in a separate section, is anonymous) thought it 'a very good book indeed' (4 November 1937, 25), and the *Times Literary Supplement* (reviewer untraced) concluded: 'This is a book to be read at leisure in the study or the drawing-room, digested in the comfort that follows a perfect meal, and put into practice in shop and kitchen the next day' (6 November 1937, 854). In more specialist journals, Evelyn, Viscountess Byng of Vimy (1870–1949), who created a great garden at Thorpe Hall, Thorpe-le-Soken, in Essex, wrote a lengthy review in *JRHS* in which she said that:

> In his latest book Mr. Bunyard, assisted by able friends, has again given us another of those ironic and witty treatises which readers of his "Anatomy of Dessert" would expect. The present volume is so filled with good things – not only gastronomical – that one is tempted to quote *ad lib.*, and excite the reader's mental appetite as well as his gastric juices to a high degree of stimulation. There is a vast store of classical knowledge, of culinary expertness, and of humour in these 528 pages, and I thoroughly enjoyed the excursion into such varying provinces. (LXIII, 1938, 142–3, p. 142)

Though Bunyard sent a complimentary copy to Fred Stoker (*c.* 1879–1943; see n. 6), it would be wrong to see in F.S.'s encomiastic review (*The Gardeners' Chronicle*, CII, no. 2657, 27 November 1937, 397–8) evidence of Gibbon's assertion that complimentary copies are the levying of 'an unavoidable tax of civility and compliment' (*Memoirs of My Life*, chap. V, '*Essai*: Service in Militia 1758–62'). Stoker speaks with the warmth of personal knowledge:

> A specialist has been defined as one who knows everything of something and something of everything. Mr. E. A. Bunyard's wide scholarship, his willingness, nay, eagerness to try all things, and his acute sense of proportion – I speak of what I know – amply qualify him both to edit *The Epicure's Companion* and to take a greater share in its compilation than any of his experienced and able collaborators. (p. 397)

He concludes:

In spite of its title and undoubted value to those for whom it is primarily written, it is a book for all who enjoy good writing and are not averse to extending their range of knowledge. (p. 398)

****

'Ah, you publishing scoundrel!'
(Henry James, *The Aspern Papers* (1888), viii)

Miss Bordereau's words to the narrator of *The Aspern Papers* are a reproof to all who would pursue the intimate life of a public figure. This biographical essay has so far concentrated on the official life – the books, articles, reviews, the plants, committees. And knowledge of the private man is, from lack of evidence, so fugitive. Of course, one could argue that this does not matter; that great medieval scholar, Helen Waddell, wrote in 1947, 'All of me that matters is in the books'.[33] It is an austere view, but preferable to the prejudice that public achievement is somehow not expressive of 'the real man'. For Edward Bunyard, books and fruit and roses, food and wine, were passions, and they tell us much about him.

None the less, we do know of some friendships. That with Norman Douglas (1868–1952), whose pocket-diaries record the sending of 310 items of correspondence to Bunyard, began in 1921 and ended only with EAB's death in 1939; as this friendship is the subject of my later chapter 'Edward Bunyard and Norman Douglas', I will say no more here.[34] Not so well known is his friendship with Basil Leng (1898–1979), and as this was, I believe, a significant relationship some fullness in my account of it is justified.[35] William Basil St. Quentin Leng was born on 20 August 1898 at Ecclesall Bierlow in the West Riding of Yorkshire. After Wellington, the

---

[33] D. Felicitas Corrigan, *Helen Waddell: A Biography* (London, 1986), 347.
[34] See also my 'E. A. Bunyard and Norman Douglas', *Norman Douglas 3. Symposium* ed. Wilhelm Meusburger and Helmut Swozilek (Bregenz, 2005), 73–9.
[35] The account here reproduces part of my 'Edward Bunyard by the Mediterranean', *The Mediterranean Garden*, no. 38, October 2004, 5–14. It gives me the greatest pleasure to acknowledge the help, by correspondence and telephone, which I have received from Mrs Gladys Clarke of Domme-en-Périgord who knew Leng.

First World War (he was a Lieutenant in the Coldstream Guards), and two years at Christ Church, Oxford (1919–21), he spent a brief period in the office of the family business of the *Sheffield Daily Telegraph,* the sale of which a year or two later to the Kemsley empire for over a million pounds would give a pecuniary vitality to his life. In January 1922 he took up a post as gardener to Compton Mackenzie on the Channel Island of Herm (an appointment recalled in Mackenzie's *My Life and Times: Octave Five: 1915–1923* (London, 1966), 214–15), and then on Jethou. It was at this time that Norman Douglas wrote on 8 December 1924 to 'Dear Bunny': 'I am sure you would like Leng, the bottanist [sic]. His address is Isle of Jethou, Guernsey. I fancy he is in London now, but don't know for certain. Why not fix up some appointment with him?' (Letter A8 in my chapter 'Edward Bunyard and Norman Douglas') In 1927 he purchased a house at Socoa, near St. Jean-de-Luz and Biarritz, and transformed a clay bank covered with rough grass into a garden of bulbs, shrubs and herbaceous plants. Bunyard had clearly taken up Douglas's suggestion to fix up an appointment with him for after a visit to Socoa in September 1930 he described in an article, 'A Seaside Garden', Leng's successes in gardening 'exposed … to the full force of the great breakers which make so grand a spectacle' (*Country Life,* 1 November 1930, 563–4, p. 563). Three years later saw Leng and Bunyard as joint authors of an article, rich in historical reference, 'The Camellia in Europe' in *The New Flora and Silva* (January 1933, 123–9). Then around 1936–7 Leng purchased an old farmhouse, La Ferme des Orangers, on Cap d'Antibes. Besides himself creating a garden full of interesting plants, he became over the years the adviser and friend of many of the great gardeners on the Riviera: Mrs George (Norah) Warre (formerly Mrs Emerson Bainbridge) and the Villa Roquebrune on Cap Martin, on which Leng and Patrick M. Synge wrote a beautifully illustrated account in the *JRHS* (October 1966); Julien Marnier-Lapostolle and the Villa les Cèdres on Cap Ferrat; Major Lawrence Johnston and La Serre de la Madone in the Gorbio valley above Menton; Arpad Plesch and the Villa La Léonina at Beaulieu; Charles, Vicomte de Noailles and the Villa Noailles at Grasse; and Pierre and Nicole Champin and their garden, La Chèvre d'Or at Biot, near Antibes. Leng was indeed a man who touched many lives: besides Norman Douglas with whom he travelled in Italy (there are several references in Mark Holloway's *Norman Douglas: A Biography,* London,

1976), we find him in a photograph of a ski party at Davos in 1939 with amongst others Eddy Sackville-West, Peggy Strachey and Cyril Connolly (reproduced in Clive Fisher, *Cyril Connolly: A Nostalgic Life* (London, 1995), facing p. 306), in the company of the composer William Walton (mentioned in Nancy Cunard, *Grand Man: Memories of Norman Douglas* (London, 1954), p. 77), and there are delightful accounts of plant-hunting expeditions in the company of his brother Kyrle and Robert Gathorne-Hardy in the latter's *Three Acres and a Mill* (London, 1939).

In May 1939 Bunyard stayed with Leng at La Ferme des Orangers; his article 'Rose Hunting in 1939' (*The New Flora and Silva*, November 1939, 11–17) opens: 'My Rose year ... began in the Riviera, where, to the tune of nightingales and the scent of Orange-blossom, I settled in a friendly house for a few weeks' holiday'. Proof that the 'friendly house' was Leng's comes in Bunyard's epicurean account, 'A Few Meals in France' (*Wine and Food*, Autumn 1939, 223–9) of what must be the same visit:

> 'Come and stay here,' said my friend B, who lives on the Cap d'Antibes, 'the roses are out and the orange blossom, too.' Who could resist such an invitation? – and I knew that the nightingales would also be singing! ... At Antibes, the nightingales were already at work and, better still, my host had an excellent Italian cook, long resident in France, who combined the best of both cuisines. Next morning came marmalade made from oranges grown on the estate, my first experience of such a home-grown product. It was curiously Oxfordian in flavour, but that cannot have been due to the accent of my host.

The location on Cap d'Antibes, 'B' for Basil, and the Oxford accent all fit; and Mrs Gladys Clarke of Domme-en-Périgord, who knew Leng, has most kindly informed me that his cook, Thérèse, was Italian (from Turin), and that the *ferme* ('estate' is rather a grand word, apparently, for its size) did indeed live up to its name with orange trees from which Leng's marmalade was made.

Leng's was not the only friendly house for Bunyard on the Riviera. His earlier article, 'Some Rose Memories of 1937' (*The New Flora and Silva*, January 1938, 116–21) begins:

> The Rose year of 1937 began very pleasantly for me in late March at Major Johnston's hospitable home near Mentone. In my room stood a generous bowl of Roses, magnificent under the electric light.

Lawrence Johnston (1871–1958) was the creator of great gardens at Hidcote in Gloucestershire and at La Serre de la Madone on the Riviera; he was some seven years older than Bunyard, and there is not quite the same indication of closeness with Bunyard as there is between EAB and Leng, some twenty years younger. Both men, like Douglas, survived beyond Bunyard's terrible death in 1939, Leng dying on 1 May 1979 (see Death Notice in the *Daily Telegraph*, 3 May 1979, 36).

Clearly, from their correspondence (seven letters from 1937 printed in the Appendix to the chapter on 'Edward Bunyard and Norman Douglas'), warm relations also existed between Bunyard and Ian Parsons (1906–80), a partner in Chatto and Windus who published the second edition of *The Anatomy of Dessert* in 1933 (and a further reprint in its Phoenix Library of Food and Drink in 1936). Parsons was a highly literary man (a First in English at Cambridge), and was behind the short-lived weekly *Night and Day* (1937), to which Bunyard contributed two articles; he was keen on both gardening and travel, and 'a capacity for friendship was perhaps his greatest gift' (*Times* obituary, 31 October 1980, 14). All these interests and qualities sparkle in the letters between the two men. There is Bunyard's playful quotation from Pope (letter 1), and there is talk of his joining Parsons and his wife for dinner in London (letter 2), and for luncheon or tea at the Parsons' Sussex home when EAB can enjoy the garden (letter 7). There is mention of fruit and gardens and the Riviera where Bunyard thinks Parsons and his wife should join him, Norman Douglas, and others in that set (letter 3). It is evident that Douglas was a key figure in a web of friends that also included David and Heather Low, Pino Orioli, and Charles Prentice, a senior partner in Chatto (see notes to letters 2 and 7 for biographical details). The tone is light and amusing – 'Chianti is a wonderful germicide' writes Bunyard (letter 3) on hearing of an infection suffered by Parsons's wife. None the less, one must also note that the epistolary forms of address are 'Dear Parsons' and 'Dear Bunyard' – not the more intimate 'Dear Bunny' used by Norman Douglas from at least August 1924 onwards (see Douglas letter, A6).

'Bunny' was also how he was called by Maurice Healy (1887–1943) in his moving obituary of EAB in *Wine and Food* (Winter 1939, 324–6). Healy was a bachelor, barrister (a K.C. from 1931), broadcaster, and an epicure of charm and humour with a 'comfortable rotundity indicative of good living' (*Times* obituary, 11 May 1943, 6; see also the Memoir by Sir Norman Birkett in Healy's *Stay Me With Flagons: A Book About Wine and Other Things*, 2nd edn. (London, 1949), 9–14). Besides *Stay Me With Flagons* (1940), he was the author of *Claret and the White Wines of Bordeaux* (London, 1934), and like Bunyard was a contributor to *Wine and Food* and on the Advisory Council of the Wine and Food Society. His obituary of Bunyard resists summary (it is printed at the end of this volume), but some aspects should be noted here. Healy wrote as one 'who cherished his friendship', and he spoke as one who knew him well: 'his silences were as companionable as his speech, and it was friendly and pleasant to have him sitting at the other side of the hearth, whether he happened to be browsing in a casual book, or listening to the gramophone, or talking.' Healy was a Catholic, but the absence of formal religion in Bunyard's outlook drew a generous response:

> Bunyard always seemed to me to be ethical rather than religious. His principles were firm and excellent; but I cannot recall any occasion when they were expressed in the language of any formal creed. Kindness was in his eyes the first of virtues; and he was not a man who failed to practise what he preached.

As a Catholic, and at a time when suicide was not only a crime but when the Everlasting's canon 'gainst self-slaughter could make condemnation seem just, Bunyard's suicide must have aroused a particular anguish in Healy, and as a friend it provoked that guilt which the friend of a suicide so often feels – could the act have been foreseen and so prevented? So Mozart's

> G Minor Quintet was his idea of perfection; and perhaps I ought to have recognized in his affection for its pathos an omen: a confession that he too knew what it was to sorrow, without Mozart's gift 'to ease his breast of melodies', and throw away sadness as a thing, beautiful but melancholy ... Many a night did we sit here and listen together; and I never guessed the secret.

It is the more affecting that in the fourth paragraph Healy moves from the earlier 'Edward Bunyard' and 'Bunyard' to the intimate sobriquet 'Bunny'. And Healy's concluding sentences have a dignity and goodness and hope which are a testament to Bunyard's qualities and Healy's friendship:

> Into the last shadows let us not follow him; we know not what they concealed, or in what secret temple his soul may have found its peace. But I hope to meet him again, as I hope for my own salvation. I feel that there is another garden, the secrets of which are delighting his newly-opened eyes; there are books he never heard of that now are beckoning him from one to another in eager and excited exploration. Mozart may not be conducting the G Minor, but the Kleine Nacht-Musik or some other gay piece is surely in his ears. But all the time he is searching, seeking. He is looking for the nurseries of Heaven. And may a divine welcome await him there.

****

> Some cold fate
> awaits us at the ends of the earth.
>
> Like the leaves we are coming within
> sight of the final river,
> its *son et lumière*
> and breath of the night sea.
> As if ghosts already
> we search our pockets for the Stygian fare.
> (Derek Mahon, 'October in Hyde Park')

The biographer, however conscious he may be of his intrusiveness, and with Miss Bordereau's accusation still ringing in his ears, must seek to penetrate a little those last shadows of which Maurice Healy spoke. By the end of December 1938 Bunyard had 'produced a report [for the Royal Horticultural Society] on the organisation of emergency food growing for

---

[36] B. Elliott, *The Royal Horticultural Society: A History 1804–2004* (Chichester, 2004), 44.

wartime';[36] it must have seemed to him a saddening echo of his 'Increasing the Home Fruit Supply' in *JRHS* (XLIII, 1918–19), and 'How to Increase Supplies of Vegetables' in *The Garden* (LXXIX, 1915). The new year, 1939, brought fresh responsibilities and honour: he replaced Frederick Chittenden as Keeper of the Lindley Library,[37] and resigned from the Council of the Royal Horticultural Society in order to become the Editor of its *Journal*.[38] The pattern of previous years continued. In May his rose hunting began on the Riviera, staying with Basil Leng (see above), and led to articles in *The New Flora and Silva*, *Wine and Food*, and *Country Life* (the last on 'Wild Flowers of the Riviera'); the tone is free of premonition – in *Wine and Food* (Autumn 1939) he promises to reveal the name of his favourite hotel in Paris 'in a month or so, after my next visit' (229), and his article in *Country Life* concludes with another promise, to write on a Damask Rose 'in another place' (29 July 1939, 488), which was his posthumously published piece in *The New Flora and Silva* (November 1939, 11–17, pp. 13–14). Other articles, notes, and letters flowed beyond the first half of 1939. There were two broadcasts on horticultural topics, the latter on 16 July (see Bibliography, s.v. 'Wireless Broadcasts').

We cannot be certain of EAB's mood in 1939. Clearly, having produced a report for the RHS on food-growing in wartime, dark prospects cannot always have been absent from his mind. But the enthusiast for plants and seed and food and wine can be remarkably disregarding of the disagreeable, of what lies beyond the range of the pleasurable pursuit. One recalls Norman Douglas's letter of 23 March 1935 (Letter C1 in my chapter 'Edward Bunyard and Norman Douglas') in which he writes: 'Don't think I should care about Germany any more, seeds or no seeds'; it sounds as if, unlike the more aware and tougher Douglas, Bunyard's determination to obtain seeds was not going to be thwarted or disturbed by evidence of Hitler's policies. In this attitude he was, of course, far from unique in the 1930s.

André Simon provides an interesting and instructive instance of how a passion can develop into a moral sclerosis. In *Tables of Content* (1933) he describes, still with a sense of astonishment and perspective, a 'dreary experience' of a dinner 'at one of the City Companies' on 24 February 1931:

---

[37] Ibid., 170

[38] *JRHS*, LXV (April 1940), xxvii.

> Some two hundred grown-up men, mostly grown old, in the same uninspiring uniform, eating and drinking something like £500 worth of food and wines, puffing away somnolently at cigars or cigarettes, whilst unemployment figures are mounting up to the three million mark, whilst India is in open revolt, Australia bankrupt and the whole world in a state of chaos. Wonderful. (107)

But by 1938 the character of superior isolation which Julian Symons detected in the Wine and Food Society (see n. 25) has developed into a pachydermatous covering which prevents a sensible and proportionate attitude to the political world and the part which gastronomy can play in it. An editorial by Simon in *Wine and Food* (Spring 1938) speaks of massacres in Spain and China, dictatorships, and class warfare, and then declares:

> But there is still a patch of blue sky, a bright patch which refuses to be obscured by all the 'black-out' orders and experiments of panicky Government Departments. It is the Wine and Food Society now in the fifth year of its useful existence. Its message is the same as ever, but it is delivered with ever-growing effect as the Society grows in numbers and influence. Its creed is the same in spite of all the depressing happenings since its foundation. It still believes and preaches that it would be far saner to give school children a plateful of good soup every morning rather than gas-masks; better to build kitchens where people could be taught how to cook rather than shelters where they can take cover during air raids. Air raids may never come, but dyspepsia is here already … Fears and hatreds, the blue and black devils which will ruin this fair world of ours if we let them, rise from acid, sour, pinched, sagging, ill-fed stomachs. They make many victims; they drive many out of their reason or of life, but they have no hold upon the sane, well-nourished optimism of the Members of the Wine and Food Society. (1)

Wonderful.

On 3 September 1939 Britain declared war on Germany; on Thursday, 19 October Edward Bunyard shot himself in his room at the Royal Societies Club, 63 St James's Street, Piccadilly. There are two accounts, both from William T. Stearn (1911–2001), then Librarian of the Lindley Library, of the day of the suicide. The first is briefly reported by Dr Brent Elliott:

> On 19 October 1939, he [Bunyard] left the Library at mid-day, telling Stearn he would be back after lunch to continue work, and went to the Royal Societies Club, where he shot himself. (Stearn, describing the incident, would remark that he must have had the gun in his pocket while talking to him.)[39]

The second, and detailed, account is in a letter to me from Dr Stearn, written in the most difficult circumstances on 19 January 2001, a little over three months before his death on 9 May; I must record my profound gratitude to Dr Stearn for his response, and the letter is worthy of quotation in full:

> 17 High Park Road
> Kew Gardens
> Richmond, Surrey
> TW9 4BL
>
> 19 Jan 2001
> Dear Dr Wilson
> Your letter of 2 Dec. 2000 came when I was lying helpless in hospital with a broken right arm. I was released only last week and am learning how to walk and write again, both with difficulty.
>   To get Mr. Chittenden removed from the directorship of Wisley, the late Lord Aberconway had him appointed Technical Adviser and Editor of R.H.S. publications and Keeper of the Lindley Library, which was subject to a Library Committee with E. A. Bunyard Chairman. I was appointed as Librarian, being interviewed by E. A. Bunyard and E. A. Bowles [in 1932: see above and n. 31].
>   One morning Bunyard said to me that we would deal with library business in the afternoon. He never came back which was not surprising. When on Air Raid Precautions this early morning someone showed me a newly arrived newspaper reporting the death of a noted rosarian, E. A. Bunyard. 'Did I know him?'

---

[39] See B. Elliott, op. cit., 170.

I went up to the R.H.S. and unfortunately it was true. He did *not* normally carry a revolver but kept it in a drawer except when he went out to his orchard to shoot bullfinches, those lovely pests of fruit trees in bloom. Evidently he had brought it to London with a set purpose. He went to the Royal Societies Club and there shot himself.

The inquest revealed that he was in good health and [?no] suspected cancer.

My supposition is that he was a victim of the War. He was now in debt; nobody bought fruit trees. Food-rationing had begun. He could no longer roam the continent for good wine. In short the good things of life for him were ceasing. There was too little to live for.

He had intended to bequeath his splendid library to the Lindley Library, but his creditors had priority. I accordingly went down to Bunyard's house at Maidstone and spent several days selecting books to be bought at valuation. I can tell you more about this.

Excuse this horrible scrawl.
Yours sincerely,
William T. Stearn

A propos the last paragraph, in a subsequent telephone conversation on 26 January 2001 Dr Stearn told me that Bunyard's library contained a remarkably large number of books on sex, including Havelock Ellis, but no specific titles were recalled.

Death was not instantaneous; according to his Death Certificate he died 'On way to St. George's Hospital' from 'Gunshot wound in head'. The notices of death placed in the newspapers were naturally euphemistic: *The Times* (23 October 1939, 1) and *Telegraph* (23 October 1939, 12) said 'suddenly in London'. A hint at more was given in the weekly *Gardening Illustrated*'s obituary: 'the death last week, in tragic circumstances' (LXI, no. 3164, 28 October 1939, 694). The *Manchester Guardian*'s news report (21 October 1939, 10) was explicit; Bunyard:

was found dead at the Royal Societies' Club, St. James's Street, London, S.W., on Thursday, after a shot had been heard. A revolver was by his side. ...

Lieutenant Colonel [F. R.] Durham, Secretary of the Royal Horticultural Society, with whom he had been working in London, said to a reporter:

"Mr. Bunyard was the greatest fruit expert alive, and one of the most knowledgeable people on all horticultural books. He had published a great many himself, particularly on fruit trees, roses, and vegetables."

Bunyard's local paper, the *Kent Messenger* (21 October 1939, 4), was equally frank; under the headline 'Head of Famous Maidstone Firm Found Shot/ Mr. A.E. [*sic*] Bunyard Dies at His Club in the West End' it reported that 'Mr. Bunyard was found shot on Thursday night, in his room at the Royal Societies' Club in St. James's Street, W.'

The inquest was held at Paddington on Tuesday, 24 October 1939, but its archival record has not survived (only 10% apparently are preserved). The *Evening Standard* (24 October 1939, 7) reported the verdict that Bunyard had 'killed himself while of unsound mind', and the account in the *Kent Messenger* (28 October 1939, 5) added that 'it was stated that he dreaded the effect of the war on his business'.

Even now, however, it is possible to advance beyond the terse reports of the inquest, and consider what may have made Bunyard's mind unsound. First, there is the fact of his bankruptcy. Whether he realized the full extent of his debts must remain unclear, but that 'he dreaded the effect of the war on his business' indicates that, at the least, he must have communicated some anxieties to others; they may have been deep enough of themselves to disturb the balance of his mind. The probate document of 1 February 1940, which wrongly locates his death as 'at Vincent Square Westminster London SW1' (headquarters of the Royal Horticultural Society), gives the gross value of his estate as £918.11s.5d, which was £311.2s.3d. net. His father's wealth at death had been £19, 268.8s.3d, though his brother Norman's was to be £58,177.[40] In his will of 19 July 1935 clause 5 declared:

> I BEQUEATH my library of Pomological Books dealing with fruit and its cultivation now at my house at Allington to the Royal Horticultural Society free of duty provided they are willing to preserve and maintain the

---

[40] See J. Morgan, 'Bunyard, Edward Ashdown (1878–1939)', *Oxford Dictionary of National Biography* (Oxford, 2004), viii, 711–12, p. 712, for the wealth at death figures for George and Norman Bunyard; the gross figure for Edward is also given.

library as a complete Collection with my name for the use of all students of Pomology and failing their acceptance of this condition then it shall fall into and form part of my residuary estate.

As Stearn's letter says, Bunyard's financial position meant that creditors had priority, and the RHS had to buy the books it wanted at valuation. The disposal of Bunyard's library was conducted by Hodgson's of Chancery Lane, London. The records of this firm are now in the British Library, and the valuation of EAB's books can be found in Additional MS. 54710, 'Valuations 1939–41, pp. 74–83, carried out on 13 April 1940 for Whitehead Thomas & Urmston of 9 King Street [the street in which Bunyard was born], Maidstone', Edward Urmston being one of two executors and trustees appointed by EAB in his will; the locations of the books included a 'study' (pp. 76–77) and a 'library' (pp. 78–81). The value of books on botany was £200 for the Lindley Library and £165 for Wisley; there were three other small valuations: for Mr G. St.Clair Feilden (author of 4 works on tropical and subtropical fruits for the Imperial Bureau of Fruit Production, East Malling, Kent, 1932–41); Mr J. Neame (presumably J. Armstrong Neame, author of *Among the Meadow and Alpine Flowers of Northern Italy*, London, 1937); and W. T. Stearn (see above).

The auction at Hodgson's took place on Thursday-Friday, 13–14 June 1940, which, oddly, was after the probate date of 1 February 1940. Bunyard's name was not mentioned, and the cover's title was 'A Catalogue of Books from Various Sources comprising Modern Books from the Library of a Gentleman … with other properties, including … the writings of Norman Douglas, several with A.Ll.s [autograph letters signed] … A Collection of Books on Botany, Horticulture, Pomology, etc. …'. Fortunately, another item in the Hodgson archive, British Library Add. MS. 54632, 'Abstract of Proprietors Jany. 1940 to August 1946', pages unnumbered, s.v. 'Sale No 6, 1939–40 June 13–14/40', identifies the owners of all the lots, giving as 'Books Bought Bunyard' lots 1–29, 73–131 (105–115 were the Douglas books), 195–223, 279–284, 375–399, 416–458 (the catalogue's sub-heading 'A Collection of Books on Botany, Horticulture, Arboriculture, Pomology, &c.' comes after lot 430, a section which runs until lot 571*), 461–504, 507–567, and 569–571*. Another Hodgson document, BL Add. MS. 54629, p. 60, gives the sums realized: on the First Day (lots 1–328) 'Books

Bought re Bunyard' came to £195.4s., and on the Second Day his books made £431.19s., giving a total of £627.3s.

The books of English and other literatures will be discussed in my chapter 'Edward Bunyard and Literature', but a few comments here can amplify Stearn's remark on the large number of books on sex (see above). The phrase 'on sex' has some ambiguity, but I would be inclined to exclude, for example, Rabelais (lot 94), Restif de la Bretonne's *Monsieur Nicolas* in translation by R. Crowdy Mathers with an introduction by Havelock Ellis (lot 97; an edition limited to 825 numbered subscribed sets); Joyce's *Ulysses* (lot 117), Wilde's *Dorian Gray* (lot 129), and probably Casanova's *Memoirs* (lots 95, 96). Only five lots seem to qualify as 'on sex' in the narrower sense: Marius Boisson, *Anthologie Universelle des Baisers*, 5 vols., 1911–12 (lot 83; not in the Bodleian or the British Library; I am indebted to Ms Sara Smith for tracing a copy); H. E. Meier, *L'Amour Grec dans l'Antiquité*, 1930 (lot 84; untraced); Hans Licht, *Sexual Life in Ancient Greece*, 1932 (lot 218); Havelock Ellis, *Studies in the Psychology of Sex*, 6 vols., 1914–18 (lot 219), and Curt Thesing, *Genealogy of Love*, 1933 (lot 220). The four lots I have seen of these five are all serious, scholarly books: Boisson's work is a sober, sociological and literary anthology of the erotic customs of the whole world (England: ii. 213–40) from ancient times to the present, covering every species of the erotic (heterosexual, homosexual, pederastic, etc.; Moinaux' poem 'Les Amours d'un Épicurien', i. 103, would doubtless have had its attractions), and with only one illustration, the frontispiece, high art and untitillating, per volume; Licht was a Professor at Leipzig; Havelock Ellis needs no comment as a serious author; and Thesing's treatment is biological, anthropological, and medical, with only one chapter out of eight on 'Love in Human Beings' (the others being on all manner of insects and animals). To lot 84 one must add 19 'others in French'; to lot 218 '10 others by Havelock Ellis'; and to lot 220 14 'others similar'. There are, then, some 47 serious but unpornographic works 'on sex'.

Knowledge or fear of bankruptcy would be bad enough, but behind the present, and the grim future, lay on the one hand what must have seemed a cursed past of Bunyards known for financial profligacy and incompetence, and on the other the stern and heroic model of George Bunyard who had rescued the firm from disaster. Bad and good examples can seem equally minatory, and Edward Bunyard had both. Charles Bunyard's 'bolting' and

Harry Bunyard's 'bunking' set an all too ready precedent that escape was an option. Throughout this chapter we have heard that EAB was more the connoisseur and scholar than the flinty man of business; the peals of the 'joy rides', as he termed his adventures in unprofitability, now sound like the tolling of a passing-bell. 1896 must have seemed a long time ago.

The *Kent Messenger* (21 October 1939, 4) said that he 'had lived a secluded life in a bungalow on the nurseries at Allington', but this ignores his metropolitan life, not only his varied work with the Royal Horticultural Society and its committees but the gastronomic clubbability of the Saintsbury Club and the Wine and Food Society. It ignores, too, his visits to his Mediterranean and Riviera friends – Norman Douglas, Pino Orioli, Reggie Turner, Basil Leng, Lawrence Johnston. And when the *Kent Messenger* reports that 'He had been extremely depressed by the war and had not had a night's sleep since it began', it is, I think, a depression caused not only by the war's financial consequences, but because it brought to a close a whole European dimension to his life, which had begun in 1900 when he went to France to learn French nursery practice, and had grown into 'that sunlit Riviera world where Death seemed not present, and all was friends, roses, and the delights of Epicurus to the tune of nightingales'.[41] Bunyard was not the only one to feel that the war was to be the end of the world he had known and loved. The medieval scholar Joan Evans has written:

> Those of my generation who would still be alive after the war would be, I felt, *survivors*: people who would dwell uneasily as aliens in a world that was not theirs. We should be like the people who lived through the French Revolution into the nineteenth century, and find ourselves strangers in a world that had forgotten the old securities, the old graces, the old forms of thought, and the old ways of living. We should seem even older than we were, for our hopes would have vanished in smoke and flame and to our tired eyes the new dawn would seem cold and grey.[42]

Bunyard was not to be a survivor. Joan Evans's elegiac words are hauntingly echoed by Stearn's:

---

[41] E. Wilson, *art. cit.* in n. 35.
[42] J. Evans, *Prelude & Fugue: An Autobiography* (London, 1964), 158.

My supposition is that he was a victim of the War. He was now in debt; nobody bought fruit trees. Food-rationing had begun. He could no longer roam the continent for good wine. In short the good things of life for him were ceasing. There was too little to live for.

Maurice Healy wrote in his obituary of the 'major shock' of Bunyard's death to all his friends. To his mother, aged 88, it was more than that. On 24 October 1939, the day of the inquest, she died of what the Death Certificate called 'Auricular Fibrillation' and 'Myocarditis'; her heart had, indeed, given out. Lorna, Edward's sister, who had edited and contributed to *The Epicure's Companion* (1937) with her brother, was present at the death, and registered it the next day. Edward's mother had lost two sons in their childhood; now she had lost a third. She was buried in her husband's grave in the churchyard at Mereworth.

****

And so it was over. The collection of 400 varieties of old roses was sold in 1939;[43] after William Stearn had purchased the volumes wanted by the Royal Horticultural Society, the remainder of Bunyard's library was sold, as we have seen, by auction at Hodgson's in London, the following year. Eventually the apples went, too, though Norman Bunyard kept the firm going until George Bunyard & Company Limited was amalgamated with Laxton Bros. of Brampton, Huntingdon, as Bunyards and Laxtons in 1964.[44] Today the sign painted on the wall of a house beside Barming Station, near Maidstone, bidding passengers 'Alight here' for George Bunyard & Co. is almost as illegible as the inscription on George and Katharine Bunyard's grave.

Edward's niece, Miss Katharine Bunyard, daughter of Edward's brother, Norman, has told me (letter of 6 November 2000) that 'His suicide was

---

[43] G. S. Thomas, *The Old Shrub Roses*, revd. edn. (London, 1979), p. 19.

[44] The first catalogue of the new firm, with a letter from Bunyard's of Summer, 1964, is preserved in the Lindley Library. For further details on the end of the old firm see A. Major, 'The Bunyards of Kent', Part Three, *Bygone Kent*, XII no. 5 (May 1991), 275–80, pp. 279–80.

a taboo subject in the family, and as I was only a schoolgirl at the time, very little was discussed at home'. However, she knew that he had been cremated, but did not know where or what became of the ashes (though she conjectured that they might have been scattered near his parents' grave at Mereworth).

Nine years earlier, at the fall of the leaf, 'E.A.B.' of 'Kent', in a letter to *Gardening Illustrated* (LII, no. 2697, 15 November 1930, 738) had contemplated his death and his memorial. He began with a description of a bed of Japanese Cherries, 'their leaves aflame with gold and red':

> Yeshino, at this time the brightest in red and gold; Hisakura, later and paler in red, but wonderful in yellow, shades; Subhirtella autumnalis, very rich in claret to scarlet; Ukon in gold; and our European Avium flora pleno, showing a richer crimson, all make a cheerful picture.

Then his last words took on a tone and tint both autumnal and shaken free of melancholy:

> And musing in the death of summer, I came to the view that for a memorial I shall have planted an avenue of Japanese Cherries; no gloomy Cypress for me, despite its age-long lore. No! Let us add a little to the beauty of the country; 50 years ahead it will need all we can provide.

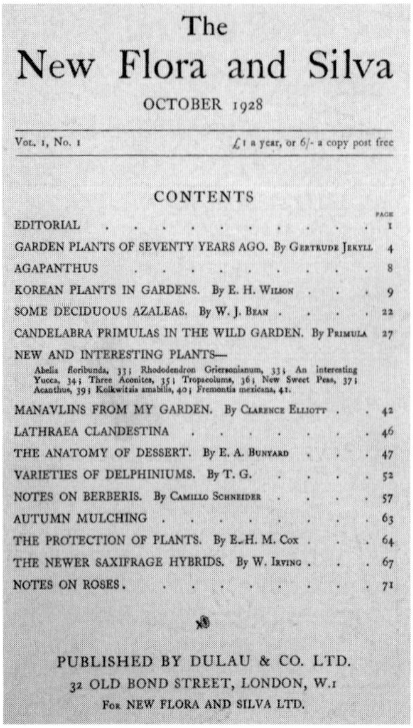

The
New Flora and Silva
OCTOBER 1928

Vol. 1, No. 1 — £1 a year, or 6/- a copy post free

CONTENTS

PUBLISHED BY DULAU & CO. LTD.
32 OLD BOND STREET, LONDON, W.1
For NEW FLORA AND SILVA LTD.

Figure 5. The cover of the first issue of *The New Flora and Silva*, published by Dulau, listing 'The Anatomy of Dessert' by EAB the full text of which would be issued in book form by the same house the next year. *(Image courtesy of David Karp.)*

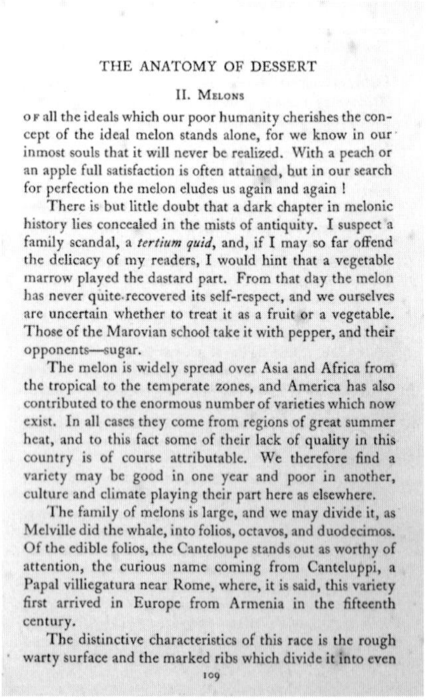

THE ANATOMY OF DESSERT

II. Melons

Of all the ideals which our poor humanity cherishes the concept of the ideal melon stands alone, for we know in our inmost souls that it will never be realized. With a peach or an apple full satisfaction is often attained, but in our search for perfection the melon eludes us again and again !

There is but little doubt that a dark chapter in melonic history lies concealed in the mists of antiquity. I suspect a family scandal, a *tertium quid*, and, if I may so far offend the delicacy of my readers, I would hint that a vegetable marrow played the dastard part. From that day the melon has never quite recovered its self-respect, and we ourselves are uncertain whether to treat it as a fruit or a vegetable. Those of the Marovian school take it with pepper, and their opponents—sugar.

The melon is widely spread over Asia and Africa from the tropical to the temperate zones, and America has also contributed to the enormous number of varieties which now exist. In all cases they come from regions of great summer heat, and to this fact some of their lack of quality in this country is of course attributable. We therefore find a variety may be good in one year and poor in another, culture and climate playing their part here as elsewhere.

The family of melons is large, and we may divide it, as Melville did the whale, into folios, octavos, and duodecimos. Of the edible folios, the Canteloupe stands out as worthy of attention, the curious name coming from Canteluppi, a Papal villiegatura near Rome, where, it is said, this variety first arrived in Europe from Armenia in the fifteenth century.

The distinctive characteristics of this race is the rough warty surface and the marked ribs which divide it into even

109

Figure 6. Page 109 of the second issue of *The New Flora and Silva* displaying the second extract from *The Anatomy of Dessert.* *(Image courtesy of David Karp.)*

CHAPTER TWO

Edward Bunyard and Literature

EDWARD WILSON

Edward Bunyard was one of those who, in his own words, 'find pleasure in that zone where good food and good literature are happily blended' (*WF*, II.6, 1935, 52). Of that blend he writes with the sensuous precision of a connoisseur of both fruit and books:[1]

> The musk-flavoured Litchi is hard to place when wine is on the table, its exact moment is surely when reading the *Arabian Nights*. The Mardrus translation, of course; (*WF*, I.4, 1934, 29)

---

1 The following abbreviations are used in quotations from Bunyard's works:

AD: *The Anatomy of Dessert with a Few Notes on Wine* 2nd edn. (London, 1933; the 1st edn. was published in 1929).

EC: *The Epicure's Companion* by Edward and Lorna Bunyard, with further contributions by others (London, 1937); each contributor's section is individually identified. In *EC*, with very few exceptions, I have referred only to authors and works embedded in Bunyard's own prose, and not to those quoted in 'An Epicure's Anthology' chosen by Edward and Lorna Bunyard and 'Varia' in Part Three.

GE: E. A. Bunyard, 'Gardening for Epicures', in *The Gardener's Companion*, ed. M. Hadfield (London and New York, 1936), pp. 13–37.

WF: articles and reviews in the journal *Wine and Food*, ed. A. L. Simon.

The script of the wireless broadcast 'In Your Garden' was supplied by the BBC Written Archives Centre, Caversham Park, Reading.

Of course, no attempt has been made to identify every allusion and quotation; my aim has been to consider those which best reflect the content and proportions of Bunyard's various reading.

or, in the same account of 'The Winter Dessert',

> A fireside chair, a Blenheim Apple, slightly warmed, and in the other hand a volume of Fielding, whose mellow wisdom and acid sap find in the Apple their perfect counterpoise.

The zone of pleasure here has a solitary, but happy, occupant – the place is the library on a frosty winter's night. But the zone could also, of course, be a convivial one, such as the meetings of the Saintsbury Club which held its first meeting at Vintners' Hall on 23 October 1931, Professor George Saintsbury's eighty-sixth birthday; Bunyard was there and presented for the menu 'Pommes d'Allington' (the Allington Pippin, introduced commercially by Edward Bunyard's father, George, in the firm's centenary year, 1896) and 'Noix à la glace' (the walnuts, too, no doubt from the Bunyard Nurseries at Maidstone).[1] Literary figures of the time were present: Hilaire Belloc, E. F. Benson, A. P. Herbert, Compton Mackenzie, J. C. Squire, A. J. A. Symons. The Toast to Professor Saintsbury was proposed by Hilaire Belloc, but in him what Bunyard had spoken of as a blend and a balance of good food and good literature had on this occasion tipped – indeed, tippled – greatly towards good wine. André Simon describes the scene:

> I shall never forget the truly awful feeling of dismay that came over me when Hilaire Belloc rose, swayed, and there were but three words he uttered: 'I am drunk.' And he was. There was an awful silence and long faces all round. Then he hummed and coughed and pulled himself together, and within a matter of minutes he had us all absolutely fascinated by the most exquisite description of the importance of the slightest differences between good and bad writing, good and bad wine: a comma wrongly placed or a cork a little loose. It was really a magnificent piece of oratory, and we were all spellbound, but nobody was there to take it down. When I asked Hilaire Belloc the next day to put down on paper what he had said, he told me

---

[1] See A. L. Simon, *By Request: An Autobiography* (London, 1957), pp. 83–4; I am indebted to Mr Merlin Holland for a copy of the printed list of members who attended the first dinner of the Saintsbury Club (and also for lists of members, including, of course, Bunyard, and their guests, who attended subsequent dinners of the Club).

quite truthfully, I am sure, that he had not the slightest recollection of it and could not possibly oblige me.

The word *literature* in this discussion will be employed in two of the senses recorded by *OED²*: (i) 'polite or humane learning; literary culture' [sense 1], first found in Middle English and last in 1880, and, as the Dictionary notes in words originally composed in 1901–3, 'Now *rare* and *obsolescent*' – 'O tempora, O mores!'; (ii) a sense not noted before the nineteenth century, 'writing which has claim to consideration on the ground of beauty of form or emotional effect' [sense 3.a]. I shall not, in the main, be concerned with *OED²*'s sense 3.b: 'The body of books and writings that treat of a particular subject', first recorded in 1860 and used in such sentences as, 'We have searched the literature for reliable radiometric ages for Late Pre-Cambrian glaciogenic rocks' (1971). Thus scientific works or works on food and wine which have no other aim than practical instruction in merely practical English (or any other language), whether by Bunyard or others, will not normally be cited. None the less, I must allow myself to observe that who but Bunyard would have ended a scientific paper on xenia ('the influence of foreign pollen upon the maternal structure'), delivered on 1 August 1906 at the Third International Conference 1906 on Genetics – at which W. Bateson proposed a new technical term, suggesting 'for the consideration of this Congress the term *Genetics*' – with a quotation from Francis Bacon:

> I cannot, perhaps, sum up the position better than in the words used by Bacon in his preface to the "Novum Organum" in reference to science in general, when he says "that it is not so much an opinion to be held as a work to be done." (*Report of the Third Int. Conf. 1906 on Genetics*, ed. W. Wilks (London, 1907), p. 300; Bateson quotation on p. 91)

Of course, there are writers who write literature in the literary sense who also know a considerable amount about gardening; as Bunyard observed in his article 'The Novelist in the Garden' in the weekly *Gardening Illustrated*:

We are all gardeners in these days, and our popular novelists, knowing this, flatter our knowledge or enlighten our ignorance by the local garden colour they introduce. Some of them, indeed, may be regarded as masters in gardening. Who in old days knew better than Mr. R. D. Blackmore the finer qualities of a Pear? And has not Mr. Eden Phillpotts himself written a book upon rare shrubs and woven a romance around a nursery with consummate mastery? Mr. Compton Mackenzie, too, has increased his knowledge with advancing years, as we all hope to do. His early horticultural excursions in "Guy and Pauline" show a faltering hand here and there, but if his specific names were over-decorated with capitals he at least flowered his Sternbergias in the right month, and he also knew the best form of Iris Vartani. (LIII, no. 2738, 29 August 1931, 533)

R. D. Blackmore (1825–1900), is now remembered perhaps only as the author of *Lorna Doone* (1869). On a sixteen-acre plot at Teddington he cultivated a range of fruits and flowers, himself taking up the produce to Covent Garden. Up to 1884 he had experimented with 79 varieties of pears and 20 of peaches, and Bunyard himself said that 'His garden at Teddington was a trial from which few fruits emerged with a *proxime accessit*' (*AD*, p. 118). He was Vice-Chairman of the Royal Horticultural Society's Fruit and Vegetable Committee from 1889–92, George Bunyard being its Chairman. Yet though Edward Bunyard refers to Blackmore's novels, his quotations (*AD*, p. 118) are from his comments on pears which were incorporated in Robert Hogg's *The Fruit Manual* (5th edn., London, 1884). The *Manual* is quoted in Blackmore's novel *Alice Lorraine* (London, 1875, I.159), and if Bunyard read this, then the scene-setting of the flirtation in the strawberry-beds between Mabel and Hilary (male, I must add these days) would doubtless have been more absorbing to him than to those readers who do not run a market-garden:

> They had straggled off into the strawberry-beds, where nobody could see them; and there they seemed likely to spend some hours if nobody should come after them. The plants were of the true Carolina, otherwise called the "old scarlet pine," which among all our countless new sorts finds no superior, perhaps no equal; although it is now quite out of vogue, because it fruits so shyly.

> What says our chief authority?* [*That admirable writer, Dr. Hogg: *footnote*] "Fruit medium-sized, ovate, even, and regular, and with a glossy neck, skin deep red, flesh pale red, very firm and solid, with a fine sprightly and very rich pine flavour." What lovelier fruit could a youth desire to place between little pearly teeth, reserving the right to have a bite, if any of the very firm flesh should be left? (I.159–60)

Blackmore continues by applying the vocabulary of Hogg's account of the Old Pine strawberry (*Manual*, p. 752) to Mabel's beauty:

> What fruit more suggestive of elegant compliments could a maid open her lips to receive, with a dimple in each mantled cheek – lips more bright than the skin of the fruit, cheeks by no means of a *pale red* now, although *very firm and solid* – and as for the *sprightly flavour* of the whole, it may be imagined, if you please, but is not to be ascertained as yet? (I.160; my italics of phrases from Hogg)

My love is like a red, red strawberry. I cannot leave Blackmore without an antiquarian footnote. He had an interest in children who were namesakes of his heroine Lorna Doone; he wrote of his 'collection' to the artist Francis Armstrong on 10 June 1881: 'There is one at Canterbury, "Lorna Bunyard", …'. Despite the reference to Canterbury and not Maidstone, where the Bunyards lived, this must surely be Edward Bunyard's sister, Lorna, born 20 August 1876, who was to collaborate with Edward in *The Epicure's Companion*.[2]

The two books by Eden Phillpotts (1862–1960) to which Bunyard refers are *My Shrubs* (London and New York, 1915) and *The Nursery (Banks of Colne)* (London, 1917). One might note that he also knew Phillpott's *A Dish of Apples*, with illustrations by Arthur Rackham (London, [1921]), poems on different varieties of apple, including the Allington Pippin (see opening paragraph above):

---

[2] Biographical information on R. D. Blackmore has been taken from W. H. Dunn, *R. D. Blackmore* (London, 1956); the reference to Lorna Bunyard is on p. 181. See also B. Elliott, 'A Novelist in the Fruit Garden', *The Garden* CXVII (1992), 488–91.

> Delicate and dainty thing!
> For the fairies you were fashioned;
> Than a flavour so impassioned
> Pine and grape no richer bring.
> Poets falter
> At your altar,
> Lacking grace your charm to sing. (st. 1; p. 69)

EAB had already quoted from this poem in *AD* (1st edn., 1929, p. 8), and would do so again in *EC* (p. 157).

Compton Mackenzie (1883–1972), like Bunyard a founding member of the Saintsbury Club, whose first dinner both would attend on 23 October 1931, under two months on from the *Gardening Illustrated* article, and when indeed 'Pommes D'Allington' were served, was a keen gardener. In his *Guy and Pauline* (London, 1915) Sternbergias flower in October (p. 39), and the Iris Vartani is discussed on pp. 69–70.

But the thrust of Bunyard's article is rather rebuke of those authors who get their botany wrong, somewhat reminiscent of Peacock's Miss Ilex: 'Truth to nature is essential to poetry. Few may perceive an inaccuracy: but to those who do, it causes a great diminution, if not a total destruction, of pleasure in perusal. Shakespeare never makes a flower blossom out of season.' (*Gryll Grange*, chap. xxiii) Thus he writes of Beerbohm:

> One would not ask, or expect, Mr. Max Beerbohm, that darling of the drawing-room (Regency style), to be an expert botanist, and, to his credit, his skill in steering clear of what he does not understand is not the least merit of his inimitability. But how sad the fall, how shattering the impact to read in "Zuleika Dobson" of the famous Horse Chestnut of Oxford, Bishop Heber's tree, "with its towering and bulging masses of verdure tricked out all over in their annual finery of catkins [chap. xix]"! Such is the price that urbanity pays for its perfection.

However, when he goes on to castigate George Moore, Bunyard is hoist with his own petard: 'We now learn from Lady Gregory that Mr. George Moore's famous Weeping Willow at Coole is not a Willow at all, but a Catalpa!' Professor John Kelly, of St. John's College, Oxford, has kindly informed me that Moore called the tree not a weeping willow but a weeping ash: 'A seat had been placed under a weeping ash …' (*Hail and Farewell*, I, *Ave* (London, 1911), Part XV, p. 349). Lady Gregory got it right: 'And I forgive George Moore his slander in miscalling my Catalpa tree a weeping ash' (*Coole* (Dublin, 1931), 'Woods, Visions, and the Lake', p. 36). One is still struck by Bunyard reading Lady Gregory so soon after publication (early July 1931).

Yet such errors were trifling compared with errors of chronology – 'Clio herself is violated' – and even the greatest are not spared censure. Virginia Woolf's picture of a venerable John Evelyn walking in his garden at Wotton, 'the butterflies flying and flaunting on his dahlias' (*The Common Reader* (London, 1925), p. 120) draws the cry: 'But, alack-a-day, why did the gifted writer make him pause at a bed of Dahlias, a flower which was to rest at least a century in its native Mexico before Europe saw it?' And in another up-to-date example, Bunyard observes: 'In her great novel, "Broome Stages" [London, 1931] Miss Clemence Dane [1888–1965] has obviously taken pains with her historical colour, though I fear that a Japanese Cherry in a garden of the Regent's day [p. 63] is a little "previous" by some years; but can we forgive the picture of Dulwich Gallery "buried in pyramids of Mulberry bloom [p. 49]"?'

For Bunyard there was a close connexion between literature and 'gustronomy' as he liked to term his subject ('GUSTRONOMY, usually spelled Gastronomy – from the Greek, *gaster*, a belly. As the Epicure's life is devoted to teaching this crude organ its place, and placing taste first, I suggest that gustronomy is a better word, more correct, decent, and desirable': *AD*, p. vi). My first two quotations above, linking the litchi [lychee] with the *Arabian Nights*, and the Blenheim Apple with Fielding, have already shown something of this connexion. Though his observations on the relationship are often made humorously, the underlying belief was a serious one. In *The Epicure's Companion* he states:

> It seems very right and proper that tea should have established itself in England in readiness for the eighteenth century; could Horace Walpole amidst the gimcrackery of Strawberry [Hill] be imagined without it? Or, at the other extreme, 'Rough Samuel' and 'Thin weedling James'? All English literature for long is musical with the tinkle of the spoons. (pp. 344–5)

Then, after quoting Lord George Brilliant's apostrophe to tea in Cibber's *The Lady's Last Stake, or, The Wife's Resentment* (1707), I.i.280ff. – in a slightly bowdlerized version, omitting 'thou innocent Pretence for bringing the Wicked of both Sexes together in a Morning' – and the *Spectator's* observations on tea-drinking (no. 10, 12 March 1711), he concludes:

> The influence of tea on literature might well be the subject of research, as that of cocoa upon the fortunes of the Liberal party; from all such investigations much of value might be learned.
>
> It would seem hard at first sight to find any common ground for Samuel Johnson and Charles Lamb, heavy tea-drinkers both, but I feel sure some underlying resemblances could and will be found by our desperate biographers of to-day – desperate, as their material is so fast ebbing away. (p. 345)

In France, however, 'the reign of tea' was 'short, for a darker rival [coffee] was stealing in from Africa' (p. 345); it was the end of an epoch: 'The decline of classicism had begun and on coffee the Romantics throve and even subsisted in times of need' (p. 346). The next chapter asks rhetorically:

> Can we imagine Dryden, Swift, Steele, Pope, and all that gay, sardonic coterie living without coffee?
>
> That other world of coffee-drinkers rather below this standard must be sought for in the impudent pages of Ned Ward [1667–1731, tavern-keeper and author of Hudibrastic scenes of London life]. (p. 349)

In his essay 'Gardening for Epicures' in *The Gardener's Companion* (1936), ed. Miles Hadfield, after toying with the idea of writing 'my vegetable interpretation of history' with chapters called 'The Effect of the Potato on Anglo-American Relationship' and 'The Potato and Prussia' – we recall comparable essay topics in *AD*: 'the Fig as an instrument of history' (p. 55), the Strawberry Grape and 'certain recent developments' in America (p. 74), and the warning concerning the Melon that 'History has been turned in its course, and dynasties hurled from their destinies, by the fatal effects of immoderate indulgence in this fruit' (p. 80), and in *EC* the heading 'The Onion in Human Life' (p. 75) – we have the conjecture:

Potatoes have had an effect too, I fancy, upon literature; the carbohydrate style is easily distinguished from the protein. The Greeks knew no potatoes, and so could write their dramas without a need of preface three times as long to explain them. Wine, meat, and bread have always produced the best literature.

The potato, however, has its place for the illiterate and those who can dispose of starch in quantity. (p. 21)

Bunyard could argue the case for the cultural influence of different foods with moderation and gravity:

History may be viewed from many standpoints, and a study of the gradual adoption of a new food or drink and its effects on social life and temperament is well worthy of consideration. (*WF*, III.10, 1936, 49)

But who would not rather thrill to the *saeva indignatio* of the denunciation of the banana in *EC*? 'The banana', Bunyard tells us, 'was designed as the staple food of the negroid races' (p. 238). After a side-swipe at Scotsmen and *their* staple food of porridge, he is off:

One cannot but deplore the infiltration of negroid standards of life and art into western Europe to-day, when the cry seems to be: 'Down with Greece, up the Congo!' Whence comes this revulsion against the accepted standards of civilized Europe? I can only attribute it to the greatly increased consumption of bananas. All the negroid characteristics, the love of the garish, of cacophony as against music, the spread of the herd spirit, and the fear of solitude – all these find their dietetic expression in the flaccid banana of commerce. (p. 238)

We must look at the remarks in their historical context. It is probable that Bunyard knew of the sensational appearance of the black artiste Josephine Baker (1906–75) when she danced in a 'cincture of phalliform bananas' (*Cambridge Paperback Guide to Theatre*, 1996) in *La Revue Nègre* at the Théâtre des Champs-Élysées in 1925, although Ean Wood, *The Josephine Baker Story* (London, 2000) says that it was in 1926 'in *La Folie du Jour* that Joséphine wore the bananas for the first time' (pp. 104–5, see also, e.g. pp. 66–7 for a general discussion of the impact of African culture at that time, and pp. 109ff. for Josephine Baker's role; see also P. Archer-Straw, *Negrophilia: Avant-Garde Paris and Black Culture in the 1920s* (London, 2000), chapter 4 for both jazz and Josephine Baker). However, Bunyard's feelings are deeper than would be provoked by one theatrical scandal, and they were also widely held. Clive Bell's *Civilization: An Essay* (London, 1928) also saw ancient Athenian life as in opposition to savagery, defining the allegedly better qualities of the latter as 'Sculpture and war-dances, friendliness, brown breasts and bananas' (chap. vii, 'How to Make a Civilization', p. 196). In pictorial form such ideas are exactly expressed in John B. Souter's controversial painting 'The Breakdown' in the Royal Academy Summer Exhibition of 1926.[3] It shows a black saxophonist seated on the helmeted head of a huge, fallen, broken statue of Britannia (or Minerva); before him a naked white woman dances, perhaps one called a break-down (*OED²* s.v. *break-down*, 2, 'A dance in the peculiar style of the negroes'): it symbolizes, in Bunyard's terms, the breakdown of the tradition of Greek art and values before a cacophonous jazz influx ultimately from the Congo. Yet the *Times* reviewer, who spoke of 'a saxophone played by a nigger', objected to the painting not on the grounds of what we might term racism, but because 'it is not true that any civilization worth a cent has succumbed to the saxophone, and if it were it would not be a pictorial

---

[3] Souter's painting is reproduced in S. Hynes, *A War Imagined: The First World War and English Culture* (London, 1990), facing p. 402, no. 23; unfortunately, this English edition, unlike the original, correct, New York one, locates the painting in the Imperial War Museum. It is not, and the photograph is from one in the Royal Academy. Joan M. Matthew, in her catalogue of the Exhibition 'J B Souter 1890–1971' held at the Perth Museum and Art Gallery in 1990, says that Souter destroyed the painting but in 1962 produced a smaller version from a small pastel and other working drawings and which is now in private hands. There can be no doubt that Bunyard would have known of 'The Breakdown' since the furore was world-wide (see Matthew, n. 8). Hynes's discussion (p. 403) silently incorporates phrases from *The Times*'s account, but does not make clear the grounds of its objection to the picture. I owe reference to Bell and Hynes to Dr David Bradshaw, Fellow of Worcester College, Oxford; I am greatly indebted to Professor Hynes for giving me a copy of Matthew's catalogue, and for other pieces of information.

subject … if it stands for the artistic truth and not for scarelines, the Academy should not encourage pictures like "The Breakdown".' (*The Times*, Saturday, 1 May 1926, p. 16)

For Bunyard the banana was 'a test of taste'. He asserts that:

> If your hostess offers you a banana trifle, you know at once what her drawing-room will be like, you know the misty and saccharine music she will prefer, that her favourite author will be – But no! My agreement with my publisher [J. M. Dent & Sons] holds me responsible for each and every libel action arising. But you know to whom I refer!
>
> In pre-banana days English men and women read Fielding and Smollett, good russet writers both, and both in the great tradition which stretched back through Rabelais and Chaucer to the crisp and juicy Greek writers. A taste for the mealy is but part of the inheritance from north Africa, from a people born to be enslaved. (p. 238)

In truth, there was much about the modern world which Bunyard disliked: scientific dieting (in which the nut, 'so long a matter for elegant trifling, has been turned into a diet, a food for Fabians and such unworldly breeds', *AD*, p. 88); cocktails ('whose appeal is that of brazen trumpets loudly overblown', *AD*, p. 159); psychology (where prejudices 'could doubtless all be explained as the abnormal activity of the subconscious mind or by some other uncheckable theory', *EC*, p. 117); aliens who try to assimilate (the English grey partridge is imagined as referring to the French one 'in the tone reserved by us for aliens who have adopted some old English family name', *EC*, p. 139); modern music ('Garlic is no more a fit subject of discussion than modern music … the cacophony of garlic', *EC*, p. 148); youth culture (of ersatz Camembert: 'To the monstrous regiment of Peter Pans, so curious a feature in our modern England, it may have a sympathetic appeal … Peter Pan, no doubt, kept on with knickers all his dream life, and wore his prep-school ties well into his second childhood. But the very essence of cheese lies in its maturity, how it stands up to life and faces it, so away with all such artificially produced cheese childhoods', *EC*, p. 206); mass-production ('In these days of standardized manufactures, mechanized music, and mass-produced food …', *EC*, p. 326). Clearly, we must not expect Bunyard to have a high opinion of modern literature, though a signal and outstanding exception was his friend Norman Douglas, 1868–1952 (see my next chapter, 'Edward Bunyard and Norman Douglas'), and see later in this chapter for his extensive ownership of modern works of literature. I have already quoted his allusion to 'our desperate biographers of to-day' (*EC*, p. 345), and it does not sound like sympathy when, discussing the qualities of Italian wine, he writes, 'I do not doubt that the proximity of Soho to Bloomsbury accounts for some of the vigorous asperities of modern poetry' (*EC*, p. 307). Henry James (1843–1916), too, had earned his disapproval; a letter to Bunyard from Norman Douglas, 8 January 1922 (see Letter D1 in the chapter 'Edward Bunyard and Norman Douglas') states: 'You are quite right in your diagnosis of these fellows – Butler [presumably Samuel Butler, 1835–1902], Henry James etc. Red blood, you say, is what they lack'; cf. too 'thin weedling James' (*EC*, p. 345). Bunyard's article 'The Newer Dessert Apples' (*The New Flora and Silva*, IX.i (October 1936), 31–4) opens with an untraced sentiment from James which is then nicely described in mock-Jamesian baroque:

> "Conservatism", said Henry James, "is the Religion of a gardener." This aphorism, I need hardly say, was not delivered in so many words; there were qualifications, and even recognitions that in certain circumstances human nature, in its infinite variability, might quite conceivably go far to prove the contrary. But we were agreed in the main it was so. I have often recalled these words when looking round a fruit show.

The last two sentences are a wonderful example of 'the art of sinking'.

None the less we have seen in his *Gardening Illustrated* article (1931) quotation from the Bloomsberry Virginia Woolf as well as knowledge of Eden Phillpotts, Compton Mackenzie, Max Beerbohm, Lady Gregory, and Clemence Dane. In 'Gardening for Epicures', published in 1936, there is a nice allusion to the recently published *Cold Comfort Farm* (1932) by Stella Gibbons (1902–89):

> Celibacy has certain advantages, amongst which I place high the freedom to lunch off spring onions and bread and cheese occasionally; after this one feels in a mood to appreciate some of our 'back to nature' authors. Cold Comfort Farm diet. (p. 20)

Otherwise, there is only a glancing allusion to the manner of P. G. Wodehouse (1881–1975):

> ... the Ciceroni, who took their name from the chick-pea. 'F. Chick-Pea, Esq.,' will not be likely to be adopted outside of a Wodehouse novel (*EC*, p. 71),

and an ironically dismissive reference to Noël Coward (1899–1973):

> the young folk striving for brightness by the aid of cocktails have yet to find their historian, unless we may consider Mr Coward on the side of the angels? (*EC*, p. 324; 'on the side of the angels' is from Disraeli, 1804–81)

In literature before the twentieth century, Bunyard was enormously widely read – Greek, Latin, English, French, and, apparently to a much lesser extent, German; he could certainly read Italian. Such knowledge was the product of private enthusiasm rather than formal scholastic instruction. For reasons of health he was educated privately (*Kent Messenger*, 21 October 1939, p. 4), and, as he entered the family firm at the age of 17 in 1896, he never attended a university. In 1900 he went to live in France for a time (script of 'In Your Garden: Novelties from the Kitchen Garden' by E. A. Bunyard and C. H. Middleton, broadcast on 2 April 1939, pp. 1–2; printed as 'Unusual Vegetables' in *The Listener*, XXI, no. 534, 6 April 1939, 749); the prime purpose was to study French horticultural methods, but a love of food and wine and a *sentiment linguistique* must also have resulted. Indeed, he had a real feeling for the tone of all four of Europe's great modern languages. In *AD* he examines how they have tried to express the qualities of the great pear, the Doyenné du Comice. Of the French effort he writes: 'Here the note of scientific aridity is surely too pronounced. "Astringente ou acidulée!"' (p. 122). Then he goes on to see if 'the phlegmatic Nordic [i.e. German] can do better', and says of his quotation:

> This has the connoisseur's note more strongly emphasised and the building up of the final climax betrays the artist, but even here we feel a lack of colour, a certain boreal chill. (p. 122)

Finally, and triumphantly, Italian: 'Here at last is the lyrical touch, the warmth and colour we are seeking. "Molto bene profumata!" Excellent' (p. 122). He concludes that, 'We cannot hope to better this in our own language, and perhaps it is not necessary, as who does not know the melting Comice' (pp. 122–3).

In English he might have made an excellent parodist – an ability which demands a scrupulous sensitivity to tone and register. After his fireworks on the topic of bananas, quoted above, he says that he will try to be an unprejudiced historian, and then gives a marvellous two paragraphs in that style of popular historical writing which in its overblown way tries to make the past vividly and tangibly present in all its sensuous quaintness:

> Let us essay the modern method: "On a day in August, in the year 1627, London lay under the stifling heat of a delayed summer. The rank smell of garbage rose from the kennel [Wardour Street for 'gutter'], and the traveller, picking his way over the uneven cobbles between which ran the discarded slops of domesticity, would stop before Johnson's dingy herbalry, where simples [more Wardour St. for 'medicines' or 'plants used in medicines'] held out their deceiving promise of gangrene cured and strangury [a disease of the urinary organs] alleviated." (*EC*, pp. 238–9)

Despite the reference to 'the modern method' I would lay a guinea hat to a gooseberry that Bunyard is satirizing the florid style of the prolific and once-popular historical novelist and, in romantic fashion, historian G. P. R. James (1799–1860); Bunyard's parody bears comparison with Thackeray's 'Barbazure by G. P. R. Jeames, Esq., Etc.', serialized in *Punch* in 1847. After another paragraph in the same manner, Bunyard cries 'But enough of the romantico-cynico style' (p. 239), though it is the style which is (mock-)romantico, and Bunyard who is cynico.

In his affectionate obituary of Bunyard in *Wine and Food* (VI.24, 1939) Maurice Healy said of his reading that 'it was sometimes to remote fountains that he went for his refreshment' (p. 325). This was true of all those literatures in which he was read, though, of course, the great figures of the canon are there as well. Thus from Greek literature Homer is, as we should expect, cited: *The Odyssey* (vii. 121) on the cultivated fig (*AD*, p. 51), and *The Iliad* (ii. 235) for Thersites' taunt of '*pepones*, or marrow-heads' (*EC*,

p. 74), but his reference to Aristophanes turns out to be remarkably out-of-the-way (more so even than Bunyard's throw-away line about obscurity implies):

> Aristophanes made many broad jokes about it [*sc.* the broad bean, *Faba vulgaris*], *vulgaris* indeed, but this was on another account which we need not go into. In any case, who, out of Oxford, reads Aristophanes to-day? (*EC*, p. 64)

It turns out that there are not 'many' jokes about the broad bean in Aristophanes but just the one, and that only in a fragment.[4] Sometimes just one work is the sole source for what look like obscure authors culled from separate reading of each of them. Thus in *AD* we have, with two deliciously humorous modesty *topoi*:

> The blending of wine and nuts has the authority and charm of antiquity. Who can forget the moving plea of Eupolis in his immortal *Taxiarchs*:
> "Give me some Naxian almonds to regale [me] and from the Naxian vines some wine to drink."
> So, too, Phrynichus, Heracleon of Ephesus, and Plutarch of Chaeronea, in lines too well known to need quotation. (p. 89)

All four authors are quoted in a single section (ii. 52) of *Deipnosophistae* (or *The Sophists at Dinner*), a cookery book by Athenaeus, 'that delightful old epicure and gossip' as Bunyard calls him in *EC* (p. 62); Bunyard's English version is from *The Deipnosophists or Banquet of the Learned* translated by C. D. Yonge, 3 vols., London, 1854, knowledge which permits one to relish Bunyard's inflation of Yonge's 'Eupolis says in his Taxiarchs' (i. 85) to 'Who can forget the moving plea of Eupolis in his immortal Taxiarchs', and the lines of Phrynicus, Heracleon of Ephesus, and Plutarch of Chaeronea

---

[4] See *Poetae Comici Graeci*, ed. R. Kassel and C. Austin, iii.2 *Aristophanes: Testimonia et Fragmenta* (Berlin and New York, 1984), 319, no. 599 (582). See also J. Henderson, *The Maculate Muse: Obscene Language in Attic Comedy* 2nd edn. (New York and Oxford, 1991), p. 149, no. 202. I owe these references to Professor Dr Arnd Kerkhecker, University of Berne.

were not 'too well known' to either Athenaeus or Yonge to omit quotation. Athenaeus is the source also for a couple of recherché-looking classical references to the cabbage in *EC* (p. 62), including even the lofty indifference to giving a precise identification: after quoting Athenaeus on the cabbage (*Deipnosophistae*, i.34; Yonge, i. 56), Bunyard adds two further quotations from Eubulus ('And Eubulus says, somewhere or other') and Niochares, both of whom are in the same section of Athenaeus ('And Eubulus says, somewhere or other', Yonge, i. 56). We may end our excursus on Bunyard and Greek literature with the playful words with which he in turn ended his chapter on figs in *AD*: 'in August and September may sycophants, in the Greek sense [lit. 'fig-shower'], flourish and abound' (p. 56).

Quotations from, and references to, Latin literature stud Bunyard's prose. Often the purpose is simply to provide a factual or historical piece of evidence: thus Juvenal's knowledge of the Richborough oyster (*EC*, p. 3; *Satire* iv. 140–2) and his comment on the Egyptian deification of the onion family ('"Kitchen-garden gods," said Juvenal', *EC*, p. 75, which squeezes the scorn out of 'o sanctas gentes, quibus haec nascuntur in hortis/numina!' what a holy race to have such divinities spring up in the garden! *Satire* xv. 10–11); or Horace's enjoyment of beans and bacon (*EC*, p. 64; *Satire* II.vi. 63–4) and his dislike of garlic (*EC*, p. 76; Epode iii). On occasion, however, direct quotation has aesthetic purpose; thus in the following two paragraphs from *EC* (p. 217),

> Autumn, as a rule, sits heavily upon the poet's pen, but my readers will subscribe rather to the 'formo[si]ssimus annus' of Ovid than the 'Autumnusque gravis' of Horace.
> From September until the year's end our home-grown fruit reaches its best, and with 'the painted partridge willing to be killed' and other game coming to our tables, we find much to compensate us for the lost leaves of summer.

The quotations from Ovid's *Art of Love* (ii. 315) and Horace's *Satire* (II. vi.19) give a brocaded richness to the account of the fruitful season, whereas in the second paragraph the mention of 'home-grown' fruit finds an apt correlative in the elided quotation from the English Ben Jonson's 'To Penshurst' (ll. 29–30), albeit 'painted partridge' is actually a calque on the *picta perdix* of Martial's description of Faustinus' simple but productive farm (*Epigrams*, III.lviii. 15). And what a happy matching of the alliterating fullness of 'painted partridge' with that of the elegiac fall of the 'lost leaves' of summer. For Horace, from whom we have had three allusions, Bunyard had an especial reverence:

> Falerno of Naples must be drunk even if only as a libation to Horace. Whether this was his Falernian or not matters little, it is an act of homage due. (*EC*, p. 307)

I have noted but two references to Tacitus: a mention of him on pearls (*EC*, p. 3) and 'omne ignotum pro magnifico est' (*Agricola*, xxx.3), wonder grows as knowledge fails, used as a tag in the essay 'Vegetable Adventures' (*WF*, II.5, 1935, p. 51). One may draw attention to the dearth of quotations from Silver Age prose writers since Bunyard's own prose style is strikingly similar to theirs.

As with Greek literature, he is ready to reach for the recondite. So, when discussing the claret Château Ausone, he expresses a devotion to a far from leading author:

> The château is believed to be built on the site of the Roman villa owned by Ausonius. One would hate not to believe this.
>
> This majestic wine matches well his no less majestical verse, and we remember his night of 'wine and flutes' [untraced] and congratulate ourselves that some of his pleasures and inspiration may be shared by us to-day. (*EC*, p. 280)

But, as with my consideration of Bunyard and Greek literature, I will conclude this account of his relation to Latin literature with a typical instance of his whimsical use of learning, this time on the growing of asparagus:

> For general directions as to cultivation we may turn to that accomplished Roman, Cato [*De Agri Cultura*, clxi], or, if preferred, to any modern garden book. (*EC*, p. 59)

When we turn to modern literatures I have noted nothing from Italian, and from German only Goethe, and him only twice. Once is in German: 'And when we again walk in the orange groves of Sorrento (Kennst du der Land?)', where *der* is a slip for *das*, from 'Know you the land where the lemon-trees bloom?' the well-known song from *Wilhelm Meisters Lehrjahre*, iii.1, in a review of a book on citrus fruits (*WF*, VI.22, 1939, p. 167). The other quotation from Goethe is not only in English but clearly from a published translation. In *EC* Bunyard wrote:

> It was Goethe, I think, who said that only children and birds knew what strawberries really tasted like – but poets are always regretting their lost youth. I stand up for adult tastes. (p. 213)

It was indeed Goethe, in an incident which took place on Sunday 15 June 1828, and was recorded by J. P. Eckermann (1792–1854) in his *Gespräche mit Goethe in den letzten Jahren seines Lebens*, Zweiter Teil.[5] However, the German has not 'birds' but, more precisely, *Sperlinge*, sparrows; and not 'strawberries' but *Kirschen und Beeren*, cherries and berries. Bunyard must have been remembering not the original German but the English translation by John Oxenford, *Conversations of Goethe with Eckermann and Soret* (London, 1850), ii. 63: '"One must ask children and birds," said he, "how cherries and strawberries taste"'; on p. 503 of *EC* in an assembly of gastronomic quotations Bunyard again quotes from Oxenford's translation (another passage), and collation shows that he was using the 1850 edition and not the slightly revised reprint of 1874. It remains to add that Bunyard's scoffing at the romantic Goethe was unfair; Goethe's remark came at the end of a performance of Tyrolean songs, including *das Gejodel*. 'Goethe seemed by no means so much delighted as we'; a taste for the Tyrolean was as immature as that of children and sparrows for cherries and berries. Goethe, like Bunyard, was standing up for adult tastes. But then, being unfair to Goethe has long been an English sport.

In the obituary to which I have already referred, Maurice Healy said: 'He read as much French as English; and in neither tongue did he care much for anything later than the eighteenth century' (*WF*, VI.24, 1939, p. 324).

---

[5] I owe this information to Professor Dr Arnd Kerkhecker.

Certainly the posthumous sale of Bunyard's books at Hodgson's in London, 13–14 June 1940 (see chapter 1) reveals a considerable number of works of French literature in French (as well as in translation): Ronsard's *Les Sonnets pour Hélène* (lot 82); Anatole France's *Œuvres Complètes* (lot 85; also in English, lot 86); as well as Michel Corday's *Anatole France...1928*, 'and other French Literature', 32 vols.: lot 88); George Sand's *Histoire de ma Vie*, 'and others', 40 vols. (lot 89); Casanova's *Mémoires* (lot 95; also in English, lot 96); and, though I am not here recording all English translations, it is worth noting Scott-Moncrieff's translation of Proust's *Remembrance of Things Past* (lot 87). Allusions to French literature are not numerous, though more so than to German; by and large, with one major exception, they conform to Healy's observation on chronological preference. We have already seen Rabelais (*c.* 1494–*c.* 1553) placed in the pomological tradition of the russet (*EC*, p. 238), and of Racine (1639–99) we are told that he 'was a tea drinker, and it would seem an ideal drink for the taut style he carried to its perfection' (*EC*, p. 345). Given Bunyard's liking for linking literature and 'gustronomy', it is no surprise to learn that 'Ortolan is, I think, the most wonderful word in the French language, sumptuous in its suggestion and musical in its refrain' (*EC*, p. 140), referring to Disraeli's 'gilded aristocrats' who 'were bred for no other purpose than to eat ortolans from silver dishes' (presumably an allusion to *The Young Duke* (1831), I.x, in which the narrator has two extravagant paragraphs in praise of ortolans: 'Let me die eating ortolans to the sound of soft music'). What is, however, surprising is the expression of Bunyard's wish that 'I hope before my dining days are over I may somewhere meet ortolans on a silver dish and see what all the fuss is about. ... A taste for eating small birds, bones and all, must, I expect, grow up from one's youth; but for all that I shall try these ortolans ... should they cross my path' (p. 140). They *had* crossed his path. The International Genetics Conference in 1906, which Bunyard attended, and from which I have already quoted, was not only a great scientific occasion but also a great gastronomic one. The *Report* of 1907 not only published the texts of the papers, but also the full menus of every magnificent luncheon and dinner. On Friday 3 August 1906 all members went for luncheon to the country house of Mr Leopold de Rothschild at Gunnersbury; the vote of thanks on behalf of the British guests was proposed by Sir Albert Rollit who said, 'The Lucullan feast of ortolans [which must have been the Mayonnaise de Volaille on the menu] and the flow of champagne has been splendid' (*Report*, op. cit. above, p. 82). Alas, that Bunyard did not remember; the flow of champagne may be why.

On the artichoke he turned to a stanza from Ronsard (1524–85), Ode XXIV, 'À Gaspar d'Auvergne' (inc. 'Gaspar, qui du mont Pegase'), in *Le Troisiesme Livre des Odes*, though mangling *Tourangeaux* into *routangeaux* (*EC*, p. 57). On Volnay he has a marvellous description of it by Bossuet (1627–1704) as '"a good funeral wine", and the author of the *Oraisons Funèbres* spoke as an expert' (*AD*, p. 184); I have not found the precise source. Truly a 'remote fountain' in Healy's phrase are three couplets describing Cos d'Estournel, a building in the Chinese style in the Médoc plain, by 'Biarnez, the poet of Bordeaux', including 'Avec des minarets groupés sur ses coteaux' (*WF*, VI.21, 1939, p. 28). The first two couplets indeed are by Pierre Biarnez (1798–1874), 'Les Vins de Médoc' in his *Les Grands Vins de Bordeaux* (Paris, 1849), 3–52, p. 46. However, Bunyard was evidently quoting from memory: his first couplet (inaccurate anyway) appears in the original six lines after his second couplet (also imperfectly quoted); the last couplet has no equivalent anywhere in Biarnez's poem and must be invented, though there is some skill in that.[6]

It is an agreeable trait of literary men to apply a phrase from a serious literary context to another, often more frivolous, situation; the reader's pleasure is heightened by knowledge of the discrepancy. Bunyard was a master of this drollery. Thus it was originally the French diplomatist and statesman, Talleyrand (1754–1838) who, to his 'attachés d'ambassade', said 'Surtout, Messieurs, point de zèle' (Philarète Chasles, *Voyages d'un Critique À Travers la Vie et les Livres*, 2 vols (Paris, 1865–8), ii, *Italie et Espagne*, 407). This instruction in statecraft is echoed by Bunyard: 'The ice-pail is almost as dangerous as the hot-water bath, "*surtout pas trop de zèle*"' (*AD*, p. 165). Of course, Talleyrand's words had clearly become a quotable tag, and, as will be discussed later, on Bunyard and English literature, Bunyard's knowledge of it very possibly derives from his encountering it in the works of Samuel Butler.

---

[6] On Biarnez see E. Feret, *Statistique Générale … du Département de la Gironde*, iii. i: *Biographie* (Bordeaux and Paris, 1889), p. 68. I owe this reference to the Archives Municipales de Bordeaux in answer to a query made on my behalf by Dr Kate Tunstall, Fellow of Worcester College, Oxford.

My final instance of Bunyard's *entente cordiale* with French literature is a particularly interesting one because it is both close and, at first blush, surprising. Under the heading 'Varia', a collection of gastronomic literary extracts, towards the end of *EC*, headlined '*Cocktail chez les Décadents*', is an English version (pp. 506–7) of part of chapter iv of J.-K. Huysmans' *À Rebours* (1884). The English is not that of the translation of 1926, *Against the Grain*, in two editions published one in Paris and the other in London; it is part translation and part summary, and is presumably by Bunyard himself. Huysmans describes a contraption in the dining-room of Des Esseintes which he called his 'orgue à bouche'. It consisted of little barrels of liqueurs and spirits; their spigots, being connected by a single rod, could be opened simultaneously, filling tiny tumblers beneath. To Des Esseintes the different liqueurs and spirits corresponded in their taste to the different sounds of musical instruments. Thus, for example, dry curaçao was the sound of the clarinet, 'aigrelet et velouté' ('velvet sharpness' in Bunyard's version); kümmel the nasal timbre of the oboe; kirsch 'fierce trumpet notes'; and so forth, in great detail, forming a full orchestra which enabled Des Esseintes to play 'symphonies intérieures' in his throat. In a further development of the analogy Des Esseintes considered that one could play string quartets 'sous la voûte palatine', with, for example, an old brandy performing as the violin (with the addition of the 'silvery vibrant notes' of a dry cumin [kümmel in Bunyard's version] one had a harp for a quintet). Thus could Des Esseintes play 'sur la langue de silencieuses mélodies', mute funeral marches, crème de menthe solos, and vespetro and rum duets.

In *AD* under the heading 'The Symphony of Wine' (p. 157) Bunyard develops an analogy between wine and music (pp. 158–60); it is repeated in *EC* (pp. 263–4, from which I quote). 'Wine can be considered as a symphony', he says: the basic vinous taste of the grape can be compared to 'the string basis of the orchestra'; to this are added 'the acid piccolo' (in Huysmans, crème de menthe and anisette are like the flute, simultaneously 'sucrée et poivrée, piaulante et douce'; 'at once sweet and peppery, complaining and sweet' in Bunyard's version) and 'the light astringency of clarinets and bassoons' (compare the 'aigrelet et velouté' of Huysmans' clarinet; Bunyard's 'velvet sharpness'); finally, we have the brass of alcohol, its 'fiery tones' recalling Huysmans' kirsch which 'sonne furieusement de la trompette', Bunyard's 'sounded fierce trumpet notes'. Thus we have our 'vinous symphony' like the 'symphonies intérieures' of Des Esseintes. Like that aesthete, Bunyard develops the analogy between wine and music to include full orchestra and string quartets:

> Wine is, therefore, a symphony, an orchestra of many tones and rhythms, and equally there are orchestras of many sizes. There is the imperial majesty of Burgundy, so richly scored, contrasting with the clean simplicity of an Anjou wine, a string quartet in comparison.

Such a debt to Huysmans may come as a surprise to readers of the mature Bunyard, 'we fogies and buffers' as he says in *EC* (p. 289), with a dislike of cocktails 'whose appeal is that of brazen trumpets loudly overblown' (ibid., p. 264), and it is hard to associate it with the rather austere face, bespectacled and hair severely brushed, which looks out at us in the photograph which accompanies his obituary in *The Journal of Pomology and Horticultural Science* (XVII.4, 1940, 294ff.), although the photograph had first appeared in *Amateur Gardening* XLIX, no. 2513, 2 July 1932, 188; but look instead at the brooding young man, without spectacles and with a mass of dark wavy hair, in the photograph which accompanies his biography in *The Journal of Horticulture and Home Farmer* (3rd series, LXI, no. 3238, 20 October 1910, 369–70, see the reproductions on pp. 16 and 30, above), who had gone to live in France for a while at the age of 21, and a flirtation with the decadent will seem but proof of his avuncular assertion that 'if youth were not up and doing the supply of old fogies would in course of time run out' (*EC*, p. 289). And he had, after all, owned Wilde's *Dorian Gray* and Lord Alfred Douglas's autobiography (Hodgson's sale, lot 129).

Yet it is, of course, English literature to which Bunyard makes the most frequent allusion. He had an excellent eye for an entertaining quotation, but proportion demands only a couple of examples here (he was at times rough and ready in his accuracy, but I give the quotations as Bunyard presents them). The first is a letter from Horace Walpole, 6 October 1775, speaking of Madame du Deffand who:

> has been so ill, that on the day she was seized I thought she could not last till night. Her Herculean weakness, which could not resist strawberries and cream after supper, has surmounted all the *ups* and *downs* which followed

her excess. (*AD*, p. 153; in the Yale edition of Walpole's correspondence see XXXIX, 269)

'Oh! admirable octogenarian' commented Bunyard; the notion of a Herculean weakness is to be relished. My second instance of the sheerly pleasurable quotation is also from a letter, this time from Sydney Smith to the Rev. R. H. Barham, 15 November 1841:

> 'If there be,' said Sydney Smith, 'one pure and elevated pleasure in this world it is a roast pheasant. Barn-door fowls for Dissenters, but for we Churchmen, the thirty-nine times articled clerk, the pheasant, the pheasant.' (*EC*, p. 137; Bunyard would have taken his text from Hesketh Pearson, *The Smith of Smiths* (London, 1934), p. 250, a reference I owe to Mr Alan Bell.)

In chronology the quotations run from Chaucer ('General Prologue'; *EC*, pp. 4, 79) to, just, the twentieth century: Eden Phillpotts's *A Dish of Apples* (1921), from which I have already quoted, is the only literary work of that century actually quoted, and its subject matter makes it a special case. However, as a further brush with modernity we may include A. C. Benson's *Coronation Ode* (1902), 'Land of Hope and Glory' as we know it, whose fourth line, 'God who made thee mighty, make thee mightier yet', is echoed in a patriotic laudation of English Cheshire cheese:

> But at its best there is nothing to touch a Cheshire as a companion for beer or to finish up a lunch of cold beef and salad. One rises with virility and patriotism enhanced – Make thee mightier yet! (*EC*, p. 202)

American literature is largely ignored; perhaps this is not altogether surprising. In his projected 'vegetable interpretation of history' in *GE*, Bunyard says that:

> 'The Effect of the Potato on Anglo-American Relationship' will describe how the prolific potato trebled Ireland's population, and then when famine and disaster came upon that unhappy country its citizens took shelter under the Stars and Stripes. There they fanned the dying embers of hatred against the old country with a result that is with us to-day. (p. 21)

It is an ingenious sequence of cause and effect. Whitman (1819–92) is mentioned once (*AD*, p. 130), but only as part of an *ubi sunt* for forgotten varieties of pear: 'Where is the honeyed Seckle so dear to Walt Whitman …?' From Melville (1819–91) he borrowed a taxonomy of whales (*Moby-Dick* (1851), chapter 32) for use with melons:

> The family of Melons is large, and we may divide it, as Melville did the whale, into folios, octavos, and duodecimos. (*AD*, p. 76)

In *EC* there is a nice echo of the humour of Mark Twain (1835–1910) when we are told that, 'Roquefort, from the English point of view, is Stilton without a college education' (p. 205); this clearly derives from one of the 'quotations' from Pudd'nhead Wilson's Calendar used as an epigraph to chapter 5 of *Pudd'nhead Wilson* (1894): 'cauliflower is nothing but cabbage with a college education'.

As would be expected – of someone educated a century ago, that is – echoes of the Bible and Shakespeare are often found, more particularly of Shakespeare in Bunyard's case. As in the example from Talleyrand noted earlier, transference of contexts is a comic delight: thus St. Paul's 'Prove all things; hold fast that which is good' (I. Thessalonians v.21) is applied to epicurean experience (*EC*, p. vii), and, over the page, in the same context, Bunyard declares 'I am with him who said: "Rejoice, and again I say, Rejoice!"' (*EC*, p. viii); whether St. Paul ('Rejoice *in the Lord* alway: and again I say, Rejoice', Philippians iv.4) would have been with Bunyard is another matter.

The same *Hamlet* soliloquy provides two echoed phrases in *AD*: early apples kept overnight will be 'flat and unprofitable' (*AD*, p. 12; *Hamlet* I.ii.133), and we learn later of 'the wonderful solidity of the Bellegarde's flesh [a variety of peach], a solidity as of good butter, and as readily melting' (p. 105; cf. I.ii.129, 'too too solid flesh would melt'). Similarly, the same speech by Brutus is plundered for imagery to tell us that if there is a chance to purchase Romanée Conti then there is a 'tide in the affairs of men' (*AD*, p. 182; *Julius Caesar* IV.iii.216), and that the 'melting moment' of Camembert cheeses 'must be taken rather before the flood' (*EC*, p. 205; cf. *Jul. Caes.* IV.iii.217, 'taken *at* the flood'). In *GE* Henry V's exhortation to 'Stiffen the sinews, summon up the blood' (III.i.7) is applied to the task of ruthless pruning (p. 34); 'Disguise fair nature with hard-favoured rage' command both Bunyard and Henry V (p. 34; III.i.8). There are, of course, more examples, but these will serve to show Bunyard's witty and creative use of transferred quotations from Shakespeare.

Though Maurice Healy in his obituary said that Bunyard in his reading did not care much for anything later than the eighteenth century, the sale of his books at Hodgson's reveals not only writers from the Middle Ages to the eighteenth century – Malory (lot 14); *The Book of the Knight of La Tour-Landry*, a modernized version of the fifteenth-century Middle English translation, 1930 (lot 77); Plutarch's *Lives* translated by North (lot 74); Shakespeare (lot 73); Sir Thomas Browne (lots 17–18); Rochester (lot 75); Ned Ward's *The London Spy* (lot 20); Fielding (lot 19); Smollett (lot 21); Richard Graves's *The Spiritual Quixote* (lot 20); Horace Walpole's letters (lot 23) – but many works of both the nineteenth and twentieth centuries. The catalogue inevitably does not list every book: thus 'Modern Miscellaneous Books 150 vols' (lot 2); Everyman's Library, 40 vols (lot 3); 'Novels by H. G. Wells, James Hanley and others 60 vols' (lot 8); etc., etc. It was clearly an impressively large library.

From the nineteenth century there are: Austen (lot 24); Keats (lot 25); Byron (lot 80); Cobbett (lot 79); Peacock (lot 26, and Van Doren's *Life*, lot 27); Borrow (lot 24); Disraeli (lot 29); Melville (lot 28); 'Erewhon' Butler's *Note-Books* (lot 102); and Wilde's *Dorian Gray*, Lord Alfred Douglas's *Autobiography*, 1929, and 14 'others' (lot 129).

More surprising, given Bunyard's playing the role of old fogey, is the number of twentieth-century works. Of those authors specified, far and away the most numerous titles are those of his friend Norman Douglas: 11 lots (105–115), most signed presentation copies with autograph letters; and there are two items by friends of Douglas and Bunyard: Edwin Cerio's *That Capri Air*, 1929 (lot 104), and Pino Orioli's *Moving Along*, 1934 (lot 126); see the chapter on 'Edward Bunyard and Norman Douglas'. We have seen already in this chapter Bunyard's knowledge of Eden Phillpotts, Compton Mackenzie, Max Beerbohm, George Moore, Virginia Woolf, Clemence Dane, Stella Gibbons, P. G. Wodehouse, and Henry James. The sale catalogue is impressively full of the modern: already noted are H. G. Wells, 1866–1946, and James Hanley, 1901–85, (lot 8), but there are also 'Novels by H. H. Munro ['Saki', 1870–1916] (4), Thomas Burke

[1887–1945, better known, if at all now, as a travel writer on England and on the taverns and restaurants of London] (5), and others 30 vols' (lot 9); '*Great English Short Stories*, Harrap 1931 [1047 pages, from Barnabe Rich to Aldous Huxley]; Modern Novels, etc. 25 vols' (lot 10); Richard Aldington, 1892–1962, *All Men Are Enemies*, 1933, together with Arnold Bennett, 1867–1931, *The Pretty Lady*, 1918, 'and others' 12 vols (lot 99); Beerbohm, 1872–1956 (lots 100–101, one volume signed); Conrad, 1857–1924, 20 vols, vol. 1 signed by the author (lot 103); Baron Corvo, i.e. F. W. Rolfe, 1860–1913, *The Desire and Pursuit of the Whole*, 1934 (lot 104); Aldous Huxley, 1894–1963, *Limbo*, 1920, *Antic Hay*, 1923, 'and others', 12 vols (lot 116), James Joyce, 1882–1941, *Ulysses*, Paris, 1925, together with Wyndham Lewis, 1882–1957, *The Apes of God*, 1930, 'and others', 12 vols (lot 117); D. H. Lawrence, 1885–1930, *The Lost Girl*, 1920, 'and others by or relating to the same' 15 vols (lot 118); works by and on T. E. Lawrence, 1888–1935 (lots 119–120); signed copies of various works by George Moore, 1852–1933 (lots 122–5); John Cowper Powys, 1872–1963, *Autobiography*, 1934 (lot 126); G. B. Shaw, 1856–1950, *Dramatic Opinions*, 1907, 'and others by or relating to' him, 18 vols (lot 127); H. G. Wells, 1866–1946, *A Modern Utopia*, 1905, 'and others', 20 vols (lot 128; see also lot 8); J. M. Synge, 1871–1909, collected edn., 1910, (lot 130), and Yeats, 1865–1939, *Poems*, 1908 (lot 131). If Bunyard really didn't care for the twentieth century, then his opinion was not based on ignorance.

Quotations and echoes from nineteenth-century authors, however, make their way quite liberally from his library to his own prose. It is true that he did not like Dickens; writing of George Saintsbury's praise of the medlar, he says:

> Each of us has some blind spots in our make-up, and it may be that a liking for Dickens and Medlars are in some strange way connected, as these are the only two things in which I cannot follow the author of the *Cellar Book* with reverence and gratitude. (*AD*, p. 145)

But he still quotes Sam Weller on oysters (*EC*, p. 4), and there are two extracts from *Sketches by Boz* in *EC*'s anthology of writing on gastronomic topics (pp. 434–5). Those who do not admire Dickens often praise Surtees, and Bunyard says that in the autumn 'the gourmet rejoices with Jorrocks to see the dahlias fall before the early frost' (*AD*, p. 117; '"Hurrah! blister my kidneys! it *is* a frost! – the dahlias are dead!"', *Handley Cross*, 1843 edn., III.ix.184; chap. lxvi of later editions). Bunyard's only other expressed preference is that of Jane Austen before Richardson; it is in a discussion of claret which he says is:

> An intellectual wine also, with a touch of astringency, perhaps a necessary quality for the preservation of classics. Richardson is forgotten while Jane Austen is still with us, preserved by the light acid of her wit and her gay, astringent irony. (*AD*, pp. 170–1)

Acidity was always for Bunyard, in apples and in books, an essential quality of classic greatness.

One nineteenth-century author from whom I have found but one direct quotation is none the less, I believe, of great import for Bunyard's own prose style. In *AD* after quoting from the posthumously published *Healths Improvement* (London, 1655) by Thomas Muffett (1553–1604), Bunyard writes:

> Let us pass to another epoch and to a writer who, even in his most intimate moments, always remains quotable. "The apricot, shining in a sweet brightness of golden velvet." Ruskin – of course you guessed. (p. 35)

The phrase 'sweet brightness of golden velvet' is from *Modern Painters*, iii (1856), part iv, chap. iii, 'Of the Real Nature of Greatness of Style' (*The Works of John Ruskin*, ed. E. T. Cook and A. Wedderburn, v (London, 1904), 68). Now consider these passages:

> There is a satisfying richness about a tree of apricots in fruit; the dark leathery leaves serve as an admirable background to the fruits. Here and there a fruit will be marked with a vinous flush and some darker freckles, indications of richness slowly maturing within. For the complete picture we need an old brick wall, mellowed by sun and rain to a rose tint, and we have a colour effect which the flower garden will not easily surpass. (*AD*, pp. 35–6)

What better end to a golden September day could be desired, as we toy with our dessert and see through the open windows a great tawny moon sailing bravely over the sleeping elms? (*AD*, p. 105)

There is a Gothic splendour in Burgundy which no other wine can match. It calls to mind the sun streaming through old glass and distant organ-notes and its music is that of Caesar [*sic*] Franck. (*AD*, p. 181)

Bunyard – of course you guessed. But something of Bunyard's stylistic DNA structure – and let us not quail at the use of such a term of a man who gave a paper at a Genetics Conference – must derive from the florid poeticism which is there in Ruskin. No doubt other authors, too, contributed to the sensuous side of Bunyard's prose: Keats's 'close bosom-friend of the maturing sun' (*To Autumn*) is quoted in *EC* (p. 214), and on the facing-page, taste 'of Flora and the country green' (p. 215) from *Ode to a Nightingale* is used to enhance an account of fresh raspberries and cream. It would be surprising if an author devoted to the epicurean did not call upon *Rubáiyát of Omar Khayyám* of Edward Fitzgerald (1809–83), and indeed in a discussion of whether to buy wine by cash or credit we are told that 'as in olden days, it is still wise to take the cash and let the credit go' (*EC*, p. 295), an unacknowledged line from *Rubáiyát* ('Ah, take the Cash, and let the Credit go', 4th edn., 1879, st. xiii). An echo from at least as sensational a poem comes at the conclusion of a section on the artichoke, *Cynara cardunculus*: 'I have been faithful to thee, *Cynara*, in my fashion' (*EC*, p. 58). Again unannounced by quotation marks, this is the refrain line of the four stanzas of 'Non Sum Qualis Eram Bonae sub Regno Cynarae', perhaps the most famous of the poems of Ernest Dowson (1867–1900), decadent aesthete poet of the 1890s, the decade of 'Non Sum Qualis …'; we recall the debt to Huysmans noted earlier, but note too that this concluding line is used by Bunyard not of a lady but a vegetable: the acid, and humour, of the maturer bachelor is at work.

Perhaps surprising in another direction is reference to Sir James Frazer's *The Golden Bough* (1890–1915, with an *Aftermath* in 1936); Bunyard talks briefly of festival processions in Greece, Egypt, and modern Calabria involving small pots of lettuce or herbs, and says, 'Readers of the *Golden Bough* will know where to look for further details' (*EC*, p. 72). Lawrence,

Eliot, Pound, Bunyard ... the *Golden Bough* was a seminal work for twentieth-century writers. Though one might not have had Bunyard down for an interest in anthropology, it may be that the relativistic attitude towards world religions which *The Golden Bough* encouraged fitted in well with his own notions; Maurice Healy's obituary (*WF*, VI.24, 1939) related that 'Bunyard always seemed to me to be ethical rather than religious. His principles were firm and excellent; but I cannot recall any occasion when they were expressed in the language of any formal creed' (p. 325). In the Hodgson's sale of his books there were 187 books on the anthropology, mythology, folklore, history, and culture of ancient societies (lots 195–217), as Swiss, Teutonic, Indo-European, Etrusco-Roman, Egyptian, Greek, Roman, Babylonian, Chinese, Asian, though Frazer is not mentioned.

It may have been this trait which drew him to Samuel Butler (1835–1902), controversialist and iconoclast on topics of religion, evolution and morality, and the author of the satiric novel, posthumously published (1903), *The Way of All Flesh*. There are two certain quotations in *AD* from *The Note-Books of Samuel Butler* (first edn. 1912; my references are to the Shrewsbury Edition of Butler's Works, xx, London and New York, 1926): '... that complete absorption of the subject which Samuel Butler thought to be love's highest expression' (p. 36; *Note-Books*, chap. xiii, s.v. 'Loving and Hating', pp. 205–6); '... the question posed by Samuel Butler (the second) as to eating [grapes] "upwards" or "downwards"' (p. 69; *Note-Books*, chap. vii, s.v. 'Eating Grapes Downwards', pp. 95–6). Earlier, in discussing Bunyard and French literature, I drew attention to his echo of Talleyrand's 'surtout point de zèle'. This has certainly now become a known tag, and it was a favourite maxim of Butler (and of his circle) in the war upon extremes. It is used twice in his *Alps and Sanctuaries* (1881; Shrewsbury Edition, vii (1924), chap. v): 'Surely [speaking of religion] there are some things which, like politics, are too serious to be taken quite seriously. *Surtout point de zèle* is not the saying of a cynic, but the conclusion of a sensible man; and the more deep our feeling is about any matter, the more occasion have we to be on our guard against *zèle* in this particular respect' (pp. 47–8); '[recommending that everyone practise a religion or denomination other than their own for a week a year] is but another phase of the wise saying – *Surtout point de zèle*' (p. 50). Whether Bunyard's immediate source was Talleyrand or Butler's quotation of him (as seems quite likely), its application to the use of an ice-bucket (*AD*, p. 165) is clearly humorous; but we should reflect that there may in the possible use of Butler here be an indication of Bunyard's serious, ethical, non-religious, wish to avoid extremes. On some topics, however, as on the cultural implications of bananas, he did not always put his principles into practice.

Other nineteenth-century authors or works cited are more as expected. Scott's *Marmion* (1808) provides 'chill and drear' and 'red and sear' for an account of November (*AD*, p. 18), and 'The horns of Elfland faintly blowing' (Tennyson, *The Princess*, iv) sound in a characterization of hock (*AD*, p. 189). Transference of contexts can freshen up an echo: 'Grow old along with me!' begins Browning's 'Rabbi Ben Ezra', and this is the recommendation for wines of the Rhone Valley (*EC*, p. 294); and the incipit of the same poet's 'Memorabilia', 'Ah, did you once see Shelley plain …?' gives the diction for Bunyard's marvelling that many alive as he wrote must have 'seen Bass "plain"' (*EC*, p. 336), Bass being 'Mr M. T. Bass the Great' of the brewing dynasty. Of prose works in the century we may also cite a reference to 'gentle Elia' for his pleasure in living in Covent Garden for the fresh peas and strawberries (*EC*, p. 83; the letter by Charles Lamb to Dorothy Wordsworth, 21 November 1817, actually speaks of 'peas and 'sparagus'; Bunyard has blended the location of the letter with the mention of strawberries and peas together in Lamb's essay, 'Old China'); the once popular *Noctes Ambrosianae* (1822–35) is quoted for an ecstatic description by Timothy Tickler of grouse soup (*EC*, p. 136; *The Works of Professor [John] Wilson*, ed. J. F. Ferrier, i. (Edinburgh, 1868), 51; the passage is also in the edn. 'selected and arranged' by John Skelton, Edinburgh and London, 1876, p. 19); as a last instance, Bunyard turned to Mrs Gaskell's *Cranford* (1853) in an uncharacteristically self-deprecating passage on the onion:

> France, facing as always the major facts of life, has never had any false modesty about the onion family. In England, unfortunately, a certain Cranford atmosphere lingers. Bashful titters, shy reluctances greet this king of vegetables. (*GE*, p. 19)

Before the nineteenth century, quotations and echoes are most common from the literature of the eighteenth century, but there is a presence from the Renaissance, too. I have already noted quotations from Shakespeare,

Bacon, and Jonson. I should like to have traced the phrase the 'innosent flaver' of strawberries, ascribed by Bunyard to Sir Philip Sidney (*EC*, p. 214), but it has so far eluded me. When writing of Dorset Blue Vinny cheese there is again a characteristic reaching for the recondite:

> I must go to Dorset without more delay; the 'hungry air of Odcombe' is, I expect, the right *apéritif* for this southerly cheese. (*EC*, p. 199)

The quoted phrase is from Thomas Coryate (1577? – 1617), *Coryats Crudities Hastily gobled vp in five Moneths trauells ...; Newly digested in the hungry aire of Odcombe in the County of Somerset ...* (1611; there was a reprint in 1905). Naturally enough for an epicure, there is a quotation (*AD*, p. 69), on grapes, from Sir William Temple (1628–99), 'Upon the Gardens of Epicurus, or of Gardening in the Year 1685', Essay II in *Miscellanea: The Second Part. In Four Essays* (London, 1690), p. 48 (there was a reprint of this essay, intro. by A. F. Sieveking, in 1908). Less recherché is the echo of

> Gather ye Rose-buds while ye may,
> Old Time is still a flying

from 'To the Virgins, to make much of Time' by Robert Herrick (1591–1674) in a passage on apples: 'Cling, however, to your apple while ye may, and thus defy time's flying' (*GE*, p. 23). Herrick's lines had been quoted in a work by his father, George Bunyard, *England's National Flower* [the rose], with photographs by Edward (Maidstone and London, [?1904]), in quotations accompanying photographs facing pp. 12 and 17. Finally, in connexion with literature of the Renaissance, Mr Ian Jackson of Berkeley, California, has drawn my attention to three notes on Drayton's *Poly-Olbion* in the edition of *The Works of Michael Drayton* by J. William Hebel (1891–1934) where, in the posthumously published 5th volume of Notes (Oxford, 1941) by Kathleen Tillotson and Bernard H. Newdigate, Newdigate (responsible for the *Poly-Olbion* notes; see p. ix) writes: 'The late Mr. E. A. Bunyard of Maidstone told me ...', p. 239, note to l. 688; see also notes to ll. 677, 689. Clearly Bunyard was the man scholars consulted on fruit.

But, as we saw earlier, if Bunyard had an apple in one hand it was generally an eighteenth-century author (Fielding) he had in the other. So far we have registered references to Ned Ward, Cibber, Addison (in *The Spectator*), Fielding, Walpole, Smollett. Swift is cited (*EC*, p. 306) for two contrasting opinions in *Journal to Stella* on Italian wine, one being 'damned wine' (Letter XIII, 4 January 1710–11) and the other he 'liked mightily' (Letter XXI, 14 April 1711); more obscure are 'Dean Swift's lines' (*EC*, p. 79):

> This is every cook's opinion:
> No savoury dish without an Onion,

which are from a poem, 'Onyons', in *Verses Made for Women who Cry Apples, &c.* Pope is there for three lines on lettuce (*EC*, p. 72) from his imitation, *The First Satire of the Second Book of Horace* (ll. 16–18). Sterne gives us his opinion that hock is 'a good wine for Curates' (*AD*, p. 192), but I have not located where. Also untraced are some splendid lines on gin ascribed by Bunyard simply to 'an eighteenth-century poet' (*EC*, p. 324):

> The starchest prude deigns the admission,
> Free from the dread of censure or suspicion,
> The flask by trusty Johnny brought her
> Seems to the sight, pure Pyrmont water.
> Gin to pained entrails gives relief,
> Makes slighted damsels lose their grief,
> Helps puffs to utter, rakes to rattle,
> Old wives to scold, and young to tattle.

'Can any cocktail do more?' asks Bunyard.

Thus must end our *tour d'horizon* of 'Edward Bunyard and Literature'. It has, perforce, been orderly: by language and by period. But *in* Bunyard's prose, quotations and echoes catch our eye kaleidoscopically, as languages and periods succeed each other for reasons not of chronology but of fresh juxtaposition and literary aptness. It is the mark of a mind which has all the richness and variety of a large and well-stocked cellar.

If, as a coda, we ask about Bunyard *in* Literature, then, stretching a point or two, we can give an affirmative response. B. F. Cummings (1889–1919) was a biologist who died aged 30 after a long and terrible illness; under the name W. N. P. Barbellion he wrote a diary, courageous, moving, and finely written: *The Journal of a Disappointed Man*, with an introduction by H. G. Wells (London, 1919). On 18 September 1912 he records an incident on holiday thus:

> The following curious conversation took place between me and the deaf gaffer, aged 76, standing in the apple tree, –
> 'These be all appulls from Kent – I got 'em all from Kent.'
> 'How long have you lived in C-----?'
> 'Bunyard & Son – that's the firm – they live just outside the town of Maidstone.'
> 'Do you keep Bees here?'
> 'One of these yer appulls is called Bunyard after the firm – a fine fruit too.'[7]
> 'Your good wife must be of great assistance to you in your work.'
> 'Little stalks maybe, but a large juishy appull for all that.' (pp. 66–7)

As a memorial, literary and pomological, with a sense of the comic absurdity of life, the scene has its merits.

---

[7] I would guess that this may be the variety which R. Hogg's *Fruit Manual* 5th edn. (London, 1884), p. 5, records s.v. 'Alexandra', with the alternative name 'Bunyard's Seedling': 'a delicious little early apple; ripe in the first week of September'. E. A. Bunyard, *A Handbook of Hardy Fruits ... Part I Apples and Pears* (London, 1920), does not record 'Alexandra' or 'Bunyard's Seedling', but , p. 85, s.v. 'Maidstone Favourite', notes that this early dessert apple, 'one of the most beautiful apples of Autumn', was raised by George Bunyard & Co. from a seed of Emperor Alexander; Hogg does not list 'Maidstone Favourite' and makes no mention of it s.v. 'Emperor Alexander' (p. 72).

Figure 7. Detail of the dustwrapper of *The Anatomy of Dessert*, as issued by Dulau in 1929. The illustration by John Nash, the type and the rules were printed in maroon ink on a mauve-gray paper. The picture was also printed in green as a frontispiece. *(Image courtesy of David Karp.)*

Figure 8. The dustwrapper of *The Anatomy of Dessert*, as published in America in 1934. *(Image courtesy of David Karp.)*

108

CHAPTER THREE

Edward Bunyard and Norman Douglas

EDWARD WILSON

It was observed in the previous chapter that Bunyard rarely draws on twentieth-century authors. Though he was a member of the Saintsbury Club, dining at its dinners with some of the prominent literary figures of the day (see chapter 1), the number of quotations from modern authors is small. It was therefore with surprise that I learned from Mr Ian Jackson of Berkeley, California, of Bunyard's friendship with the writer Norman Douglas (1868–1952); it is to Mr Jackson that I owe knowledge of the material printed below in the Vorarlberger Landesbibliothek, Bregenz, and in the catalogue 'A Norman Douglas Collection', produced *c.* 1980 by Dawson's Book Shop, Los Angeles. Before discussing Bunyard's relationship with Douglas, I will print the known surviving primary sources.[1]

A. *8 letters in the Vorarlberger Landesbibliothek, Bregenz, Austria.*

See the brief account by Wilhelm Meusburger, 'The Norman Douglas Collection at the Vorarlberger Landesbibliothek, Bregenz' in the catalogue

---

[1] The following abbreviations are used in the annotation:
  Holloway: Mark Holloway, *Norman Douglas: A Biography* (London, 1976).
  Woolf: Cecil Woolf, *A Bibliography of Norman Douglas* (London, 1954).
  The marks ` ´ are used to indicate authorial interlineation. Square brackets are used for editorial interventions in the letters.

of the exhibition 'Norman Douglas (1868 Thüringen – 1952 Capri): Schriftsteller' held at the Vorarlberger Landesmuseum, Bregenz, 25 November 2000 – 28 January 2001, pp. 199–202 (Bunyard correspondence mentioned p. 200), and his 'Der Nachlass von Archibald Douglas' in *Norman Douglas Symposium: Thüringen, Vlbg., 25.11.2000* (Bregenz, 2001), pp. 10–12 (Bunyard correspondence mentioned p. 10).

A1.

c/o T. Cook & Son
Via Tornabuoni
Florence[1]
3 Dec 1921

Dear Sir

Many thanks for your very kind and all-too flattering letter of the 14 Nov. I am so glad to think you liked *Alone*.[2]

Yes – a supplementary volume of that book, printed for the initiated, is to me an attractive proposition. But the wherewithal … ? Anyhow, we might have discussed this and other matters, were I not rather too far from London just now.

Don't bother about the book of short stories[3] – a preposterous production. It is quite unprocurable; in fact, to the best of my knowledge, there are only four copies in existence. And that is four too many.

Yours very truly

Norman Douglas

---

[1] Cf. Holloway: in 1921 Douglas 'had already begun to adopt a practice of never divulging his address except to intimates, of using Cook's as his postal address' (p. 300).

[2] *Alone* (Woolf, A21(a)) was published in November 1921, and the 2nd impression in January 1922; Bunyard was thus smartly off the mark in reading the first impression and in writing to Douglas by December 1921. It is a rambling and ruminative travel book on Italy, and Bunyard had evidently survived the ironic reference to 'your professional gardener [who] knows everything; it is useless for an amateur to offer him advice; worse than useless, of course, to ask him for it' (p. 27).

[3] Bunyard had evidently been prompted by a sentence in *Alone*: 'I dedicated to her [Ouida] a book of short stories; they were published, thank God, under a pseudonym,

and eight copies were sold' (p. 113). *Unprofessional Tales* (Woolf, A6) was Douglas's first book, written in collaboration with his then wife, Elsa FitzGibbon, and published under the pseudonym 'Normyx' in 1901; most copies were pulped.

A2.

c/o T. Cook & Son
Via Tornabuoni
Florence
12 December 1921

Dear Mr Bunyard
Thanks for your kind letter of the 7th. I am not sure where I shall be next Spring; *I move in a mysterious way*:[1] it is the sole point of resemblance between myself and a certain old gentleman whom you may have heard of; but if I should be in Florence, it would give me great pleasure to meet you.[2] Not that I could be of the slightest use in your delightful hobby of tracking our fruit trees backwards! I only know that plums are not mentioned 'in Homer' and that Pliny the Elder is a perfect mine of information on old horticultural matters, and that V. Hehn's book on the wanderings of cultivated plants[3] used to give me much pleasure – one or two odd facts like that. My friend Sprenger the botanist ("asparagus Sprengeri")[4] would have been the ideal man for you; he made a special study of these things and discovered a Roman variety of apple in the country behind Naples, but it is too late to apply to him. He has now been "gathered" himself.
Yours very truly
Norman Douglas

Very kind of you offering to send me that book which, I hear, is admirable.[5]

---

[1] Cf. 'God moves in a mysterious way', one of the Olney Hymns of William Cowper (1731–1800).

[2] Bunyard visited Florence in 1922 (see letters A4 and 5) and he refers to his article, 'Some Early Italian Gardening Books', *Journal of the Royal Horticultural Society*, XLVIII (September 1923), 177–87, as being 'the fruits of a hurried search in Italian bookshops and street barrows' (p. 177); I know of no earlier visit.

3 Victor Hehn (1813–90) published his *Kulturpflanzen und Haustiere in ihrem Übergang aus Asien nach Griechenland und Italien sowie im das übrige Europa: Historisch-Linguistische Skizzen* (Berlin, 1870). There were in all 8 German editions between 1870 and 1911; there was also an English translation: *The Wanderings of Plants and Animals from Their First Home*, ed. J. S. Stallybrass (London, 1885).

4 Carl Ludwig Sprenger (1846–1917); he lived in Naples 1877–1917, and Douglas had lived first on the Posilipo, on the Bay of Naples, and then on Capri 1896–1916. According to Holloway, when Douglas was renovating the house and garden of his Villa Maya on the Posilipo: 'By December 1896 … shrubs and trees had been ordered from Dammans, and Douglas had made the acquaintance of Carl Sprenger, the distinguished botanist who worked for that firm and had given his name to *Asparagus sprengeri*, and was later to give Douglas so many tropical orchids that they had to be removed in a taxi' (p. 112).

5 One would guess that this is the book on Tahiti mentioned in the next letter.

A3.

c/o T. Cook & Son
Via Tornabuoni
Florence
30 Dec 1921

Dear Mr. Bunyard,

I have only this morning returned from Volterra – wonderful red Etruscan town – to find the book on Tahiti[1] waiting for me. How very kind of you to send it! I am ever so much obliged. It looks as if it were going to be enjoyable reading.

No doubt you got my letter of the 12th., to say that I could be of mighty little use to you in your researches on fruit-trees etc. I am keeping my ears open, however, in case I hear of any literature dealing with the subject, or of any student here who might be able to put you on the track of what you want. Such things and people must exist. If one could only put one's hand on them! I suppose you have tackled Kew – its officials and library? I used to find them very amiable. Well, with my best wishes for 1922, and hoping to have the pleasure of meeting you ere long. I remain
Yours sincerely
Norman Douglas

1 This must be *Tahiti by Tihoti* (George Calderon), London, 1921. The account of the island would presumably have a particular interest for Douglas as a travel-writer. In *How About Europe?* (London, 1930), p. 259, Douglas quotes ('a writer on Tahiti') a paragraph from p. 128 of this work. See also letter D1.

A4.

c/o T. Cook & Son
Via Tornabuoni
Florence
6 February 1922

Dear Bunyard,

Many thanks for yours of the 1st. It is ten to one that I shall be here when you arrive – almost certain, in fact. A propos of introductions, if I happen to be away and you want to look at English papers etc. etc. do go to the British Institute (3 Via dei Conti – near cathedral) and ask for my friend Deane *Perceval*, the Secretary, who will arrange everything for you and whom you will find so sympathetic that it is quite needless my giving you a card to him. Just mention my name! The Director, Spender (brother of Westminster Review,)¹ is also a friend of mine, but you will find Perceval more useful. [*In left-hand margin*:] `Perceval might also be useful to you in your researches. He is very obliging. Don't hesitate to use, and abuse, him!´

This hotel (Nardini) has one passable room.² It is 2 bedded, but a friend of mine, last year, who could only stay two days here on his way through to Greece, took it, and was "pleasantly surprised." The Hotel Baglione is much better and only 5 minutes walk from here (near Station); it is steam-heated and quite comfortable. You can feed there, which you can't here. You can get a room there for about 5/- a night – good! There are a few taxes to pay, but 6/- would be the outside, *and might even include a bathroom*. You can do easily on £1 a day, if the exchange keep [*sic*] near where it is: (95 lire to the £1); *excluding*, of course, railway tickets.

As you are coming over the Riviera I should be sorely tempted to meet you at Ventimiglia where I have some very *urgent* and pleasant and personal business to transact,³ if you could manage to arrive there on a Saturday and leave on Monday morning (But train `to´ Florence from Ventimiglia leaves V. at 8. a.m). But I fear my finances won't bear the strain.

Thanks for the pamphlet. I am sending you two ancient ones of mine [*In left-hand margin:*] 'I have not corrected their numerous misprints'[4]

I know the person who made the speech of which you enclosed me the report – at least, I knew him years ago. Very good-looking, in those days; uncommonly so. If any one tried any of those injections on me, I should fight like a demon.[5] Damn their eyes! What next?

So sorry you find a difficulty in getting *Siren Land*.[6] I have had more than the usual bad luck with my books. The first one (short stories) cost me over £100 to get printed; less than 10 copies were sold; and the publisher pulped the entire lot, *without consulting me*.[7] One would have liked to have bought a few copies, to give to a friend. To the best of my knowledge, there are only *four copies* in existence, one being at the British Museum. *Siren Land* came next. Having got no account from Dent for five years as to sales, I wrote and learnt that there were over 900 copies "wasted." What did that mean, I asked? Why, pulped! And without saying a word to me, or offering them to me at cost price. One would have liked to be able to give a copy to a friend! *Fountains in the Sand*[8] sold fairly well, but Secker,[9] *without consulting me*, remaindered the entire edition. I would have been glad to buy a dozen copies, to give away. Of course I never got a penny out of the remaindered copies; in fact, *for that whole edition*, I received £15: neither more nor less. Publishers are SWINE. No wonder I have been, and practically am, on the streets! Not much harm done, of course, so long as one has good health. But I simply can't afford to get ill, and have not even been able to give myself the luxury of an influenza this year.

I enclose the latest photo of myself. I don't know whether it looks more like President Harding[10] or a prizefighter out of work: which do you think? Or a disfrocked Baptist Minister? Or the "heavy father" in some American cinema film?

Yours sincerely
Norman Douglas

---

[1] J. A. Spender was editor of the *Westminster Gazette* (not *Review*) 1895–1921. See further, Alyson Price, 'Norman Douglas and the British Institute of Florence', *Norman Douglas 3. Symposium* ed. W. Meusburger and H. Swozilek (Bregenz, 2005), 26–32.

[2] Douglas himself lived at the Hotel Nardini from 1921–3 (Holloway, pp. 293, 297, 311); given his reticence over revealing his address (cf. A1 n. 1), it is remarkable that

within a couple of months of the start of the correspondence Douglas can contemplate Bunyard staying at his hotel. Amongst the people Douglas met in Florence at this time were H. G. Wells, Rebecca West, Aldous Huxley, and D. H. Lawrence (Holloway, p. 297); Bunyard was potentially in heady company.

3   Douglas's serious paedophilic relationship at this time was with René Mari who was 14 when they first met at Menton in 1919; his parents lived at nearby Ventimiglia (Holloway, p. 263) which was doubtless why Douglas was going there on urgent, pleasant and personal business.

4   There is no way of determining the titles of Bunyard's gift to Douglas and Douglas's to Bunyard, though for the latter see below H1 and 2.

5   If the report of the speech was in *The Times*, then I can find nothing relevant in the period January/early February 1922.

6   Woolf, A13(a); the only edition at this date was that of 1911. To describe it as an Italian travel-book would be a distortion; concerned with the Naples area, 'it is discursive, moving from one topic to another, a series of brief disquisitions ranging lightly and speculatively over the whole extent of a capacious, enquiring and well-stocked mind' (Holloway, p. 182).

7   See A1 n. 3.

8   Woolf, A14(a), 1912; second edition, Woolf, A14(b), 1921. It is a travel-book about Tunisia. Douglas frequently complained about the financial return on this work (Holloway, pp. 237, 259, 266–7). Cf. Letter F1 below.

9   On Martin Secker, Douglas's publisher, see Holloway, *passim*.

10   President of the United States, 1921–3.

A5.

c/o T. Cook & Son
Via Tornabuoni
Florence
11 Oct 1922

Dear Lenin[1]

Moby Dick[2] is very good, tho' I ain't got very far, as I have to do such a *bloody* lot of writing of my own. Hope to be done with my present book – full of botanical errors (put in on purpose, to make you laugh) – in 5 weeks' time.[3] Some energy!

   Got yours of the 1st. WE ARE EXPECTING YOU HERE, within the

next month.⁴ So don't forget. I have to get up at 5 a.m. tomorrow to go with [?] motor-bus to Siena to meet Edward Hutton;⁵ shan't be gone more than 2–3 days, and perhaps you will have already arrived by the time I return. Getting cool now. Florence very pleasant. Baglione⁶ waiting for you.

As to *Villa Said*,⁷ I have noted it down but can't afford just now, as I have had to pay 400 odd francs for a waterproof which I needed (possessing none) and shall have to pay another 100 for a pair of boots (possessing only one single pair). You bullionists⁸ don't realize these house-keeping difficulties of the impecunious author.

Bishop⁹ is here, and *howling for you*. He declares that the man you saw at the Club¹⁰ must have been somebody else, who resembles him – possibly the Duke of Litchfield [-*t*- *sic*].¹¹

So hustle up!

Yours ever

N d

---

¹ The term 'Lenin' is clearly ironic; Bunyard was far from advocating the brotherhood of man (cf. his remarks on 'negroid characteristics' quoted in the last chapter). Partly through the words 'Dear Lenin', but mainly above, is a drawing of a very fierce-looking owl; Dr Howard Booth of Manchester University has suggested to me that it might be an allusion to Reggie Turner (*c.* 1870–1938) who under the name Algy Constable was described by D. H. Lawrence, *Aaron's Rod* (1922), ed. M. Kalnins (Cambridge, 1988), as 'flapping his eyelids like some crazy owl' (p. 215); certainly Richard Aldington, *Pinorman* (London, 1954), describes him 'Flapping his eyelids like a demented owl, as Lawrence wickedly but exactly described him' (p. 8), a blinking commented on by others (e.g. p. 80) and owing 'to some small eye trouble he refused to have treated' (p. 75). For Turner's letters to Bunyard see later in this chapter, K1–7.

² By Melville. Bunyard had evidently put Douglas onto it; as noted in the last chapter, Bunyard borrowed from *Moby Dick* in discussion of the taxonomy of melons in *AD*.

³ The book was *Together*, 1923 (Woolf, A22(a), (b), (d)). It 'was the result of two successive visits to the Vorarlberg [where Douglas was born] with René [see A4 n. 3], in 1921 and 1922. It was written easily and quickly, between the end of July and the end of December of the latter year, and with three kinds of love – in the present, for his companion; for present sights and sounds and experiences; and for the past, for his childhood and its associations' (Holloway, pp. 319–20).

⁴ One cannot tell whether this is a second visit to Florence (cf. A4), as would be implied

by the possible owl-allusion to Turner (cf. n. 1), or the result of the postponement of earlier plans.

⁵ Edward Hutton (1875–1969): a prolific author, especially of travel books on Italy (as well as on its art); for his relations with Douglas see Holloway, *passim*, and Neil Ritchie, 'Norman Douglas and Edward Hutton: Two Friends', *Norman Douglas 3 Symposium* ed. W. Meusburger and H. Swozilek (Bregenz, 2005), 22–25.

⁶ The Hotel Baglione (see A4 para. 2).

⁷ I do not know to what this refers.

⁸ *OED²*'s definition 'one who advocates a metallic currency', recorded between 1811–78, throws no light.

⁹ Bishop is untraced. Mrs Alyson Price, Archivist of the Harold Acton Library, the British Institute of Florence, has told me that a Warner Bishop was a member of the Institute 1922–3. However, if this is William Warner Bishop (1871–1955), Librarian of the University of Michigan, then though he did go on book buying expeditions to Europe, he was in the States in October 1922, not leaving for France that year until 11 November (see C. Glenn Sparks, *Doyen of Librarians: A Biography of William Warner Bishop* (Metuchen, N.J., and London, 1993, 161). The expression 'howling for you' is extreme.

¹⁰ Untraced.

¹¹ Another puzzling reference as Lichfield is an earldom, not a dukedom.

A6.

Gasthaus Krone
Bludesch¹
Vorarlberg
Austria
15 August²

Dear Bunny

Thanks for yours of 11ᵗʰ with address of typist. I will send her some stuff tomorrow – *the last*. I have finished a book of reprints of old articles *etc*;³ about 50000 words; it's all I am good for just now; and am looking for a cheap but super-excellent printer who will do me 250 copies – edition de luxe at 2 guineas each. I find I make nothing with publishers; can't make less than nothing! So why not try a new dodge? I suppose you don't know of such a printer, I am ½ thinking of having them done *here*, in Gothic characters, just for a joke.

Archie[4] may come here sooner than he expects. Or perhaps I shall join him down there. The next week will decide. Why don't you turn up. Send me some shag.[5] I have not a grain of tobacco left, or so much as the stump of a cigar. Simply bloody. Enclose cheque for baccy. Send as registered letter[6]

Why don't you come here

The boots you sent me ages ago are going stronger than ever. Last longer than 4 pairs of Italian ones – in fact, show no signs of wear. What is the fellow's address?[7]

---

[1] Born at Thüringen in the Vorarlberg, Douglas had begun his education at the local school at Bludesch (Holloway, p. 19); for this later visit see Holloway, pp. 329ff.

[2] No year is stated, but this letter is clearly immediately prior to the next letter (no. 7) of 22 August which can definitely be dated to 1924 (see n. 2).

[3] This eventually appeared as *Experiments* in 1925, privately printed in Florence, and commercially in America and England (Woolf, A24(a), (b), (c)); see Holloway, pp. 329, 330–1, 337–8, 347–8. Bunyard received a copy (see below G1 and H4); see also A7 and A8.

[4] Douglas's elder son (1899–1977). Archie was in Italy revising for a Consular examination, but as he could not get the money to go to Austria, his father joined him on Capri (Holloway, pp. 329–30).

[5] Holloway notes that Douglas 'wrote to everyone in England he could think of – such as Straus, Hutton and Secker – to send him tobacco, as there was none in the Vorarlberg' (p. 307).

[6] The last two words are in a drawn oblong box.

[7] Unidentified.

A7.

Gasthaus Krone
Bludesch
Vorarlberg   Austria
22 August[1]

Dear Bunny,

You will have got my card of this morning. *I shan't move* until Archie assures me he can't come here (which I hope he can). He is now presumably on Capri. *Shan't move anyhow till 1ˢᵗ week in Sept.*

Ever so many thanks for yours of 20^(th). and baccy just arrived. It's awful, not having either baccy, or as much as the stump of an Italian cigar: nothing but local cigarettes. But it needn't be such high-class stuff. Anything will do: anything! Shag. Only not "St. Iulian"

There is a "Fragment" of mine coming out in the Sept^(r). number of the *First* ['First' written above an undeciphered crossed-out word] *Edition* (23 Gerrard St. W1)²

As to printing – your catalogue has not yet arrived. I want a luxi edition of 250 copies on hand made paper (to sell at 2 guineas a-piece, but *don't tell your man this*) The size should be octavo or royal octavo; large margins; paper faintly coloured; and about 220 words to the page. The book consists of reprints of old things: all improved or at least touched up. `About 50,000 words.´ He need not bother about binding; he could send me the sheets to Florence where I can get them bound cheap and yet so tastefully that the fool-amateurs [?] will think they are getting their money's worth. The book is ready in type-script. Now can he send me a specimen page, to show his type and paper? And what's his address? If you do [hear]³ from the Pelican you might ask their price (approximate: and only *sheets*. 270 [another earlier number crossed-out] copies, as 20 are sure to go wrong one way or the other).⁴ As to putting down money – I shall try to get other people to do that. I have not had a single account from any publisher since last December! [`not a´ crossed-out] (except one from Secker, overdue *2 years*!) One simply *can't* go on like this

The *Anatomy of Dessert*⁵ is excellent. Best luck to it! How far are you.⁶ I wish you could come out here! *No distance at all*. A week-end??

                          Yours   N

---

¹ The year must be 1924; see n. 2 below.

² Douglas's 'A Fragment', an Assyrian mythological fantasy, appeared in *The First Edition and Book Collector*, no. 2, September–October 1924, 57–64; Woolf, C166; see Holloway, p. 325; the address is the publisher's.

³ 'hear' omitted in the manuscript.

⁴ The printer is not named in the Florence edition, Woolf A24(a); cf. A6 n. 3. The reference to the Pelican remains obscure; it is not the famous Pelican imprint which began in 1937. See also A6, A8, G1 and H4.

⁵ Bunyard's *Anatomy* was first published in a limited edition of 1000 copies, signed by the author, in 1929.

⁶ Though this sentence could refer to how far on Bunyard was with his *Anatomy*, I think it more probable that it means the distance from Bludesch.

A8. (cf. G1 below)

Florence
8 Dec 1924

Dear Bunny

So glad to hear from you again.

Yes; the boots fit perfectly! It was ever so kind of you to send them.

I have been laid up with neuritis; also an abscess on the jaw which, the doctor tells me today, may have to be x-rayed. No fun at all! And this is my birthday. I hoped to get south over Christmas, but who knows?¹

The book proceeds slowly:² 200 out of 300 are already sold: it ought to be ready middle or end of January. I enclose Table of Contents. Don't trouble to return. [in head margin of the letter:] 'If you know any one who wants copies of that book, drop me a line. I shall keep about 50 for myself. Two guineas each, however.'

I am sure you would like Leng, the bottanist [sic].³ His address is Isle of Jethou [with an asterisk, Douglas also spells the name in block capitals in the head margin: 'JETHOU'], Guernsey. I fancy he is in London now, but don't know for certain. Why not fix up some appointment with him?

Archie's address is British Passport Office, Prague.⁴ He seems to be doing well – which is more than I am.

The cherries in Turkey are wonderful. They grow as high as an Alpine fir-tree. In fact, if you go to a place like Broussa, you will find it any [sic] eye-opener. Apricots …

I hear from Scott-Moncrieff⁵ now and then. He talks of coming here this week.

Yours in despair   N

---

¹ Further on these ailments see Holloway, p. 331.

² *Experiments*; see letters A6 and 7, and also s.v. G1 and H4 below.

³ Basil Leng (1898–1979), botanist and landscape gardener; he became a friend of

Bunyard's (see further on him in chapter 1).
4 See Holloway, p. 330.
5 C. K. Scott-Moncrieff (1889–1930), famed translator of Proust.

B. *1 letter in the National Library of Scotland, Edinburgh (MS 9752, f. 126)*

B1.

Florence

24 Aug 1929

My dear Bunny.

Here we are again, after a pleasant but all-too chaste holiday,[1] and I don't think I shall move again, as it is perfectly cool.

What have you been doing?

Now is the time, if you can, to send me Harriett Wilson.[2] She will make a nice pendant to Hickey, whom I have already done.[3] I should not keep the old tart longer than a fortnight; then return her to you.

By the way – about *a month ago* was published a fantastic book on Vegetarian Cookery, giving all sorts of recipes with attractive classical names, such as Venus soufflée etc (in order to induce people to eat the muck).[4] I stupidly mislaid the reference, and don't know the title or author. Have you any means of finding out? I think the book might produce matter for another little footnote in my *Europe*,[5] which Mavro[6] is at present poring over amid loud cussings at me, no doubt.

Are you ever coming here again?

Do you see Archie now and then?[7] He writes me once a century, nowadays.

Hutton is in London just now.[8]

I am *all alone* in Florence – not a white man within 500 miles. Yours ever

N D

P.S. When you kill babies by bedclothes, I thought it was *over-laying* – at least, that is what my East-End boys' mothers used to call it.
I find somebody calls it *over-lying* – in a printed book.
Which is correct?[9]

¹ In the pursuit of boys; other holidays were less chaste: see Holloway, pp. 378–9.
² Harriette Wilson (c. 1789–1846), celebrated courtesan; her *Memoirs*, to which presumably Douglas is referring, were much printed.
³ The *Memoirs of William Hickey*, covering the period 1749–1809, ed. A. Spencer, had been published in four volumes (London, 1913–25); they were discussed by Douglas in *How About Europe?: Some Footnotes on East and West* (London, 1930), pp. 75–84; privately printed in Florence, December 1929 (Woolf, A30(a)), with the first English edition in 1930 (Woolf, A30(c)); there is no mention in them of Harriette Wilson (cf. n. 2 above). Cf. also letters G2, 3, and 6.
⁴ Untraced. Douglas's mind was much on culinary matters at this time. *Paneros: Some Words on Aphrodisiacs and the Like* appeared in a private edition in Florence, 1930 (Woolf, A34(a)), and Bunyard received an inscribed copy (see below, H7); the first English edition was in 1931 (Woolf, A34(b)); see Holloway, pp. 366, 381, 383–5. He had also begun work on *Venus in the Kitchen or Love's Cookery Book* (Woolf, B9(a)), which was offered to Chatto and Windus in 1932 (Woolf, p. 140) but published only posthumously in 1952; see Holloway, pp. 366, 371, 380–1. There is no mention of the vegetarian cookery book in either.
⁵ See n. 3 above for *How About Europe?* which has no mention of the vegetarian cookery book. Bunyard received an inscribed copy of *Europe* (see below, H6).
⁶ J. N. Mavrogordato (1882–1970); a lifelong friend of Douglas, he had in 1919 become the first holder of the Koraes Chair of Modern Greek Language, Literature and History at London University; see Holloway, *passim*.
⁷ Douglas's elder son (see A6 n. 4, above). After working in a bank in Paris (Holloway, p. 350), Archie now had a job with the Royal Horticultural Society (ibid., p. 377), but later lost it or gave it up (ibid., p. 389). Bunyard's extensive and deep involvement with the Society leads one to suppose that he had got Archie the post.
⁸ On the back of the letter is written (in an unknown hand) '114 Clifton Hill/N.W.' which was the address of Edward Hutton (see A5 n. 5 above); see *Who Was Who in Literature 1906–34* (Detroit, 1979), s.v. Hutton, Edward.
⁹ OED^2 records the sense 'to smother by lying upon (a child, etc)' both s.v. *overlay*, v., 5.a (between 1557–1863) and *overlie*, v., 2.a (between 14th C.–1856).

C. 1 letter in the Department of Special Collections, University of California, Los Angeles (Collection 111, Box 2)

C1.

Florence
23 March 1935

Dear Bunny

I got your letter just after sending you a postcard to say I was back.[1] Refreshed, yes; but I twisted my thumb – right hand, *of course* – and now it is not much use. It will have to undergo some diathermic treatment. Meanwhile it is troublesome and hurts me even to write.

No more writing books, so far as I am concerned. The business is wound up.

By the way, Prentice (Chatto & Windus)[2] is here just now, on his way to Greece, and strongly recommends me to read "A Year amongst the Persians – 1887/8" by E. G. Browne (Cambridge Univ. Press.)[3] Have you read it?

I remember Seawright [4] well, tho' I saw him for only one evening. I heard about his artistic efforts, but have seen nothing of them. I have a young ex-undergraduate friend living in Rome:[5] if you give me Seawright's address I might bring them together, to their mutual advantage.

No; don't send me anybody's European History – I am past that stage, and Fisher[6] always struck me as a shit, tho' I am glad he doesn't spenglerize.[7] You mean the ex-minister of Education? That what *I* mean.

Had a note from Basil[8] who says he is sick of France (who isn't) and going to his old man in April.

I don't know Trier or Erfurt. Don't think I should care about Germany any more, seeds or no seeds.[9]

When do we meet again?

Yours ever
N

Note: this letter is closely followed by D2.

[1] After a visit to Ceylon and India; see Holloway, pp. 412–15.

[2] Charles Prentice (1892–1949), senior partner in Chatto, Douglas's publisher; see Appendix I to this chapter, Letter 7 n. 5.

[3] First published in 1893; the CUP edition was in 1926.

⁴ Presumably an artist or sculptor, but untraced.
⁵ Untraced.
⁶ H. A. L. Fisher (1865–1940); his *A History of Europe*, 3 vols., was published in London in 1935, vol. I, *Ancient and Mediaeval*, which Bunyard must have offered to Douglas, in February, and vols. II and III in July and November. He had been President of the Board of Education 1916–22, though I do not know why Douglas found him so objectionable. See further on Fisher in the *Oxford DNB*.
⁷ A reference to Oswald Spengler (1880–1936) whose *Untergang des Abendlandes* (1918 and 1922), English translation *The Decline of the West* (1926–9), argued for a predetermined cyclical view of history as a process of growth and decay; the English translation was in lot 375 of the sale of EAB's books (see chapter 1).
⁸ Presumably Basil Leng; see above A8 n. 3.
⁹ Certainly Erfurt was a great seed distribution centre, especially the world-famous Benary Company founded in 1843 by Ernst Benary (1818–93), and Haage und Schmidt, the Haage family being a noted German gardening family from the eighteenth century onwards.

D. *2 letters owned by Professor Arthur S. Wensinger of Higganum, Connecticut, U.S.A.*
I am greatly indebted to Professor Wensinger for telling me of these letters, and for sending me xeroxes of them.

D1. (cf. G5 below)

c/o T. Cook & Son
Florence
8 January 1922

Dear Bunyard,
　I am dropping, with your permission, the "Mr"; after so charming and illuminating a letter as your last,¹ I feel that such formulas would be a kind of insult to the intelligence of both of us. As to "Tahiti",² I have now read it with great care, and enjoyed it hugely. Shall go through it again, ere long. What a pity the fellow died so young!³
　Fruit History. You might note the name and address of this friend of mine, in case I am not here when you come to make your researches. Cecil

Pinsent, 5 Via delle Terme, Florence.[4] He is an architect by profession, but likes nothing better than following up any other kind of intellectual by-way. His (and my) friend, Reginald Temple (3 Costa Scarpuccia, Florence) is an artist by profession, and knows the galleries of this town like the inside of his pocket.[5] Would you like introductory cards to him?

The "sample of your delvings" has not yet arrived. I am leaving Florence tomorrow, but only for a week or so. Perhaps I shall find it on my return.

I have never read anything of Aldous Huxley, tho' I know him personally, and his father. He is an over-tall and rather frail personality. One of these days I may get hold of *Chrome* [*sic*: *for* Crome] *Yellow*.[6]

You are quite right in your diagnosis of these fellows – Butler,[7] Henry James etc.[8] Red blood you say, is what they lack. *Guts and balls* is what I should call it. But I fear this verges on the obseen [*sic*]. Yours sincerely
Norman Douglas

---

[1] In sequence, closely after letter A3 (30 December 1921).

[2] By George Calderon; see letter A3 n. 1.

[3] Calderon (1868–1915) was hardly young when he died at Gallipoli in 1915; see *Times* obituary (5 May 1919, 19).

[4] Cecil Pinsent, with his partner, Geoffrey Scott, 'were building and adapting Tuscan villas for foreigners' (Harold Acton, *Memoirs of an Aesthete* (London, 1948), 64).

[5] Reginald Temple (*c*. 1869–1954); see *Times* obituary (8 May 1954, 8), and a vivid account by H. Acton, *More Memoirs of an Aesthete* (London, 1970), 63–5: 'Under his primness and neatness was an obsession with the macabre: he gloated on a Chamber of Horrors of his own creation. ... our last exponent of the naughty nineties and he played the part with unction'.

[6] *Crome Yellow* was published in 1921. Novels by Huxley were in lot 116 of the sale of EAB's books (see chapter 1); see also the chapter on 'Edward Bunyard and Literature'.

[7] Presumably Samuel Butler (1835–1902), author of *Erewhon* (1872), *Erewhon Revisited* (1901), and *The Way of All Flesh* (1903). His *Note-Books* were in lot 102 of the sale of EAB's books; see also the chapter on Bunyard and Literature.

[8] Henry James (1843–1916). Bunyard, once, quoted James, and in the second sentence below there is an amusing parody of the constantly qualifying quality of a Jamesian sentence: '"Conservatism", said Henry James, "is the Religion of a gardener."

This aphorism, I need hardly say, was not delivered in so many words; there were qualifications, and even recognitions that in certain circumstances human nature, in its infinite variability, might quite conceivably go far to prove the contrary. But we were agreed in the main it was so. I have often recalled these words when looking round a fruit show …' ('The Newer Dessert Apples', *The New Flora and Silva*, IX .i (October 1936), 31–4, p. 31).

D2. (cf. G7)

Florence

8 April 1935

My dear Bunny

Very glad to get yours of the 5th. Don't' bother about that Swinnerton book.[1] The publisher – Frere Reeves of Heineman [*sic*],[2] a nice fellow – sent me a copy. Finished it today. I like what he says about me, though my mother wasn't an Austrian, and I can't imagine why he thinks that "Keith" is a self-portrait. That idea never entered my head, at all events.

And Prentice,[3] who arrives in Greece today, has caused to be sent to me Browne's Persian travel.[4] Promises to be interesting, but a bald style. I've barely glanced into it. If you get that other 7/6 book, let me know whether it is worth reading.

Glad to hear about your onion article,[5] but why not make a book of it? Garlic: I cannot imagine a salad without it. And do say a good word for chives; grossly neglected in England. Martial and a lot of others consider onions to be aphrodisiac; if they were, there would be no holding me, as I eat them all the time. Garlic = also aphrodisiac. I wish it were. There are some notes on onions in Athenaeus, who mentions various kinds. I hope you will not forget *sauce soubise*. As to Jews and garlic, there is a German couplet beginning "Garlic is a Jewish fare", but I forget the second line (may try to remember it, if you want me to).[6] Also Turks eat garlic on mountain walks, as it makes breathing easier. There was also a much-advertised remedy for coughs etc – can't remember its name – which was exposed in the *Daily Mail* [*in margin*: About five years ago.] by some analyst as being only garlic. The exposure ruined the sale, and the *Daily Mail* printed it only because the proprietor had refused to advertise the stuff in that filthy rag. And what about a good French potage à l'oignon, and their even better leek soup? And

pommes lyonnaises – one of the few ways in which that horrible vegetable can be made fit for man's consumption? Aren't there special ships bringing onions from Spain to England every year?   Yours ever
N

---

[1] Frank Swinnerton, *The Georgian Literary Scene: A Panorama* (London, 1935); Douglas is discussed on pp. 167–73 (the two comments complained of are on p. 167).
[2] A. S. Frere-Reeves, then managing director of Heinemann; he is mentioned briefly (oddly as 'A. S. Frere') in Holloway, pp. 386, 388.
[3] Charles Prentice (1892–1949), senior partner in Chatto and Windus; see Appendix I to this chapter, Letter 7 n. 5.
[4] See above C1 n. 3.
[5] Bunyard's article 'The Onion in Human Life' appeared in *Wine and Food* II.6 (Summer 1935), 42–6.
[6] I have not traced the couplet. Bunyard uses Douglas's information in his discussion of garlic in *The Epicure's Companion* (London, 1937), 76: 'I hear of an old German couplet which begins: 'Garlic is a Jewish fare,' but I expect the whole subject has been worked out by an erudite anti-Semite, and lies buried in some forgotten *Verhandlung*.'

E. 1 letter in the Beinecke Library, Yale University.
I owe knowledge of this letter to Professor Arthur S. Wensinger.

E1.
c/o Thomas Cook
Via Tornabuoni
Florence
11 Sept[1]

Dear Bunny

I'll send you the limerick book[2] in 2–3 days and only hope it will reach your hands and nobody else's. *It would be a great relief if you dropped me a postcard when you get it.*[3]

There is heaps of room for suggestions on your part written in pencil, and excisions proposed, and corrections and enlargements and anything else you like.[4] Do just put down what strikes you. How about punctuations? My English is getting very groggy. In short, *improve all you can.*

Won't write more, as I am fussed to death just now. Drop me that card.

Wrote you on the 4th Sept

      Yours ever

      N D

---

[1] No year is stated, but it must be 1928; *Some Limericks*, the book referred to in this letter, was first published in Florence in November 1928 (Woolf, A27 (a) and (b)).

[2] *Some Limericks* is described by Woolf as an 'anthology of limericks, collected and edited by Douglas with a long and witty introduction and erudite satirical commentary on the text' (p. 93); their sexual candour and colloquial language may still startle, and this accounts for Douglas's nervousness in the first paragraph. See also Holloway, 367–70.

[3] This sentence is not only underlined, but is pointed to by three large arrows in the left-hand margin.

[4] It is possible that we can discern one of Bunyard's suggestions incorporated by Douglas in his commentary on this limerick (one of the mildest in the book):

> There was a young man of Australia,
>
> Who painted his bum like a dahlia.
>
> The drawing was fine,
>
> The colour divine,
>
> The scent – ah! that was a failure. (p. 47)

In his commentary, Douglas states: 'My bottomical expert writes: "Dahlias are first mentioned by Hernandez in his History of Mexico, 1651; later on by the Frenchman Ménonville, who went out there to steal the red cochineal insect from the Spaniards. Named "for" Andrew Dahl, Swedish botanist, and introduced into England by the Marchioness of Bute; afterwards by Lady Holland to Holland House. All dahlias, including the variety *cocksinia* [a re-spelling, to suit the ethos of the anthology, by Bunyard or Douglas, of *coccinea*], are scentless" (p. 48). Not only does the word-play on 'botanical expert' and the historical knowledge point to Bunyard, but in Bunyard's article, 'The Novelist in the Garden', *Gardening Illustrated*, LIII, no. 2738, 29 August 1931, 533, an article, like the note on this limerick, concerned with historical accuracy, he had criticized Virginia Woolf for her horticultural solecism in describing John Evelyn as growing dahlias: 'But, alack-a-day, why did the gifted writer make him pause at a bed of Dahlias, a flower which was to rest at least a century in its native Mexico before Europe saw it?'; see also my chapter on 'Edward Bunyard and Literature'.

F. *1 letter in the Berg Collection, New York Public Library.*
I owe knowledge of this letter to Professor Arthur S. Wensinger.

F1.

Florence
17 Oct 1923

Dear Bunny

Thanks for yours of 10th. I am still here; don't know how much longer I can stay, nor where to go afterwards. No flats; and probably no prolongation of my rent [rent *crossed out*] lease of this place.[1]

Why don't *Lotus* do a retail job?[2] Do you mean to say you buy your boots wholesale – fifty-dozen pairs at a time? I should not be surprised. Here, anyhow, is the plan of my foot, and I hope your local man is enough of a retailer not to insist on my buying more than ten pairs, to begin with. BLACK. And do explain the *mystery of the Lotus people*.

The letter from Cambridge, which I return, is pleasant reading.[3] These have been my profits – income – since Dec 1922: *South Wind £39; *Fountains £2–9–6[4] *Alone* £9–13–0. *Street Games* £1–9. say £50 altogether *Calabria* nil (I still owe £3–10–0); *They Went* nil (I still owe £24–5–0) *Sirenland* nil (Still owe about £30). I mention these figures in case you come across any bloated capitalist whose pocket you might be able to pick for me, after making him drunk. And I think you know that I have no other income whatever. What a life! Now comes *Together*, of course; but will be ages before I can get anything else written.

No, I have not yet seen that story of my son's.[5] The silly British Institute don't stock the E.R.

I should like to read Golding's latest which of course he hasn't sent me, after promising to do so. No doubt flamboyant – and a little restlessly self-conscious.[6]   Yours ever

N D

1 On Douglas's flat-hunting at this time see Holloway, pp. 318–19, 323.
2 Letters A6 (15 August 1924) and A8 (8 December 1924) refer to Bunyard's purchase of boots on Douglas's behalf.
3 Correspondent unidentified.
4 In the left-hand margin, with an asterisk, Douglas has written '*minus* 10% to Lit. Agent'. Letter A4 (6 February 1922) also informs Bunyard of the financial returns on his books.
5 Robin Douglas (1903–?62), ' "Fiddlin' Dick" ', *The English Review*, XXXVII, no. 179, October 1923, 493–9. Set in 1922, it is a romantic, some would say mawkish, short story.
6 Louis Golding, *Seacoast of Bohemia* (London, 1923); a novel. I do not know if Bunyard ever knew Golding (1895–1958); Louis Golding and André L. Simon, *We Shall Eat and Drink Again: A Wine & Food Anthology* (London, [1944]), reprints, 69–71, Bunyard's 'The Wine List' from *Wine and Food*, III, no. 12, Winter 1936, 32–4.

G. *8 letters in the catalogue 'A Norman Douglas Collection', c. 1980, of Dawson's Book Shop, Los Angeles.*
I print in full below (save for nos. 1, 5, and 7) the text of the extracts as given in the catalogue; the second number given is its item no. in the catalogue, and which I have followed for its identifications from Woolf.

G1. No. 36. In a copy of *Experiments* (Florence, 1925); Woolf, A24(a); see above A6 n. 3, A7 n. 4, and H4 below.

The date and text of the extract are identical with A8 above save for misprinting '200' as '100' and, probably, 'that' as 'hat [sic]'.

The catalogue notes that 'With the letter Douglas included a proof sheet of the table of contents, lacking page numbers' (cf. above A8, para. 4).

G2. No. 44. In a copy of *How About Europe?* (1929); Woolf, A30(a); cf. B1 n. 5 above, and below G3 and 6 and H6. There are two letters (for the second one see no. 3 below).

'The first is dated 30 August 1929, one page closely-written. "Mavro went through 'Europe'[1] and made some very valuable suggestions. I don't think, however, it's the sort of thing he likes (don't tell him this) and as I am very anxious not to be tripped up over errors of fact, I'll send it to you as well … Heaps of room at the bottom of each page for scribbling in pencil anything that strikes you as wrong. I can cut out wholesale, 10 pages at a time – it makes no difference! So just write what you please, but it's no good writing anything unless you are perfectly *merciless*. Maul it about; the more the better."'

---

[1] For a discussion of *Europe* see Holloway, pp. 373–5; he describes it as 'a verbal guerrilla war against occidental civilisation. … The chief targets … are Christianity, education, antiquated or absurd legislation, war and its effects, and petty restrictions of all kinds. … It implies that a return to a simpler and more dignified way of life, even if it were basically a feudal system or a society incorporating slavery, would be preferable – at any rate for a gentleman' (pp. 373, 374, 375).

G3. No. 44. Also in *Europe* (cf. no. 2 above).

'The second letter is dated 11 September [1929]. "I have been obliged to buy other paper for printing that damned 'Europe' on, else they would have kept me waiting till Christmas. So I am now ready to go ahead, as soon as you return the typescript, in which I hope you have picked 500 holes (as I have, even since sending it to you). We have a filthy wave of Scirocco just now. Everything limp, and can't be straightened out."'

G4. No. 49. In a copy of *Looking Back* (London, 1933); Woolf, A36(a); cf. H8.

Dated Florence, 22 October 1933, beginning "My dear Bunny", and 'stating in part "So glad to hear your business is looking up. Mine is looking down – especially as I can't produce any more. No! I can't write hors d'oeuvres, or even entremets, though your title about 'Emotion remembered in tranquility [sic][1]' is most suggestive – it would have to be personal again, and my last one was that infernally personal 'Looking Back' "'.

---

[1] From the preface to Wordsworth's *Lyrical Ballads*; Wordsworth had written '… recol-

lected in ... '. As Douglas indicates, the book is an autobiographical work, organized into reminiscences suggested by his collection of calling-cards.

G5. No. 67. This and the next three items appear under the heading 'Autograph Letters by Douglas'.
   This letter is now owned by Professor Arthur S. Wensinger of Higganum, Connecticut, U.S.A.; it is printed above, D1.

G6. No. 68.
   'To E. A. Bunyard, 23 September (probably 1929). A hurried note, one page. "Began printing today. He won't be long over it." The reference is probably to *What About Europe?*'

Cf. letters B1, G2 and 3.

G7. No. 71.
   This letter is now owned by Professor Arthur S. Wensinger of Higganum, Connecticut, U.S.A.; it is printed above, D2.

G8. No. 72
   '17 March (no year).[1] Two pages, one to E. A. Bunyard and one a letter of introduction for Bunyard to the mayor of Capri.[2] The latter reads "The bearer is my friend Mr. Bunyard, a great lover of Italy. What he don't know about apple-trees and *Convolvulus cneorum*[3] is not worth knowing. If you make it worth his while, he may possibly discover a new plant on the island, but it would require several bottles of *Capri vecchio*."'

---

[1] Cf. earlier letters indicating a visit to Italy by Bunyard in 1922 (see A2 n. 2; A4, A5). This date would be confirmed by the mayoralty of Edwin Cerio (see n. 2 below).

[2] This is most probably Douglas's friend, Edwin Cerio (1875–1960) who was Mayor of Capri, 1920–3 (*Times* obituary, 29 January 1960, p. 17; see also Holloway, p. 505 n. 69). Apart from his mayoral good offices, Cerio would have common interests with

Bunyard, being according to *The Times* the writer of, amongst others, three books on the flora, pergola, and gardens of Capri.

3 Probably a personal and pointed reference since it may well have been a favourite of Cerio's. In his sketch, 'Consule "Costanziello"', in *That Capri Air* (London, 1929), a translation of part of his *Aria di Capri* (Naples, 1927), Cerio had written of: 'floods of convolvulus, white and blue, and that choice flower, the *Convolvulus Cneorum*' (p. 15). A copy of this book was owned by Bunyard (Lot 104 in the posthumous sale of his books at Hodgson's in London, 13–14 June 1940; see chapter 1).

H. *8 books in the catalogue 'A Norman Douglas Collection', c. 1980, of Dawson's Book Shop, Los Angeles, which are either inscribed by Douglas to Bunyard or, if lacking an inscription, may none the less probably be regarded as gifts from Douglas to Bunyard. Bunyard's copies of Douglas's books were lots 105–115 in the sale of his books in 1940; see J below.*

The second number given is the item no. in the catalogue which I have followed for its identifications from Woolf.

H1. No. 3. *On the Herpetology of the Grand Duchy of Baden*; reprinted from *The Zoologist*, 1891 (London, 1894); Woolf, A3.
  'inscribed on the front cover "E. A. Bunyard from Norman Douglas"'.
  Cf. H2 below, and A4 n. 4 above.
  A study of reptiles and amphibia; see Holloway, pp. 73–5.

H2. No. 8. *Fabio Giordano's Relation of Capri* (Naples, 1906); Woolf, A9.
  'inscribed on the title page "To his friend E. A. Bunyard from Norman Douglas"; Douglas has additionally signed his name on the last page and added a bibliographical note some time after 1915'.
  Cf. H1 and A4 n. 4 above. 'It consists of an account of Fabio Giordano [16th century] and his *Historia Napolitana* from which Douglas here edits and prints for the first time *De Capreis Insula*' (Woolf).

H3. No. 35. *D. H. Lawrence and Maurice Magnus: A Plea for Better Manners* ([Florence], 1924); Woolf, A23.

'Inscribed on the half title "To Bunny, hoping he will approve of these sentiments from Norman Douglas, Florence, 30 Jan 1925"'.

Maurice Magnus (1876–1920), an American who, like Douglas, had abandoned a wife to pursue his homosexual orientation, had, under pressure of debt, killed himself in Malta. He joined the French Foreign Legion in 1915, but deserted a year later, and wrote an account of his experiences called in manuscript *Dregs*. After his suicide this was published as *Memoirs of the Foreign Legion by M. M. with an Introduction by D. H. Lawrence* (London, 1924); both the *Memoirs* and Lawrence's Introduction were expurgated by the publisher, Martin Secker, with the removal of references to both homosexual practices in the Legion and Magnus's own orientation. Douglas in his brief (54 pages) *Plea* took exception to Lawrence's account of both Magnus and himself (blaming repeatedly 'the novelist's touch. It falsifies life', p. 31). See further: (i) K. Cushman (ed.), *D. H. Lawrence: Memoir of Maurice Magnus* … (Santa Rosa, 1987); *inter alia*, Cushman prints two of the passages (pp. 139–47) excised from *Dregs*, as well as the censored passage on Magnus's own homosexuality (pp. 93–6); (ii) H. J. Booth, ' "To desire, to belong": homosexual identity in the lives and writing of Compton Mackenzie, Norman Douglas and D. H. Lawrence', University of Kent at Canterbury Ph.D. thesis, 1997, chapter four: 'The same-sex desiring subject in the social sphere: Douglas and Lawrence's responses to Maurice Magnus', pp. 181–216.

H4. No. 36. *Experiments* ([Florence], 1925); Woolf, A24(a).

'… unopened; in a dust-soiled wrapper. One of 300 copies numbered and signed by Douglas. … With the letter [see A8 above] Douglas included a proof sheet of the table of contents, lacking page numbers'.

Though this copy does not apparently have Bunyard's name, the presence in it of letter A8 above together with the table of contents mentioned in the letter make it clear that this copy was presented to him by Douglas.

It consists of reprints of old articles and reviews concerning travel, history, literature, etc.

Cf. above A6 n. 3, A7 n. 4, A8 n. 2, and G1.

H5. No. 42. *Nerinda* (Florence, 1929); Woolf, A28(a).

'One of 475 copies, this one unnumbered but inscribed "For E. A. Bunyard from Norman Douglas and G. Orioli, Florence, 5th April 1929"'. This was Orioli's first venture as an independent publisher.

Of Douglas and Orioli (1884–1942), Holloway writes that they 'had enough in common to ensure a strong foundation for friendship. They both liked and had a wide knowledge of good food and drink, of literature, anecdote and gossip; they both had a Rabelaisian turn of mind; they both, in their different ways, were without pretensions; both, in their different ways, had boundless curiosity; both liked travelling; and both were interested in the younger members of their own sex, though in Orioli's case, less young than in Douglas" (p. 311).

A variant of the Pygmalion myth, *Nerinda* is set in southern Italy and takes the form of a diary; though fictional, it 'is an imaginative attempt to describe the kind of progressive mania which engulfed his friend Luigi Guerrieri-Gonzaga, who died insane in 1895, in his late twenties' (Holloway, p. 129; *Nerinda* had first been published in 1901).

H6. No. 44. *How About Europe? Some Footnotes on East and West* (Florence, 1929); Woolf, A30(a).

'One of 550 copies numbered and signed by Douglas; … this copy is further inscribed on the half title "For Bunny from Norman, 23 Nov. 1929"'.

For a description of this polemical work see above, G2.

H7. No. 47. *Paneros* (London, 1930); Woolf A34(a).

'One of 250 copies, this one unnumbered but inscribed in Douglas's hand "For Bunny from Norman Douglas & G. Orioli, 6 Dec. 1930" (Orioli has signed his own name). … Privately printed for subscribers by G. Orioli.'.

On various foods, etc., as aphrodisiacs.

H8. No. 49. *Looking Back: An Autobiographical Excursion* (London, 1933); Woolf, A36(a).

'One of 535 sets numbered and signed by Douglas'.

Though this copy does not apparently have Bunyard's name, the presence in it of letter G4 makes it clear that this copy was presented to him by Douglas.

I. *Other literary links between Bunyard and Norman Douglas.*

I1. *Birds and Beasts of the Greek Anthology.*

In his *Birds and Beasts of the Greek Anthology* (London, 1928; Woolf, A25(b)) Douglas added a paragraph not present in the Florence edition of 1927, p. 119 (Woolf, A25(a)):

> My friend E. A. Bunyard draws my attention to the analogy between *xouthos* and the Latin "purple" or its Greek equivalent. He quotes from Chevrier's (*Ampélographie Retrospective*, p. 64) comment on Columella's "purple" grape: Purpureus signifie aussi éclatant: on dit, en ce sens, nivea purpurea d'une neige parfaitement blanche (confusion between lustre and tint). So Homer applies the same word to the brightness of the rainbow. And a writer quoted in Daremberg and Saglio [C. Daremberg and E. Saglio, *Dictionnaire des Antiquités Grecques et Romaines* (Paris, 1877–1917), 40th fascicle (1907), s.v. *purpura*, 769–78, p. 772, col. 2, 'l'agitation, la rapidité'] say it characterizes also "agitation, rapidity" (the same obscure ingredient of motion). (pp. 113–14)

The reference to J. Roy-Chevrier, *Ampélographie Rétrospective* (Montpellier and Paris, 1900), p. 69 [sic] is inaccurate: Roy-Chevrier's comment is actually on *purpureae* in Virgil's *Georgics* II. 95, and is towards the end of his discussion of *Georgics* II. 89–108. Two-thirds of the way down p. 69 is the heading 'Columelle', but though *purpureae* is found in Columella's *Rei Rusticae* III.ii.1, which is quoted, it is not commented on and Douglas's French passage relates wholly to Virgil's use of the word. It is hard not to see the error of attributing Roy-Chevrier's comment on Virgil to the following author Columella as other than Bunyard's.

It is uncertain whether the reference to Homer (where the word is applied to a rainbow once, *Iliad* XVII. 547, and means not 'bright' but 'dark-shimmering, lurid, grimly-threatening') and Daremberg and Saglio derive from Bunyard or are Douglas's contribution. However, it may be noted (i) that Daremberg and Saglio's *Dictionnaire* was cited by Bunyard on Roman horseshoes in a letter to *The Times*, Wednesday, 14 September 1938, p. 6 e; (ii) this work was lot 279 in the sale of Bunyard's books (see chapter 1).

I2. Quotations from Douglas in E. and L. Bunyard, *The Epicure's Companion* (London, 1937).

In the section 'An Epicure's Anthology. Chosen by Edward and Lorna Bunyard' is an extract, 'The Perfect Cook and some Imperfections' (pp. 443–6), from Douglas's *South Wind* (London, 1917), chapter 30 (pp. 350–4); it would not seem adventurous to attribute this selection to Edward Bunyard.

In the section 'Varia', whose chooser(s) are unascribed, are two extracts from Douglas's *Alone* (London, 1921): the first, 'Cave Strega' (p. 498), is from the chapter 'Soriano' (p. 217), and the second, 'Food and Philosophy' (pp. 498–9), is from the chapter 'Rome' (p. 119). Again, it seems reasonable to attribute the selections to Bunyard.

I3. Two quotations from Douglas ante-date the beginning of the Bunyard-Douglas correspondence in 1921.

(a) In his article 'Figs in Pots' in *The Garden*, LXXX, no. 2332, 29 July 1916, Bunyard writes:

> It was for many years a puzzle to me why Figs are so often called black or white when they are green, brown or purplish-brown. However, in a recent book of Italian travel, I came across a possible explanation. In the South of Italy, the country *par excellence* of the Fig, it seems that the colour sense of the inhabitants is extremely limited. Blue is out of their range and dark colours are generally called black, while green and yellow are called white. The Mediterranean blue is lost to the native, who calls it lead colour! (p. 374)

The source is made clear in (b) below.

(b) In a letter titled 'Greek Colour Perception' in *The Garden*, LXXXI, no. 2399, 10 November 1917, Bunyard gives his source as *Old Calabria* (London, 1915):

> A curious light is thrown upon the colour sense of the Mediterranean peoples in a passage which I have before quoted in THE GARDEN from the ever-delightful "Old Calabria" of Norman Douglas. Speaking of the Calabrians, he says: "Of Blue they have not the faintest conception. … Figs are white or black [hence I suppose our White and Black Ischia], Wine is white or black," &c. The author asked a lad as to the colour of the sea, in his own eyes a brilliant sapphire blue. The reply was "A sort of dead colour." The sky on a cloudless day is "white." A Beech in full leaf is "half black" or "tree colour." "Rosso" is not red, but rather dun or dingy, all of which will make us careful in discussing what Homer or other writers meant by their colour terms. (p. 478)

The quotation is from Chapter viii, 'Tillers of the Soil', pp. 51–2.

J. *Bunyard's ownership of Douglas's books.*

In the Hodgson's sale of Bunyard's books sold on Thursday, 13 June 1940 (see chapter 1) are a number of Douglas's works. All but one (H3 above) of those in the Dawson's catalogue are mentioned by name, plus several others. I reproduce the entries in the Hodgson's catalogue (my numbering is followed by the Hodgson lot no.), together with reference to my listings above.

J1. 105. Douglass (G. Norman) On the Herpetology of the Duchy of Baden *(only a few printed), Presentation Copy, with A.L.s.* [Autograph Letter signed], *wrapper.* 1894.
Cf. H1 above.

J2. 106. Douglas (Norman) Fabio Giordano's Relation of Capri, *front., Presentation Copy, with MS. note at end, wrapper.* Napoli 1906.
Cf. H2 above.

J3. 107. Douglas (N.) London Street Games, *First Edition with A.L.s. relating to "my profits – income" from four books, and losses from three, "17 Oct. 1923,"* buckram. 1916.

J4. 108. Douglas (N.) They Went, *Presentation Copy,* N.Y. 1921, and South Wind *(one of 150 on blue paper, signed)*, 1922, 2 vols.

J5. 109. Douglas (N.) Alone, *with A.L.s.*, 1921, and Together, 1923, *First Editions,* and 3 others by the same 5 vols.
Cf. A1 and A5 n. 3 above.

J6. 110. Douglas (N.) Together, 1923, and Experiments, 1925, *both First Editions, Large Paper, signed, and both with A.L.s.* 2 vols.
Cf. A5 n. 3 and H4 above.

J7. 111. Douglas (N.) Experiments, *with A.L.s.*, 1925, and Birds of the Greek Anthology [sic], 1927, *both Limited Editions, signed,* and 1 other. 3 vols.
Cf. H4 and I1 above.

J8. 112. Douglas (N.) Paneros, *Limited Edition,* 1930, etc., *Presentation Copies,* 2 vols, *with* 2 *A.Ll.s.*, and 3 others by the same. (5 [vols.])
Cf. H7 above.

J9. 113. Douglas (N.) In the Beginning, *with A.L.s.*, 1927, The Last of the Medici, 1930, and 1 other, *Limited Editions,* 2 signed. 3 vols.

J10. 114. Douglas (N.) Nerinda, 1929, and How about Europe?, 1929, *Limited Editions, both Presentation Copies, with A.L.s.* 2 vols.
Cf. H5 and H6 above.

J11. 115. Douglas (N.) South Wind, *illus. by J. Austen*, 2 vols, 1929, and Looking Back, *Limited Edition, signed*, 2 vols, 1933, *both with A.L.s.* 4 vols.
Cf. H8 above.

It is time now to ponder this evidence. Of course, it must be remembered that we do not have every letter that Douglas wrote to Bunyard; indeed, Dr Wilhelm Meusburger, of the Vorarlberger Landesbibliothek, Bregenz, has informed me that Douglas's pocket diaries, now in Yale University Library, mention just the name 'Bunyard' 310 times, between 3 December 1921 and 12 July 1939, probably recording the sending of correspondence. We have no letters from Bunyard to Douglas. In the surviving correspondence we know what topics Douglas himself raised, and by inference from Douglas's responses some of the matters which Bunyard had expressed. None the less, the task is like trying to construct a jigsaw puzzle picture without having all the pieces.

Bunyard's admiration for Douglas had begun as early as 1916–17 (I3(a) and (b)), and once their correspondence started, it is clear that the relationship developed rapidly. Douglas's terms of address move within a little over a month from 'Dear Sir' (3 December 1921; A1) to 'Dear Mr Bunyard' (12 December 1921; A2) to 'Dear Bunyard' (8 January 1922; D1), with the playful 'Dear Lenin' on 11 October 1922 (A5), and the first 'Dear Bunny' being found on 15 August 1924 (A6). They had shared interests in botany, travel, culinary art, and literature; Douglas makes reference to family matters, especially his elder son Archie (for whom Bunyard probably obtained a post: B1 n. 7), and makes requests for the purchase of tobacco and boots; there are grumbles about publishers and illness. On occasion Bunyard evidently gave considerable help in the practicalities of obtaining typing and printers for Douglas, as well as suggesting improvements to the texts, and naturally received presentation copies, sometimes jointly with Douglas's Florentine publisher and bookseller friend, Pino Orioli. Notably, Bunyard sent *The Anatomy of Dessert* (in draft or typescript version) to Douglas five years before publication (A7). Indeed, in a praise of the apple as the most English of fruits, the *Anatomy* has a covert, humorous reference to Douglas, three-quarters Scottish and one-quarter German, born at Thüringen, educated at Yarlet Hall in Staffordshire and then at Uppingham, and currently living in Florence:

> In a careful pomological study of my fellow-men I have met but one who really disliked apples, but as he was a Scotchman born in Bavaria, educated in England, domiciled in Italy, he is quite obviously ruled out. (p. 1)

Bunyard certainly visited Douglas in Florence at least once in 1922 (see A2 n. 2, A4, A5 n. 4), and a letter of 1935 implies further visits (C1), confirmed by letters of 1937 in the Bunyard/Ian Parsons correspondence (see Letters 1, 2, and 7 in Appendix I to this Chapter). There is evidence that Bunyard saw not just Douglas but also other members of the expatriate

Anglo-Florentine colony. The flavour of that world has been well caught by Harold Acton: first, in *Memoirs of an Aesthete* (London, 1948):

> In Florence there was a plethora of writers, and you were bound to meet them in the Via Tornabuoni; D. H. Lawrence with his Rubens *frau* and his string bag after marketing; Norman Douglas chewing the cud of a *Toscano*; Ronald Firbank capering into a flower-shop; Aldous Huxley who maintained that in Florence 'every prospect pleases, but only man is vile'; Scott-Moncrieff, who kept up a doggerel offensive against the Sitwells in *The New Witness*: dining at Betti's, scandal-mongering in Orioli's bookshop, drinking vermouth at Casone's, there was no avoiding one of these in the city … (p. 107),

and secondly, in *More Memoirs of an Aesthete* (London, 1970):

> In the 1920s a younger generation of writers, Aldous Huxley, D. H. Lawrence, Richard Aldington, Scott Moncrieff, became temporary residents. … Reggie Turner kept up the gay persiflage of Oscar Wilde; and Norman Douglas, who was printing his books privately for the bibliophiles, scoffed at the art critics and damned the Cinquecento. … (p. 365)[1]

We have already encountered some of these names: the presentation (H3) in 1925 of Norman Douglas's book attacking D. H. Lawrence 'To Bunny, hoping he will approve of these sentiments …', an inscription which indicates Bunyard's familiarity with the context; Bunyard's reference (D1) to Aldous Huxley, though the date, 8 January 1922, must have been before Bunyard's first visit to Florence; Douglas's casual reference (A8) at the end of 1924, 'I hear from Scott-Moncrieff now and then'. From Reggie Turner,

---

[1] On Florence and the Anglo-Florentine colony see most recently D. Leavitt, *Florence, A Delicate Case* (London, 2002); there is a useful bibliography. See also J. Pemble, *The Mediterranean Passion: Victorians and Edwardians in the South* (Oxford, 1987), especially pp. 78–80, 159–64; I. Littlewood, *Sultry Climates: Travel and Sex Since the Grand Tour* (London, 2001), esp. pp. 131–3 (on Norman Douglas), and the same author's 'Crossing Frontiers: Norman Douglas and the Sexual Motives of Travel', *Norman Douglas: 2. Symposium* (Bregenz, 2003), 57–62.

however, there survive printed extracts from seven letters to Bunyard, and these are reproduced below from Stanley Weintraub, *Reggie: A Portrait of Reginald Turner* (New York, 1965); page references are to Weintraub; all are addressed to 'Bunny', unidentified by Weintraub (but not mis-assigned to David Garnett, also known as Bunny, but with no known connexion with Turner).

K. *Extracts from letters from Reginald Turner to Bunyard.*

K1. 27 June 1931: 'When you can, send me a line. Letters sent here will always find me wherever I am – except, of course, in the grave, & I may make arrangements with Sir Oliver Lodge [1851–1940; English physicist, much interested in psychical research and the evidence for life after death] to have them sent on there.' (p. 217 and n. 44)

K2. 25 October 1933: 'In my old age I want to warm myself with the sight of a nice, friendly girl. I am getting vicariously fond of young-ish females, so long as they are kind & not too boisterous.' (p. 224 and n. 12)

K3. 28 November 1933: 'I am a real sceptic, who hopes everything, believes everything, & trusts everything but the likelihood that men will ever be real Christians – the saints apart, & even they were often not Christians but only saints.' (p. 243 and n. 53)

K4. 25 June 1935: Weintraub introduces the letter thus: 'In the midst of his own anxieties, he wrote to a bereaved friend, "I am never sorry for anyone who *is* dead, however bright & promising life may have looked for him; I am only sorry for the suffering & the dying."' (p. 242 and n. 52)

K5. 28 December 1935: Weintraub introduces the letter thus: 'Worry about war in Europe, Reggie wrote one American friend, was "sickening, a great torture"' (p. 241 and n. 48)

Why Weintraub calls the 'Bunny' to whom this letter is addressed American is unclear. If this is the same Bunny as in K1, then that letter's reference to Sir Oliver Lodge would mean more to an Englishman than an American; certainly the American Weintraub does not appreciate the eminence of Lodge in English intellectual life at the time (' … with a tangential gibe at a mutual acquaintance's dabbling in spiritualism', p. 217).

K6. 27 December 1936: with reference to the American presidential election in 1936 and the American colony in Florence's support for Alfred Landon against Roosevelt: 'But they are thinking really only of their moneybags, which are getting less bulgy. I am sure that the American people are sound and that they are probably going to lead us on the road which lies ahead of us.' (p. 235 and n. 37)

K7. 3 February 1938: in discussion of his treatment for cancer, he said that he was recovering well 'but for having to have a preventive after-cure of radium which I am having in my own house – thank heaven – but which on the eighth day of the ten of the cure has tired and confused me … It is the first time in my life I have been of any value as I have 100,000 Lire worth of radium round my neck – a fact I don't broadcast among my bargain-hunting friends.' (p. 244 and n. 56)

As noted above, the presumption, despite K5, must be that 'Bunny' is Bunyard. At a time when Douglas was writing to Bunyard also from Florence and using the same nickname this is the most reasonable inference. Turner (*c.* 1870–1938) was essentially an Æsthete and at one time a homosexual, though from the turn of the century he largely abandoned this predilection, even claiming to find women attractive (cf. K2 above). Essentially a surviving part of the detritus of the Wilde set, of which he had been a member, he formed a close but tormented friendship with Douglas, characterized by Weintraub thus:

> Although Reggie Turner had known Norman Douglas before the War, their close friendship dated from the War's end. It was a strange relationship, based upon malice, suspicion, jealousy and the knowledge that each found life vastly more amusing in the company of the other. "A mixture of Roman emperor and Roman cab driver," Reggie characterized Douglas. Douglas on Reggie, often in public, especially when inebriated, was less printable.

Douglas and Turner would often meet for lunch or dinner, then – over wine, and more wine – swap stories or argue late into the night. Although Douglas often complained to others about Reggie's blinking nervousness [cf. A5 n. 1] and oldmaidish ways (he told Richard Aldington that Reggie ought not to have been in Florence but in Kensington handing round the tea cakes), for him Florence was incomplete without Turner.[2] (pp. 189–90)

Though all Turner's letters to Bunyard quoted by Weintraub date from the 1930s, there is some evidence that the two may have known each other from the time of Bunyard's first visit to Florence in 1922 (cf. A5 nn. 1 and 4).

If Turner's actual practice of homosexuality was by the 1920s mainly a thing of the past (though his manner did not suggest the *monde viril*), Douglas's paedophilia was active and frequent in expression. Others mentioned in Douglas's dealings with Bunyard were also members of what was an Anglo-Florentine homosexual set: Orioli (1884–1942), who joined Douglas in some presentation copies of his works to Bunyard (H5 and H7); Scott-Moncrieff (cf. A8 n. 5); D. H. Lawrence, though not homosexual, had an undoubted interest in and complex relationship with the issue.[3] Of course, Bunyard had initiated the correspondence with Douglas simply as an admirer of his Italian travel book, *Alone* (A1), and before going to Florence had expressed an interest in Aldous Huxley and his 1921 novel *Crome Yellow* (D1). Huxley was not a homosexual, and indeed in a letter to his brother, Julian, 21 April 1925, had given a less genial description of the city than Harold Acton's:

> a third-rate provincial town, colonized by English sodomites and middle-aged Lesbians, which is, after all, what Florence is …[4]

---

[2] This whole chapter (x), 'The Twenties: Norman Douglas and D. H. Lawrence', pp. 189–217, is worth consulting.

[3] See H. J. Booth's thesis, cit. s.v. H3 above, chapters 3 (pp. 136–80) and 4 (pp. 181–216), and his article 'D. H. Lawrence and Male Homosexual Desire', *Review of English Studies*, n.s. liii (2002), 86–107, pp. 104–7.

[4] G. Smith (ed.), *Letters of Aldous Huxley* (London, 1969), p. 246.

All that said, one cannot consider the relationship between Douglas and Bunyard without examining, if possible, Bunyard's attitude to Douglas's inversion, and whether their friendship was in part based on a comparable sexual commitment.

The evidence is not rich. There is certainly not in what survives or in what is quoted from Douglas's letters anything as gross and overt as we find in a letter he wrote to J. R. Ackerley.[5] None the less, there are some indicators. At first, it seems that Douglas veils his homosexuality – there is a secretive, personal, pleasurable knowingness in his early reference (6 February 1922) to his 'very *urgent* and pleasant and personal business' in Ventimiglia, a reference to his relationship with René Mari (A4 and n. 3), which at that stage Bunyard can hardly have understood. Likewise, in the same letter, Douglas's reference to a man as 'very good-looking' (A4 and n. 5) would seem more something that he could not desist from observing than a shared intimacy of reference. However, by the end of that year (11 October 1922), after a possible earlier visit to Florence by Bunyard (cf. A5 n. 4), Douglas is telling him that 'Bishop is here, and *howling for you*' (A5 n. 9) which has an extremity of ardour further emphasized by Douglas's underlining. The reference at the end of 1924 (A8) to Scott-Moncrieff, an active homosexual,[6] may be indicative by its very unstudied nature, but little or no weight can be placed on this. However, when in 1929 Douglas writes that his holiday has been 'all-too chaste' (B1) it is hard to imagine not only that Bunyard did not know to what he was referring but also that, at the least, he was expected to be indulgent rather than shocked or disapproving. On the other hand, a letter of 1936 from Bunyard to Edward Hutton (see Appendix II to this chapter, below) shows that Bunyard, in common with all Douglas's friends save perhaps Orioli, was not someone to whom Douglas could reveal the shame of his expulsion from Austria following a charge of rape. Finally, on the question of Douglas's quarrel with D. H. Lawrence over the depiction of the homosexual Maurice Magnus the tone of Douglas's inscription in 1925 in the copy of his *Plea* (H3) is confidently associative. On the question of book inscriptions, as noted above, Douglas's

---

[5] P. Parker, *Ackerley: A Life of J. R. Ackerley* (London, 1989), p. 55.

[6] There is a good account of him in Leavitt, op. cit. in n. 1, pp. 11–15. Leavitt's chapter 3 (pp. 73–113) is on Florence and homosexuality.

homosexual friend, Pino Orioli, joined him in the presentation of two of them (H5 and 7).

Little evidence from Bunyard's side survives. We have none of his personal papers, which seem to have been destroyed in the wake of his suicide, though we do have the late W. T. Stearn's observation that Bunyard's library contained a remarkably large number of books on sex, including Havelock Ellis (see chapter 1). Although Ellis's originally six-volume *Studies in the Psychology of Sex* (1897–1910) included as its first volume *Sexual Inversion* (1897) this was only a part; no conclusion as to orientation can be drawn from this, and in any case it is surmise that this particular work, out of Ellis's many, was what Stearn saw.

He was, of course, unmarried, but his writing does on occasion make play with conventional romantic notions. Thus in *The Anatomy of Dessert* (1929) he writes of 'the queen of fruits':

> The Pear must be approached, as its feminine nature indicates, with discretion and reverence; it withholds its secrets from the merely hungry. Fickle and uncertain it may too often be, concealing an inward decay by a fair and smiling cheek; but when all is said, how well are we rewarded by her gracious self at its best! Forgotten are our ardours and endurances in the soft rapture of attainment. (p. 94)[7]

We may be inclined to see a suspiciousness of the feminine beneath an air of old-world gentlemanly gallantry, but he is, after all, only discussing a pear.

Perhaps the opacity thins a little in some sentences of Maurice Healy's obituary of Bunyard in *Wine and Food* (VI, no. 24, Winter 1939):

> His intimate friends were generally younger than himself; some of them a generation younger. To these he never condescended: they were his equals,

---

[7] Cf. T. Longville, 'Tim Longville's Snippets', *Hortus* no. 67 (xvii, no. 3), 2003, 18–27: '*The Anatomy* is a strange book by a strange man, a sort of Kama Sutra of fruit by the Humbert Humbert of horticulture. Its prevailing tone is a heady combination of sexism and sheer sex. Bunyard's fruit-connoisseur is always a man, the fruit he is about to eat is always a woman' (p. 21).

to be treated as equals, not pupils to be instructed. You see, they never suspected the instruction. But I cannot imagine a more valuable course of education for a young man than the companionship of Edward Bunyard. Wise, tolerant, full of knowledge, with a mind that not only discriminated but taught discrimination, his gentle guidance lost nothing through the lightness of the rein. (p. 326)

Yet no certainty on the topic is possible. Bunyard was, at the least, tolerant of Douglas's sexual taste, but the friendship, which had many elements, could not have survived without that tolerance. Such was the nature of Florence at the time that contact with members of its homosexual set was unavoidable. That Bunyard's bachelor life had its tensions is evident from Stearn's recollection of his library. He seems to have been more at ease in the company of men than of women, but why Bishop 'howled' for him we shall never know. Inevitably, and not entirely with regret, we may be put in mind of Gladstone's comment on a biography of George Eliot: 'It is not a Life at all. It is a Reticence, in three volumes.'[8]

APPENDIX I
Correspondence between E. A. Bunyard and Ian Parsons

Although only three letters (nos. 1, 2, and 7) concern Norman Douglas, the surviving Bunyard-Parsons correspondence is given in full since it is a rare source of letters from EAB and because the exchange itself has its own flavour. The correspondence is in the archive of the publishers Chatto and Windus, now housed in Reading University, ref. CW 68/17; I am indebted to Mr Michael Bott, Keeper of Archives and Manuscripts at Reading University for his help.

Ian Macnaghten Parsons (1906–80), after a First in the English Tripos at Cambridge, entered Chatto and Windus in 1928, became a partner two years later, and was Chairman 1954–74. Chatto had published the

---

[8] E. F. Benson, *As We Were* (London, 1930), p. 111.

second edition of EAB's *The Anatomy of Dessert*, adding *with a Few Notes on Wine*, in 1933, and Parsons was the driving force behind the weekly humorous magazine *Night and Day*, mentioned in Parsons's last letter, which ran from July to December 1937 and to which EAB contributed two articles (see Bibliography). The *Times* obituary (Friday, 31 October 1980, p. 14) observed that 'A capacity for friendship was perhaps his greatest gift', and that, *inter alia*, he was 'a keen gardener, a good traveller', and an author himself; he was keen on publishing contemporary poetry and work by members of the Cambridge English Faculty. See also O. Warner, 'Chatto and Windus: A Brief Account of the Firm's Origin History and Development', in *A Century of Writers 1855–1955: A Centenary Volume Chosen by D. M. Low & Others* (London, 1955), 11–26, pp. 20–6; O. Warner, *Chatto & Windus: A Brief Account of the Firm's Origin, History and Development* (London, 1973), 19–33, and the *Oxford DNB*.

Letter 1
(apart from the printed letter-head, hand-written)

THE EPICURE'S
COMPANION

From	*From*[1]
EDWARD A. BUNYARD	MISS LORNA BUNYARD
Allington, Maidstone	25 Bower Mount Road, Maidstone
Kent	Kent

Editors: Edward and Lorna Bunyard
To be published shortly in the
'Companion' series (7*s.* 6*d.* net)
by J. M. Dent & Sons Ltd.

2.3.37

Dear Parsons,

Here you see my latest graft and I want to know what you think of quoting some of the notes on Wine from Anatomy. Above[2] a companion to Gardeners [*sic*] Companion[3] (150–170 thousand words). I shall treat fruit briefly & shortly so as not to cut into Anatomy but I thought the Wine part with reference to 'A of D.' might not be a bad advt.⁴

I delighted in your Xmas Card both the drawing & the poetry – I wonder if you remembered Pope
> "For if the nights seem tedious, take a Wife
> Or, rather, Truly, if your point be Rest
> Lettuce & Cowslip Wine probatum est.⁵

I am just recovering from a mixture of bronchitis laryngitis & a few other oddments & though I've no Voice I don't notice any one seems seriously put out – I'm not!

Hoping you are both well
> Yours sincerely
> Edward A Bunyard

I'm planning to go to Riviera end of month & then on to Italy where I hope to see N.D.⁶

---

[1] Lorna Bunyard's name and address crossed through in ink as the letter is from EAB.

[2] With reference to the heading *The Epicure's Companion* (published by Dent in October 1937).

[3] *The Gardener's Companion* ed. by Miles Hadfield published by Dent in 1936, and to which EAB contributed a chapter.

[4] *The Anatomy of Dessert* had been published in 1929 by Dulau & Co. Ltd. of 32 Old Bond Street, London, in a limited edition of 1000 numbered copies signed by EAB; in May 1933 it was published by Chatto & Windus in a 2nd edn. which added *with a Few Notes on Wine*; in November 1936 (but still imprinted 1933) it was included by Chatto as the first volume in its 'The Phoenix Library of Food and Drink'.

[5] Quoting from memory Pope, *The First Satire of the Second Book of Horace Imitated*, 16–18.

[6] 'N.D.' is Norman Douglas; see further Letter 2 n. 3, and Letter 7 n. 3.

Letter 2
(carbon of typescript)

IMP/DRS

6th March 1937

Dear Bunyard,

Very many thanks for your delightful letter. No I'm sure we shouldn't mind your quoting from the Notes on Wine in your new 'Companion', though I hope you won't quote more than enough to whet people's appetite for the 'A. of D.' itself. It's doing very nicely in its new 3/6d. form.[1]

So glad you liked our Christmas effort. We were hoping it might serve to remind you of your promise to come and dine with us one night in London and drink some wine. Is there any chance of your doing so before you abscond to the Riviera? I do hope so.

David and Heather Low,[2] who are in Florence at the moment, write that N.D. is in good form but toying with the idea of going to India again.[3] How I envy you going on to Italy and seeing them all. My wife, like you, has been afflicted with a variety of noisome germs in her nose and throat. She sends her best wishes for the speedy return of your voice, and joins with me in hoping we may see you in London before very long.

With kindest regards,
Yours sincerely,

Edward Bunyard, Esq.,
Allington
Maidstone
Kent.

---

[1] The Phoenix Library edition (see above, Letter 1 n. 4); the 1933 edition had cost 5s.

[2] David Morrice Low (1890–1972) and his wife Heather (died 1953); though *The Times* obituary (Monday, 26 June 1972, p. 14) does not mention his first wife's name, it is confirmed by letters to David Low from Charles Prentice of Chatto (now in the D. M. Low Archive at King's College, London, where Low had been a lecturer in Classics, 1945–57). Low is known principally as a Gibbon scholar, but he also published two novels, one of which, *Twice Shy* (London, 1933), is dedicated to Heather [Low]. He was a friend of Norman Douglas, and in 1955 edited *Norman Douglas: A Selection*

from His Works. I owe this identification, and reference to the D. M. Low Archive, to Mr Ian Jackson of Berkeley, California.

³ For the visit to India, December 1934 – March 1935, see M. Holloway, *Norman Douglas: A Biography* (London, 1976), pp. 412–15. See also Letter C1 n. 1.

Letter 3
(apart from the printed heading, hand-written)

From MR. E. A. BUNYARD, ALLINGTON, MAIDSTONE.

8.3.37

Dear Parsons,

Thank you for your letter – no – I shan't quote any *dessert* only some Wine bits – as I really don't think they can be bettered!¹ I fear I shall not be able to get to London before I go as my Doctor says 'no going out till this wintry weather is over'. I am very sorry to hear 'that' your wife has also been attacked I think you had better both join us² on the Riviera & in Italy Chianti is a wonderful germicide.

    Yours sincerely,
    Edward A. Bunyard

---

¹ In the *Anatomy of Dessert* the Notes on Wine run from pp. 157–208, and most of this section is incorporated in the *Epicure's Companion: AD* 157–77 (*EC* 262–71); *AD* 178–80 (EC 290–1); *AD* 181–6 (*EC* 283–5); *AD* 186–94 (*EC* 299–303); *AD* 196–9 (*EC* 303–4); *AD* 199–200 (*EC* 305–6). Parsons may well have been surprised at how much Bunyard's 'bits' covered.

² Bunyard was travelling alone, and so 'us' doubtless refers to Norman Douglas, his friend Pino Orioli, the Lows, and others of the English expatriate set (see this chapter above).

Letter 4
(on Company writing paper; typed)

ESTABLISHED 1796

GEORGE BUNYARD & CO. LTD
NURSERYMEN

HEAD OFFICE

TO WHICH ALL COMMUNICATIONS

DIRECTORS	SHOULD BE SENT	TELEPHONE
EDWARD A. BUNYARD	BROADWAY	2204 MAIDSTONE
G. NORMAN BUNYARD	MAIDSTONE	

OUR REF	YOUR REF	DATE
		28th May, 1937

Dear Parsons,

   I fear an incompletely addressed letter slipped in the post yesterday. As it may not have reached you I must repeat it.

   Boulestin has written for the 'Epicures [sic] Companion' an article on 'Food and modern authors' in which he quotes about five hundred words from your translation of Proust about the dinner to M. Norpois.[1] May I have your special permission to quote this with due acknowledgement?

   I was very glad to get back from London to the green country again.

All good wishes,

Yours sincerely,

Edward A Bunyard [*signed*]

Alan [sic] Parsons, Esq.,
40 Chandos Street
W.C.2.

---

[1] In his article 'Gastronomes in French Literature', X. Marcel Boulestin quoted two passages from the C. K. Scott-Moncrieff translation *Remembrance of Things Past*, 'Within a Budding Grove', Part I, 'Madame Swann at Home' (*EC*, pp. 492–4).

Letter 5
(carbon of typescript)

IMP/NW

29th May, 1937.

Dear Bunyard,

Very many thanks for your two letters, both of which arrived safely.

We're delighted for our part to give Boulestin permission to quote about 500 words from Proust's "Within a Budding Grove", but as we only hold the translation copyright I'm afraid we must refer you to Messrs. A. M. Heath & Co., Ltd., 188 Piccadilly, W.1. They are the English agents for Gallimard the French publishers. I will send your letter on to Messrs. Heath, and tell them that we're not making a charge as it is such a small quotation, but I don't know how they will feel about it.

I quite agree that the country is infinitely preferable to London at the moment.

Yours sincerely,

E. A. Bunyard
Allington,
Maidstone,
Kent.

Letter 6[1]

From MR. E. A. BUNYARD, ALLINGTON, MAIDSTONE.

17.6.37

Recd. from Messers Chatto & Windus the sum of £4.1.11
Royalties Anatomy of Dessert
    [signed over a 1½d. and a ½d. stamp:]
        Edward A. Bunyard
        17.6.37

---

[1] Not a letter but a receipt. Hand-written apart from the printed letter-head.

Letter 7
(carbon of typescript)

22ⁿᵈ June, 1937.

IMP/NW

Dear Bunyard,

Very many thanks for your letter of the 8th,[1] which I'm ashamed not to have answered before this, but we're just about to give birth to a new humorous weekly called "Night and Day",[2] (which I hope you'll read and like) and its [sic] been keeping us all pretty busy.

What's all this about Norman? None of us here know anything definite except that he's left Italy.[3] Letters from Pino[4] and Charles Prentice[5] haven't referred to the fact. Have you any later information?

The garden at Herstmonceux[6] is looking its best just now, and I do hope you'll be able to come over to lunch or tea one weekend soon. But we've no fruit to speak of, alas – except the irrepressible gooseberry.

All good wishes,
Yours sincerely,

E. A. Bunyard, Esq.,
Allington,
Maidstone.

---

[1] This does not survive.
[2] The first issue was published on Thursday, 1 July 1937.
[3] See M. Holloway, op. cit. Letter 2 n. 3: Norman Douglas fled from Florence on 31 May 1937 (p. 431) to Menton for one night (p. 430), and then on to Vence (p. 430). At the age of 68 he had had to 'hop it' (p. 425) following relations of some sort with – surprisingly for a homosexual with a predilection for young boys – an Italian girl, Renata, aged 10½ (pp. 424ff.).
[4] Pino Orioli (1884–1942); Florentine bookseller, publisher, author, and close companion of Douglas; see Holloway, op. cit., *passim*, and this chapter above, H5 and 7. He was evidently a friend of EAB's, too.
[5] Charles Prentice (1892–1949; d.o.b. *ex inf.* Mr Michael Bott); senior partner in Chatto and Windus; see above, Letter C1 n. 2; O. Warner, art. cit. in the Introduction

to this Appendix, pp. 21–22, and his book (1973), pp. 16, 19–22; Holloway, op. cit., *passim*.

⁶ Where Parsons lived in Sussex.

APPENDIX II
Letter from E. A. Bunyard to Edward Hutton

I owe knowledge, and a photo-copy, of this hand-written letter to Mrs Alyson Price, Archivist of the Harold Acton Library, the British Institute of Florence, where it is preserved in the Edward Hutton Collection (HUT: I:C:1:f1).

On Edward Hutton (1875–1969) see above, Letter A5 n. 5.

[printed]
THE BUNGALOW,
ALLINGTON,
MAIDSTONE.
24.ix.36

Dear Hutton

Archie's address – the public one – is Conservative Club Hastings.¹

I've just had a long letter from N.D. No word of illness & a request for Hakluyt to read – doesn't sound very like a serious collapse!² 8 vols!

He says he has grown a beard & moustach – Ye Gods – he must look like one of Blakes [*sic*] ancients of days³ – we must get a photo of this incredible transfiguration.

Yours ever
EAB

---

¹ Norman Douglas's son, Archie, at this date had a private address at his cottage in Sussex (Holloway, p. 421).

² On 20 September 1936 ND had written to Archie from Florence, saying that he had suffered 'heart trouble' on a visit to Bludenz. This was either a euphemism or a complaint brought on as a result of his arrest on a charge of rape; he was detained

in Bludenz from 11–18 September when he was ordered to leave the country within twelve hours; he never returned. Holloway observes: 'Once again, he had gone too far; but this time it looks as though there was an element involved which had not been present on previous occasions: it looks as though he was ashamed. It looks as though no one, with the possible exception of Orioli, was told the truth of the affair; as though, having invented illness as a convenient signal of urgent distress to Archie, he clung to it as a disguise for a scandal that he was not, in this case, ready to admit even to friends' (p. 421); Hutton, like Archie, had evidently been fed the illness story, and EAB had not even been told that. The beard and moustache ND had grown (see next para.) can hardly have been needed for a real disguise; rather a change in the externals was a psychological escape mechanism for the man who had been arrested and shamed in the land of his birth.

[3] On Blake's 'The Ancient of Days' see G. E. Bentley Jr., *William Blake's Writings*, I, *Engraved and Etched Writings* (Oxford, 1978), s.v. *Europe a Prophecy*, pp. 204, 222, 707–8.

CHAPTER FOUR

Bunyard on Xenia

SIMON HISCOCK

In the summer of 1906 Edward Ashdown Bunyard attended what became known as The Third International Conference on Genetics held at The Royal Horticultural Society, Vincent Square, London, where he delivered a paper 'On Xenia',[1] in which he reviewed the subject and described some of his studies of hybridization in fruit trees and other crop plants (Bunyard, 1906). At the time of the meeting its title was 'The Third International Conference on Hybridization and Plant-Breeding', as it followed two similar meetings of the same name held in 1902 and 1899 at New York and Chiswick, respectively. The reason for the name change at the third meeting was the introduction to our language of the term 'Genetics' by William Bateson, the conference president, at his inaugural address[2] (Bateson, 1906). After the 'rediscoveries' of Mendel's rules of heredity in 1900 (reviewed by Sturtevant, 1965, Olby, 1997), Bateson championed Mendelism and saw it as a way of unifying the scientific studies of hybridization and plant-breeding and animal-breeding under a single discipline – 'genetics', where 'not even the time honoured distinction between things botanical and zoological is valid', because genetics is 'devoted to the elucidation of the phenomena of heredity and variation' which are common to all living organisms (Bateson, 1906).

---

[1] Xenia f. Gr. ξένος (guest) Bot. 'A supposed direct action or influence of foreign pollen upon the seed or fruit which is pollinated': *OED²*.

[2] Bateson first used the term 'Genetics' in 1905 in a letter to Cambridge zoologist Adam Sedgewick.

This was clearly a pivotal moment in the history of the biological sciences. While the Mendelian rules were acknowledged and discussed at the New York meeting of 1902, their wider applicability to all organisms was yet to be appreciated. By the summer of 1906 however, the universality of Mendel's rules was more widely appreciated by scientists and practical plant and animal breeders alike, so Bateson thought it time to introduce this new science of 'genetics' formally to the world. Bateson is therefore rightly considered to be the founder of modern day genetics, an accolade perhaps anticipated by the editor of the conference proceedings, RHS secretary, the Rev. W. Wilks, as he hastily changed the title of the conference to include the term 'genetics' before the proceedings went to press. The significance of this meeting was duly recognized and the titles of the previous two conferences were changed retrospectively so that they became the first and second conferences on genetics (Sturtevant, 1965, Olby, 1997).

In the audience along with Bunyard on Tuesday 31 July 1906 for the 'baptism of genetics' (Olby, 1997) were some of the most eminent proponents of the new science, including Hugo de Vries, Carl Correns, and Erich von Tschermak who are jointly credited, along with Bateson, for the rediscovery of Mendel's rules (Sturtevant, 1965, Dunn 1973, Olby, 1997). Also present was Wilhelm Johannsen who three years later would introduce the concept of the 'gene' as the unit of inheritance, together with the now familiar terms 'genotype', as the sum of an organism's genes and 'phenotype' as the outward expression of the genotype (Sturtevant, 1965, Olby, 1997).

Today, the terms 'gene' and 'genetics' are so familiar and inter-linked that it seems strange to think of a time when one existed and the other didn't; but that was the situation in 1906: genetics had yet to be defined as the study of 'genes' and for the present it was the study of the inheritance of those 'factors' (a term used by Mendel) that determined the physical characteristics or 'characters' of an organism (Bateson, 1906). From Mendel's work and that of de Vries, Correns, Tschermak and Bateson the audience of 1906 would have known that such 'factors' (genes) exist in pairs, one inherited from the mother and the other from the father and that usually two different forms of a factor ('allelomorphs')[3] could occur,

---

[3] Allelomorph, now usually referred to as an 'allele': one of a pair or more of alternative forms of a gene controlling alternative forms of a character.

each responsible for controlling two facets of a character, e.g. tall and dwarf forms of the common pea (*Pisum sativum*), Mendel's experimental organism. In such cases, one allelomorph (e.g. tall) was usually 'dominant' to the other (e.g. dwarf = 'recessive'), such that where both were present together (e.g. one tall and one dwarf) the character observed would be that controlled by the dominant allelomorph (e.g. tall). Individuals carrying pairs of identical allelomorphs (e.g. tall/tall or dwarf/dwarf) were referred to as 'homozygous'[4] whereas individuals carrying both allelomorphs (e.g. tall/dwarf) were referred to as 'heterozygous'.[5] If two homozygous individuals of the same kind ('true-breeding')[6] were crossed (or in plants, selfed) all of the offspring would be identical for that character, and homozygous. If however, two heterozygous individuals (e.g. tall/dwarf) were crossed (or selfed) the offspring would appear in a ratio of 3 tall: 1 dwarf, owing to the dominance of the tall allelomorph. Bunyard was clearly familiar with these basic genetic concepts as he referred to the effects of 'Mendelian dominance' in his paper on Xenia.

Wednesday August 1st was the day of Bunyard's paper, delivered in the third session of the conference. His was to be the last in a relatively short session of just five papers, a session kept short to allow delegates ample time to board a special train from Victoria to Burford, near Dorking in Surrey, where a luncheon was scheduled at the home of the President of the RHS.[7] The session began with a paper by von Tschermak (Hochschule für Bodencultur, Vienna) on 'The Importance of Hybridization in the Study of Descent'. In the previous year von Tschermak had delivered a similar paper to the 1905 International Congress on Botany in Vienna (the equivalent meeting was held in Vienna one-hundred years later) where he spoke of the new science of Mendelism, 'but his was a lonely voice' (Olby, 1997), and the subject was greeted with little interest. Now, however, thanks to Bateson and the RHS, Mendelism, the science of genetics, was receiving

---

[4] Homozygous: having two identical allelomorphs (alleles).
[5] Heterozygous: having two different allelomorphs.
[6] True-breeding: remaining uniform for one or more characters from one generation to the next.
[7] *Report of the Third International Conference on Genetics*, ed. W. Wilks, Royal Horticultural Society. p. 5.

its due recognition and von Tschermak was speaking to the converted, or at least those that were open to conversion, Bunyard among them. Papers followed on 'Cytological Investigations on Plant Hybrids', 'Castration and Hybridization in the Genus *Hieracium*' and 'The Germination of Orchids': with 'Lantern Slides'[8] – perhaps one of the first slide presentations at such a meeting.

Then came Bunyard 'On Xenia' (Bunyard, 1906). The session was scheduled to finish promptly at 12.15 so that delegates would have sufficient time to catch the special train taking them to the lunch hosted by the RHS President, Sir Trevor Lawrence, and his wife. No doubt Bunyard, anticipating a fine luncheon, kept one eye on the clock because his paper was brief and very much to the point. His subject, 'xenia', he introduced as 'the influence of foreign pollen upon the maternal structure' – 'maternal structure' in his opinion, referring particularly to the fruit, produced as a consequence of pollination. Of xenia he said: 'on few subjects has there been expressed greater difference of opinion', a fact that he attributed to there not being a sufficiently exact definition for xenia, which resulted in its 'somewhat vague' usage by many writers. This was clearly a controversial topic and Bunyard aimed to set matters straight and clarify the subject by focussing on xenia as an effect on the *fruit*.

The term 'xenia' was first used by the German Botanist Focke (a delegate to the meeting) in 1881 to describe the effect of foreign pollen on the development and characteristics of the fruit and *seed* (Focke, 1881). Bunyard did not refer to this work, and attributed the earliest observations of xenia[9] to Darwin who mentioned the phenomenon in his classic work, 'The variation of animals and plants under domestication' (Darwin, 1868). At the time of Darwin, and later Focke, it must be remembered that neither the Mendelian basis of character inheritance, nor the cytological details of the fertilization process in flowering plants were known.[10] Xenia must

---

[8] Ibid.

[9] Ibid. p297.

[10] Although Mendel's experiments on hybridization were published in 1866 in Brno, the work remained in obscurity and largely unread or unappreciated until its rediscovery in 1899–1900. Despite reading Mendel's paper and referring to it in his book, Focke (1881) 'failed to appreciate or even understand the work' (Sturtevant, 1965).

therefore have appeared to be a very mysterious phenomenon. As Bunyard goes on to explain, it is only through an understanding of Mendel's rules and the unique process of fertilization in flowering plants that the effects of 'supposed' xenia upon the *seed* could be explained. It is one of the great tragedies in the biological sciences that Darwin did not live to become aware of Mendel's work (he died in 1882) because it would have helped him clarify so many of his ideas on evolution and heredity, including his observations of xenia. It is therefore fitting that Darwin's third son, Francis ('Frank'), himself an eminent botanist at Cambridge and a Fellow of the Royal Society, was present as a delegate at this meeting.[11]

A year before the rediscoveries of Mendel's laws in 1900, two important papers (cited in Dunn, 1973), one by a Russian botanist, Sergei Nawaschin (not cited by Bunyard) and the other by a French botanist, Jean-Louis-Léon Guignard (cited by Bunyard), independently announced the discovery, by microscopic study in lily, of the process of 'double fertilization'. The observation of 'two acts of fertilization' was truly unexpected and marked the sexual process in flowering plants as distinct from that of all other organisms. Pollen contains two sperm cells, one of which fertilizes the egg to produce the embryo (plant), while the second sperm fuses with another pair of nuclei (the polar nuclei) in the embryo sac to produce the endosperm, the nutritive tissue of the seed. As Dunn (1973) points out, 'these two papers produced the botanical sensation of 1899'. These findings were duly confirmed for maize by de Vries and Correns who were studying xenia and character inheritance. Indeed, from his studies of xenia in maize Correns inferred the existence of double fertilization before Nawaschin's and Guignard's observation of the process (Dunn, 1973).

Correns and de Vries were studying the inheritance of certain seed characteristics in maize (work that would later be included in papers recording the experimental 'rediscovery' of Mendel's rules) (Dunn, 1973). Both were seeking to determine how foreign pollen exerted a direct visible effect on the form and colour of the seed when the parental plants differed in such characters. For instance, if a variety of maize with sugary endosperm was crossed with the pollen of a variety with starchy endosperm, the resul-

---

[11] *Report of the Third International Conference on Genetics*, ed. W. Wilks, Royal Horticultural Society. p23.

ting hybrid seeds all had starchy endosperms. This is clearly xenia *sensu* Focke (1881) and can now be explained easily in the light of the influence of a parental pollen factor (a dominant gene for starchiness) inherited by the hybrid endosperm. Double fertilization can therefore explain xenia effects on the endosperm character of the hybrid seed. This Bunyard was clear about as he stressed that most of the hitherto reported cases of 'supposed' xenia could be explained by the fact of double fertilization and 'Mendelian dominance'.

Bunyard, unlike Focke and others (de Vries and Correns among them) did not view xenia as being a 'gift' from pollen to the seed, Bunyard saw xenia as 'a gift', from the pollen to the fruit. He therefore asked the conference to accept a definition of xenia in line with that advocated by Tschermak that 'xenia shall be applied to all those cases where the pollen shall have caused, apart from the egg-cell and embryo-sac (=endosperm), variation corresponding to the pollen-parent upon the vegetative parts of the mother-plant', i.e. the fruit. Bunyard wanted xenia focussed on the more obscure, genetically unexplainable effects of foreign pollen on the resulting fruit, and for the remainder of his paper he addressed current evidence for incidences of xenia, *sensu* Tschermak and Bunyard on the fruits of peaches, nectarines and apples.

Interestingly, by advocating Tschermak's stricter definition of xenia Bunyard pre-empted a later division of xenia into xenia and 'metaxenia' (Swingle, 1928, reviewed by Denney, 1992) to distinguish xenia effects in fruit and seed. Metaxenia refers specifically to the effects of foreign pollen on fruit tissues of maternal origin that have no male genetic contribution (Denney, 1992). Today the term 'xenia' is generally applied to seed phenomena arising as a consequence of double fertilization (Denney 1992). So what were Bunyard's conclusions on xenia (= metaxenia) in fruits?

Bunyard described crosses between distinct varieties of nectarines and between varieties of peach concluding that 'in none was any influence visible to the unaided eye'. He then moved to his favourite fruit, the apple where 'xenia had been most often recorded'. He described a case of xenia reported by Darwin (no reference): 'The case of the St. Valery apple, which produced no pollen, but on being pollinated by other varieties gave fruits which resembled those of the male parent'. Bunyard sought 'corroborative evidence' for Darwin's observations and reported: 'My experiments, with one presumable exception, have so far failed to augment this stream'. He describes crosses made between apple varieties with fruits differing in size and colour such as Sturmer Pippin (small) x The Queen (large) and Gloria Mundi (green) x Hoary Morning (distinct stripes) but 'in all cases no change was seen, though the crossing of a russet skin with a smooth green would seem to offer an easy and exact method of detecting xenia'.

He ends his report with 'the only case of presumable xenia I have ever seen': describing a cross between Sandringham (large faint stripes) and the pollen of Bismark (bright, non-striped red) which resulted in a fruit which 'was in shape and colour quite out of character, resembling a fine fruit of Cox's Orange' rather than the fruit of either parent. He went on to state that 'This case was reported in the JOURN. R.H.S. vol. xxiv. part 4, p. 1899'. So far, however, I have been unable to trace this report because no such article exists in this volume of the journal.[12] Clearly, xenia *sensu* Bunyard is extremely rare, if it even exists at all. Of xenia then, Bunyard concludes: it 'is of rare occurrence, and in my opinion, considerably more experiment is needed to establish the phenomena on a firm basis of positive fact', ending with a quote from Bacon's preface to the 'Novum Organum',[13] referring to science in general, as a metaphor for the current situation with respect to xenia: 'that it is not so much an opinion to be held as work to be done'.

Perhaps with thought of 'work to be done' Bunyard set off with fellow conference delegates to Burford where they were 'warmly welcomed by Sir Trevor and Lady Lawrence', luncheon being served 'in a marquee most charmingly decorated to harmonise with the surrounding foliage'.[14] And a splendid luncheon it must have been too:

---

[12] Librarians at the RHS Lindley Library were unable to trace such an article.

[13] *The New Organon or True Directions Concerning the Interpretation of Nature*, Francis Bacon, 1620.

[14] *Report of the Third International Conference on Genetics*, ed. W. Wilks, Royal Horticultural Society. p. 66.

DÉJEUNER DU 1ᵉʳ AOÛT, 1906
Darnes de Saumon. Sauce Remoulade.
Côtelettes de Mouton à la Norvégienne.
Pâtés de Pigeons à la Française.
Poulets et Langues au Cresson.
Salade de Laitues. Salade jardinière.

———

Jambon à l'Aspic.
Rond de Bœuf à l'Anglaise.
Quartier d'Agneau. Sauce Menthe.
Roast Beef à la broche.

———

Entremets.
Gelée aux liqueurs.
Riz à l'Impératrice.
Tartes aux fruits.
Macédoine de fruits.
Glaces panachées.

Reading the account of this afternoon in the *Proceedings*, I could not help but compare this idyllic scene with today's much larger schedule-obsessed conferences where perhaps an hour at most is set aside for a 'lunch', usually consisting of a sandwich, a cake and a piece of 'fruit' (often a banana!) served with a fizzy drink, all packaged in a cardboard box and obtained at a counter from a surly official in exchange for a lunch-ticket with that day's date stamped upon it.[15]

Lunch ended, Professor Wittmack of Berlin thanked the President and his wife for their hospitality and proposed a toast to their health. Sir Trevor responded and spoke of his love of orchids and orchid breeding but assured delegates that his interests extended 'to every class of flower and fruit and vegetable'. The speeches over, Rev. W. Wilks goes on to say: 'The guests then rambled about the beautiful park and visited the gardens and plant houses'. Whilst they 'rambled' they were entertained by music from the band of the Royal Artillery. At half-past four, tea was served on the lawn before the

---

[15] XVII International Botanical Congress, Vienna, 17–23 July 2005.

delegates and their friends left by special train arriving back in London by 6.15 'having enjoyed one of the most delightful excursions possible'.

So, what of xenia, or more correctly metaxenia, today? Bunyard was right in his conclusion that xenia relating to the fruit is rare, but the experimental work that he advocated to confirm its existence has been 'done' and metaxenia, although still a somewhat obscure phenomenon, has been recorded conclusively in a wide range of plants including: date palm (Swingle, 1928), apples (Nebel and Trump, 1932), cotton (Harrison, 1931), almonds (Garcia-Gusano et al., 2005), cacti (Mizrahi et al., 2004), durian (Lim and Luders, 1998), blueberry (Ehlenfeldt, 2003), poppy (Bernath et al., 2003) and pistachio (Hormaza and Herrero, 1998). Unfortunately, metaxenia does not appear to attract the same amount of scientific interest as xenia (relating to the seed) perhaps because of its rarity and because its physiological basis is not yet fully understood. Using the search engine 'Web of Science' I could locate just 21 papers on metaxenia published between 1945 and 2005, compared to 193 papers on xenia. Recent papers on maize cultivation highlight how xenia can be used as a strategy to increase yields by selecting pollinating plants that consistently impart a larger endosperm upon the seeds that they sire (Bulant and Gallais, 1998; Weingarter, 2002; Weingarter et al., 2002a, 2002b, 2004).

Xenia effects in the seed are clearly due to the effects of expression of paternal genes in the hybrid endosperm, but how can such pollen-derived genes affect the development of the fruit (metaxenia) when these tissues contain only maternal genes? Various authors since Swingle (1928) have suggested that the effect of the pollen source on the fruit is most probably mediated by plant hormones produced in the seeds, either by the embryo or the endosperm (discussed in Mizrahi et al., 2004). As one of the most widely reported examples of metaxenia in fruits is time taken to ripen (Mizrahi et al., 2004), plant hormones would seem to be the obvious mediators of this metaxenia effect. Clearly much work still needs to be done on metaxenia before a full physiological explanation of the phenomenon is forthcoming. In August 1906 Bunyard asked for more experiments to be carried out to confirm the existence (or not) of what we now call metaxenia. In the ensuing ninety-nine years this existence has been confirmed for many different fruits, but the physiological basis of metaxenia has still to be elucidated – today, as in 1906, on metaxenia there is still 'work to be done'.

REFERENCES

Bateson, W. (1906), 'The progress on genetic research', *Report of the Third International Conference on Genetics*, ed. W. Wilks, Royal Horticultural Society, pp 90–7.

Bernath, J., Nemeth, E., Petheo, F. (2003), 'Alkaloid accumulation in capsules of the selfed and cross-pollinated poppy', *Plant Breeding* CXXII, 263–7.

Bulant, C., Gallais, A. (1998), 'Xenia effects in maize with normal endosperm: I. Importance and stability', *Crop Science* XXXVIII, 1517–25.

Bunyard, E.A. (1906), 'On xenia', *Report of the Third International Conference on Genetics*, ed. W. Wilks, Royal Horticultural Society, 297–300.

Darwin, C. (1868), *The Variation of Animals and Plants under Domestication*. John Murray, London.

Denney, J. O. (1992), 'Xenia includes metaxenia', *HortScience* XXVII, 722–8.

Dunn, L. C. (1973), 'Xenia and the origins of genetics', *Proceedings of the American Philosophical Society*, CXVII, 105–11.

Ehlenfeldt, M. K. (2003), 'Investigations of metaxenia in northern highbush blueberry (*Vaccinium corymbosum* L.) cultivars', *Journal of the American Pomological Society*, LVII, 26–31.

Focke, W. O. (1881), *Die Pflanzen-Mischlinge: ein Beitrag zur Biologie der Gewachse*. Borntraeger, (Berlin).

Garcia-Gusano, M., Matinez-Gomez, P., Dicenta, F. (2005), 'Pollinizer influence on almond seed dormancy', *Scientia Horticulturae*, CIV, 91–9.

Harrison, G. J. (1931), 'Metaxenia in cotton', *Journal of Agricultural Research*, XLII, 521–44.

Hormaza, J. I., Herrero, M. (1998), 'Pollen effects on fruit and seed characteristics in pistachio (*Pistacia vera* L.)', *Annals of Applied Biology*, CXXXII, 357–64.

Lim, T.K., Luders, L. (1998), 'Durian flowering, pollination and incompatibility studies', *Annals of Applied Biology*, CXXXII, 151–65.

Mizrahi, Y., Mouyal, J., Nerd, A., Sitrit, Y. (2004), 'Metaxenia in the vine cacti *Hylocereus polyrhizus* and *Selenicereus* spp.', *Annals of Botany*, XCIII, 469–72.

Olby, R. C. (1997), 'Mendel, Mendelism and Genetics', Mendel Web (www.mendelweb.org/MWolby.html).

Nebel, B. R., Trump, I. J. (1932), 'Xenia and metaxenia in apples II', *Proceedings of the National Academy of Sciences USA*, XVIII, 356–9.

Sturtevant, A. H. (1965), *A History of Genetics*, Cold Spring Harbour Laboratory Press.

Swingle, W. T. (1928), 'Metaxenia in the date palm, possibly a hormone action by the embryo or endosperm', *Journal of Heredity*, XIX, 257–68.

Weingarter, U. (2002), *Combined effect of male sterility and xenia on grain yield and yield components in maize (*Zea mays *L.)*, PhD. thesis, Swiss Federal Institute of Technology, Zurich.

Weingarter, U., Camp, K. H., Stamp, P. (2002), 'Impact of male sterility and xenia on grain traits in maize', *European Journal of Agronomy*, XXI, 239–47.

Weingarter, U., Kaeser, O., Long, M., Stamp, P. (2002), 'Combining cytoplasmic male sterility and xenia increases grain yield of maize hybrids', *Crop Science* XLII, 1848–56.

Weingarter, U., Prest, T. J., Camp, K. H., Stamp, P. (2004), 'The plus-hybrid system: A method to increase grain yield by combined cytoplasmic male sterility and xenia', *Maydica* XLVII, 127–34.

CHAPTER FIVE

Bunyard and the Saintsbury Club

ALAN BELL

Edward Bunyard, with his agreeable and very well-informed writings on desserts and Epicureanism, is sometimes compared with the much older George Saintsbury and his writings on wine. Saintsbury, born in 1845 and exceedingly – perhaps excessively – productive as a scholar, had been a professor of English literature and a journalist and free-lance author long before he became a don. His much celebrated, and still enjoyable, *Notes on a Cellar Book* was published in 1920, after his retirement from his Edinburgh chair. It is a causerie based on the detailed memories prompted by an old exercise book recording the contents of a cellar long since consumed, a mellow work full of elongated sentences and literary allusions, some of them rather obscure. The *Notes* were deservedly well known at a time when serious wine writing was only just starting; a reminiscent, 'baroque' approach was pardonable. For Saintsbury, who had made a book out of a series of articles prepared for the *Piccadilly Review*, a new magazine that soon failed, the *Notes* were a useful source of modest literary income in his retirement.

Bunyard, by contrast, was a practical nurseryman with many technical publications on pomology to his credit as well as a substantial output of weekly horticultural journalism that made him well known as one of the leading gardening columnists of his day. His *Anatomy of Dessert* (1929 and 1933) and *The Epicure's Companion* (1937) are (like Saintsbury's *Cellar Book*) more relaxed in manner. Like Saintsbury's *Cellar Book*, they are free from the demands of weekly journalism, of writing to a set length and a regular deadline, that can make even the most hardened columnist chafe at editorial demands. The two writers had much in common, not least in their industrious output, even if Bunyard's prose style was much less ornate.

The two seem never to have met. By the time Bunyard was rising to prominence in horticultural journalism, the emeritus professor, already something of a legend, was living reclusively in Bath, where he died in 1933. Clubland might have provided an opportunity for a memorable encounter, but Saintsbury's exile to Bath was complete and his memberships had lapsed. Bunyard was an active member of the Royal Societies Club, a sodality formed in 1894 from among the fellowships of the various senior learned societies; he qualified through his fellowship (since 1914) of the Linnean Society. It was a club that came to an end in the 1960s, after a marsupial existence in other establishments; finally it was subsumed by the East India Club in St James's Square, and none of its records appears to have survived.

Saintsbury's plight in old age, when he was on medical grounds virtually forbidden wine, became a matter of anxiety, indeed of misleading speculation, in the vinous circles of London. On 5 February 1931, André Simon, that great showman for wine, even then a senior figure in the London trade (he died at the age of 93 in 1970), held a small luncheon party at his city office. The company included Maurice Healy, the voluble Irish barrister now remembered for his excellent anecdotal *Stay Me with Flagons* (1940) and also among lawyers for his reminiscences of *The Old Munster Circuit* (1939). Guy Knowles, about whom less is known, was also of the company. There was the bibulous J. C. Squire, editor of *The London Mercury*, and that exotic young bibliophile A. J. A. Symons, already founder of a literary society, the First Edition Club, and from 1930 first editor of *The Book-Collector's Quarterly*. After luncheon the talk moved on to the Sage of Bath. They all wished Saintsbury might have been at their table, and soon resolved to ask him to a testimonial dinner.

Saintsbury was duly invited but, being confined to his house, he had to refuse. His handwriting was universally reckoned to be appalling, and age had not improved it. Some have mistakenly thought he turned down the invitation abruptly (André Simon elaborated this story), but it is pretty clear that Saintsbury was flattered and intended no discourtesy in his refusal. Undeterred by the absence of the guest of honour, the informal committee went ahead and convened a dinner as a compliment to the professor. There was a banquet at the Connaught Rooms in May 1931, with D. S. MacColl in the chair. A dining club was proposed, to meet twice yearly beginning on the honorand's eighty-sixth birthday, 23 October 1931, and holding its other meeting on or near St George's Day each year. The second dinner, in April 1932, had the Ambassador of France present as a guest, and Hilaire Belloc took the chair, delivering an impromptu oration that was much acclaimed but never recorded.

Bunyard was one of the founding members of the brotherhood of fifty, then as now half 'men of wine' and half 'men of letters' (many of the latter nowadays lawyers or doctors). It has met twice a year ever since, at Vintners' Hall in the city of London where the first dinner was held. The aim was to honour Saintsbury 'by bringing together men whose love of wine and letters is catholic and articulate'. These criteria still apply, and the pattern of meetings has changed little over the years. From the start there was an oration later printed for the membership, though this is less frequent nowadays; discussion at table of the wine and food is detailed, well-informed and good-tempered. A cellar was soon established, it becoming the custom for new members to give 'some good wine' at the time of their election.

Bunyard was an obvious choice for membership, and must have been well known to many of the founders. Not only was he a notable figure in the horticultural and gastronomic worlds of his day, but the second edition of his *Anatomy of Dessert*, prepared after he had joined the Saintsbury Club, had included by way of postscript 'a few notes on wine'. These are still helpful, even after fourscore years of now widespread education, and even allowing for some elaborated orchestral similes. Bunyard's *Anatomy* is good, for example, on the absolute necessity of simple and capacious glasses. Coloured ones, he tells us, 'may best be left to those who revel with Wallaboola Burgundies and medicinated "Ports"', and he adds (rather daringly for 1933):

> If the wine has not been gradually warmed before it is poured, it must be warmed by the hands of the drinker, lovingly clasping the wine glass, making love, as it were, to the reluctant nymph. And here comes the justification of the thin glass: Could you, Sir, or you, Madam, make love to anyone in cut-glass pyjamas?

He reckoned himself 'an average person who falls short … of expert rank', taking refuge in further orchestral figures of speech to attempt distinctions between various classed-growth clarets. He is more successful when concrete and practical. As a guide to quantity, for example: 'a quarter of a bottle – reticence; a half – sufficiency; three-quarters – eloquence; and a whole bottle – benevolence.' And Bunyard's horticultural experience comes in useful when seeking vinous partnerships for the various fruits likely to be on offer – always excluding 'the viscid Banana'. He is original in recommending a Beaujolais with strawberries ('the strawberry likes a little roughness in its wooing, so a young wine may be used'); but he shows himself conventional for his time, and by no means wrong, in urging German wines as good partners for dessert fruits. The exceptional Rhineland vintage of 1921 made them an ideal choice at the time; there are some fashions that well deserve revival, and after a recent run of fine vintages the sweeter Hocks and Mosels must surely now be among them.

The menus of the Club's early meetings have survived, and were indeed published with a commentary by André Simon as its long-serving Cellarer. They show sound seasonal tastes, notably for partridge at the autumn dinner. 'Pommes d'Allington' accompanied the Quarles Harris 1851 ('remarkable for its vitality') at the first meeting; 'Les Ribstons d'Allington' were tabled eighteen months later, matched by a venerable Sercial. 'Ananas glacé' at the next dinner may not have been altogether welcome to one of Bunyard's firm opinions, and one hopes that 'Le Dessert' unspecified at subsequent meetings contained suitable offerings from the family orchards.

From an early stage the wine was good – some of it 'supernacular', to use one of George Saintsbury's own favourite terms. There is frequently a first-growth claret, some from the excellent Bordeaux vintage of 1921, and occasionally pre-phylloxera wine that was still available to connoisseurs from country-house sales. The presence of Sir Stephen Gaselee, Cambridge don and classical scholar as well as librarian to the Foreign Office, assured the Club a generous supply of ancient Madeira (pre-1851 Sercial and Terrantez) from impeccable reserves he had located on the island. They must have increased Bunyard's knowledge considerably, for the *Anatomy*, even when revised in 1933, has all too little to say about Madeira as a suitable accompaniment to dessert.

Even though it meets but twice a year, the Saintsbury Club, perhaps especially in those early days, is much more than a dining facility. Its members gradually get to know each other well, not least during the visits to European vineyards that are occasionally arranged by the Club. Bunyard's sudden death on 19 October 1939 must have been a very sad loss to the Saintsbury Club, which was by then, in spite of the lean wartime years soon to come, firmly established.

CHAPTER SIX

The Epicurean Context of Edward Bunyard

RICHARD SHARP

'When war was declared ... my friend A. J. A. Symons and I, the Secretary and President of the Wine and Food Society, must have been disconcerted, desolated, distressed ... To preach the gospel of gastronomy in wartime was sheer folly'.[1] The words of André Simon add force to the overwhelmingly probable assumption that the breakdown of international peace in September 1939 contributed substantially to Edward Bunyard's tragic decision to end his life very shortly afterwards. Unlike some,[2] Bunyard had no comfortable illusion that epicureanism might somehow continue to flourish for the duration of hostilities, in spite of the fact that remarkable advances had been made with regard to the provision and appreciation of good things to eat and drink in

---

[1] A. L. Simon, *In the Twilight* (1969), p. 108

[2] Many members of the Wine & Food Society (founded in 1933) went on to demonstrate a capacity for disregarding the Axis that surpassed even their earlier indifference towards the Slump. In 1944, as Allied forces pushed inland from Normandy to liberate France, Simon himself, who had remained a French citizen, eagerly anticipated the benefits of returning peace by publishing, with Louis Golding, *We Shall Eat and Drink Again: A Wine & Food Anthology*. This included a complacent appraisal of his own contribution to the war effort: 'There are some who believe that the continuance of ... [*Wine & Food*] ... during these war years was the keeping alight of a torch, as gracious a thing as the keeping alive of ballet and music and the other fine arts'. (p. 9)

Britain since the end of the Great War in 1918. The following survey will attempt to provide a short outline account of the many ways, both practical and theoretical, in which the understanding and enjoyment of food and wine was promoted in the 1920s and 1930s. As nurseryman, scholar and anthologist, Edward Bunyard played a central part in this process.

The beginnings of a new approach to wine and food were evident before 1914, as rising material prosperity and the development of new techniques for distribution, preservation and preparation created new markets and levels of interest. After nearly half a century, the supremacy of Isabella Beeton's *Book of Household Management* (1859–61) was challenged by other writers with a wide market appeal, like C. Herman Senn, whose *Practical Gastronomy* (1894), *Ices and How to Make Them* (1900), *The New Century Cookery Book* (1901), *Senn's Century Cookery Book: Practical Gastronomy and Recherché Cookery* (1901), *Practical Cookery Manual* (1906) and *Chafing Dish and Casserole Cookery* (1905) frequently went into multiple editions and remain common to this day in second-hand booksellers' stock. Other widely-read authors of the period included Florence Jack, whose *Cookery for Every Household* (1914) followed earlier titles like *Cold Sweets, Jellies and Creams* (1904), and Janet Ross, compiler of the influential *Leaves from Our Tuscan Kitchen* (1899). Interest in diet of a more austere variety was evinced by the numerous customers of Eustace Hamilton Miles (1868–1948), whose first vegetarian restaurant opened in Chandos Street, Charing Cross, in 1906, to be followed by the Milestone in the King's Road, another restaurant with similar ideals, and by health-food shops, one (hardly surprisingly) in Bloomsbury, and others in North and South London. These attracted '…theosophists, simple-lifers, aspiring writers, healers and others of an idealistic bent'.[3]

The Times published its first Wine Supplement in June 1914, shortly before events in Sarajevo cast a temporary shadow over the epicurean world. At first, the impact of war was felt only gradually, and even in 1915 the appearance of works such as Mrs E. W. Bowdich's *New Vegetarian Dishes* (first published 1892) and Nancy Lake's *Menus Made Easy, or How to Order Dinner and Give the Dishes their French Names* (first published 1884) looked back – and forward – to more comfortable times. However, by 1917, works like *The Eat-Less-Meat Book* by Mrs C. S. Peel reflected the impact of

---

[3] *Oxford DNB*, 'Miles'.

shortages and rationing on housekeeping during the later stages of the war. The return of peace after 1918 brought an end to shortages, but in many other ways the war had deep and enduring effects, not least by bringing about a rapid and irreversible decline in the numbers of domestic servants. The implications of these changes for the development of household catering were profound, as those who had previously entrusted the running of their kitchens and cellars to paid staff were suddenly obliged to take an active interest for themselves, resulting in a rapid stimulation of technical and culinary innovation.

These developments were faithfully reflected in the much expanded quantity and range of post-war publications relating to wine and food. Works like Elizabeth Craig's *The Way to a Good Table: Electric Cookery* (1918, frequently republished) and G. F. Scotson-Clark's *Kitchenette Cookery* (1925) revealed technical novelty, while in 1928 one of the earliest publishing ventures of the new B.B.C. was a collection of cookery recipes entitled *Home, Health and Garden*. National newspapers and magazines also responded with alacrity to the new interests of their readers. At one level, there was the *Daily Mail Cookery Book* (1919, frequently republished) and *Good Housekeeping*, with a series of popular guides, including a *Cookery Book* by Florence B. Jack (1925) and a *Menu and Recipe Book* by D. D. Cottington Taylor (1928). At another level there was *Country Life*, which published a range of works including Frances Keyzer's *French Household Cooking* (1909) and Helen Edden's *County Recipes of Old England* (1929) and *The Times*, whose regular food writer, Lady Jekyll, reprinted some of her newspaper articles as a collection in 1922 under the title *Kitchen Essays*; subjects included 'Luncheon for a motor excursion in winter', diet 'for the too thin' and 'food for the punctual and unpunctual'.

Lady Jekyll was one of several prominent writers on food and wine from the 1920s whose works were later singled out for praise by Bunyard in *The Epicure's Companion* (1937). Others included Major Hugh Pollard, author of *The Sportsman's Cookery Book* (1926);[4] P. Morton Shand, the writer and

---

[4] The student of Bunyard will be immediately struck by Pollard's robust declaration that this work was 'for bad lots who openly admit that they like the pleasures of the table and who enjoy life … [rather than for] … intense and progressive people [who] count the calories in carrots and the vitamins in veal and advise us to live on raw cabbage'. (p. v)

architectural critic, who as well as being the author of *A Book of Food* (1927) also published extensively on wine; Sir Francis Colchester-Wemyss, who was not only the author of *The Pleasures of the Table* (1931) but also the inventor of the Improved Croquet Hoop (Pat. no. 192,928), and X. Marcel Boulestin (1878–1943), the author of numerous recipe-books, including *Subtle Seasoning* (1926), *A Second Helping* (1925) and *The Conduct of the Kitchen: How to Keep a Good Table for Sixteen Shillings a Week* (1925). It has been well observed that Boulestin's *Simple French Cooking for English Homes* (1923), which introduced such novelties as aubergines and pipérade, 'suited the new, often servantless, pared-down sophistication of post-war domestic arrangements'.[5]

A close friend of Bunyard, who contributed an essay on 'Gastronomes in French Literature' to *The Epicure's Companion*, Boulestin was one of the most influential figures in the inter-war culinary world. In addition to publishing twelve recipe books between 1923 and 1937, he wrote columns for the *Daily Telegraph, Country Life, Harper's Bazaar* and the *Evening Standard*, and in 1937 achieved celebrity as the first ever TV chef. In 1928 he began to run a successful series of cookery courses, which were later operated in conjunction with Fortnum and Mason's, and in due course he was appointed to the Council of the newly-founded Wine & Food Society (1933). His first restaurant, on the corner of Leicester Square and Panton Street, was opened in 1925 and proved an instant success despite having no full alcohol licence. In 1927 he opened Boulestin's in Covent Garden, decorated in the latest Parisian style, with silk velvet curtains by Raoul Dufy and panelled walls and ceilings by Marie Laurencin and Jean-Émile Laboureur. Although probably the most distinguished from a gastronomic and aesthetic point of view, Boulestin's was only one of many new restaurants established in the post-war years. Rising appreciation of Italian cuisine was reflected in the success of Joe Bertorelli (1893–1994), who arrived in England from New York in 1922 and became a naturalized British subject in 1936. Having expanded his first restaurant in Charlotte Street, Fitzrovia, from 5 to 100 seats, he opened further restaurants at

---

[5] *Oxford DNB.*, 'Boulestin'. Boulestin became an enthusiastic supporter of the Bunyard nurseries, and contributed the guest preface to the firm's annual catalogue 'Vegetables for Epicures' in 1932.

Shepherd's Bush Green and Queensway (the Monte Carlo) in 1928. The new level of interest in non-English food was reflected in the titles of works published during the 1920s, such as *The Cook's Decameron: ... Over 200 Recipes for Italian Dishes*, by Mrs W. G. Waters (1920; first published 1901) and *French Household Cooking*, by Frances Keyzer, published by *Country Life* in 1922 (first published 1909). Similarly, the rapidly-growing interest in opportunities for eating outside the home was signified by the publishing success of A. E. Manning Foster, writing under the pen-name 'Diner-Out', whose *London Restaurants*, *Through the Wine-List*, and *Dining and Wining* appeared in rapid succession between 1924 and 1925, and by demand for works such as Julian Street's *Where Paris Dines, with Information about Restaurants of all Kinds...* (1929).

One keen observer of such gastronomic progress was André Simon (1877–1970), whose best-selling *The Art of Good Living* (1929) looked forward to yet further improvements. Noting contentedly that 'we are happily approaching the greatly to be desired stage when the art of good living is again receiving proper attention', he went on to explain the grounds for his optimism: 'Cocktails and jazz belong to ... a now passing age: they belong to the previous generation – the one that went through the strain and anxiety of the War and lost their sense of balance, harmony and art. The young people of today ... do not like cocktails and jazz. They crave for something that is better balanced, more harmonious, more artistic.'[6] It was hardly to be expected that something like the Wall Street crash in October 1929 would curb confidence of this order, and therefore little wonder that Simon and A. J. A. Symons were able to establish the Wine & Food Society with such success in 1933, a full three years before the first hunger marcher had set out from Jarrow. As Symons's brother, and memorialist, observed: 'the professional and semi-professional section of the middle class had made few sacrifices in the depression, and were well prepared now to make believe that no depression had ever disturbed the even tenour of their lives.'[7]

---

[6] A. L. Simon, *The Art of Good Living* (1929), pp. 4, 14–15. Events in the 1930s were to belie Simon's estimate of the future prospects for both cocktails and jazz, but his views and Bunyard's coincided closely on these matters.

[7] Julian Symons, *A. J. A. Symons: His Life and Speculations* (1950), p. 145.

This claim is amply vindicated by the record of publishing, where the patterns established in the 1920s continued without interruption throughout the following decade and the volume of published material expanded substantially. Ever-widening public interest in the subject of wine was reflected in the titles of works such as Ellert Forbes's *Wine for Everyman* (1937), and by the market for books like Boulestin's *What shall we have to drink?* (1933). To meet new levels of demand the wine trade began to open chain-stores, and to make helpful advice available in user-friendly form with works such as *Here's How: Being a Symposium of Recipes of Good Cheer*, published by the Victoria Wine Company in 1937. More specialized information was made available for the first time to a general level of reader through the medium of Constable's Wine Library, a series begun under the editorship of André Simon in 1933. Simon himself contributed volumes on *Madeira* (with Elizabeth Craig, 1933) and on *Port* and *Champagne* (both 1934), while other volumes were commissioned from a growing circle of professional or semi-professional writers, most of whom were also prominent in the Wine & Food Society and in the Saintsbury Club, which had been founded in 1931 to honour the elderly – and decidedly reluctant – Professor George Saintsbury.[8] The volume on *Sherry* (1933) was written by H. Warner Allen (1881–1968), a sometime classical pupil of T. E. Page at Charterhouse, who had combined a distinguished journalistic career on the staffs of the *Morning Post* and the *Yorkshire Post* with the writing of detective fiction and books about wine, including *Claret* (1924), *The Wines of France* (1924) and *The Romance of Wine* (1931). In a remark that might apply with equal justice to Edward Bunyard, it has been said of Warner Allen that 'in all his publications on the subject, vinous information was nicely interwoven with literary and historical allusions'.[9] *Burgundy* (1934) was contributed by Stephen Gwynn (1864–1950), another classicist, who had sat as MP for Galway from 1906–18 and led the moderate Nationalists in the Irish Convention following the death of John Redmond. He later became a regular contributor to *Wine & Food*. *Claret and the White Wines*

---

[8] 'The enthusiasts … were not to be dissuaded from their resolution to hold a dinner by the mere fact of the chief guest's unwillingness to attend it' (Symons, op. cit., n.7, p. 141).
[9] *Oxford DNB*.

of Bordeaux (1934) was written by Maurice Healy (1887–1943), who had contributed the foreword to Simon's *The Art of Good Living*. He was a close friend of Edward Bunyard, writing a sensitive obituary notice for him in *Wine & Food*, and was an enthusiastic patron of the Hind's Head restaurant at Bray in Berkshire, whose advertisements were a regular and noted feature of that publication.[10] The volume on *Wine in the Kitchen* (1934) came from the well-known writer Elizabeth Craig, a long-established protagonist of cooking by electricity and author of best-selling works such as *The Stage Favourites' Cook Book* (1924), *The Up-to-date Cookery Book* (1932) and *Woman, Wine and a Saucepan* (1936), while Hugh Rudd contributed *Hocks and Moselles* (1935).

Just as Constable's Wine Library provided systematic and accessible information for those who were developing an interest in that subject for the first time, so writing on food in the 1930s enabled the enthusiastic or merely curious beginner to accumulate encyclopaedic knowledge by easy stages. Inexpensive works like Mrs Mollie Stanley-Wrench's *The Complete Illustrated Cookery Book* (Associated Newspapers, 1934) or the seasonal 'Spring' and 'Summer' *Good Housekeeping* cookery books (1935) were regularly republished, while more specialized advice was available for the more ambitious. A notable contribution at this level was made by Ambrose Heath (1891–1969), cookery correspondent for the *Morning Post* and a regular patron of Boulestin's restaurant. A prolific writer, Heath produced four books on food, including *The Book of the Onion* and *More Good Food* (with woodcut illustrations by Edward Bawden) in 1933. By 1939 he had published eleven more titles, including *Good Savouries* (1934), *Good Soups* and *Good Potato Dishes* (1935), a translation of *Madame Prunier's Fish Cookery Book* (1938) and *Good Drinks* and *From Creel to Kitchen: How to Cook Fresh-Water Fish* (1939). In 1937 he collaborated with C. H. Middleton, the well-known 'Radio Gardener', to produce *From Garden to Kitchen*, a practical and accessible guide to the growing and preparation of vegetables aimed at the widest-possible market. Heath also provided guidance for those who were keen to experience restaurant cuisine for

---

[10] Healy's enthusiasm for the Hind's Head found poetical, if uninspired, expression in his verses 'The Liquor of Bray', reprinted in L. Golding and A. Simon (eds.), *We Shall Eat and Drink Again: A Wine and Food Anthology* (1944), pp. 197–9.

the first time, publishing *Dining Out: How and What to Order, What to Drink, What the Menu Means* in 1936. Restaurant-goers received further encouragement in 1937, with the publication of the first of the 'Bon Viveur' Guides, *Where to Dine in London*. For the first time, too, the range of restaurant experience moved beyond Europe, with the introduction of Chinese and Indian cuisine,[11] and books were available to assist those who were adventurous enough to experiment at home with new and exotic recipes. S. K. Cheng, of the Shanghai Restaurant in London, published *The Shanghai Restaurant Chinese Cookery Book* in 1936, and in the same year Marie Pickering published *Tropical Cookery*. Other new areas were explored by Lilla Deeley, with *International Cookery* (1933) and *Hungarian Cookery* (1938); Inga Norberg (*Good Food from Sweden*, 1935) and David Bethel (*The Tyrolese Cookery Book*, 1937).

The rapid and successful growth of the Wine & Food Society, which recruited more than a thousand members in the twelve months following its foundation in October 1933, can be seen both as a result and as a cause of this widening public interest. However, the Society's appeal was not universal. Julian Symons, the brother of its co-founder, A. J. A. Symons, later maintained that it had been conducted in a way that many found exclusive and even offensive,[12] and a rival organization, the Half Hundred Club, came into being for those who preferred to combine their gastronomic enthusiasm with the spirit of social awareness. Founded by

---

[11] Indian and Chinese restaurants were few, and almost entirely confined to London. An early provincial exception was the Taj Mahal in Turl Street, Oxford, which opened in *c.* 1935. Edward Bunyard's sister, Marguerite, contributed an anecdotal account of 'A Dinner in India' to *The Epicure's Companion* (1937).

[12] See J. Symons, *A. J. A. Symons: His Life and Speculations* (1950), p. 144: 'if, in fact, the Society's chief concern was to raise the standard of cooking in Britain … they went about it in a very odd way. During the whole of its existence the Wine and Food Society has made little attempt to give practical advice to the working-class housewife; it has made no attempt at all to set up those bureaux of advice and practical assistance which might really have transformed, in pre-war days, the nature of English cooking; its members, from the President and Secretary downwards, are open to the charge that they have educated others merely by setting an example in good living themselves, without moving on to the mundane ground of ways and means.'

Philip Harben (1906–70), later a well-known cookery writer and television chef, and by Raymond Postgate (1896–1971), its dinners cost a maximum of 10/-.[13] Members, like Harben himself, were drawn from the milieu of the Hampstead Left. Postgate, for example, the son-in-law of George Lansbury and brother-in-law of G. D. H. Cole, had been a founder member of the Communist Party of Great Britain in 1920, but is now probably best remembered as the editor of the *Good Food Guide*, established in 1951. Similarly, Francis Meynell (1891–1975), another prominent member, was a socialist and sometime conscientious objector, Bolshevik sympathizer, and assistant editor of the *Daily Herald*. Yet, as other aspects of Meynell's career serve to demonstrate, those who differed politically could still have much in common, even in the era of the Spanish Civil War.

As a poet, publisher, connoisseur of typography and founder in 1923 of the Nonesuch Press, Meynell was a natural associate of A. J. A. Symons, who ran the First Edition Club from 1922–31 and established the *Book Collector's Quarterly* (1930) before combining with André Simon, a fellow-bibliophile, to found the Saintsbury Club (1931) and the Wine and Food Society (1933). When Symons, now best remembered as the author of *The Quest for Corvo* (1934), established the Corvine Society, celebrating the memory of the curious Frederick Rolfe, Meynell attended their second dinner, held at the Ambassador Club. It was a remarkable occasion, not least because of the attendance of Maundy Gregory, the notorious honours-broker, but the guest-list was in many other ways distinguished and demonstrated the extensive overlap between the worlds of literature and gastronomy. Shane Leslie and Wyndham Lewis mixed with Vyvyan Holland, son of Oscar Wilde, translator of Escoffier's *Ma Cuisine* and later a member of the Saintsbury Club and of the Wine and Food Society's Council; with Ralph Strauss (1878–1924), biographer of George Augustus Sala and of Dickens and later a regular writer for *Wine & Food*, and with T. Earle Welby, editor of Swinburne and of Walter Savage Landor, and author of *Away, Dull Cookery!* (1932, a work singled out for praise by Bunyard

---

[13] Food, 2/6; Wine 5/-; service 2/6. By contrast, the Wine and Food Society's grand banquet at the Brighton Pavilion in 1934, marking the centenary of the death of Antonin Carême, cost its members 2 guineas.

in *The Epicure's Companion*) and of *The Dinner Knell: Elegy in an English Dining-Room* (1932), dedicated to André Simon.

Enough has now been said to indicate why it is not surprising that Bunyard was regarded so highly by the founders and other members of the Saintsbury Club and the Wine and Food Society. His wide reading equipped him admirably to write about wine and food, as well as about flowers and fruit, in a manner enriched by apt literary reference and quotation. Like André Simon, whose collection of early books and manuscripts relating to cookery constituted one of the more distinguished exhibitions staged by the First Edition Club, he had a very important working antiquarian library, and as one whose eye for good design led him to commission work from John Nash[14] for *The Anatomy of Dessert* and the Bunyard Nurseries' list of 'Vegetables For Epicures' in 1934 he had a natural affinity with those who, like A. J. A. Symons and Francis Meynell, were responsible for maintaining the highest standards of book production in England during the inter-war years. As an anthologist, in *The Epicure's Companion* (1937) it is striking to find Bunyard undertaking a very similar task to that attempted in the same year and with equally memorable success, by another member of the Council of the Wine and Food Society, Sir John Squire (1884–1958). A poet, and patron of poets, Sir John Squire has been described as 'a central figure in Georgianism':[15] he was also the founder and, from 1919–34, the editor of the *London Mercury*, where an advertisement for Bunyard's *Anatomy of Dessert* had appeared in October 1929.[16] His anthology, *Cheddar Gorge:*

---

[14] John Northcote Nash, RA (1893–1977). One of Nash's other patrons, Horace Annesley Vachell (1861–1955), novelist, writer and contributor to *Wine & Food*, had much in common with Bunyard. Vachell's *The Best of England* (1930), with wrappers by Nash, was an appreciation of 'hunting, shooting, fishing, racing, cricketing, golfing, sight-seeing, wining and dining [and] country house visiting', while his best-selling *This was England: A Countryman's Calendar* (1933), described itself as 'a pilgrimage through the by-ways of yesterday, through the England that used to be, with its flowers and fields and trees and birds, with its legends, stories and fables, its quaint customs and folk-lore' (title).

[15] *Oxford DNB*.

[16] A regular contributor to the *London Mercury* was Martin Armstrong (1882–1974). Like Sir John Squire, he was closely involved with Walter de la Mare, Edmund Blunden,

THE EPICUREAN CONTEXT

A Book of English Cheeses (1937), with illustrations by E. H. Shepard, is as much a monument to literary epicureanism as *The Epicure's Companion*. The writer and critic Osbert Burdett,[17] author of the entry on Double Gloucester, had contributed (with Edmund Blunden, T. S. Eliot, Edith Sitwell, A. J. A. Symons and Rebecca West) to *Tradition and Experiment in Present-Day Literature* (1929). Oliver St John Gogarty (1878–1957), who wrote on Irish cheeses, was a friend of Augustus John, James Joyce and W. B. Yeats. Henry Stevens (Leicester) was the compiler of *Book Auction Records*, and Ernest Oldmeadow (1867–1949, Caerphilly) was noted as a writer on music and 'an expert on frugal cookery'.[18] The novelist and writer Horace Annesley Vachell (1861–1955) contributed the entry on Cheddar, while Cheshire cheese was appraised by Vyvyan Holland, translator from the French of Henri Barbousse's *Stalin: A New World Seen Through One Man* (1935). Moray M'Laren, author of *Return to Scotland: an Egoist's Journey* (1930) wrote on Dunlop, and Ambrose Heath and André Simon, notwithstanding their differences of opinion about the conduct of the Wine and Food Society, contributed respectively on Wensleydale and Blue Vinny. Simon also contributed two pieces to Bunyard's *The Epicure's Companion*, on 'Recent Bordeaux Vintages' (pp. 314–6) and 'Thirst and the Law' (pp. 474–8).

Although there can be no doubt that Bunyard found the urbane and prosperous milieu of the Wine and Food Society profoundly congenial, it is also clear that his origins as a practical nurseryman ensured that he

---

and other 'Georgian' poets. He also took a critical interest in book-production: his *Selections from Jeremy Taylor* (1923) was published by the Golden Cockerel Press, and his *Saint Hercules* (1927), with illustrations by Paul Nash, was published by the Curwen Press. Author of *The Major Pleasures of Life* (1934), he reviewed *The Anatomy of Dessert* in the *Saturday Review* (14 December 1929) and became a close associate of Bunyard. He contributed five pieces to *The Epicure's Companion*: 4 poems on wines (pp. 251–4, 282–3) and 'Spanish Holiday' (pp. 479–82).

[17] Burdett's other published works at this point included *A Little Book of Cheese* (1935) and *The Art of Living* (1933), an idiosyncratic discourse embracing Wine, Food, Dress (including Thoughts on the Corset), the Character of a Tory, Manners, Literature and the Art of Prose, Architecture, Local Museums, Travellers' Tales, Bonfires, the Savour of Eccentricity, Over-Beliefs, Fun, the Art of Persuasion and Anniversaries.

[18] *Oxford DNB*, 'André Simon'.

never made the mistake of confusing connoisseurship with mere opulence. Indeed, some of his most eloquent writing was devoted to demolishing this illusion: 'Bread and cheese are good things and can be enjoyed on the lee side of a haystack as well as anywhere – and if you want to know where the best cheese can be got don't ask in the suburbs, ask Hodge in the farmyard – *and* the best bacon – *and* the best beer!'[19] It is certain that, when perusing a work like Dorothy Allhusen's *Unusual Savouries* (1935), he would have been more interested in the recipe for Welsh Rabbit, contributed by the Duchess of Wellington, than in the editor's more fanciful offerings 'in these cocktail days, when savouries are so much in demand'. In the list of works recommended by Lorna Bunyard, EAB's sister, for 'The Kitchen Bookshelf' in *The Epicure's Companion*, it is similarly significant to discover that although space is found for *Au Petit Cordon Bleu* (1936), a reference work produced by Dione Lucas and Rosemary Hume, who had set up the prestigious cookery school of that name in Sloane Square in 1935, it was placed alongside other works of a rather different nature. *Good Things in England* (1932), advertised itself as 'a practical cookery book for everyone's use … containing Traditional and Regional Recipes suited to Modern Tastes contributed by English Men and Women between 1399 and 1932'. Its compiler was Florence Louisa White (1863–1940), author of *Flowers as Food: Receipts and Lore from Many Sources* (1934), who had founded the English Folk Cookery Association in 1928 in conjunction with Alice Bertha, Lady Gomme (1853–1938). In 1936, Florence White established her own Domestic Training School, or House of Studies, at Fareham, and in the same year she published *Where Shall we Eat or Put Up?* This included an eloquent summary of the highlights of English domestic cuisine: 'a roast pheasant with celery sauce and English salad sauce; a boiled pheasant with celery sauce. The correct way of making a Lancashire Hot Pot with oysters and serving it with home-made pickled red cabbage. The stuffing of grouse with red whortleberries. The jugging of hare and serving with redcurrant jelly. The making and frying of sausages.' Such a vision would have delighted both EAB and Lorna (who insisted that 'simple native cookery', with nothing 'beyond the powers of the good plain cook' could add 'unending zest to adventure on a motor tour in England

---

[19] *The Epicure's Companion*, p. vii.

and Scotland').[20] Accordingly, *The Epicure's Companion* also recommended *Farmhouse Cookery* [1936] by Mrs Arthur Webb, and *The Scots Kitchen* (1929) by F. Marian McNeill (1885–1973), a journalist, sometime Vice-President of the Scottish National Party, and, like Lady Gomme, a prominent folklorist and former suffragist. It is certain, too, that Bunyard would have welcomed the steady publication of local recipe books, such as those for Cornwall (1933), Gloucestershire (1936) and Westmorland (1937), produced by County Federations of Women's Institutes. For him, such diversity was part of a much grander vision.

Beyond the limits of epicurean circles, the wider context in 1937 was already ominous. Unlike those who preferred to ignore realities, or pretended that gastronomy might still be practised with a ration book, Bunyard had no illusions about the seriousness of the situation. In the preface to *The Epicure's Companion* he complained that 'the most depressing sign of these days is the placid acceptance of the second-rate … the deadening influence of machine-made things.' The remedy was clear: 'we must hold on at all costs to our freedom of choice wherever it still remains to us.' Left at that, Bunyard's words might be seen as conventional enough: the commonplace grumblings of a St James's Street bore. However, that was not all. 'This mental attitude of freedom', he continued, 'cannot, I fancy, be maintained in one thing and abandoned in another. Gradually closing down on us comes the view that "Father knows best", "father" being the dictator of the day, whether political, literary, artistic, or any other self-appointed parent. To this appalling threat I answer, and I am sure many with me: "*I know best what I like.*"'[21]

Much was at stake. 'The epicure … will be first of all an individualist … [with] … a curious and inquiring mind … , a joyous person, as he will find so much of interest in this inexhaustible world of ours … He will not eat his dinner without a word of gratitude … In short, he will be a civilized man.'[22] Looking at the prospects for civilization in 1937, Bunyard found optimism difficult. In spite of eventual victory in 1945, his work still speaks to us today.

---

[20] *The Epicure's Companion*, p. 526.
[21] *The Epicure's Companion*, p. vii.
[22] Ibid.

CHAPTER SEVEN

Edward Bunyard the Epicurean Nurseryman

JOAN MORGAN

Edward Bunyard has enjoyed enduring fame as the fruit connoisseur who brought alive the colours, perfumes, textures and, above all, the flavours of fruit in his acclaimed celebration, *The Anatomy of Dessert*. This evocative and unique account of the diversity and subtleties to be found in the complete range of temperate fruits then grown in England continues to guide the fruit-lover and gardener in their choice of the most flavoursome variety, although the book was published as long ago as 1929. Bunyard's reputation rests on this literary treatment of fruit, but he was no amateur: he was the pomologist of his era, studying the botany, history and cultivation of fruit, and author of one of the bibles of fruit research, *A Handbook of Hardy Fruits*, which remains a key text. His talents extended beyond fruit to vegetables and ornamental plants: Bunyard was also a distinguished rosarian whose repopularization of old 'European' roses through another of his well-known books, *Old Garden Roses*, kindled a passion for these treasures of

---

In the preparation of these chapters I thank my son, Dr Morgan Clarke, for much help. For many discussions and information, I thank Tom La Dell and Dr Alison Lean; also Edward Wilson, Hugh Pudwell, Brian Self, Dr Brent Elliott, Dr Ken Tobutt and Robert White. My thanks are due also to Simon Brice, Bill Chowings, Dr Peter Dawson, Sir Garth Doubleday, Nick Dunn, Rev Edmund Hatton, Dr Judith Scheele and my son Dr Parry Clarke; and to Tom Jaine for his skilful editing.

the past that continues to this day. His perceptive judgements of quality – whether it be the flavour of a pear, the form of a flower or the most desirable strain of a vegetable – gained him lasting renown for exquisite taste, to be relied upon in all matters pertaining to fruits, plants and gardening. His advice still pervades the literature. Equally, Bunyard delighted in good food and wine and produced an engaging and authoritative book on the pleasures of the table, *The Epicure's Companion*.

Bunyard's scholarship and expertise gained him a prominent place in the horticultural establishment, most notably the Royal Horticultural Society in London, Britain's premier horticultural organization. As a member of its Council and a number of committees, he played an influential role in the Society's affairs, but he was also active in the wider spheres of scientific and commercial horticulture, directed towards helping fruit growers meet the new challenges of international trade. The Society, on the other hand, provided Bunyard with the companionship of plant enthusiasts and in particular of book collectors; tracking down rare books was one of his greatest interests throughout his life. Bunyard's magnificent library, which he began collecting as a young man, now forms the heart of the RHS's world-renowned collection of works on fruit. The Society also provided a fellowship of many like-minded devotees of every aspect of good living, a pastime to which he was increasingly drawn during the 1930s.

All Bunyard's achievements in the literary world, his promotion of fruit, his academic work in pomology, his role as a trend-setter in the field of roses and dedicated committee man depended on the fact that he was first and foremost a commercial nurseryman, raising and selling an exceptionally wide range of fruit trees, roses and other plants. As head of the Maidstone family business during the 1920s and 1930s, he made the name Bunyard a byword for fine quality and the source of the most desirable stocks, while the nursery supported and fostered his eminence as pomologist, gourmet and rosarian. The nursery was always a pivotal force in his life and Bunyard was promoting the nursery and searching for fresh gems to include in its lists right up to his death.

******

In his career as a nurseryman, Bunyard was tutored by his father, George Bunyard, a towering example of an industrious, self-made, successful businessman. George Bunyard had the good fortune to profit from the fundamental changes that occurred in fruit growing for market at the end of the nineteenth century, when the modern British fruit industry was founded. Fruit became of great commercial importance and also triumphed on the most fashionable dining-tables as the dessert of fresh fruit, the grand finale to the formal dinner: a position that fine fruits had enjoyed since antiquity, but which was at its zenith in Victorian England when, with the advent of glasshouse technology and ample funds, the challenges of our climate were overcome and every type of fruit from temperate to tropical, from apples to pineapples, was grown in the gardens of large country estates. The turn of the century was in many ways the glorious swansong of this splendour, when economic interest and connoisseurship combined to greatest effect. These leisurely and deliberate tastings of an array of the most perfectly ripe fruits, delicious morsels at the close of a meal, were the inspiration for Edward's writings, which he tailored to the mood of the inter-war years.

The Bunyard Nursery came to prominence in the 1890s, a time of opportunity for nurserymen. The revolution in transport brought an unprecedentedly high demand for fruit trees from market growers as the new railway network stimulated an expansion of orchards in traditional counties such as Kent, one of the main fruit-growing centres for the London markets, and allowed new areas to find an outlet for the more profitable fresh fruit, rather than turning their apple crop into cider. Improved transport also led to increased competition from abroad. Continental fruits, for centuries English growers' main competitors, were now joined by apples from New York, Boston and Halifax, as the eastern United States and Canadian industries developed and exported vast quantities to Britain. The barrels of bright, attractive apples captured the markets to the extent that English producers feared they would be completely overwhelmed. Growers across the Channel were protected by import duties, but the British government's free-trade policy, designed to help its manufacturing industries, did the fruit farmers no favours, although competition galvanized everyone into action. A 'Fruit Campaign' was launched to 'beat the Yankees' and demonstrate to the public, through exhibitions, shows and congresses, the quality that could be grown in England's much-maligned climate. The historic RHS National Apple Congress of 1883 launched the campaign, which made apples the stars of shows of the 1890s.[1] For several years Cox's Orange Pippin was voted the finest flavoured variety of all, so beginning the English love affair with Cox. The campaign was also Edward's initiation, during his teenage years, into the complexities of the vast selection then cultivated in gardens and grown for market.

The apple became our national fruit, discussed over dining-tables in as much detail and with as much passion as the claret, not only because it was the focus of attention in the market place as English apples struggled against the foreigners, but also because it was seen as the salvation of British agriculture. Mainstream agriculture suffered a long depression from the 1870s up to the First World War due to a combination of factors – bad harvests, disease in cattle and, not least, competition from cheap prairie wheat and imported frozen meat. Landowners and farmers looked for other crops to supplement their incomes and, especially, invested in fruit. By the end of the century every county grew fruit and the major areas of the new fruit industry had been established: in Kent the area under fruit doubled; the traditional cider counties – Hereford, Worcester, Gloucester, Somerset and Devon – invested in fresh fruit; new plantations emerged in East Anglia; and market gardeners' orchards expanded everywhere, especially in the Thames Valley and the Vale of Evesham.

Changes in garden fashions were also encouraging the planting of orchards and fruit gardens. Designers, especially the followers of the Arts and Crafts movement, had looked for their inspiration to Tudor and Stuart England, where walled enclosures filled with fruit trees and flowers typified, it was believed, a truly English style, in contrast to the reviled Italianate terracing and massed parterres of the high Victorian era. At a time of rapid technological change, they recalled a quieter age, in which the apple was perceived to be quintessentially English: now alarmingly threatened by extinction. Not only was a large fruit garden or orchard deemed an essential part of a country dwelling, but apple trees became decorative as well as

---

[1] For a brief survey of English fruit growing from the late nineteenth century up to World War II see Morgan, J. and Richards, A., *The New Book of Apples*, (London, 2002), chapter 5, pp. 105–135.

useful, recommended for planting in shrubberies, sited as specimen lawn trees, trained over arches to form a tunnel of fruit, or used to create the backdrop to a flower border. Artistic orchards underplanted with spring bulbs were in vogue. Gertrude Jekyll, a leading exponent of the new, more natural styles, advocated garlanding old apple trees with roses. Every aspect of the apple tree became of interest, even its blossom.[2] Naturally, it became the most important fruit for the Bunyard Nursery. The new gardening aesthetics also influenced Edward's own values as a plantsman and, in particular, as a rosarian.

Bunyard's Nursery was in the centre of the most active and forward-looking county at a time when a good nurseryman could hardly go wrong. George Bunyard, a man of energy and drive, capitalized on these changes to satisfy all potential buyers. The new market growers' needs were different from the nurseryman's traditional best customer – the large estate garden. Commercial growers needed a reliable selection, not the great range and successions of varieties grown for the country-house dining-table. George Bunyard shrewdly provided 'profitable' apples, as well as traditional favourites. Although he publicly marked a century of the nursery's history in 1896, the year Edward was welcomed into the firm, the business had been set on its feet in 1880–81 by an order for half a million fruit trees and bushes for the Toddington orchards of Lord Sudeley in Gloucestershire: the largest fruit complex ever seen, with its own railway connection and jam factory. Toddington orchards had invested heavily in Bunyard's new apple, which was renamed Lady Sudeley in 1885: it was said its showy, red skin was reminiscent of her ladyship's dresses at court. Bunyard's also launched Allington Pippin, originally South Lincoln Pippin but renamed after their new nursery, and Gascoyne's Scarlet, raised by a fruit grower near Sittingbourne, both widely taken up by fruit farmers.

Like a number of nurserymen, George Bunyard published widely. With *Fruit Growing for Profit* in 1881, he subscribed to the rationalization of fruit varieties; while he kept diversity alive in *The Fruit Garden* of 1904, written in collaboration with the royal head gardener, Owen Thomas. His guidance to every sort of customer did not stop there. Other books touched on the rose (*England's National Flower*, 1904), and larger specimens (*The Planters' Handbook of Hardy Trees and Shrubs*, 1908). But fruit made the nursery's

---

[2] Ibid., pp. 95–98.

reputation and this he celebrated in all its splendour in *The Fruit Garden*, which covered every candidate – from apples and pears to grapes and even citrus fruits and pineapples – for the fresh-fruit dessert. Fashionable as ever, he highlighted apple varieties with striking flowers and included an evocative photograph of spring bulbs growing in a grassy orchard at blossom time.

'Tall and gifted with a fine presence, endowed with great ability as an organiser', George Bunyard's achievements were outstanding and he became a member of the innnermost circles of the fruit and horticultural worlds, honoured with every accolade that could be bestowed. He was elected to the RHS Council and was among the first sixty recipients of the RHS Victoria Medal of Honour (VMH), its most prestigious award, inaugurated in 1897 to commemorate the Queen's Jubilee. He was made a freeman of the City of London in recognition of his part in the Guildhall Fruit Show of 1896. This was one of many in which George Bunyard played a prominent role in his capacity as chairman of the RHS Fruit and Vegetable Committee and as a member of the Worshipful Company of Fruiterers, the fruit producers' and sellers' livery company.

By the early 1900s, the Maidstone nursery was one of the largest in the country, selling 'From the Garden of England … 800 Kinds True to Name' – that is, varieties correctly labelled and what they claimed to be – of apples, pears, cherries, plums, cob nuts and all the soft fruits. The business had begun close to the town centre but, as Maidstone developed and their own trade expanded, George Bunyard bought land nearby in Allington, which he built up to nearly 300 acres. It was an ideal site, with deep, light, fertile soil that could produce his prime objective – good quality trees with a well-developed root system and plenty of healthy growth. The ground was on a gentle slope, encouraging any frosts to roll away rather than settle and damage the young plants and the fruit blossom.

The nursery occupied the land to the right and left of the London Road (now the A20), leading into Maidstone.[3] It was skirted by the railway line and extended along to Barming station where, in faded lettering, you can still see painted on the gable-end of the station master's house the sign,

---

[3] 'The History of the Bunyard Firm; from 1796 to 1911', privately printed and dated Maidstone, 1911; see pp. 30–31. See also Ordnance Survey maps for 1908 and 1933/36.

'Alight here for Bunyard's'. A lodge was built at the entrance to the nursery and opposite, on the land to the left of the London Road, a reception area for customers was developed. Bunyard's owned other parcels of land around Maidstone and retained a shop in the town centre. On the edge of Penenden Heath, near to the Chiltern Hundreds public house, they had some 70 acres of strawberry fields and other crops, and were sending fruit to market as well as raising plants. There were further plots of ground close to the shop and a small nursery in Bower Mount Road attached to the family home.

Their main production ground for raising fruit trees and ornamentals was the Allington nursery, where there were also extensive glasshouses for tender plants and fruits – grapes, peaches, nectarines and figs. From Allington tens of thousands of trees were sent all over Britain and even across the globe. It is tempting to imagine that Barming station, which is a mile or more from the village of Barming, was specially sited for the nursery's convenience in the dispatch of goods and reception of customers. From this little fiefdom, George Bunyard took promotional exhibits of fruit up to London and to other shows from Aberdeen to York and Chertsey to Oban. He even went in 1887 to Hamburg and, as he proudly boasted in the nursery catalogues, received the 'only Gold Medal given to a British Trade Exhibit'.

The Bunyard Nursery's head office and shop was on the Broadway in Maidstone at the junction of the London and Tonbridge roads, near Maidstone West railway station. Boldy advertised by a ten-foot high metal sign, it was a landmark that everyone knew and could not fail to see, at least in the 1930s, as they crossed over the Medway. Here they sold plants, cut-flowers, seeds, bulbs, books and horticultural sundries, such as tools, insecticides and fungicides, including their own patent remedies – 'Bunyard's Tar Oil Wash', 'Lime Sulphur' and 'Uno Dust'.

******

When Edward joined the family firm in 1896, trade was buoyant. With his father in full control and confident that he could be spared, Edward was sent in 1900 to gain experience in France, where he also acquired his lifelong love of the country, its language, cuisine and wines. We may surmise that, following the usual practice, Edward was 'apprenticed' to one or several nurserymen during his stay, working and gaining practical knowledge of every aspect of the business. He may have been placed with one of the many nurseries based around Paris in the Île de France. This was also the centre of the luxury fruit trade, then at its height, where all the latest techniques to produce high-quality peaches and grapes, and also pears, cherries and apples were employed, bringing serious competition to London market gardeners. Belgium and Holland, important horticultural areas, may also have been on his itinerary. In 1901, after his return, Edward became a Fellow, that is, member of the RHS, where his father was a leading figure. He no doubt helped stage the nursery's exhibits at the RHS shows and began attending conferences and the formal dinners and banquets that always accompanied a Society event. Edward explored the more academic side of fruit, which was soon to become a consuming passion. Trips to the Continent continued in search of both items of interest for the nursery, and rare fruit books for his collection, which was developing into his favourite indulgence.

Even if Edward had wished for another career, it was unlikely that George Bunyard would have permitted his eldest (living) son to have done anything other than join the family business. Edward, being delicate, had been educated at home by a tutor, which left many hours of spare time to foster his love of literature. Edward's penchant for long hours of private study poring over fruit samples and reference books would suggest that, at the age of nearly 18, he might have preferred the opportunity to continue studying rather than immediately join the nursery staff. Something as unpractical as going away to university was clearly not on his father's agenda, and 1896 was a little too early to have considered enrolling in Kent's own agricultural college at Wye, some 20 miles away, although a number of local farmers' sons were among its first students.[4] Bunyard's was a family business and continued to be so under Edward's management, involving, in one way or another, most of those of his siblings who remained in Maidstone: his younger brother, Norman, and at least three of his five sisters. His eldest sister, Lorna, helped with Edward's books as she did with the leaflets and posters produced for the nursery in her father's time. Frances, the artist who illustrated two of George Bunyard's publications, also produced botanical

---

[4] The South Eastern Agricultural College opened at Wye in 1892, became one of the 'schools' of the University of London in 1898, and is now part of Imperial College. A degree syllabus for Wye College was agreed in 1903.

watercolours for Edward's books, papers and the nursery catalogues, to which another sister, Marguerite, also contributed. Edward, in turn, helped in his father's book on roses by taking the photographs and very likely contributing to the text.

In the early 1900s George Bunyard still held the reins, although in 1903 Norman, who was then 17, had probably also joined the firm when it was converted into a private limited company, with all the stock owned by the family. George gave the opening lecture to the RHS Conference on Fruit Growing in October 1905, on those varieties likely to cope best with foreign competition, and was not showing any signs of slowing down. In addition to, and perhaps to the exclusion of his nursery duties, he was an officer of the Worshipful Company of Fruiterers: in 1904 he became Renter Warden, then Upper Warden in 1905 and Master in 1906.[5] Not until his seventieth birthday approached in 1911 does he seem to have been stepping out of the limelight. A life-time of work was beginning to take its toll and 'though wearing well,' he now needed to 'winter carefully'.[6] Edward and his brother were given greater responsibility. In 1919 George died, a victim of the influenza epidemic. It was the end of one era but under his sons' management the nursery remained at the forefront of horticulture.

******

Edward Bunyard, as one of the up-and-coming fruit experts, had achieved public recognition in 1912 when he was invited to give a keynote lecture at the conference which accompanied the Royal International Horticulture Exhibition. This drew contributions and displays from all over Britain, the Continent and the furthest corners of the Empire. Bunyard covered the developments in fruit over the nearly 50 years since the first International Horticulture Exhibition of 1866. He saw not too many changes in country-house gardens, where there were still small armies of gardeners and villages of glass houses producing grapes all year round. Although the growing of

---

[5] My thanks to R. S. Gothard, Hon. Archivist to The Worshipful Company of Fruiterers for this information.

[6] 'George Bunyard', *Journal of Horticulture and Cottage Gardening*, vol. 60, 1910, p. 197.

pineapples had faded with the influx of good imported fruit by the end of the nineteenth century, peaches, grapes and figs would be ready for Easter and successions of the choicest apples and pears ripened from late July right round to May. The major development in fruit lay with market growers, in the husbandry of orchards and the improvements in the appearance of fruit on sale, but Edward feared demands for heavy crops were inevitably going to overshadow the merits of quality.[7]

The following year, Edward began to make his mark on the nursery's public image when he took charge of producing its catalogue. It proudly displayed a picture of the Shropshire Cup the nursery had won at the 1912 Exhibition as the frontispiece. Meanwhile, his other careers as scholarly pomologist and committee-man were progressing rapidly. In 1911 he became a member of the RHS Library Committee and in 1913 joined the Fruit and Vegetable Committee. He was writing papers, giving lectures, building up notes and records for his *Handbook*, while opening his long connection with the gardening press on all matters to do with fruit, thus keeping the Bunyard name in every gardener's mind.

Edward was not called up for military service because of his health; he later recounted a 'tardy convalescence' under the care of a 'devoted nurse', although we do not know when this occurred.[8] Neither his health nor the war halted his writing or research, and the nursery continued to exhibit at RHS Shows, although these were reduced to one- rather than two-day events. The war years did, however, prove difficult. Demand for fruit trees was inevitably reduced and there were probably manpower problems. The nursery business calls for many hands to graft or bud the trees, care for them, then lift, package and dispatch them. The staff, which stood at over 100 in 1910,[9] must have been severely depleted. Nursery workers were not exempt from military service, and by 1917 a third of the country's work-force was in the army or navy or employed in munitions factories. The nursery's problems were compounded by the need to increase British food production as German submarines took their toll on the supply ships and the country could no longer depend on imports. Food rationing was

---

[7] Bunyard, E. A., 'Fruit', *The Horticultural Record* (London, 1914), pp. 153–162.

[8] Bunyard, E. A., *The Anatomy of Dessert* (London, 1933), p. 195.

[9] 'George Bunyard', op. cit.

introduced in 1917 and grassland compulsorily ploughed up for corn and potatoes. Some of the nursery land was taken – Bunyard commented in 1919 that 'the necessity of producing food has caused a great decrease in the number of fruit trees raised.'[10]

With the death of their father in the January of 1919, they had lost their guiding hand. Edward, and Norman when he returned from the army, faced some trying years before the nursery was at full capacity again. In the catalogue of 1921, they 'thank many of their customers for their forbearance in the unavoidable delays and disappointments during the past few years. ….. We regret that the supply of fruit trees has not yet anything like reached demand and it cannot do so for many years, as many of the trees take some three to six years or more to produce.' Nevertheless, they were still capable of staging a Gold Medal-winning exhibit at the RHS Great Autumn Show in October 1919, when the nursery made the grand gesture of introducing the 'Bunyard Silver Cup', awarded annually for the most promising new apple or pear.

From his first encounters with French and Continental horticulture in his prentice years, Bunyard would have appreciated the benefits that accrued from contact with fruit experts in other countries. In England, however, there was no forum for sharing this specialist knowledge, even of progress made in the country's own, recently established, fruit research institutes. Bunyard was nothing if not a man of action. Accordingly he began publishing in 1919, at the nursery's expense, *The Journal of Pomology*, to keep the whole fruit community abreast of developments at home and abroad. He did not miss the chance to advertise the nursery: the *Journal* opened with a picture of the apple, Maidstone Favourite, which Bunyard's had introduced. He featured notes on a number of pears that the nursery was promoting and closed with an advertisement for his forthcoming work, *A Handbook of Hardy Fruits*, published the following year. The *Journal* and the *Handbook* belong with Bunyard's pomology studies to which we will return later, but in all his writings he never lost sight of his main task, the success of the nursery business.

At some point between 1908 and 1910, 'The Bungalow', which became Bunyard's home, was built in the midst of the orchards at the Allington

---

[10] Bunyard, E. A., ' A Pomological Pilgrimage', *Journal of Pomology*, vol. 2, 1921, p. 58.

nursery site. In its garden were 'interesting trees and shrubs', a collection of ornamental apple and pear species, with a range of glasshouses close by.[11] At the Bungalow, probably from 1922, he was looked after by William Buss, whom Bunyard described as his 'man servant', although Buss considered himself the butler and chauffeur. Buss, who, one imagines, was the son of the nursery's foreman Frederick Buss, drove Bunyard everywhere and acted as his general factotum, keeping his clothes brushed and shoes mended and polished. Buss's wife, Ada, was Bunyard's housekeeper and an excellent cook preparing wonderful food, if Bunyard's later writings can be taken as evidence of her prowess at Allington. Life at the Bungalow appears to have been cosy and quite intimate. The Buss family lived in the Bungalow or in an extension; Buss's daughter was born in the Bungalow, went to school from there and learnt to play the piano on Edward's instrument.[12]

Edward Bunyard remained a bachelor. Surrounded by fruit trees and roses, free from the commitments of wife and family, he studied and cultivated his hobbies. He was a talented pianist and a keen photographer from an early age, owning perhaps one of the fashionable Leicas. Bookshelves were plentiful to house his expanding library and there must have been cupboards, or perhaps a cellar, for his burgeoning wine collection.

An expansion in the scope of the business under Edward's management was indicated at its headquarters in the centre of Maidstone – although no change was made to the name, which continued as George Bunyard & Company Ltd. *The Gardeners' Chronicle* reported the double-fronted shop proclaiming 'in big gold letters the nature of the business, which is made to include that of pomologists',[13] thus bringing Bunyard's research, his careful work on fruit identities and variety evaluations contained in the *Handbook*, within the nursery's remit and substantiating their claims to sell the best, 'true to type'.

---

[11] 'Nursery Notes, An Afternoon with a Pomologist', *Gardeners' Chronicle*, vol. 82, 1927, p. 213. See also Ordnance Survey map 1908, which shows a small building on the site of the Bungalow, but the first reference I have found to the Bungalow occurs in *Kelly's Directory* of 1910, when the resident is E. A. Bunyard.

[12] My thanks to Nick Seymour, grandson of William Buss, for information on his grandfather and grandmother.

[13] 'Nursery Notes', op. cit.

The post-war years brought a fresh set of circumstances for the nurseryman. The demand for fruit trees from commercial growers soon returned, but there was renewed foreign competition as well as changes in the social circumstances of many potential customers.

Fruit production had not been interrupted during the war, but rather the reverse: with restricted imports, everything home-grown became valuable, irrespective of quality, and the Bunyard Nursery must have made money out of their orchards. After the war there were no longer guaranteed prices, competition from imported fruit returned with a vengeance and growers once again had to address the question of quality. A renaissance was seen to be underway by the mid-1920s, with renewed demand as market fruit growers responded to advice from the new government research institutes and planted new orchards. They bought fruit-graders and built stores to produce the quality required by the Ministry of Agriculture's Nation Mark scheme introduced in 1928.

Even good English produce, however, faced severe challenges. Exotics such as bananas, oranges and canned pineapple were imported from the Empire, and temperate fruits from the southern hemisphere fulfilled out-of-season demand from late winter until summer. In the 1920s and 1930s, the British Empire, then at its largest extent, was seen as the motherland's salvation. Its economic development was encouraged, ties were strengthened and the short-lived British Empire Board (1926–33) promoted all Empire goods, including fruit. The British market, in particular for apples, was a battleground in which American and Continental imports fought it out with those from the Empire. Home-grown produce struggled to stay in the field at all. Such competition was encouraged by the launch of the 'Eat more Fruit' campaign by Liverpool shippers in 1923: seized upon by the fruit trade in general as a means of encouraging fruit consumption. The Imperial Fruit Shows, held in a different city each year, were shop windows for home-producers and importers of Empire fruit. 'Fruit is stored sunshine' was the slogan, promoting apples as health-giving, simple and easy to prepare. As further encouragement, the policy of Imperial Preference imposed import duties on non-Empire goods in 1932. This did not entirely stop the challenge posed by North American apple varieties, whose bright colours caught the public's attention. Although American imports were penalized, American varieties were now being planted all over the world and, using the opposing seasons of the southern hemisphere, a trend began towards the continuous availability of a single variety almost all the year round. Jonathans were Bunyard's particular *bête noire*, which although attractive were almost flavourless.

All these factors influenced English fruit development and the way nurserymen focussed their promotion. The business remained highly competitive, with many more fruit nurseries than today. Bunyard's main rivals were the Thomas Rivers' Nursery in Sawbridgeworth, the giant of the Victorian era, and Laxton Brothers in Bedford, headed by Thomas Laxton's son. Laxton's made the breeding of new fruits its speciality. There were also Cheal's in Crawley, Seabrook's in Chelmsford, Allgrove's in Slough, Cranston's in Hereford, Scott's in Merriott, Somerset, Pearson's and Merryweather's, the introducers of Bramley's Seedling, in Nottingham and many others, each seeking to capture a portion of the market and battling to find their own niche.

An expanding market lay with the commercial fruit growers, boosted by the government's encouragement to 'Eat more Fruit'. Bunyard's continued to supply farmers with trees of their signature varieties, such as Allington Pippin, grown in Kent and elsewhere. Also a popular exhibitors' apple at the autumn fruit shows, it was so well known that the playwright and author Eden Phillpotts composed an ode to Allington Pippin. Gascoyne's Scarlet remained a commercial variety, as did Grenadier, which they had first promoted in 1883, and widely planted in the 1920s and 1930s. Another Bunyard introduction, Ben's Red, for a while rivalled Worcester Pearmain in orchards.

Bunyard's were important cherry tree producers for Kent farmers, who also grew plums, gooseberries and currants alongside apples and pears. Cobnuts were another Kent speciality, together with strawberries. However, there was increasing competition. Seabrook's was successful during the inter-war years and an important supplier to growers, especially in Essex. Wholesale nurseries which supplied the horticultural trade also sold direct to growers.[14] The best known, producing the main varieties by the thousands, were Brinkman's, a Dutch family with a business at Bosham in Sussex, and Frank

---

[14] For information on the wholesale nursery trade my thanks to Andrew Dunn, Director of Frank P. Matthews Nursery and son-in-law of Frank Matthews.

Matthews', today's largest fruit-tree nursery, then at Hayes and Harlington in Middlesex. Competition also came from across the Channel, where Holland had always been, and remains, a major producer, causing Bunyard to preface the catalogue of 1927–8 with the following: 'In view of the importation of plants from abroad, we would ask purchasers to remember in comparing prices that it is values which should be first considered. The stock, the hardiness of growth (not to be obtained in plants grown on Peat soils), accuracy of nomenclature, are some of the factors of value.'

While market growers were satisfied so long as they could buy good quality trees of the right varieties, the private garden presented a rather different scenario from the pre-war years. At the top end of the trade, on larger estates, gardeners carried on much as before, furnishing perfect fruits for the dining-table and writing gardening columns on how to look after the vinery, peach house and herbaceous border. However, the 1920s saw the rise of the owner-gardener, in charge of all developments on his or her demesne, although often continuing to leave the fruit and vegetables in the hands of the head gardener. Some families, of course, were suffering the loss of their sons in the hostilities, others from the burdens of wartime taxation and staff shortages; but fortunes had been made during the war in shipping and armaments, sufficient to preserve a flourishing demand for exciting new varieties and old favourites.

The post-war years also saw the rapid increase of gardening as a hobby, a weekend suburban pastime, as well as the emergence of the middle-class housewife in charge of culinary matters, no longer able to call on cooks and servant-maids who had found better employment elsewhere. Both the leisure-gardener and the housewife were looking for some domestic luxury after years of restrictions and shortage. Cookery books written by society hostesses and fashionable restaurant owners offered practical solutions and inspiration; while foreign travel, now far easier, broadened English horizons. For the gardener, instructions and encouragement poured from magazines and manuals designed for the amateur, who found extra stimulus from local flower and produce shows.

Fruit was democratized: more readily available, within the average middle-class budget, no longer a privilege of those with large gardens and a staff to match. Yet the middle classes were acquiring that age-old badge of upward mobility, a pleasure garden and its consequent aspirations. New suburban villas were modelled on country houses with their multiplicity of rooms and large gardens, offering plenty of space for a line of trained cordon fruit trees against a fence, espaliers to separate the vegetables from the flowers, and even room for a couple of large standard trees. Their owners needed careful guidance, however, to gain an appreciation of home-grown fruit, especially in the face of competition from tinned pears, peaches, plums, cherries, as well as fresh and canned exotics.

******

Bunyard's Nursery was ideally placed to take up the challenges, as it had been in the 1890s. It was in the centre of the most forward-looking fruit-growing county, now with its own fruit research station at East Malling near Maidstone. It was also in the prosperous south-east, accessible to thousands of suburban villas being built within commuting distance of London, each needing plants and advice to develop their gardens. Edward directed the nursery so as to attract all potential customers, but especially these new amateur gardeners. He masterminded its promotion through the catalogues and the many shows at which Bunyard's staged an exhibit, while his brother Norman seems to have borne most of the burden of running the business.

Most nurseries like Bunyard's sold a range of traditional apples such as Blenheim Orange, Ribston Pippin and, of course, Cox's Orange Pippin, as well as newer introductions like James Grieve, Charles Ross, Ellison's Orange, Newton Wonder and Early Victoria. But other lists were not always as extensive as Bunyard's. Rivers', for one, promoted about half as many in 1935. Laxton's list, on the other hand, was as long, but each variety was not treated to so comprehensive a presentation. Bunyard was promoting each one of over 100 apple varieties as well as all the other fruits with an enthusiasm and style designed to appeal to the new leisure-gardeners. Rather than providing the barest details sufficient for the well-informed head gardener or commercial grower, Bunyard gave a rounded portrait of each variety, telling its story, pointing up its distinctive qualities, and guiding his customers in their choice in a more inviting fashion than his peers. He promoted the fruits as highly desirable epicurean treats, almost collector's items and, of course, many of the connoisseur entries were old varieties.

A nursery, however, always has to come up with new acquisitions, something exciting and tempting for the forthcoming season. One of the best routes to novelty was to raise your own new varieties which, if successful, brought exclusivity. Other sources of new stocks were either amateurs who had planted a pip and raised a good fruit, as in the case of Bramley's Seedling, or head gardeners who might be breeding in a more systematic way – this is the origin of Charles Ross. Both were looking for nurserymen to take up their seedlings. A third route was to rejuvenate old varieties, Bunyard's favoured approach. In many ways this followed naturally from his bookish and scholarly proclivities. Bunyard later remarked that 'all novelties are not new, some of them are old plants lost to most gardens and rediscovered by some enthusiast's sharp eye and so reintroduced to our gardens. …Very much the same thing, I believe, happens in ladies' fashions.'[15]

Edward or his father 'discovered' Orleans Reinette, an old Continental apple, mixed up in a basket of Blenheims that had been sent in for identification. Realizing that it was a different variety, it was introduced as Winter Ribston in 1914, but later under its true identity with the tribute that it 'cannot be too highly recommended … and … must be placed in the best six apples.'[16] This connoisseur's choice, aromatic and nutty, was endlessly promoted by Bunyard at committee meetings, shows and in articles for the gardener, but its often dull appearance and erratic crops would not make it a commercial money-spinner. The tiny golden Pitmaston Pineapple with a 'honey-musk' quality had also been received in a box of apples for naming from Llandrindod Wells.[17] It had originally been brought to notice by the amateur fruit enthusiast John Williams of Pitmaston, outside Worcester, in the early nineteenth century and was reintroduced by Bunyard's in 1927 as 'nearly lost to cultivation … with the surety that all amateurs will appreciate the remarkable flavour.' The pear Emile d'Hyest was rescued from semi-oblivion and became widely planted through the efforts of Bunyard, who also repopularized Egremont Russet, now everyone's idea of a 'russet' apple.

---

[15] Bunyard, E. A., 'Plant Hunting at Home', BBC radio broadcast made on 16 July 1939. My thanks to Alison Richards, formerly of the BBC, for obtaining copies of the broadcasts.

[16] 'Apple Winter Ribston', *Gardeners' Magazine*, 9 Jan. 1915, p. 19.

[17] 'Fruit Notes', *Journal of Pomology*, vol. 1, 1920, p. 141.

This direction taken by Bunyard was in strong contrast to that of his main rivals. Laxton's were introducing a stream of new varieties with little suggestion of Bunyard's epicurean slant in their promotion, although they did name one of their apples Epicure. Laxton's still sold many old varieties, but their trade-mark was their own new ones. In the case of apples, these combined the exciting colours of American fruit, such as bright red Wealthy, with the aromatic quality of the best English apple, the Cox, to give Laxton's Fortune, for example. There were many more which found a ready sale, from Laxton's Superb apple, to Beurré Bedford pear, Laxton's Delicious plum, and many strawberry varieties to follow Thomas Laxton's lasting success, Royal Sovereign. Such introductions sold at double the price of established varieties. At the outset, they were exclusive to Laxton's – which must have given them a decided financial edge over Bunyard's. Laxton's was almost the only successful fruit breeder in the inter-war years; varieties raised at the research institutes were not introduced until after the Second World War. Bunyard's had no tradition in fruit breeding and Edward showed no inclination in that direction. Maidstone Favourite, a chance apple seedling that arose on the nursery at Allington is the only variety they could claim as their own.

The Rivers' Nursery, which boasted '205 years reputation' in 1930, was continuing to capitalize on its earlier successes – Early Rivers and Czar plums, Early Rivers cherry, and Fertility and Conference pears, all raised in the nineteenth century by the great Thomas Rivers and his son. Rivers' also specialized in fruit trees in pots and citrus fruits for growing under glass in a large airy orchard house, the invention of Thomas Rivers, and were resting on their laurels with their grandfather's many peaches and nectarines. Neither Rivers' nor Bunyard's had any new 'profitable' varieties for fruit farmers under development and, while Seabrook's were promoting their latest addition, Monarch, and Allgrove's were pushing the Reverend W. Wilks, Edward relied more and more on rediscovering old ones.

Another way to expand your lists and gain publicity was by introducing new fruits or varieties from abroad, although there was always the risk they might not thrive in the English climate. Bunyard had discovered this early in his career with the 'salicina' plum, also known as Japanese, Californian or Cape plum, which appeared in English markets as South African imports.

Bunyard trialled them at Allington by 1914.[18] Originating from the Chinese plum, but introduced from Japan, *Prunus salicina* was developed by Luther Burbank, the Californian fruit breeder, as a 'shipping' plum capable of withstanding the journey across America. Its firmer flesh made it more suited to long-distance travel than the conventional 'European' plum. Bunyard may have wished to introduce it to a wider public but as the 'salicina' plum flowers very early, it is usually damaged by spring frosts. The nursery could only recommend it for the orchard house. European cultivation remains restricted to southern France, Italy and Spain although the Burbank plum and more modern varieties have almost overwhelmed English plums in shops and markets.

A successful nurseryman needs to balance his love of plants against the necessity to produce marketable stocks. Rare gems are expensive indulgences if no one wants to buy them, and Bunyard was probably a victim of his own enthusiasms. He found it difficult to restrain his collecting instincts. The unfortunate 'salicina' plums were still on sale in 1939. He was also offering the Chinese cherry (*Prunus pseudocerasus*) which, because it flowered very early, was similarly confined to a glasshouse. It did have the compensation of prolific crops and, although small, was welcome 'as … the first fruits ripening in a cool orchard house.' The nursery supported collections of all the fruits used by Bunyard in his academic studies; indeed, in the case of the strawberry, far more – over 80 varieties – than the number offered for sale. Similarly there were over twice as many cherries in his collection as listed in the catalogue and over 200 gooseberries as compared with about 30 advertised.

Bunyard continued to be adventurous, introducing many European stars, in particular apples: Belle de Boskoop, which he had seen successfully growing in Holland and Luxemburg in 1920; Reinette Rouge Étoilée, Belgium's beloved favourite; and Transparente de Croncels, popular in northern France on account of being one of the few varieties that survived the great frost of 1879. The nursery brought in varieties that became international celebrities. One was the red-skinned Delicious apple from America – until recently the most widely planted apple in the world. Its

---

[18] Bunyard, E. A., 'The Japanese or Cape Plums', *The Garden*, 14 March 1914, p. 135.

drawback was to need warmer summers than England could provide: 'after 15 years' trial we think this is not an apple for England' concluded the catalogue of 1935. Canada's famous McIntosh, with its brilliant red colour and snow-like flesh, was deemed 'well worthy of trial'; but it was too soon to pass judgment on Granny Smith, offered for the first time in 1939 as 'this favourite Australian apple'. It sold at 5/-, double the usual price but 'many may wish to try its suitability for this country'.

In 1926–27, Bunyard introduced what could have been an enormous coup, the infamous Golden Delicious, with the following comment: 'This American apple is probably the most highly advertised fruit of modern times. A book has been published in its honour and all the Liberal professions of America have sung its praise. We think therefore that our customers may like to try this variety, which we offer for the first time in England.' Golden Delicious can be good, sweet and perfumed as Bunyard says, but it became the epitome of the commercial apple in the most disparaging sense – undeveloped and unripe as witnessed in the French imports of the 1970s. It has never gained a footing in English farmers' orchards, where its crop cannot match those of France and warmer countries, but Bunyard might still have had a winner on the Continent, if not in England. Bunyard was unlucky, yet the irony of its history would surely have amused him.

The diverse selection of other fruits that Bunyard's sold included new, larger quinces from the Balkans; a mirabelle, the small French plum of jams, liqueurs and tarts, which sadly has never caught on in England; and a German quetsche, the heavy-cropping cooking plum. But Bunyard's selection of the best-flavoured varieties of all fruits remain on every fruit lover's wish-list to taste and to grow. That he caught the public's imagination at the time is evident from the varieties that arrive nowadays for identification, at centres such as Brogdale, from orchards planted in the inter-war years, especially in Kent and the south-east. With samples of Orleans Reinette, Claygate Pearmain, Ross Nonpareil, Roundway Magnum Bonum, Pitmaston Pineapple and occasionally Reinette Rouge Étoilée and Transparente de Croncels, one can imagine a Bunyard catalogue at work in the background.

******

RHS Shows were the nursery's main advertising forum: exhibits were staged, catalogues displayed and orders could be taken. Exhibitions and shows were part and parcel of the horticultural world: a social event and a public demonstration of excellence in garden plants, and to an extent also commercial crops, by nurserymen, market growers, head gardeners from large country estates, and amateur enthusiasts of more modest means. The fortnightly RHS London shows held in Vincent Square consisted of exhibits, mainly from nurserymen, and competitive classes centred on seasonal flowers, fruits and vegetables. Through the year there were other events – Chelsea Flower Show in May, and the Autumn Show at Holland Park, Crystal Palace or Olympia. Rarely did the Bunyard Nursery miss an important show or fail to gain a prize; the office at Allington must have been covered in award cards and the drawers filled with medals. The aim was not only to show off the breadth of the nursery's stock and highlight the newest acquisitions, but to secure the coveted Gold Medals which, then as now, boosted the nursery's prestige. This required perfect fruits: well coloured, evenly shaped, blemish free and correctly named. A certain artistic flair was also needed to fill the space with interest, yet without over-crowding the exhibit.

Bunyard clearly had a talent for display. In 1925 the Bunyard stand at the Autumn Fruit Show in early October won not only a Gold Medal, but also the Society's highest award, the Lawrence Medal, for the best exhibit staged throughout the year. This was usually awarded to floral exhibits, although vegetables gained it several times in the inter-war years, but Bunyard's was the only fruit exhibitor to capture the coveted prize. The winning display was of apples and pears 'arranged in ornamental baskets, of which the majority were elevated on stands, with a central pyramid of Apples crowned with hanging baskets containing the richly coloured Lady Sudeley Apple and other hanging baskets were filled with the brilliantly-coloured Ben's Red. …The group was decorated with Ferns, Crabs and Nuts.'[19]

The nursery exhibited fruit throughout the year. In January 1927, at the first Vincent Square show, they began with a 'particularly meritorious collection' of 'sixty seven varieties of apples and pears'. There followed other displays, often of novelties or little-known varieties. Come the autumn, the

---

[19] 'Societies', 'Royal Horticultural', *The Gardeners' Chronicle*, 3 Oct. 1925, p. 278.

many possibilities for promoting apples and pears again returned. Another outstanding Gold Medal-winning exhibit was staged at the Holland Park Show in late September, followed in October by 'a very attractive display' of 'Apples, Pears, Grapes, Nuts, Plums and Crabs'. On 1 November, they staged another winner that drew ecstatic comments from the gardening press: 'Such an extensive exhibition is seldom seen on the show table, and probably not since the war has this firm – noted for its Apples and Pears – staged such a wonderful exhibit.' Over 200 varieties were 'tastefully displayed, and in no single case was the quality below first class exhibition standard. Many of the varieties were little known to the public, but arranged in this exhibit each appeared to show some good quality.'[20]

Cherries, gooseberries, plums, and glasshouse peaches and nectarines had their turn in July and August when Bunyard was striving to make fruit a prominent part of the summer shows. He encouraged competitive exhibitors with the introduction of the Bunyard Medal in 1923, and the following year brought the Kent cherry-growers to London to help boost attendance. Bunyard's cherries were usually on display at the July shows, to be followed by large collections of gooseberries, and often an exhibit of as many as 60 plum trees in pots.

In many ways, Bunyard's greatest achievements were his early-summer exhibits at Chelsea Flower Show of 50 or more varieties of apples – when most home-grown apples were long past their best. They often gained Gold Medals. Chelsea was the occasion for nurseries specializing in ornamentals to shine, where the stars were rhododendrons and orchids, but it was one of the best opportunities to secure big orders. The cream of the gardening world attended: the large estate owners, with their head gardeners in tow, as well as less opulent home-owners eager to pick up the latest fashions in plants and place orders with reputable nurseries. Only the main fruit firms, Bunyard's, Laxton's and Rivers', exhibited at Chelsea. In May, however, Bunyard would have found it impossible to compete with Laxton's on strawberries, or with Rivers' orchard-house pots of peaches, nectarines and, often, citrus fruits. Nonetheless, it was essential to have an arresting exhibit, and a display of English apples in May was certain to gain everyone's attention. Even Bunyard's friend,

---

[20] 'Societies', 'Royal Horticultural', *The Gardeners' Chronicle*, 29 Jan. 1927, p. 80.

fellow Library Committee member and Harley Street physician, Dr Fred Stoker, confessed to not knowing 'that it was possible to have English apples from August until May.'[21] For these exhibits, Bunyard used fruit from their 'Fruit Room', a store that had gained them the Shropshire Cup in 1912 and many other prizes over the years. It was kept, according to a small notice, 'without ice or other artificial cooling'. This made it clear that the fruit had been maintained in pristine condition, not by the use of the new refrigerated stores recently introduced to Kent fruit farms, but in natural conditions. Bunyard's 'Fruit Room', introduced in 1884–5, was a trade mark. It resembled a thatched cottage, and was designed to keep fruit in a cool, equable temperature throughout the winter by virtue of its thick walls, insulated with cork and thatch. Plans of the 'Fruit Room' were sold by the nursery and it became popular with owners of country houses. Built examples are still to be found.

An important message underlined these Chelsea exhibits. They demonstrated that there were plenty of English apple varieties that would keep until springtime and beyond, at a time when Empire fruits from the southern hemisphere were pushing the late varieties out of private and commercial orchards. Bunyard's stocked many of these late-maturing apples and pears, which they exhibited at the winter shows in Vincent Square, but Chelsea was an even better place to promote their virtues.

The effort required for shows was immense. Fruit needed to be picked with painstaking care to ensure perfect samples, although plenty of spares would be necessary on the day. Fruits would have been taken from the store and packed in boxes, each one separately wrapped. To stage a large exhibit would take several people all day and into the night. Judging took place in the morning before the show opened. In the 1920s and 1930s, at Westminster, Chelsea and other shows, the nursery was staging both fruit exhibits and displays of irises, Norman's speciality, for which they also received a number of medals. Herbaceous plants were often exhibited too: one year, michaelmas daisies; 'hedging plants, screen trees and shrubs' to coincide with the Conifer Conference of 1931; and roses, Edward's particular interest by the late 1930s. The cost in time, labour, stress and

---

[21] Stoker, F., 'Notices of Books; "The Epicure's Companion"', *The Gardeners' Chronicle*, 27 Nov. 1937, pp. 397–398.

money was high, but necessary if Bunyard's was to keep up with the formidable competition. Not only Laxton's and Rivers' staged spectacular displays of fruit, but Allgrove's in Slough were frequent Gold Medal winning exhibitors, as well as Cheal's in Crawley. To an extent, it was also expected that a member, not only of the RHS Fruit and Vegetable Committee but also of Council, which Bunyard had become in 1923, would support the Society in this way and thus promote and encourage high standards.

Capturing customers did not stop with the shows. Visitors were welcome at the nursery, where they could see and taste an array of fruits in season, as well as view roses, herbaceous plants and shrubs. The vineries, peach and nectarine houses and orchard houses were open for inspection. Various forms of apple trees could be seen, such as cordons and espaliers, and it seems likely that the one-hundred-foot pergola of trained pears, called 'Beauty and Utility Reconciled' in the catalogue, was growing at Allington. The nursery dispatched parcels of fresh fruit 'at the customer's own risk'. Like most firms, it also offered a number of services: 'Mr E.A. Bunyard will (as time permits) endeavour to name fruits of all kinds for customers' and, no doubt, they could obtain on-the-spot advice on how to prune and care for their fruit trees.

Bunyard's gained an international clientele. George Bunyard had boasted of 'the many Colonial Governments, as well as County Councils and the Trade that had bought stocks from the Nursery.' According to the catalogues of the 1930s, it could dispatch consignments to North America, South Africa, India, Australia and New Zealand as well as Europe. Skilled packing of dormant plants would have been necessary for them to survive the months of sea voyage, and there was the problem of the reversed season. A customer in South Africa told Bunyard that 'when he opened the crate the trees were all in full flower – "a beautiful sight. ... We planted them out and they all had splendid crops that year." ' Trees sent to Island Port, West Newfoundland, had to be planted before the soil had thawed out, but no harm was done.[22] In a letter to *The Times* in 1933, Bunyard wrote of a customer in Nova Scotia who was ordering trees from Allington rather than America, on grounds of cost, however, not exclusivity.[23]

---

[22] Bunyard, E. A., 'Late Planting', *Gardening Illustrated*, 28 Feb. 1931, p. 128.
[23] Bunyard, E. A., 'Ottawa and After', letter to *The Times*, 24 Feb. 1933, p. 10 d.

Edward Bunyard's own reputation was an important nursery asset. By the 1920s, he was not only the country's leading pomologist and author of the definitive work on the subject, but also a well-known and prolific writer of popular articles, blessed with an ability to dash off a few hundred words whenever required. He was writing both under his own name and, I suspect, anonymously and under the pseudonym 'Pomona', after the nursery's telegram address – 'Pomona Maidstone'. It was surely Bunyard alias 'Pomona' writing in the *Gardeners' Chronicle* on 'Some Useful Late Apples' in 1925, and who else would have concluded a piece in its 'Fruit Garden' series in 1927 with that familiar phrase – 'Orleans Reinette is, I consider, one of the best six dessert apples'? At the same time, he was shamelessly promoting his new introductions, even Golden Delicious which had been launched the previous year. He contributed to the column 'The Fruit Register' under his own name and as 'Pomona', advertising his 'rediscoveries' such as the old Duchess's Favourite, and Mrs Phillimore, introduced by the nursery in 1900.[24] He had probably begun his clandestine writings many years before with a 1904 piece on quinces in *Flora and Sylva* credited enigmatically to 'B'. It is difficult to see who, other than Bunyard, would have written so knowledgeably about quince varieties, or known of quince marmalade made in Rye and that 'many an old pond in Kent and Sussex is fringed every autumn with its loaded Quinces.'[25] He never stopped writing – any excuse would turn a visit or a discovery into an article.

******

Running throughout Bunyard's work as a nurseryman was his strategy of appealing to the aspirations of his customers. Britain was still class-ridden, despite some redistribution of wealth and the social change brought about by the war. Food and dining had become a particularly sensitive measure

---

[24] Pomona, 'Some Useful Late Apples', *The Gardeners' Chronicle*, 10 Jan. 1925, pp. 26–27; 'The Best Dessert Apples for Cordons', *The Gardeners' Chronicle*, 5 Nov. 1927, p. 371; Pomona, 'Fruit Register', *The Gardeners' Chronicle*, 10 Dec. 1927, p. 472; Pomona, 'Apples raised by the Late Mr. Charles Ross', *The Gardeners' Chronicle*, 6 Nov. 1926, p. 375.

[25] 'B', 'The Fruiting Quinces', *Flora and Sylva*, vol. 2, 1904, pp. 377–381.

of one's place on the social ladder. Many were the pitfalls waiting to expose the nuances of class distinction. In Bunyard's opinion, the middle classes fell between the two stools of snobbery and ignorance. While the upper classes were well catered for because of their money and the lower classes had local knowledge of where the best food could be found, the middle classes lacked good information.[26] Bunyard offered this in abundance. In his writings and the way he orientated the business he supplied direction: he sold the best-flavoured fruits, with lyrical descriptions of their taste and erudite notes on their provenance, marketing the whole as an epicurean feast with associations of refinement and high quality. 'His judgments were deliberate, shrewd and impersonal' a colleague later remarked,[27] suggesting this strategy was calculated to attract those looking for that extra gloss of 'real' quality and exclusivity associated with the upper classes.

The nursery business was a trade. But through adding this intellectual dimension to the marketing, he secured social advancement for himself, or at least ensured the high status of his father's name persisted. Class was always a sensitive issue for nurserymen, despite being large landowners and often leading figures in their local communities. At one point during the nineteenth century, the RHS had tried to exclude them from its council, though eventually conceding that it needed both nurserymen and head gardeners involved in its governance. There is a story told of an old Kent nurseryman in the 1950s who, when visiting a garden, never went there again if he was shown the tradesman's entrance. Bunyard, too, distanced himself from the vulgar necessities of trade when he remarked in 1912, that 'Any nurseryman who is worth the name is an enthusiast for his "speciality"; in tracing the development of any flower and fruit we are brought again and again in touch with such men who have made a hobby of their work.'[28] He may himself have erred too much in this direction for the financial good of the firm, but he was selling to just that sort of person: the lover of plants who was also a member of the RHS. After the First World War the RHS had pledged to support the horticultural trade and, in Bunyard's case, RHS members were probably his best customers.

---

[26] Bunyard, E. A., and Bunyard, L., ed., *The Epicure's Companion* (London, 1937), p. viii.
[27] Stoker, F., *Proceedings of Linnean Society*, 1940, p. 362.
[28] Bunyard, E. A., 'Fruit', op. cit., p. 156.

Bunyard founded his commercial strategy and the composition of his catalogues on fruit for the epicure who cared more about its eating quality than its cropping. This was often the reverse of the marketplace, but had always been the case at the country house. The luscious Kirke's Blue plum, for instance, was 'a rather shy bearer, but too good to omit on that account.' Early Sulphur gooseberry was 'indispensable'; and who would not like to have a tree of Thomas Rivers apples which, when cooked, uniquely retained an aromatic quality with a 'distinct pear-flavour and quince-like acidity'? The Thomas Rivers Nursery could only promote its own product in much more mundane fashion – 'very rich flavour, in fact requires no sugar when cooking'. Bunyard seduced his customers by combining inspirational anecdote with practical direction. The Louise Bonne of Jersey pear, he wrote, thrived 'under so many various and trying conditions that it will surely be found in Pomological Paradise.' This is Bunyard the purveyor of fine fruit to the discriminating. Claygate Pearmain was 'one of the indispensable dozen; Cox, 'without doubt the best flavoured apple'; and Margil, 'nearest to Cox in flavour … deserves the connoisseur's attention.' While the country house garden had space for a collection of 50 or more varieties, a dozen trees would still provide a choice succession for the suburban villa. Bunyard was selling the orchard of everyone's dreams.

As soon as Edward took over editing the catalogues in 1913, and more particularly after the 1918, their presentation changed. Instead of a cover busy with images, it became plain buff with simply the nursery name in stylish, embossed maroon lettering. The catalogues were elegant, with spacious, well-illustrated pages. Placed side by side with his peers' rather more routine lists and bright colour photographs, the Bunyard catalogues exude good taste and authority.

The catalogues aimed to attract a wider range of customers than was to be met at the London shows or locally. His pursuit of a stylish image was encouraged and influenced by Maidstone's many high-quality paper-makers such as Whatman's (Edward was the grandson of a paper-maker on his mother's side). A polished presentation was ensured by the services of the long-established printers Vivish & Baker, who had produced two of George Bunyard's publications as well as a number of his own. He experimented with different formats, at first larger, then reverting to the usual size for a very Edward-inspired reason: 'as our catalogue of Fruit Trees is valued as a work of reference we now adopt a size more convenient for bookshelves.' The 120-page main catalogue, combining fruit and ornamental plants, was almost double the size of that produced by Laxton's or Rivers'. He glamorized all the nursery's catalogues from 'Bunyard's Roses' to ornamental shrubs and trees, herbaceous plants, seeds, bulbs, strawberry lists, alpine and aquatic plants, and 'Bunyard's Irises'; the last three named being Norman's responsibility. The Bunyard catalogues can provide hours of dreamy pleasure, as they must have done for customers in the 1920s and 1930s. At the end of the list of currants, for example, is the advice to 'all gourmets to try the wedding of Black Currants and Rum a marriage [that], if not made in heaven, deserves celebration on earth. A teaspoonful of Old Jamaica to a dish of stewed fruit or tart is ample.'

Production of the catalogues was a family affair. His sister, Frances, provided watercolours of a number of fruit varieties, which were reproduced as black-and-white images thus accurately portraying their appearance and adding to the general tone of refinement. It is clear from the similarity in style to his father's book on roses, where Bunyard is credited as the photographer, that he also provided the pictures of charmingly posed roses and presumably of other ornamental plants. His sister Marguerite helped by making detailed notes on the colours of flowers, and provided from 1935 the unique feature of exact colour descriptions for the roses.

******

One should perhaps see Bunyard's literary output – *The Anatomy of Dessert*, *The Epicure's Companion* and the booklets entitled 'Vegetables for Epicures' as an integral part of his marketing strategy. *The Anatomy of Dessert*, Bunyard's loving tribute to the most exquisitely flavoured varieties, was an extension of the nursery publications that, as he said in its advertisement, 'allowed more space to be devoted to the important characters, flavour etc than a catalogue permits.' It may have been that Bunyard's literary friends encouraged him to develop his notes into a book, which was in draft form when his friendship with the novelist Norman Douglas began in 1922.[29] In London, he often enjoyed the company of the barrister and wine-writer, Maurice Healy,

---

[29] For Bunyard's friendship with Norman Douglas see chapter 3.

whom Bunyard had known since 1924, if not earlier. Healy later described sampling some Orleans Reinette with 'dear Edward Bunyard'. 'They were the most delicious apples that I have ever tasted, … and although I begged him shamelessly every year for a repetition of the favour, even his generosity was not able to grant my request. His trees more often failed him.'[30] The trials of an irregular cropper.

The Anatomy of Dessert, at first sight, resembled a slim volume of verse rather than a work on fruit: it was printed on thick, high-quality paper, elegantly laid out and prefaced with a line drawing by the well-known artist, John Nash. Not only beautifully produced, *The Anatomy of Dessert* was witty, full of charm and scholarship and raised its subject almost to an art-form. In this respect it belonged to a new style of the 1920s that the social historian Nicola Humble has identified for cookery books,[31] and which also included those about gardening. It offered, as did his catalogues, an entrée into the most privileged dining-rooms in the land at a time when markets were bringing uniformity and fruit was losing its exclusivity. Bunyard presented his subject in its most traditional and luxurious context, the dessert of fresh fruit. He evoked the pleasures of diversity in a setting of leisured contemplation, as the finale to a perfectly orchestrated dinner, or a quiet sampling in the privacy of one's own library or garden. The 'whole technique of gustatory appreciation', Edward explained, could not be hurried: first one should 'savour the various qualities separately and then the symphony as a whole.' The colour, the rosy glow on a peach for instance, its texture, juice and aroma all contributed to the delicious experience. As contemporary wine-writers dwelt on flavour distinctions and the celebrity of different regions and châteaux, so Bunyard talked of the complexities of fruit flavours. He discussed how these varied from variety to variety, often from year to year, and were influenced by the nature of the site. A reviewer in the *Countryman* wrote: the 'fourteen chapters are a very orchard of fruity wisdom, vintaged for the delight of a gourmet fruit grower and gardener'.[32]

---

[30] Healy, M., *Stay Me With Flagons* (London, 1940), p. 270.
[31] Humble, N., *Culinary Pleasures* (London, 2005), pp. 48–9.
[32] Quoted in Bunyard Nursery, 'Catalogue of Fruit Trees Roses Shrubs 1938–1939', p. 59.

Bunyard's standard of excellence required that every variety was savoured in its right season and at the point of perfection. The cherries would be so ripe that, as he says, 'they were fit to burst out of a bushel basket.' The pears would be superb – buttery and juicy, their sweetness balanced by lemony acidity and perfumed with rosewater or musk or other exotic aromatics. Naturally the apple, which 'for the English is King', was given the largest section in the book with a succession of varieties from the refreshing yet rich Irish Peach in August, to the complex blend of aromas of the autumn Cox and Ribston, nutty Blenheim Orange and the sweet-sharp, acid-drop flavour of Ashmead's Kernel in the new year. Among the plums, the Transparent Gage was incomparable: 'in it are blended all the flavours that a plum can give in generous measure. … Its French name, Reine Claude Diaphane, exactly describes its clear, transparent look; a slight flush of red and then one looks into the depths of transparent amber as one looks into an opal, uncertain how far the eye can penetrate.'[33]

At one level, these delights were at risk as varieties were rationalized and the public accepted 'foreigners'. But many wealthy homes continued to serve a dessert of fresh fruit. The RHS Fruit Shows and its Fruit and Vegetable Committee remained dominated by head gardeners of the Victorian 'school' all through the 1920s and 1930s; and Bunyard, in connection with strawberries, knew of 'a wealthy bourgeois of Mayfair [who] sends a car to his country seat each evening to bring these delicacies fresh to his table, in their season.' To preserve this aura of country-house privilege he advised never to let 'the butler's fingers intervene' between the picking and serving of peaches.[34] Bunyard himself presumably went out to his own glasshouse and picked them with no help from William Buss.

Bunyard treated the new exotics severely: the popular banana, for instance, was dismissed with disdain as merely farinaceous. Its death-blow to the dessert gooseberry – by arriving on the markets at the same time of year, the early summer – was much regretted. He stressed how in gardens the gooseberry could remain 'the fruit *par excellence* for ambulant consumption. The freedom of the bush should be given to all visitors.'

---

[33] Bunyard, E. A., *The Anatomy of Dessert* (London, 1929), p. 137.
[34] Ibid., pp. 93, 128.

Foreign apples such as the ubiquitous Jonathan were censured too. They were proof of widespread ignorance, even among the well-informed on most aspects of the pleasures of the table. This did not, of course, include fellow-RHS Council member Sir William Lawrence, who suggested that Bunyard should 'practice what he preaches; in the restaurant of the RHS there is virgin soil to be tilled, and it is surely not too much to hope that at the fortnightly meetings we shall find in that restaurant not Jonathan apples and Jamaican bananas but rather the best Nordic fruits in prime condition!'[35]

The decision to write a book about the dessert, Bunyard says, was because none existed, which was true. Tasting notes were buried amongst the fruit descriptions in the pomonas and manuals; while the selection and presentation of the dessert had always been the head gardener's preserve. Cookery books rarely contained information on the fruit for the dessert, which in the formal dinner followed the last offerings from the kitchen, the puddings, that is the pastries, soufflés, jellies and so on. There had been no book devoted entirely to the flavours of fruits, but it was a lacuna that he stylishly filled to captivate readers in literary and dining circles – 'One of the most fascinating books I have read for many a moon … a piece of literature destined to a very long life,' wrote the novelist E. V. Lucas in his review in the *Sunday Times*. And the book had a broader impact both on his business and the wider fruit community.

By the 1920s and 1930s, the term dessert was already changing its meaning. The English classification of fruit into dessert and culinary varieties had been introduced early in the nineteenth century but had no validity elsewhere. Dessert signified the best quality for fresh eating: fruit exclusively for the dining-table. By the 1920s dessert was coming to mean any sweet dish that followed the main course, as it does today, rather than specifically the finale of fresh fruit. Nonetheless, Bunyard's use of the term exalted the unique attributes of English varieties and home-grown fruits, when the shops were being flooded by imports. Bunyard had already written on the theme of the dimensions of flavour the previous year, and he continued to promote the idea of a succession of good quality fruits, which could only be gained

---

[35] Lawrence, Sir William, 'Notices of Books', 'Dessert Fruits', *The Gardeners' Chronicle* 26 Oct. 1929, p. 329.

from English produce. This was the message that he introduced into the new journal of the Wine and Food Society, founded in 1933, with which Bunyard was closely associated and where he found an appreciative audience

******

Bunyard's epicurean approach encompassed vegetables as well as fruit. In 1931, he launched a booklet entitled 'Vegetables for Epicures', which was issued annually until 1939. This was a fabulous production for what was no more than promotion of the nursery's vegetable seed list; a lavish presentation for humble sprouts and carrots. It had a different cover each year, which ranged from a simple title page to an image of a jolly chef and a cornucopia of vegetables drawn by John Nash, who had earlier provided the frontispiece for Bunyard's book. Another dash of class was given by the inclusion of introductory pieces from his contacts in the RHS and London dining scenes who were well-known writers and arbiters of taste in culinary matters.

That Bunyard should have chosen to give vegetables the epicurean treatment was not totally surprising. There had been a decade of interest in food and gardening circles. After the war, vegetables had played a more important role as dining fashion had shifted from many-coursed Victorian and Edwardian meals to simpler fare. This had been fostered by the experience of growing your own vegetables during the shortages of the war years and was encouraged in post-war cookery books. Vegetables occupied by far the largest section in, for instance, *The Gentle Art of Cookery* of 1925, written by Mrs Hilda Leyel, of *Herbalist* and Culpeper House fame. Her imaginative recipes and strong sense of the aesthetic pleasures of vegetables – to be served in their own right rather than as adjuncts to meat – presaged an increasing interest in vegetarian food. *Cantelope to Cabbage*, published in 1929, was devoted entirely to vegetables (given that melons grew on the ground), and was the second lively and influential cookery book written by the much-travelled Lady Alice Martineau.

Within horticulture and the RHS, where Bunyard was at the centre of affairs, vegetables were the subject of an ongoing debate surrounding the 'preposterous size and consequent coarseness of the vegetables usually found on exhibition tables, particularly at local shows', as Sir Austen

Chamberlain wrote in a letter to Council on 21 September 1920.'[36] He asked 'whether the influence of the Society could not be exerted to eliminate coarseness and to improve quality. The Society responded positively and promised that eminent chefs would be recruited to assist in making the awards. The vegetable men, however, argued that cottagers needed the largest size consistent with good quality. The squabble passed over but the question came up again in May 1928, when Godfrey Palmer sent 'A Memorandum on the Use and Abuse of Vegetables and Salads in England'. Although it was not discussed until November 1930, Bunyard, as a Council member, would have known of its contents, which took everyone to task, from the cottager's lack of information to the seedsmen's promotion of gigantic vegetables and the poverty of knowledge when compared with France.[37] Bunyard would have sensed that it might be an opportune time to give his seed list a boost, although 'Vegetables for Epicures' took it into another league. The support of F. A. Secrett, a Thames Valley market gardener, was a bolster to confidence. Secrett was the star-turn of the annual RHS 'Home Grown Produce' Exhibitions, launched in April 1933 as part of the government's campaign to encourage market growers who faced competition from the Continent and the Channel Islands. Secrett introduced the most advanced practices for forcing early salad crops and the tender vegetables that epicures sought. He soon made his views known on monstrous vegetables, suggesting that a new class be introduced into the show schedule with the aim of encouraging 'the growing of small sized delectable vegetables.'[38] The vegetable message was pushed home by lectures which accompanied the exhibitions. Bunyard, one imagines, through his contacts with wine and food writers, arranged for André Simon's lecture 'Unusual Vegetables' in 1938; and in 1939 Ambrose Heath gave a talk on 'Salads and Salad Making'.

Bunyard's decision to promote vegetables may have also been influenced by economic circumstances. The late 1920s and early 1930s saw fortunes lost on the stock market, causing many grand families to downsize to smaller homes and greatly affecting middle-class spending. Fruit trees,

---

[36] Elliott, B., *The Royal Horticultural Society* (London, 2004), p. 262.
[37] RHS Lindley Library, RHS Council Minutes, 25 Nov. 1930.
[38] RHS Lindley Library, RHS Council Minutes, 8 Oct. 1935.

perhaps, were not selling as well as usual. The early 1930s were described by one nurseryman as a time when 'a Bramley tree could be bought for sixpence.' Bunyard could have been looking for other areas to promote. Seeds had a broad market with a less expensive outlay in time and space for the nursery.

By gathering together 'a few vegetables that will appeal to those who prefer dining to exhibition,' Bunyard spoke to the connoisseurs and hooked into the current debate on size versus quality. He urged his customers to bear in mind that vegetables were 'at their best when cooked while still alive'; to follow the French gardener who cuts them when very young; and to remember that not every vegetable need be boiled.[39] Presented as a booklet for the discerning, it was nevertheless a platform for advertising Bunyard's own selections of seeds, such as Bunyard's Noisette Sprout, Bunyard's Delicate Carrot and Bunyard's Last Word Pea, as well as more unusual items such as Continental waxy potatoes, celeriac and fennel. Bunyard did not, of course, neglect his majority customers. The nursery's main seed list, a twelve-page illustrated booklet, continued to carry a wide range of varieties for every need, including the exhibitors' favourites – those that could achieve 'majestic contours', which 'like a race horse are a class apart admirable for their purpose.' Exhibitors who won prizes with such varieties as Bunyard's Scarlet Perfection carrot, Bunyard's Giant leek, or Bunyard's Exhibition broad bean (which remains a much-favoured show vegetable) would have their prize-money doubled by Bunyard's and suitable cards could be procured to advertise their source – the Bunyard Nursery.[40]

To maintain novelty each year, Bunyard began collecting vegetable seeds. After the initial acquisition these would have had to be bulked up before sale. Seeds of vegetables and flowers were, at that time, produced on farms around Colchester in Essex, where the dry climate allowed the seeds to fully mature. Bunyard's and other nurseries subcontracted their requirements to one of these Essex farmers. Obtaining improved forms of vegetables or new ones altogether took seedsmen all over Europe: northern Italy, the south of

---

[39] 'Vegetables for Epicures', 1931, pp. 1–2. Seven issues are held in RHS Lindley Library.
[40] See Bunyard's 'Seed Catalogue, 1938'.

France, Brittany and the Nantes region, Erfurt the centre of Germany's seed trade, Belgium, Holland and the big capital cities, such as Paris, Berlin and Amsterdam. They might to be able to beg or buy only a very small quantity of seed of a valuable new strain from the growers in, for instance, Brittany – who would not want to give away the advantage that they were enjoying at London's Covent Garden Market. Bunyard's frequent trips across the Channel to attend conferences afforded him opportunity to track down seeds as well as fruits. He also obtained new acquisitions from close friends and, no doubt, from American contacts.

In the issues of 'Vegetables for Epicures', the number and range of entries increased year by year. The novelties included the American lima bean: 'not so hardy as the Runners but are so excellent in flavour that a sheltered corner should be found for a few'; the Quintal d'Alsace cabbage, thought excellent for 'Pheasant au Choux' and an economical dish of 'Choux aux Pommes'; the attractive 'Labrador Kale which makes a low cushion-like plant – a vegetable pouf', which he offered 'through the kindness of that Emperor of Vegetables, Mr Beckett', his colleague on the RHS Fruit and Vegetable Committee; and from Barry Neame, owner of the well-known restaurant, The Hind's Head at Bray near Maidenhead, he obtained seeds of the 'excellent small African marrow' which made an 'admirable luncheon dish'. He branched out further to include really unusual vegetables, ones often praised by fellow-Council member Sir William Lawrence, such as Japanese artichoke, which was not in fact an artichoke but with a similar flavour and 'the most recent vegetable to gain wide acceptance'; Chinese cabbage, Pe Tsai; and the list of herbs increased to 'offer all those varieties likely to be wanted in the kitchen or still room.'[41]

Bunyard's portraits of the vegetables – based on trials at Allington – were a combination of cooking and gardening hints that would have attracted the ambitious housewife and the experimental gardener. His cook Mrs Buss must have been kept busy. Never more so than when salsify was on the menu. The preparation was a long business that he might have learned during his first visit to France from Marie, his landlady. It called for washing, steaming and then 'after the roots are soft, take each separately and wipe the skins with soft paper … early in the day if the roots are for dinner.'

---

[41] For comments on vegetable varieties, see 'Vegetables for Epicures'.

They could be heated in a good sauce or deep-fried – 'nothing is nicer as an accompaniment to roast fowl or guinea fowl.'[42]

'Vegetables for Epicures' drew appreciative letters from customers as well as requests for recipes. Bunyard fulfilled these, writing also as Rosine Rosat. He was keenly interested in every stage of the procedure and had maybe taken up cooking himself, although he does drop hints from time to time that Mrs Buss was mistress of the kitchen – artichokes 'should never be served when a small, restive staff is anticipating "an afternoon off."'

The introductory pieces from the famous names of London's smart dining-circles imparted extra glamour. It also hints at Bunyard's powers of persuasion, or his very wide sphere of friends. The first guest-writer, in 1932, was Marcel Boulestin, owner of one of London's most fashionable restaurants, Boulestin's at the top of Southampton Street in Covent Garden, which opened in 1926. Boulestin, who was a tireless advocate of good eating both at home and outside it, practised in his restaurant what he preached in his cookery books. He introduced the British to simple French bourgeois food, made with the freshest and highest quality ingredients, such as Bunyard had experienced on his first visit to France. That he contributed a piece suggests Bunyard's acquaintance was more than that of an admiring reader, but rather of a frequent customer at the restaurant. Boulestin had other horticultural connections, however, and had collaborated in 1930 with 'Jason Hill' in *Herbs, Salads and Seasonings*. Jason Hill was the pseudonym of Dr Frank Hampton, a psychiatrist whom Bunyard also knew well, since they judged roses together for many years. Whatever the link with Boulestin, the Frenchman supported Bunyard in condemning 'gouty carrots and obese marrows', advocating diversity, using the correct variety for a particular dish, and dismissing 'this mania for tastelessness, that rage for standardization which is bound to end, gastronomically in dullness, that is in disaster.'

Lady Alice Martineau, who provided the introduction in 1935, would have been known to Bunyard through her cookery and gardening books and as a member of the RHS – she showed Jamaican oranges to the Fruit and Vegetable Committee on one occasion. She enthused over Bunyard's innovations: 'Mr Bunyard has proved that the Lima bean, another exquisite vegetable from America, can also be grown here' although, it has to be said,

---

[42] 'Vegetables for Epicures', 1937, p. 4.

not reliably. Since moving back to England from California, she had missed the meaty, crimson American tomatoes, but now these were available as the Ponderosa variety of Bunyard's list. This included another favourite – Orache Blonde 'looking like a golden spinach', with a 'most delicate flavour' which 'never bolts in hot weather.'

Others responded to his call. His friend of many years, the cider and perry authority Dr Herbert Durham, praised his skills in 'sifting out for the diner' the best strains and varieties. Durham, in return, had provided Bunyard with seeds of a small 'Russian' cucumber 'the size of a trowel handle' to be served with 'chopped Dill, Vinegar and Oil'. And in 1939, André Simon, as President of Wine and Food Society, exalted the need to search for the best variety of a particular vegetable.

His promotion of vegetables took many forms. The results of his potato trial in October 1932, along with an exhibit of salad potatoes, were displayed at the RHS Show at Vincent Square. This last reinforced the nursery's claim to be the only British firm offering both 'floury' and 'waxy' to cater for both schools of potato-lovers. English taste was for floury, but French cooks favoured firm, yellow-fleshed, waxy tubers – 'unequalled for frying' as well as salad. Of these he sold four varieties including Kipfler, with a mysterious history: 'a Viennese variety known to all who dined or lunched with the regretted Mme Sacher.' At the RHS Fruit and Vegetable Committee, he brought up lima beans for inspection, as well as neglected vegetables such as Welsh onions. Here, he was joined by Sir William Lawrence in highlighting unusual ones, such as 'Purple leaved Sorrel and Hibiscus sabadariffa [okra]', which his gardener grew in the tomato house. Bunyard also wrote much on peas, onions and other vegetables in the gardening press and for the journal of the Wine and Food Society. He even made vegetables the subject of his talk to the Horticultural Club in 1934. After surveying the history and prejudices that have surrounded some of our best-known vegetables, he ended with the call for 'a spirit of adventure in the vegetable garden', reminding his audience of the current success in France of the Japanese artichoke – his own latest introduction.[43]

Remarkably, vegetables came first in his chapter 'Gardening for Epicures'

---

[43] Bunyard, E. A.,'The Introduction of Vegetables', *The Gardeners' Chronicle*, 3 March 1934, pp. 148–149.

in *The Gardener's Companion*, edited by Miles Hadfield in collaboration with Bunyard, Jason Hill and other garden writers in 1936.[44] Bunyard 'opens the door to the new Garden of Epicurus, a garden not only of fruits, but also of vegetables'. Encouraging exploration of the varieties, just as he had done with fruit, he wrote that cabbages 'have their "prerogative and ranks" as Athenaeus knew in olden days.' The text was an extension of the booklet and featured his prized introductions: lima beans, African marrows and potatoes 'for keeping "new" all through the winter, Kipfler, the Viennese favourite.' It was, no doubt, Bunyard who selected the pieces for the accompanying anthology, including an extract from an article very likely written by him on the quince in 1904. *The Gardener's Companion* was published by Dent as part of a series of Companion books. They must have been pleased with his contribution since the next year, 1937, Dent produced Bunyard's own guide to the art of good living – *The Epicure's Companion*.

******

Bunyard wrote that 'the most depressing sign of these days is the placid acceptance of second rate.' A disregard of quality in pursuit of modern convenience was unacceptable, a sentiment echoed by Sir William Lawrence who commented that the English had become 'a people that count petrol more precious than Pears and would have arterial roads rather than Apple trees.'[45] Nevertheless, food had become a subject of wide interest. Scores of books about cookery, wine and food in general, as well as magazines, had been published. West End restaurants were a focal point of London social life, while food was now acceptable as a topic of sophisticated conversation. In the opinion of the wine connoisseur André Simon, the generation that had revelled in nightclubs, cocktails and jazz in the 'Roaring Twenties' was now in a position to appreciate the finer points of life.[46]

---

[44] Bunyard, E. A., 'Gardening for Epicures', in Hadfield, M., Bunyard, E. A., Hill, Jason, Giffard Woolley, R.V., and Daglish, E. F., ed., *The Gardener's Companion* (London, 1936), pp. 14–23.

[45] Bunyard, E. A. and Bunyard, L., ed., op. cit., p. vi; Lawrence, Sir William, op. cit.

[46] Simon, A. L., *The Art of Good Living* (London, 1929, 2nd edition, 1930), pp. 14–15.

The epicurean Bunyard – 'one to whom a flavour on the tongue is as important as the air he breathes and infinitely more deserving of advertisement'[47] – found plenty of scope for providing a life-line to an audience sometimes lost in the maze of social niceties associated with entertaining and dining-out. *The Epicure's Companion* was written and compiled with his sister Lorna. A compendium of ideas rather than recipes, arranged as a menu from oysters, fish, meats, vegetables and cheese, to fruit, wine, cider and spirits, it was the complete guide to dining. It drew on both their experiences at home and abroad, particularly at Paris markets and, in Lorna's case, in Geneva and Berlin.

Bunyard trotted out once more his account of the seasonal dessert as well as a discourse on vegetables, but he also dealt extensively with wine (even helping his readers with phonetic spelling), meats and cheese. Lorna covered soups, fish, sausages and baking. His sister Marguerite, who had visited India, provided information on spices, while Frances Bunyard supplied the illustrations. The book was rounded out by an anthology of literary extracts on the matter of food, chosen by Lorna and Edward and a number of 'After Dinner' essays written by friends from the Wine and Food Society. The versatile Bunyards abounded in knowledge and good counsel and 'are indeed the epicure's Good Companions', concluded a lengthy review in *Wine and Food* by K. Kinninmont, who had already renamed it 'the Bunyard book'.[48]

The Bunyards' call to arms included Edward's immortal words on the apple pie and English cooking apple.[49] The uniquely English 'cooker' developed by the Victorians was a large, sour apple (of which hundreds of varieties existed), which cooked easily into a juicy, brisk purée, flavoursome enough to need no further embellishments and specially selected for traditional puddings. Today, alas, the only well-known example is Bramley's Seedling. Culinary apples were ideally suited to baking whole and serving simply with a little cream; they made a smooth, savoury apple sauce for

---

[47] Stoker, F., 'Notices of Books', 'The Epicure's Companion', *The Gardeners' Chronicle*, 27 Nov. 1937, pp. 397–398.

[48] Kinninmont, K., 'The Epicure's Companion', *Wine and Food*, vol. 16, 1937, pp. 70–72.

[49] Bunyard, E. A., and Bunyard, L., ed., op. cit, pp. 155–158.

goose and pork; and were perfect for apple dumplings and apple pie, the pride of the English kitchen. But English puddings and apples were under threat from Americanization and other foreign influences. Elsewhere, apples tended to be multipurpose. Eating apples were used for cooking but, being much less acidic than proper 'cookers', held their shape. The American apple pie had chunks of apples to spike with a fork and the essence of the French 'Tarte aux Pommes' was its carefully arranged slices of cooked apple. These foreign apples made poor substitutes in an English pie, Edward trumpeted, for they had 'not learnt the art of collaboration. Their idea is a confection of stewed wood holding its own against any crust.' Bunyard railed against the caterers' apple pie made probably, heavens above, with imported Jonathans. Yet there was a succession of choices for every need among the many varieties that were in danger of being forgotten and even lost. The early codlins, such as Keswick Codlin, were just right for baking, rising up into a juicy fluff like a soufflé, but too insubstantial for a pie. Golden Noble in late September and on into October and November fulfilled all the criteria for an apple pie, 'golden before and after cooking … and every way delectable'. Then came Bramley's Seedling, planted in their thousands during the 1920s and 1930s, but pushing out Wellington, also known as Dumelow's Seedling, which, like Bramley, kept its acidity right through to the spring: remaining brisk and full of flavour with a 'crisp translucency quite ideal for pies'. Bunyard ends with a resounding call to readers to reject 'any vicious travesty of a pie' they might be served in a restaurant: 'Send back such vile mockeries' that resembled 'a mess of apples crowned by a slab of paste looking like an anaemic dog biscuit, but without its nutriment.'

Edward was an outspoken defender of our fruit heritage and a brilliant advocate for diversity, but he never lost sight of his main objective – the success of the nursery, which of course sold a wide selection of 'cookers'. His writings, his prize-winning displays at the London shows, his engaging catalogues and, from 1937 to 1939, his broadcasts with the Radio Gardener, C. H. Middleton – which included contributions on 'Apples for the Epicure', novelty vegetables, and roses – ensured that the nursery remained in the public eye. He succeeded in maintaining the family business at the leading edge of the nursery trade, not only because they sold a great range of high-quality plants, but because of his marketing flair and imagination. In modern terms, Bunyard branded his product perfectly for his target market, capturing the mood of the times by combining the traditional and the aspirational. He added credibility through his well-known professional expertise and his genuine and enthusiastic love of his subject. Edward was undoubtedly a versatile and talented nurseryman, despite his eventual personal financial problems. After his death, the nursery continued under his brother's management but did not survive into the next generation. If it had, Bunyard's would now be everyone's favourite fruit centre.

Following the Second World War, as Britain sought to increase home-grown produce, commercial orchards expanded and their needs dominated the nursery trade. The most successful fruit nurseries were wholesale businesses producing trees of a small number of varieties. Few of the well-known names of the interwar years were able to keep their large and varied stocks and remain profitable, or even continue, during the years 1960–1990. Now we have come full-circle. Large-scale commercial orchards have diminished, especially in the last decade and particularly in Kent. The English apple industry has gone into decline under the pressures of global trade and the particular demands of large supermarkets. With fruit farmers no longer major customers, wholesale nurseries have diversified into the gardening sector and greatly expanded the number of varieties they offer. Specialist fruit nurseries with very extensive lists have emerged. They cater for the widespread interest in recovering past diversity and for renewed enthusiasm for the home orchard. Fruit has gained a place on many agendas, from conservation of varieties and landscapes to regional foods and health. The environmental charity Common Ground has embraced orchards, launching in 1990 the now annual 'Apple Day'. Local societies have formed devoted to rescuing their regional fruits and planting them once more in community orchards. Smaller fruit farms producing good traditional and modern apples for local markets are thriving. 'Heritage' has become one of the most valuable assets in marketing. A range of fruits and varieties such as Bunyard's and their contemporaries sold is the goal of many nurseries both here and around the world. Edward's wisdom, and his emphasis on home-grown produce in its right season, is more than ever appreciated. Not only are *The Anatomy of Dessert* and *A Handbook of Hardy Fruits* invaluable guides, but the Bunyard's Nursery catalogues are also sought-after works of our best-loved fruit connoisseur.

CHAPTER EIGHT

Edward Bunyard the Pomologist

JOAN MORGAN

Edward Bunyard always styled himself a pomologist, thereby revealing his true vocation, the study of fruit. Bunyard's fruit studies, although not as well known as his literary output, were an outstanding contribution to British pomology and he was by far the most active figure of the twentieth century in this field. Doubtless he would have preferred to spend most of his time among his fruit trees and books rather than running the nursery from day to day. Nevertheless, this did support the large collection that formed the basis of his *Handbook of Hardy Fruits*, a directory to all the fruits grown in Britain which remains an essential part of every pomologist's library. Bunyard's collection, probably the most extensive in the country, allowed him not only to bring the records up-to-date but also fostered his particularly rigorous and meticulous approach that advanced the whole subject. His breadth of learning and lifetime of experience underpinned substantial contributions to the development of the fruit industry and made him a key figure in the creation of Britain's National Fruit Collections: the world's largest collection of temperate fruits growing on one site, in Kent.

As a young man Bunyard did not immediately direct his scholarly energies towards the detailed examination of fruit varieties, but was caught up in the major advances in biological sciences occuring at the turn of the century. Bunyard's first excursion into the more academic aspects of fruit, and into print, may have come soon after he joined the family nursery. He claimed to have made a brief report to the Royal Horticultural Society's International

Conference on Hybridization in London in 1899. This had been staged at the instigation of the biologist William Bateson, then secretary of the Royal Society's Evolution Committee. He believed that evolutionary studies could gain from the experience and knowledge of practical plant breeders. He urged the RHS to encourage its Fellows – amateur enthusiasts, gardeners, botanists and nurserymen – to make accurate records of their successes and failures. An appeal was sent out and record cards made available. No doubt it was one of these that Bunyard completed.[1]

At the Third International Conference on Hybridization and Plant Breeding in 1906, again in London (the second had been in America), Bunyard gave a paper on the same theme, entitled 'On Xenia', a Greek word meaning 'foreign' or 'guest'. In this case it referred to the pollen from one variety of apple which had fertilized the blossom of another variety and the effects this might have on the subsequent fruit. He also experimented with other plants. This question continues to be debated.[2] Bunyard was not the only son of a distinguished nurseryman to speak at the conference. H. Somers Rivers spoke about his breeding of peaches and nectarines, work initiated by his grandfather Thomas Rivers; and William Laxton described the new path that he and his brother Edward were taking in raising hardy fruits, following in the footsteps of their father Thomas Laxton.

This introduction to horticultural conferences was at two historic events that launched the new science of genetics. In 1899 the essence of Mendelian inheritance was expressed in certain conference papers. The following year Mendel's work was rediscovered and delivered to the Society in a lecture given by Bateson. And at the 1906 Conference, over which he presided, Bateson coined the term genetics. For Bunyard and his young contemporaries the meetings were an opportunity to meet leading international plant breeders as well as to imbibe this new scientific ethos.

---

[1] Bunyard, E. A., 'On Xenia', *Report of the Third International Conference 1906 on Genetics, Journal of the Royal Horticultural Society*, vol. 32, 1907, pp. 297–300. Quoted on p. 299 is the reference to Bunyard's contribution in 1899, 'J. R. H. S. vol. XXIV part 4, p. 1899'. Volume 24 of *JRHS* is the report of the Conference of Hybridization of 1899, which suggests that Bunyard made some contribution, but I have been unable to find it.

[2] See chapter 4.

Bunyard had also been brought into contact with C. C. Hurst, a pioneer geneticist then working with orchids, and E. A. Bowles, who was just beginning his writing career and laying the foundations of his reputation as a plantsman. Hurst and Bowles, together with Sir Harry Veitch, the famous nurseryman, and Dr Benjamin Daydon Jackson, the bibliographer, were the sponsors for Bunyard's successful application in 1914 to become a Fellow of the Linnean Society, Britain's leading botanic society.[3]

As far as the experimental sciences were concerned, however, Bunyard made few more forays. He dabbled in cross-breeding experiments with redcurrants and gave a lecture at an RHS meeting on the physiology of pruning in 1909, but by this time his interests had focussed on the study of fruit varieties which became a consuming passion.[4]

******

Bunyard was a pomologist in the broadest sense of the word, possessing wide expertise. His great strength lay in systematic pomology. The distinct and constant botanic features that characterize each fruit were resolved by the middle of the eighteenth century. Since each of these features varies from variety to variety, accurate records could be compiled of fruit populations. In Europe, and by the early 1800s in the United States, pomologists recorded their stock of varieties and combined with the most celebrated painters of the day to create magnificent pomonas. England and the London [Royal] Horticultural Society, founded in 1804, became an international focal point. The Society formed very large fruit collections at its gardens in Chiswick; extensive records were compiled; and its circle of botanic artists created incomparable fruit books. The Society's fortunes, however, went into decline by the 1850s and it was no longer able to take the lead in pomology. Studies were continued by the redoubtable Dr Robert Hogg, author of the encyclopaedic *Fruit Manual,* published in its final, fifth

---

[3] Bunyard's application to the Linnean Society is held at the Linnean Society Library, London.

[4] Bunyard, E. A., 'The History and Development of the Red Currant', *JRHS.*, vol. 42, 1916–17, p. 269 ; Bunyard, E. A., 'The Physiology of Pruning', *JRHS*, vol. 35, 1909–10, pp. 330–334.

edition in 1884. Hogg was the fount of all Victorian fruit knowledge and Bunyard's immediate British predecessor.

The emphasis of pomological research at this stage was overwhelmingly directed towards the needs of the country-house garden – whose fruit collections were, in effect, the main trial grounds of old and new varieties, along with those of the nurserymen. Their evaluations were reported in the gardening press where Hogg presided over one of the two leading weeklies. By the end of the century, however, the centre of attention shifted to commercial production, to provide the burgeoning fruit industry with a level of assessment commensurate with fruit farmers' often substantial investments in orchards. Now, the trend was to concentrate on the best and most useful varieties. There was, however, no one body driving matters forward. Although the RHS had revived to lead the fruit campaign of the 1880s and 1890s, their Chiswick fruit collections were neglected. Suffering in the pollution and westward expansion of London, they seem to have been disbanded when the RHS acquired its Wisley Gardens in Surrey in 1904. Collecting had to start all over again, but was not seriously undertaken until the 1920s. Into this vacuum, and to help the British fruit industry, three fruit research stations were set up in the early decades of the twentieth century, initially privately funded but later government financed. The first was the National Institute for Cider Research in 1903 near Bristol, which became Long Ashton Research Station. Next was the John Innes Research Institute at Merton, South London, in 1909. Finally, in 1913 Wye College set up its Fruit Experimental Station at East Malling. With the support of Kent fruit growers, this became the independent East Malling Research Station in 1921.

The consequence of this fractured history of pomological research in England was a gap in the records since the issue of the final edition of the *Fruit Manual* in 1884. Meanwhile, pomologists were busy in France and, more especially, in America. Bunyard was well aware of the situation and took up the challenge. Whether by inclination or circumstance, he found time to commence serious studies by 1911, when evidence of his work began to stream out of Allington in articles and lectures given to the RHS and the Linnean Society.

Edward Bunyard regarded this meticulous work as fundamental to his nursery business. Indeed, it underpinned the claim to always sell 'true to name'. The level to which Bunyard developed his studies was, however, far beyond that which a nurseryman might usually go to ensure that his stocks were 'true', but rather closer to that of an academic. It satisfied his intellectual needs and nicely justified his passion for collecting books. It also placed him in distinguished company. Since antiquity, pomology had been the pastime of the learned and leisured with libraries, money and time to indulge. The discipline attracted Roman orators, Renaissance princes and, closer to home, the English gentry who had established the Royal Horticultural Society and earned its early fame as leader in the subject. Heroes such as Thomas Andrew Knight who, in the seclusion of his Shropshire walled garden, had undertaken the first experiments in fruit breeding and, on his trips to the capital, presided over the Society. Pomology was an occupation that Edward's father could be proud of and one that provided respected status within the horticultural community. It was the badge by which he was known throughout his long committee-life, together with the honour and appellation FLS (Fellow of the Linnean Society).

Bunyard was well placed to take up the baton of pomology. He had easy access to the first essential, a comprehensive collection of varieties. The 'mother' trees and plants which formed the basis of the nursery's stocks, to which the latest varieties were being continually added, were excellent research material. Again, whether by choice or happy chance, it was convenient for his studies that the nursery continued to sell the old varieties and that he brought in the best-known and new fruits from abroad. Bunyard's collections were probably unique in this country. There was no 'national' collection and although a wide range of varieties was still grown by other nurseries such as Laxton's and Rivers' and in large estate gardens, it seems clear that none matched Bunyard's in size or diversity. Collecting fruit varieties was, of course, part and parcel of being a nurseryman, a good reason for other pomologists to have themselves followed this occupation. André Leroy, for example, author of the six-volume *Dictionnaire de Pomologie* (1867–1879), was said to have the largest fruit nursery in the world at Angers in the Loire Valley. Dr Robert Hogg, the *éminence grise* of Victorian fruit studies, was the son of an Edinburgh nurseryman and for a short while a partner in the Brompton Park Nursery at Kensington, fruit specialists since the seventeenth century.

Bunyard was an excellent linguist, an invaluable asset for the pomologist.

He needs to match his fruit to its first and most comprehensive description, then trace its history, as it was distributed from country to country, through a trail of synonyms in many different languages. Edward 'read as much in French as English', which gave access to the important Belgian as well as French literature. He was fluent in German, which was particularly useful for cherries and plums, and understood Italian, although his Latin, helpful for checking descriptions in the early herbals, did not equal Hogg's skills in the ancient languages. Bunyard had to turn to his Linnean Society colleague Daydon Jackson for translation of a botanic paper on gooseberries written in Latin. Checking the identity of a fruit, he wrote, was a painstaking task of 'thousands of references to literature, not all in one language, and of which each writer's idiosyncrasy requires weighing.'[5]

The third essential, a well-stocked library, was also being fast acquired by Bunyard. As early as 1899 he began book collecting and, judging by the evidence of his articles in 1911, he owned, even then, most of the key pomonas and fruit texts of Europe and America. Bunyard's search for rare books had taken him to 'libraries in France, Holland, Germany, Belgium and at home', as well as book dealers around the world. He spared no effort in tracking down a precious volume, as in the case of the early nineteenth-century Dutch work *Pomologia Batavia* of Van Noort. It was known to exist, but no description had been made and it appeared so elusive that he 'began to fear it was one of those flying Dutchmen who are more talked about than seen.' A copy did turn up, however, at a sale in Holland. It was in his possession by January 1917, but only just. It had been brought to England by a friend, 'which prevented it from being sent on the mail boat captured by the Germans.'[6]

In May 1922, Bunyard bought *Le Bon Mesnager*, published in Paris in 1536, a French translation of Pietro de Crescenzi's widely influential thirteenth-century estate manual (he also owned an Italian translation of 1542), from the bookseller and publisher, Leo Olschki, in Florence. The bill that accompanied the parcel remains in Bunyard's own copy in the

---

[5] 'The Pears of New York', a review uncredited, but almost certainly by Bunyard, *Journal of Pomology*, vol. 3, 1922–1925, pp. 153–155.
[6] Bunyard, E. A., 'A Rare Pomological Work', *The Gardeners' Chronicle*, 20 Jan., 1917, p. 30.

Lindley Library. We do not know how frequently he may have bought from Olschki, as these records are now lost, but his friendship with Norman Douglas brought him to Florence on many occasions. His purchases on that first visit in 1922 prompted an article on some 30 neglected Italian works, probably all from his own library.[7] Norman Douglas's friend Pino Orioli, who ran a shop specializing in incunabula and early printed books, was another fruitful contact.

Bunyard's own library provided the material for his entry into pomology. He contributed two substantial bibliographic articles to the *RHS Journal* in 1911–12: 'An Index to Illustrations of Apples' and 'An Index to Illustrations of Pears'. There he detailed the sources of paintings for each one of nearly 2,000 varieties. More evenings spent by the fireside reading old books resulted in 'A Guide to the Literature of Pomology' in the same journal in 1914–15. The previous year he had commenced a series on 'The History of Cultivated Fruits as Told in the Lives of the Great Pomologists' in the weekly *Gardeners' Chronicle*, beginning with the Belgium pear-breeder van Mons. He also wrote scholarly pieces on the history and development of the redcurrant, strawberry and cobnut. Bunyard wore his learning lightly, a skill that derived from great familiarity with the fruits and the literature. He had the gift for combining botanic insight and evidence from many sources, weaving the often dry details with an apposite quotation from an old fruit book into an engrossing story.

For pomology, as with any subject that relies on historical accuracy, it was important to know when and by whom innovations, that is the new techniques and varieties, were introduced and popularized. In order to unravel the origins of a variety, it was crucial to be aware of the different synonyms. In the case of the very old varieties the tracks were often confused by the lack of references to their first mention in the works of the previous generations of herbalists, physicians, botanists and collectors. An individual might be credited as the premier originator when in fact he was merely

---

[7] For information on Leo Olschki, I thank Alessandro Olschki – 'the firm "Libreria antiquaria editrice Leo S. Olschki" was divided into two separate firms in 1946; the antiquarian side was later sold in England.' For Bunyard's friendship with Norman Douglas see chapter 3 of this volume. Bunyard, E. A., 'Some Early Italian Gardening Books, *JRHS*, vol. 48, Sept., 1923, pp. 177–87.

copying from an earlier authority. Bunyard was particularly talented in what he described as the sport of hunting plagiarisms, a satisfying occupation for those with fluency in many languages and given to long hours of poring over old books, especially seventeenth- and eighteenth-century gardening texts, in which their authors had tended to translate from one language into another without any concern for crediting the original writer. He found, for instance, through skilful research among the scarce and much-translated authorities of the seventeenth century, that *The Dutch Gardener* by Henry van Oosten, published in English in 1703, was in large part culled from French sources. The fruit chapters were taken from *L'Art de Taillier les Arbres Fruitiers* of 1683 by a physician of la Rochelle, Nicholas Venette, and the culture of oranges was copied from Louis XIV's gardener, Jean de la Quintynie's *Instructions pour les Jardins Potagers et Fruitiers* of 1690. Bunyard left another to unravel the origins of the floral section and the date of the original Dutch edition. Here, Bunyard's colleague on the RHS Library Committee C. Harman Payne, 'with his usual industry has discovered that the first edition was published at Leyden in 1700', as *De niewe Nederlandse bloem-hof*, but no advance was made on resolving the source of further plagiarisms.[8]

English authors, Bunyard confessed, were especially 'guilty in this matter, and for the natural reason that France was the home of gardening, and the obiter dicta of its experts were received here with becoming reverence.' This he confirmed one day when looking for certain varieties of cherries in a 'scarce French book entitled "Instructions pour les Arbres Fruitiers"' of 1653. He realized the resemblance of this text to that of *The Planter's Manual* written, supposedly, by Charles Cotton, poet and continuer of Walton's *Complete Angler*. Cotton's *Planter's Manual*, published in 1675, was exposed with characteristic Bunyard diligence as a translation of the earlier French work, written by François Vautier, physician to Louis XIV and in charge of the Jardin des Plantes in Paris.[9]

The days of great bibliographic bargains were, however, over after the

---

[8] Bunyard, E. A., 'Henry Van Oosten and the "Dutch Gardener"', *Journal of Pomology*, vol. 1, 1920, pp. 37–40; 'Van Oosten's Dutch Gardener', p. 144.

[9] Bunyard, E. A., 'Cotton's "Planter's Manual"', *The Gardeners' Chronicle*, 27 April, 1918, pp. 174–5; Wilson, E., *Notes and Queries*, vol. 248, 2003, pp. 189–90.

war. He believed demand had increased from amateurs and also from 'the many experimental stations all over the world ... tombs which swallow up books for ever.' With prophetic irony, Bunyard concludes that this had its compensations for the amateur collector since 'booksellers prefer to sell to him, as there is always the chance of death or bankruptcy stepping in to bring his books on the market once again'. In fact, both tragically happened in Bunyard's case.[10]

******

Bunyard's research into the history of fruit was only one aspect of the work involved in making systematic records; the main activities lay outside, in the orchard and at his desk recording the information. Systematic pomology calls for painstaking observation and noting details of each variety. For long hours, Bunyard would have sat describing the samples, making measurements, magnification-glass and callipers to hand, cutting sections to reveal and record the inner structures and, of course, tasting. Descriptions often demanded difficult judgments on key features: the typical shape of a particular pear, the usual colour of a certain gooseberry variety. To write a book required 'thousands of observations ... in many cases of varying characters as to which the author must at some time take his courage in his hands and decide where the average line is to be drawn.'[11]

The pomologist must also be skilled in recognizing a variety. George Bunyard had been a master of the art. He attributed his 'quickness in discerning minute differences in fruits and flowers' to his early interest in studying lepidoptera.[12] He had won his spurs at the National Apple Congress of 1883, checking and identifying hundreds of varieties gathered from all over Britain. His precision was on show in the descriptions for *The Fruit Garden*, in which line drawings by his daughter Frances provided botanically accurate outlines. Edward may also have helped with this book

---

[10] 'News and Notes'; 'The Price of Old Books', not credited but almost certainly written by Bunyard, as editor, *Journal of Pomology and Horticultural Science*, vols. 3–4, 1922–25, pp. 207–208.

[11] 'The Pears of New York', op. cit.

[12] 'Mr. George Bunyard', *The Garden*, 10 Aug., 1901, p. 95.

and certainly early training would stand him in good stead. While a French colleague reflected that the pomologist's skill, 'acquired by long years of practice usually arrives a trifle late in the life of those who possess it',[13] the young Bunyard could probably tell a Cox from Ribston as easily as an apple from a pear. As he later reflected when discussing Latin nomenclature: 'Those of us born into gardening families learn these names unconsciously in their youth.'[14]

The skills of father and son were kept honed by the fruit-naming service offered by the nursery. This ensured they were sensitive to the wide variation in a variety when grown under different conditions. In comparison to a Kentish fruit, something from Scotland, for instance, may be smaller, often of a somewhat different shape, with its other features battered by frost and wind and showing little of its characteristic taste. Although decades of experience permeated the very air at Allington, it was a huge undertaking to bring the English records up to date, especially since Bunyard proposed studying not only the tree fruits but also soft fruits and the tender fruits grown in England under glass. It had taken a team of workers in New York more than 30 years to bring into print the records of their own orchards.

Bunyard was an enthusiast, undaunted by the task, methodical and thorough. He gave it his wholehearted commitment, at least as far as nursery work allowed, but reflected in 1914 that he was already one of a dying breed in some countries: the 'day of the nurseryman and amateur as pomological authors is now fast disappearing in America, and their place is filled by a benevolent Government which provides unlimited funds and expert specialists to write the books. The result of this combination is a happy one, and it is no exaggeration to say that never has pomology been so well supported as it is to-day in America.'[15] Government funding of horticulture had begun in the USA in 1862. At the New York Agricultural Station in Geneva an apple collection, commenced in 1883, had risen to over 700 varieties by 1900. The first of their new pomonas, *The Apples of*

---

[13] Chasset, L., 'The Determination of Pears', *Journal of Pomology*, vol. 2, 1921, p. 11.
[14] Bunyard, E. A., 'The Meaning of Plant Names', *The Listener*, 15 Dec., 1938, p. 1313.
[15] Bunyard, E. A., 'A Guide to the Literature of Pomology', *JRHS*, vol. 40, 1914–15, p. 437.

New York by Professor Spencer A. Beech, was published in 1905. All the fruits were covered by 1925 in the New York series.

In England, Bunyard wryly reflected, horticulture had to rely on private enterprise. It was some time before the English government supported this type of work. He wrote with a degree of envy in 1922 that in America the authors of fruit books occupied 'positions which enable them at once the opportunity for research and the time to present their conclusions in book form.' Bunyard fitted pomology in between his other work and did not have the budget to support lavishly illustrated pomonas: the 'Englishman cannot but reflect that his country has not produced even one pomological treatise to compare with the detailed, sumptuous volumes which come from Geneva.'[16]

******

Bunyard's research was directed towards his own *magnum opus, A Handbook of Hardy Fruits,* his most enduring contribution to pomology, published as two volumes in 1920 and 1925. A directory to the fruits grown in England, it provided the definitive description of each variety, its history and an indication of its value. He judged that a succinct and sound guide was needed, not necessarily a great tome; but the *Handbook*'s modest title concealed a wealth of erudition and knowledge. Three volumes were originally planned: the first devoted to apples and pears, the second to stone fruits and the third to soft fruit, nuts, quinces and medlars. For some reason, volumes two and three were condensed into one. Post-war problems at the nursery and Bunyard's increasing RHS commitments were probably part of the reason for the curtailment.

His stated intention for the *Handbook* was 'to provide information in a popular form without any loss of accuracy', Although the New York books are very different in appearance, being large and well illustrated, his aim was similar.[17] The New York series were reference books aimed at the home and

---

[16] 'Pears of New York', op. cit.

[17] Bunyard, E. A., *A Handbook of Hardy Fruits*, vol. 1, 'Apples and Pears' (London, 1920), pp. 5–6; Beach, S. A., *The Apples of New York,* vol. 1 (New York, 1905), pp. vii–ix.

commercial grower, nurseryman and fruit seller, but with no compromise on the factual information, as was the case for the other contemporary work, *Les Meilleurs Fruits au début du XXe Siècle* published by the Société Nationale d'Horticulture de France in 1907. Bunyard achieved his objective, but it was a no-frills production – a neat, handy, inexpensive volume – with no illustrations, not even line drawings such as could be seen in the French book, let alone the early examples of colour photography that featured in the New York series. Instead, Bunyard turned to the indexes of illustrations he had published in 1911–12 (page 237, above), including a reference to a coloured plate wherever one existed in the literature. He extended his original index of apples and pears (published separately as pamphlets, see Bibliography) to cover all temperate fruits for the second volume.

Classification tables were included in the *Handbook* for all the tree fruits and gooseberries: that is, a grouping of the varieties in a way that would allow the identity of an unknown sample to be worked out, in a similar fashion to a botanic key. Devising a satisfactory classification system had long been the Holy Grail for pomologists. The Germans were particularly zealous in this field, but inevitably geared their approach to Continental varieties. For the apple, Hogg had devised a system based on the fruit's internal features, which was too elaborate for most people to make use of, and his system for pears was only preliminary. Bunyard concluded, in a lecture and subsequent article on the subject in 1915, that 'while the authoritative naming of Apples will doubtless always remain in the hands of experts … such grouping is extremely desirable. … For these reasons the writer thinks such a system worth making, and hopes that some leisured enthusiast may be found to attempt it.'[18] He remarked later, however, 'I doubt greatly if it is possible to make a grouping or key which will enable the inexperienced to run down a fruit with, let us say the accuracy that he can identify a postage stamp.'[19]

Bunyard hardly fitted the profile of someone with time on his hands but, with typical single-mindedness and clarity, he produced a simple classification system following the principles of the latest German work and

---

[18] Bunyard, E. A., 'The History of the Classification of Apples', *JRHS*, vol. 41, 1915–16, p. 456.

[19] Chittenden, F. J., ed., *Apples and Pears, Varieties and Cultivation in 1934* (Royal Horticultural Society, London, 1935), pp. 48–49.

based on the varieties in his *Handbook*. He provided tables for apples, pears, plums, cherries and gooseberries. It was a masterly achievement. Bunyard's system has been expanded as new varieties have been introduced, but never bettered and remains the most useful of all guides to naming a fruit.

The *Handbook* rapidly gained acceptance as the definitive reference work. It was quoted in articles in the gardening press and Bunyard was lauded as its author. It became everyone's guide, but it was distilled from yet more extensive work taking place at Allington. To provide the best possible material for research, stocks had been increased to enable Bunyard to realize his aim of making all his own observations on a living collection. He established his own pomological research station: an exceptionally large collection supported by extensive, meticulous records. His contemporaries in America had large collections, but also large staffs of record-keepers and assistants. Bunyard soldiered on by himself. He had his father's energy and determined perseverance to keep going season after season, working through, for instance, climatic problems, when the frosts played havoc with the pear and plum crops and strawberry plants became diseased. To do it well, as he said, there could no short cuts. Bunyard did not 'make a large collection of descriptions by quoting from other authors' and there was only one way to resolve confusions and ensure a correctly named collection: 'nothing short of growing the plants side by side and comparing their characters over a series of years can clear up doubtful identities.'[20] He wished 'to fill the place formerly occupied by Dr Hogg's Fruit Manual' since 'there are a large number of fruits which have not yet been described save in the weekly gardening Journals'. His intention, however, was to be more thorough than his predecessor. For his own book Bunyard was selective, describing only those varieties that were 'more commonly grown in Great Britain' – some 350 apples and 150 pears. Hogg, on the other hand, had been inclusive and described every variety he could find, which included over 900 apples and almost as many pears.

Hogg had had large collections at his home in Sussex and access to those of the RHS, but he probably made a number of his descriptions from fruit that he had seen on his travels around the country, at shows, or from

---

[20] Bunyard, E. A., *A Handbook of Hardy Fruits*, vol. 2, 'Stone and Bush Fruits, Nuts etc.' (London, 1925), p. 5.

parcels of fruit that came in for identification at the office of his *Journal of Horticulture*. Bunyard was in a more ideal position – with all the varieties growing under the same conditions at Allington – and he was aiming to record a more comprehensive view of each one. Hogg, in his opinion, had treated fruits as 'museum pieces', describing only the fruit. Bunyard's contemporaries, particularly the French, now looked at the whole tree and recorded the foliage and habit, that is the natural shape of the tree. As a nurseryman, he was well aware of the importance of these details. Trees were often sold before they had fruited, particularly cherries, which take a long time to come into bearing. The tree's habit and leaves were often the only criteria by which to judge whether there had been a propagation mistake. Bunyard mused that the experienced nursery foreman can identify his stock as 'the shepherd who recognizes all his sheep.'[21]

Bunyard was critically re-evaluating the key characters that were used to build a description and searching for new ones. The 'winter need not be an off season for the pomologist' he wrote: the winter buds and the appearance of the shoots provided distinct features with which to help resolve an identity. He brought to notice the value of examining the blossom in apples and pears, which can often be used to distinguish between varieties when the fruit has failed.[22]

Bunyard's profiles in the *Handbook* do not include all the details that he was exploring, for the work was on-going and he was aiming at a broad readership. As he said, the pomologist has to 'take a firm seat either on the stool of exact botanical descriptions or that of popular terminology, but all who have attempted such work will sympathize. It is extremely difficult to draw a line between the extremes of systematic description.'[23] Bunyard's descrip-

---

[21] Bunyard, E. A., *Old Garden Roses* (London, 1936), p. 70.

[22] Bunyard, E. A., 'The Winter Study of Fruit Trees', *JRHS*, vol. 47, 1922, p. 18–25; Bunyard, E. A., 'The Winter Aspect of the Buds of Plums', *The Gardeners' Chronicle*, 19 Jan, 1918, p. 23; Bunyard, E. A., 'The Flowers of Apples as an Aid in Identifying Varieties' *JRHS*, vol. 38, pp. 1912–13, pp. 234–237; Bunyard, E. A., 'The Basis of Classification in Apples and Pears', in Chittenden, F. J., ed., *Apples and Pears, Varieties and Cultivation in 1934*, op. cit., pp. 47–74.

[23] 'Recent Pomological Literature', uncredited but written almost certainly by Bunyard as editor, *Journal of Pomology and Horticultural Science*, vol. 3, 1922–24 p. 114.

tions are concise, less discursive than Hogg's and considerably less so than the New York series, but he has the knack of usually including the most telling features. As well as habit and foliage, the variety's cropping performance had also been noted and, where possible, its susceptibility to pests and diseases. Bunyard could not, however, resist lifting the content above mere facts. The pear Napoleon, for example, which has numerous synonyms, 'such as Roi de Rome, Gloire de l'Empereur and Captif de St. Helene, tell their story of Imperial ambitions and their result.' The foliage of Colmar d'Été pear turned 'a fine "sang de boeuf"', while Gravenstein apple with 'its fragrant aroma and digestible flesh make it deserving of wider cultivation.'

Compilation of good records for apples was an onerous task, but pears required considerably more effort. Hundreds of new varieties had been introduced following what was in many ways the birth of the modern, buttery pear in Belgium in the late eighteenth and early nineteenth centuries. They had been eagerly taken up in country-house gardens, but their critical evaluation was far from complete. Hogg had included almost no details on the performance of the varieties introduced later in the century except for a few, usually wholly disparaging, remarks from R. D. Blackmore who, as well as writing novels, ran a Thames Valley market garden. Blackmore's frequent comment was 'worthless at Teddington'. A pear trial was thus much needed. Clearly, there could be varieties with undiscovered potential. Bunyard discussed only those he considered the most suited to the English climate in the *Handbook*. There were many more in existence and probably in his collection. A visitor in 1927 wrote of 200 pear varieties at Allington and, Bunyard said, 'I might easily have quadrupled' the list. He succeeded in sifting out a number of promising, yet forgotten varieties – Émile d'Hyest, Beurré Six, Comte de Paris and Admiral Gervais – for promotion to the nursery's catalogue.

To maintain these large collections required continuous monitoring and labelling of the trees and re-propagation of any that appeared sickly. This task was even more demanding when it came to the subjects of the second volume of the *Handbook*. Here he described 75 cherries and 107 plums, to which he added the additional details of their flowers, leaves and stones – the latter being important identification features, especially for plums. Some 80 or so peaches and nectarines are covered as well as 20 apricots, 42 dessert grapes and 16 figs. Again, this was an enormous task. Even to grow

20 varieties of apricot in England was heroic. These, like the other tender fruits, were grown under glass, to ensure that they fruited and so that he could make sound descriptions. The volume also included 14 varieties of cobnuts and all the soft fruits. No temperate fruit was forgotten in his wide-ranging research.

Cherries had proved particularly tricky. Not only was their fruiting season short, but often the nature of the flowers and leaves were essential to confirm an identity. 'A great deal of work remains in settling the nomenclature and synonymy of Cherries, such work is radical, as without certainty in this matter much of the research, for example, in pollination in this and other countries loses its value to the grower.' Very true, and he only included varieties that he had grown and fruited and found satisfactory at Allington, leaving out many on which he had notes. Space limited the number of synonyms that could be included. Alas, Bunyard's notes, his laborious work in tracking the names of the varieties of all the fruits across Europe through the centuries, which required all his language skills, have not survived. This lost body of work would have been invaluable. For instance, he had traced Tradescant's Heart cherry through 50 synonyms, but only included two in the *Handbook*. Bunyard had concluded that the cherry that John Tradescant had brought back from the Low Countries in 1611 to the garden of his patron, Lord Salisbury at Hatfield was one and the same as Noble, a recently introduced variety. The trail had taken Bunyard to Hatfield to examine the original manuscript accounts recording Tradescant's purchases of an 'exceedyng great cherye called the boores cherye 12s'. He then traced its Continental origins back through the sixteenth century and the course of its subsequent wanderings when it became known by a host of synonyms, including Bigarreau Gros Noir in France and Grosse Schwarze Knorpelkirsche in Germany. Bunyard, however, decided its English name should be kept as reminder of Tradescant's pioneering work. This name, however, did not endure and recent research has cast doubt on some of Bunyard's conclusions. Frustratingly, we will never know the ramifications that he uncovered in connection with this and many other entries.[24]

---

[24] Bunyard, E. A., *Handbook of Hardy Fruits*, vol. 2, op. cit., p. 22; Bunyard, E. A., 'John Tradescant, Senior', *Journal of Pomology*, vol. 1, 1920, pp. 188–196. Personal

For this second volume, some the nursery's collections had needed augmentation. We hear of numerous blackberries being grown, many obtained from America, but only a few appear, including the much-publicized Himalaya Berry – nothing to do with the Himalayas, but with enormous berries and crops. Among the berry fruits, it was currants and gooseberries that received the most attention. For currants, fruit alone was insufficient to distinguish one variety from another: leaf and flower characteristics were also essential. Redcurrants were 'in a state of confusion' for many reasons; not least, he believed, because, 'no one seems to have thought it worth while to publish an accurate botanic description of so unimportant a thing as a Currant.'[25] To build a collection, he gathered together 'in 1912 all the varieties I could procure from gardens and nurseries in England and from America and the Continent; these amounted in all to over seventy.' After close observation over several seasons, many names turned out to be synonyms. He wrote in 1920 that 'it has been an extremely difficult matter' to sort out the identities and names and decide which was the original variety. His careful research was the subject of his début and, it appears, only lecture to the Linnean Society in 1916, which was followed by further work reported in the *Journal of Pomology*, illustrated by his sister Frances's paintings.[26]

Gooseberry studies began two years later in 1914. Hundreds of varieties had been raised in the nineteenth century, mainly as candidates for the 'heaviest berry' competition at shows held in the northern counties. Only a couple of dozen varieties were well known, although 'there are probably five hundred or even more still grown in nurseries and gardens.' Bunyard collected some 250 varieties – double the number in today's collections – and which he studied over the next seven years.[27] This was primarily for

---

communication Dr Emma-Jane Lamont, Dr Alison Lean, Imperial College, Defra National Fruit Collections – molecular analysis of cherry varieties suggest it is unlikely that Noble is the same as Grosse Schwarze Knorpelkirsche.

[25] Bunyard, E. A., 'A Revision of the Red Currants', *Journal of Pomology*, vol. 2, 1921, p. 38–55.

[26] Bunyard, E. A., 'The History and Development of the Red Currant', op. cit.

[27] Bunyard, E. A., 'Notes on a Trial of Gooseberries', *Journal of Pomology and Horticultural Science*, vol. 3–4, 1922–25, pp. 148–152.

his *Handbook*, which carried descriptions of some 105 varieties, but also, as always, to see if there were some neglected yet promising varieties awaiting rediscovery for the nursery. The gooseberries were grown as single-stemmed cordons for reasons of space but, since they had all been propagated in the nursery, important criteria such as their ease of rooting from cuttings and their habit of growth had been noted before they were trained. Bunyard never missed an important detail. The evocative names of gooseberries make this a fascinating section, in which the champion heavyweights make their mark and are represented in all the four colour categories: green, King of Trumps; yellow, Hit or Miss; white, Antagonist; and deep red, London, which had weighed in as the heaviest berry for 36 seasons in the nineteenth century. Dessert gooseberries, now an almost forgotten concept, are just as full of charm and can be luscious and fragrant when fully ripe: for instance, Lily of Valley – 'milky white' and 'very sweet'; Snowdrop – 'very delicious'; Red Champagne – 'deep claret … aromatic and sweet'; and the intriguing Yellow Warrington which could, unusually, produce fruits striped in red.

Bunyard's strawberry collection of over 80 varieties was particularly large and interesting to the botanist and epicure. It contained most of the species and many of the varieties that made up the story of its domestication. The wild strawberries of Europe, the woodland and the alpine, were well represented and he laced their entries in the *Handbook* with anecdotal comment: the White Alpine strawberry, which was 'most delicious,' he suggested should be added to ordinary strawberries for jam making – a handful to a gallon. He had plants of the American species – the Virginian and the Chilean – that had crossed to produce the modern, large-berried strawberry in eighteenth-century France, and a number of the very early hybrids – Keen's Seedling, for example, which had created a sensation when it was introduced with its large fruit carried high off the ground. It had been raised by a London market gardener of that name in the early 1800s, and was still cultivated in Bunyard's time. Nowadays, it is impossible to find. Others that he was keeping going are probably lost too, such as a number of those with a distinct 'pine' flavour (i.e. pineapple), formerly the most sought-after quality, found in many of the varieties that had made up the Byzantine complexity of strawberries grown by Victorians. The historic Ananas, 'rich' Filbert Pine, 'remarkable' White Pine, and Dr Hogg 'with a delicious pine flavour' which was 'still the best flavoured in cultivation and worth every effort to bring it to perfection' are examples. Strawberry collections, however, are demanding to maintain and require propagating every two or three years to keep them disease-free; a problem that, from his remarks, Bunyard was encountering.

******

Fruit collections are only as good as their records which hold information about the variety and are proof of its identity. Bunyard remarked that 'pomology is largely a matter of tradition, knowledge being handed on from one generation to the next, and whilst this actual practical knowledge is of the first importance, and without it the merely book-learned would fail dismally, the converse also holds some truth. The traditional pomologist cannot afford to dispense with records'[28] – a comment, perhaps, on his father's methods. He would not fall into this error. When recommending the proper facilities for the task of identifying fruit varieties to be undertaken by the RHS, he stated at a Council meeting on 28 February 1928 that technical knowledge, a living fruit collection, a reference library and a fruit room to keep the samples were essential, as well as an herbarium of leaves and flowers and photographs of tree habit. Suggesting provision of '10,000 herbarium sheets', he remarked that 'the work of specialists is too often lost at their death when valuable collections are dispersed.'[29] This reflected, one might imagine, the level of data collection undertaken at the nursery, but these too have been lost, together with all his work on synonyms.

The unofficial research team at Allington probably included a trusted member of staff given the time-consuming task of helping pick typical samples of the fresh fruits, labelling and storing them in the Fruit Room ready for his employer to describe. The herbarium, an archive of pressed leaves and flowers, also contained the stones of cherries, plums, peaches, nectarines and apricots. Bunyard's sisters were, no doubt, persuaded to help collect and press leaves and flowers, extract and wash the fruit stones, and pack them into individually labelled bottles. Taking photographs of the trees was a winter activity, since the habit was easier to perceive when all the leaves

---

[28] Bunyard, E. A., 'The Flowers of Apples as an Aid in Identifying Varieties', op. cit.
[29] RHS Lindley Library, RHS Council Minutes, 28 Feb., 1928.

had fallen. It was also the time to study the buds and shoots. Before that they would have recorded the autumn leaf colours, another identification feature useful in cherries and pears. In spring, as well as collecting blossom to press and describe, the dates of flowering would be noted.

His sister Frances was certainly part of the Allington team in her role as botanic artist. Watercolour paintings were the traditional way to record details of a fruit. They are often superior to a photograph, even today, for the artist can arrange and tilt the sample so as to highlight its key features in a manner impossible with photography. Colour photography was then in its infancy and Bunyard was not enamoured of it. In commenting on *The Apples of New York* he wrote that its illustrations suffered from 'the disadvantages of all photographic work – the lack of emphasis of important detail.'[30] Choosing a typical specimen for the painting was essential, but Edward and Frances had the ideal situation, although one that is not always possible – the combination of artist and pomologist side by side – with her brother always there to select the fruit and advise on its features. They collaborated and built up what must have been an extensive collection of botanic plates. Some were used to illustrate the nursery catalogue, Edward's articles and as lantern slides to accompany his lectures, but their main role was surely that of permanent record.

Frances's paintings are visually exquisite, technically brilliant and rank among the best examples of botanic art. At the time her work drew public acclaim and she received the Silver Gilt Grenfell Medal, the highest award that the RHS could give to a botanic artist, in 1931, 1932, 1934 and 1935. She also won a Silver Medal in 1932 for her plates of fruit and flowers. Sadly her paintings have not remained together in a single collection, nor probably have they all survived. One can only imagine that after her brother's death no one thought to reclaim the paintings that had been lent to various people over the years. The RHS Lindley Library still owns 53 cherry plates, mostly depicting fruits and stones, and there is a further, considerably larger, collection at East Malling Research and with the East Malling Trust. Taken together, these comprise paintings and drawings of cherries, plums, apples, pears, quinces, figs and a peach. Alas, they include none of her paintings

---

[30] Bunyard, E. A., 'An Index to Illustrations of Apples', *JRHS*, vol. 37, 1911–12, p. 154.

of gooseberries, strawberries, currants, nuts and nectarines nor any of the roses that illustrated the catalogues and Edward's *Old Garden Roses*.

At East Malling there are, altogether, 21 watercolours of apples, 21 of pears and two of quinces; each variety is shown as a single fruit, as they appear in the catalogues, and a number of the plates correspond with these published images. The 22 paintings of plums are also depicted as single fruits, though some include their stones. There are 46 drawings of plum stipules, the tiny leaves at the junction of the stalk and the stem, which Bunyard must have been exploring as another fruit identification character. But there are no winter fruit buds of plums, however, which we know Frances painted. In addition, there are 16 pen-and-ink drawings of plum stones and ten black and white plates of plums, some with their leaves. At least one of these was used in the catalogues. The large number of cherry plates reflects Bunyard's special interest in this fruit. There are 38 watercolours at East Malling, 34 of which are of the same varieties as those held in the Lindley Library. She made 15 paintings of winter fruit buds of cherries, 65 pencil and ink drawings of cherry stones and four pencil drawings of cherry leaves. The drawings of cherry stones are particularly beautiful, showing in perfect detail the sutures that run across the surface. These markings differ for each variety, and Bunyard would have wanted a precise record for identification. Figs are represented by four varieties: the fruit is coloured and set against a background of leaves which have been left as a black and white drawing. Those she painted for Bunyard's article 'The Cultivation of the Fig' are missing. She used the same style of coloured fruits and uncoloured leaves in the four larger plates of De Larchipel fig, Belle de Louvain plum, Doyenné du Comice pear and Sea Eagle peach which hang framed at East Malling. These, like many of the other paintings, are signed by Frances. Several of this group held in Kent are dated to 1925 and 1926.[31]

Perhaps Edward and Frances had in mind one day producing an illustrated pomona with Edward's detailed descriptions and historical research. An appreciative friend, R. T. Pearl, in paying tribute to a lecture given

---

[31] My thanks to Dr Ken Tobutt of East Malling Research, Mr Adrian Padfield and the East Malling Trust for allowing me to see the paintings and also to Dr Alison Lean for help in examining them.

by Bunyard in 1934, said: 'I hope that one day we shall to be able to look to him to replace Hogg's *Fruit Manual* with a work conceived on the spacious lines of the works of Alphonse Mas. I look on this paper as an appetizer for the banquet that must surely follow.'[32] Mas, the great French pomologist who had devoted all his life to studying fruit, produced very detailed illustrated works. What a sumptuous pomona the Bunyard family might have compiled. Sadly, it was not to be realized. Mas could have been Bunyard's role-model, but Mas had a very different and enviable life-style. He had great personal wealth and did not need to run a business nor earn a living. Mas maintained his own collection and probably financed his very expensive publications.

******

Bunyard's opinions on the correct procedure for recording and identifying varieties spilt over into his committee work at the RHS, where he wore several hats – pomologist and exhibitor, but also judge and promoter of high horticultural standards. One of the Fruit and Vegetable Committee's tasks – he was chairman from 1929 – was to identify samples sent in for naming by Fellows. These were usually apples and pears, but any fruit was possible: for example, grapes from the South African High Commissioner in April 25 1933; peaches and figs in August from English gardens; followed by the identification of numerous fruits in early October. Bunyard once remonstrated at the abuse of this service by the gardening press forwarding readers' queries to the Society

Fruits were sent to Wisley Gardens and to 'Fruit & Veg.' at the Society's headquarters in Vincent Square. Both places were inadequately equipped, Bunyard opined in a memo delivered to the Council on 28 February 1928: fruit-naming was one of his specialities as well as a hobby-horse. Wisley was developing a fruit collection, but lacked a comprehensive reference library. Vincent Square had the library, but no fruit samples. Members had to rely on their memories: a vast data-bank in itself. But to do the job properly Bunyard recommended one centre at Vincent Square, equipped

---

[32] Chittenden, F. J., ed., *Apples and Pears, Varieties and Cultivation in 1934*, op. cit., p. 87.

with all the facilities he had at Allington. If this plan were followed, the Society would be taking the lead by forming the first 'National Herbarium for Fruit'. To add further weight to his proposal, he informed Council on 27 March that 'it was his intention to present his library of books on fruit and his herbarium to the Society with the wish expressed that the two be housed in one room.' The question of a fruit room was discussed again in April, when Council wondered if it could be located in the basement.

Bunyard's inducements proved unnecessary, for according to the editorial on 'The History of the R.H.S. Fruit Committee' in the *Gardeners' Chronicle* on 8 June 1929, possibly written by Bunyard, everything necessary was in hand. 'Thanks to the recent provision of a fruit room in the new hall, the presence of a herbarium now in the process of formation, and a collection of works of reference for their special use, the Fruit Committee should now be able to undertake this onerous duty under better conditions.' Perhaps he was a little too swift with the publicity, or the space proved inadequate, for three years later Bunyard is asking again whether accommodation for a fruit cold store could be made next to the Committee room.[33] The outcome is unclear, but a fruit room was subsequently made in the main house at Wisley. Until recently, this room served as the fruit identification centre. Reference fruits were arranged on shelves around the walls, and the fruit officer retired for long, chilly hours to name the fruit sent in by members. The beginnings of the 'Herbarium', envelopes containing leaves of apple varieties, were discovered at Wisley some years ago and have now been mounted as herbarium specimens. A surviving plum-stone collection may also have been formed at the same time.

******

As early as 1919, Bunyard had achieved wide recognition for his work as a pomologist. He was in touch with research institutes and societies in Europe and America and interacting with those in England. He became

---

[33] RHS Lindley Library, RHS Council Minutes 28 Feb, 1928; 27 March, 1928; 24 April, 1928; 21 June, 1932; 'The History the R.H.S. Fruit Committee', *The Gardeners' Chronicle,* 8 June 1929, p. 415. My thanks to Jim Arbury, RHS Fruit Officer, for information on the herbarium and plum stone collection.

great friends with [Sir] Ronald Hatton, director of East Malling Research Station, which was only a mile or so away from his home at Allington. Hatton's son, the Reverend Edmund (Christopher) Hatton, remembers his father proudly showing him a copy of *The Anatomy of Dessert*, its author's name being mentioned with great respect. Hatton was one of the most influential figures in modern fruit growing through his development of new dwarfing rootstocks. These revolutionized orchards, providing growers with more compact trees producing higher quality fruit. He had come to Wye College in 1912 and during the war years was in charge of its Fruit Experimental Station, which evolved into East Malling Research Station. We can imagine many discussions on the finer points of some aspect of fruit research between Hatton and Bunyard. At East Malling also, he would share knowledge on raspberries and cherries with Norman Grubb, who became a renowned authority on cherries; and he was in touch with the fruit breeder M. B. Crane at John Innes Research Institute, who was investigating the problems of pollination. This topic was of importance as commercial orchards were increasingly restricted to only a few varieties thus risking poor pollination and crops. Bunyard's own records of the flowering dates of pears, apples, cherries and plums provided most of the data for a survey undertaken at Wye College;[34] there could have been no other place with a collection as extensive as that at Allington.

Abroad, Bunyard was a member of the French Pomological and Horticultural Societies and attended their meetings as soon as he could after the war. The first of the annual French Pomological Society conferences took him to Metz in September 1919, where new apple introductions were on display, contacts to be made with French authorities and friendships strengthened over the *banquet familiale*.[35] On the final afternoon he visited the famous nursery of Simon Louis Frères, where 'such of the Nursery as the war had spared' included 500 apple varieties. On his return journey he stopped in Paris for another international conference. We find him

---

[34] Hooper, C. H., 'Order of Flowering and Pollination of Fruit Blossoms', *The Gardeners' Chronicle*, 20 April, 1929, pp. 298–299; 4 May, 1929, pp. 332–333; 11 May, 1929, pp. 351.

[35] Bunyard, E. A., 'The Pomological Conference at Metz', *Journal of Pomology*, vol. 1, 1920, pp. 59–61.

the following year attending the French Pomological Society conference, this time in Lausanne, where he made friends with the leader of the local Society. He was sufficiently well known for the Luxemburg government's horticultural representative to spend several days escorting him around nurseries, vineyards and orchards on his return journey.[36] He may also have been a member of the International Federation of Professional Horticulturalists, which convened each year in a different European city. When they met in London in 1929, Bunyard helped organize the meeting and led a discussion session.[37] His network of contacts and correspondents stretched to America, including particularly Professor Ulysses Hedrick, Beach's successor in New York, and the Canadian fruit breeder Dr W. T. Macoun in Ontario.

******

Bunyard appeared to move easily from conference, to collection, to commercial plantation through his contacts among pomologists and the nursery trade. However, information did not necessarily flow freely from one body or individual to another, so he did what any academic might do and started a journal. In 1919 he conceived, produced and published the quarterly *Journal of Pomology*. Its intention was to fill the void that existed in horticultural communication in England, where the work of the research institutes was only published in their annual reports, but it was immediately international in scope. An indication of Bunyard's prestige was provided by the list of contributors to the first and second volumes. The breadth of coverage in the articles, the mix of topics, and the international character of the authors would have made any learned society proud. All this was achieved single-handed, with no apparent support from editors or assistants and probably not even a secretary to help with correspondence. Articles embraced all aspects of the subject: fruit varieties, breeding, cultivation, pollination, pests and diseases, and included work from the English research institutes and the home-station, 'Notes on Fruits on Trial at Allington'.

---

[36] Bunyard, E. A., 'A Pomological Pilgrimage', *Journal of Pomology*, vol. 2, 1921, p. 62.
[37] 'Fédération Horticole Professionelle Internationale', *The Gardeners' Chronicle*, 13 July 1929, p. 37.

History was part of its remit, with accounts of rare books and the activities of John Tradescant being in the first issue. There were book reviews and the editor's 'News and Notes' which even included book auction prices. It was a glorious mélange, reflecting the founder's wide range of interests. There were papers from Hatton on the classification of blackcurrants, which Bunyard complemented with his own work on redcurrants, and further lengthy communications on Hatton's research into rootstocks, with Bunyard providing an historical perspective through a piece on the origins of the Paradise (dwarfing) rootstock. Other contributions to the first volumes included his friend Dr Herbert Durham of Hereford describing his records of perry pears and the etymology of fruit names; L. Chasset of the French Pomological Society; several from Hedrick in New York; one from Owen Thomas, the Royal head gardener, on grapes; and Edward Laxton on breeding apples. Bunyard everywhere leavened and filled up the pages with amusing notes: on the monuments that have been erected to commemorate famous apples, to cite just one.

The *Journal* was well received. It continued for three years before it was taken over at the end of 1922 by the research institutes, one imagines much to the relief of Edward's brother Norman and their accountant. At the end of the first year, Bunyard confessed that 'on the financial side, as was anticipated the Journal has been run at a loss' due to 'very substantial increases in materials and costs of printing'.[38] To keep the subscription at the same level, he urged his readers to recruit new subscribers. Aside from the worries of how to fund the *Journal* and fill the pages, one can only marvel at how he managed to fit in the nursery business and everything else around the pressure of producing a hundred illustrated pages four times a year. Bunyard achieved his aims to inform, to share knowledge and enthuse others. However, once he gave up as editor in 1923, the *Journal*'s content became considerably heavier.

One little-known spin-off from the *Journal* was the publication in 1928 of *The Catalogue of Fruit Trees of Le Lectier*. This was an obscure list of fruit variety names belonging to a seventeenth-century lawyer and fruit collector at Orléans. In many ways it was an extraordinary undertaking, but so typical of Bunyard's indulgence, with little thought for costs, of his beloved hobby

---

[38] The Editor (Bunyard), 'Editorial Note', *Journal of Pomology*, vol. 1, 1920.

of collecting and studying old books. Beautifully produced with a blue marbled paper cover and a cream spine lettered in gold, it measures just 18 cms high and is only 39 pages long. It bears no indication of the identity of the publisher, although it was clearly Bunyard. The printers were Vivish & Baker, the same firm that produced the *Journal*. This *Catalogue*, indeed, in exactly the same format as it was finally produced, was printed in the *Journal* in 1919, when it was described as a 'bibliographic rarity'. The original survived as a single copy in the National Library at Paris. It had been reprinted, although not in its entirety, by the nurseryman and pomologist, André Leroy, but Bunyard's version was complete and recopied for him by the Librarian to the French National Horticultural Society, 'revealing several mistakes in the first reprint', he pedantically commented. A copy of this little book has survived in Wye College Library and inside, written in Bunyard's hand, is 'No 32 of 100'. Possibly Bunyard produced the book as a gift for friends (the College copy belonged to R.T. Pearl), for it is never mentioned for sale in the nursery catalogue.[39]

******

Like all pomologists, Bunyard was intrigued by unusual fruits. Among the curiosities growing at Allington were the Chinese flat peach, for example, and the White Apricot, which he believed was one of Tradescant's introductions from Algeria. He was also interested in the Chinese cherry, *Prunus pseudocerasus*, bringing it up to RHS meetings and exhibiting trees at Chelsea Flower Show. Although not a fruit for the English climate it proved to have unexpected value. Bunyard had obtained his material from America, but it appears to have also been introduced from Japan at the same time by 'Cherry' Ingram, the ornamental-cherry collector, who lived not far from Allington at Benenden. The Chinese cherry had the virtue, Bunyard found, of fruiting by itself and hence, presumably, being self-fertile. Most cherry varieties require another tree close by to act as pollinator and they are particularly fussy as to which variety. A self-fertile cherry was an attractive proposition, but its early flowering ruled it out for England. It did, however,

---

[39] 'The Catalogue of Fruit Trees of Le Lectier', *Journal of Pomology*, vol. 1, 1920, p. 244; a copy of the book is also held in the RHS Lindley Library.

prove valuable to British cherry growers for another reason. It roots readily from cuttings, unlike most varieties, and was exploited at East Malling to produce the Colt cherry rootstock when crossed with the native mazzard (*P. avium*). Colt became the main cherry rootstock and has only recently been overtaken in commercial orchards. It seems likely that the research station received its original material from Bunyard, although there are no surviving records to prove it, but he did give East Malling some 40 cherry varieties.[40] Bunyard was part of the British network of plant exchanges, sending not only cherries, but numerous parcels of graft and bud-wood, and trees of all the fruits to East Malling and, without doubt, to John Innes also.

His studies and searches for new material for the nursery took him to many European countries – and further afield to Algeria and South Africa. Bunyard visited Algeria in 1921. To be more accurate, he talked to the Horticultural Club in London in May 1922 about Algerian horticulture, presumably having made his trip at harvest-time the previous autumn. An introduction to the country may have come via his French contacts: there was then much interest in Algerian orchard crops and vineyards. His talk, unfortunately, was not printed in any journal, so it is impossible to know if he found any noteworthy local fruits or practices. Later, when writing about the distribution of the apple, he confirms visits to both Algeria and Tunis, where he found one lone variety of apple growing 'under the shade of Palms in the island of Sfax.'[41]

South Africa was his destination in March 1927. Their fruits were the most prominent southern-hemisphere Empire imports on English markets and it is easy to understand why he might wish to visit the Western Cape, where most of these were produced and where, furthermore, Bunyard's nursery had customers. The invitation may have come from the pioneer nurseryman H. E. V. Pickstone, who had lectured in London in 1903 and probably supplied Bunyard's with its stock of Cape plums. The Cape growers' community acted as hosts. Bunyard visited Worcester, where the

---

[40] My thanks to Dr Ken Tobutt of East Malling Research for the information on the Colt rootstock and for allowing me to examine the East Malling accession books.
[41] Tjaden, W. L. *The Horticultural Club*, 1975, p. 11 (this booklet is held in the RHS Lindley Library); Bunyard, E. A., 'The History and Development of the Apple', reprinted as a booklet from *The School Science Review*, No 77, Oct. 1938, pp. 69–76.

Pickstone nurseries were based, the government Experimental Station at Stellenbosch, and the headquarters of the Cape Town shippers: in his view, the best cold-storage facilities in the world.

In March the fruits were ripe and it was an ideal time to visit the historic vineyards at Constantia near Cape Town although, by the 1920s, many had been turned over to table grapes for the English market. He motored north into the Drakenstein Valley to see the peaches and nectarines around Stellenbosch, Wellington and Worcester, where the English varieties of Thomas Rivers occupied the premier place. He tasted Cape plums, well ripened on the tree, but was not converted – 'rather one fruit of Transparent Gage than a bushel of Kelseys!' Climbing up to Paarl he continued into the Hex Valley to see pear plantations and then further north to the cooler climate of Ceres where he found, for the first time, a rare occurrence in his experience – good apples and a first-class Jonathan. As in Algeria, water was the main problem for these fruit growers, not an English concern; but, on the other hand, their hot, dry climate did give them much less worry over disease and blemished fruits. He returned with a photograph of a solitary protea in bloom – March was not the time to see South African flowers – but there do not seem to have been any fruit finds. [42]

******

Bunyard was quick to see the possibilities of technical innovations and to make these available to the public. The nursery, like most others, sold trees grafted onto dwarfing rootstocks using 'Rivers' Broad Leaf Paradise' for apples and the quince for pears. Catalogues show that Bunyard's were early users of the latest rootstocks emerging from East Malling Research Station and were grafting onto the more-dwarfing 'Type IX' (M9), which remains the main apple rootstock used today.

He was also an early advocate of the Lorette system of pruning. This regime of detailed summer pruning was slowly adopted in a modified form

---

[42] Bunyard, E. A., 'Fruit Growing in the Western Cape Province', *The Gardeners' Chronicle*, 14 May, 1927, pp. 338–340; 21 May, pp. 357–358; Bunyard, E. A., 'Two Valleys in the Western Cape Province', *The Gardeners' Chronicle*, 6 Aug., 1927, pp. 110–111.

in England. It was essential for keeping a line of cordons fruitful and giving some touches to the new, more-dwarfed orchard trees. It had been developed by Louis Lorette of the Horticultural School at Wagonville, outside Douai in north-west France. His techniques came to prominence following an article by a Versailles colleague which had brought 3,000 visitors to Wagonville in June 1912. They may have included Bunyard and Herbert Durham, then President of the Herefordshire Fruit Growers' Association. Durham would lecture the RHS on the subject in July 1917, at a meeting chaired by Edward. The system gained wider acceptance following the English translation of Lorette's book in 1925. Bunyard had helped with this, particularly in rendering abstruse technical jargon.[43]

******

Bunyard was much involved in the wider politics of horticulture, one strand of which was the setting-up of the first British trials of fruit varieties for the market grower. As we have seen, evaluation remained largely in the hands of nurserymen, head gardeners and members of the RHS Fruit and Vegetable Committee. A variety might win an award but this was not necessarily a measure of its commercial potential. No independent assessment for the commercial grower existed.

In a paper published in the first issue of the *Journal of Pomology* in 1919 – not credited, but almost certainly written by EAB – the author discussed the 'strong movement [that] has been started in this country and in France to pass a law which will give the raiser of a new plant exclusive rights in their propagation and sale for a period of years, so as to recompense him for the considerable outlay which such work entails.' Such protection in Europe was not achieved in Bunyard's lifetime, but many of the points raised in this article were embodied in the aims of the Commercial Fruit Trials set up jointly in 1922 by the Ministry of Agriculture and the RHS at Wisley Gardens.[44]

This article was not entirely in favour of patenting new fruits, pointing out the major difficulty in deciding with certainty that the fruit was new

---

[43] Lorette, L., *The Lorette System of Pruning* (London, 1925), translated by W. R. Dykes, p. 14.

[44] 'The Patenting of New Fruits', not credited, but almost certainly written by Bunyard,

rather than a reintroduction under a new name – an age-old practice, contributing mightily to confusion. The only solution was a large collection of fruit trees for, as the author wearily observed, 'even if we assume the existence of Pomologists so skilled in fruit knowledge that they would undertake to recognize any of the 5,000 or more Pears that have been introduced, it is quite certain that a Committee of such men or super-men could not be expected to recall at any moment these varieties from their inner consciences.' A second problem was proving the worth of a new fruit. This could only be gauged after many seasons' growth and observation. The 'vigour and fertility of the tree, its capacity to grow well in soils other than its own, are points of the first importance, and the most richly flavoured fruit which does not possess these primary qualities is worthless for the great bulk of growers. The value of a new fruit can only be determined after trial in different localities.' Here was the essence of the new trials: rigorous evaluation, side by side with a large fruit collection. It seems likely that Bunyard was contributing to the discussions before they were presented to the RHS Council on 13 December 1921.[45] Although he was not yet a Council member, he was nominated along with three Council members to form a committee on the matter. The Ministry of Agriculture's negotiator and Chief Scientific Advisor was Sir Daniel Hall. Hall, a soil scientist and pioneer of university agricultural education, was Wye College's first principal. His meteoric career took him to the office of Secretary to the Board of Agriculture in 1917, then Chief Scientific Advisor. A polymath and bon viveur, he would have had plenty of common ground with Edward.

The stated purpose of the trials had all the signs of Bunyard's influence: 'The primary object in the testing of new varieties of fruit is to show their potential value for market purposes in order to bring prominently before growers varieties of exceptional promise at the earliest possible moment,

---

Journal of Pomology, vol. 1, 1920, pp. 50–53. In USA, the Plant Patent Act was passed in 1930; the European International Union for the Protection of New Varieties of Plants was signed by five nations in 1961 and by three more countries, including the UK, in 1962. My thanks to Dr Alison Lean, UK Plant Variety Rights Officer for Fruit, for this information.

[45] RHS Lindley Library, RHS Council Minutes, 13 Dec, 1921.

and to afford an opportunity to them to see them growing on sufficient scale. Other objects are to define the characters of varieties under trial and to compare them with known varieties, so that accurate descriptions may be made, synonyms determined and the nomenclature of the fruits made more exact.'[46]

The work of the trials was carried out by Wisley staff, assisted by a grant from the Ministry and administered by a joint-committee of ten under the chairmanship of William Bateson, then director of the John Innes Institute. At his death in 1926, he was succeeded, at John Innes and on the committee, by Sir Daniel Hall.[47] The committee, with equal representation from the Ministry and the RHS, included Bunyard, Charles Nix (chairman of the Fruit and Vegetable Committee), Cuthbert Smith (a Maidstone commercial fruit farmer based at Loddington), Wisley's director F. J. Chittenden, and the chairman of the Wisley Garden Committee. The Ministry representatives were headed by its horticultural controller, [Sir] William Lobjoit, and deputy-controller H. V. Taylor. Varieties to be tested were first submitted to the Fruit and Vegetable Committee, who made the selections for trial. After some years of observation, the best were then sent out for further evaluation at ten stations in different parts of the country, that in Kent being at East Malling.

By the end of 1931, the first trials of strawberries, currants and raspberries had been completed and 110 varieties of apples were under investigation. The first report was published and an exhibit of apples from the trials displayed at the Imperial Fruit Show held in Manchester, which Bunyard attended.[48] There was one important fruit, however, that could not be trialled at Wisley – cherries – which did not thrive in its sandy, acid soil. At Bunyard's suggestion, made to the RHS Council in September 1932, it was agreed that cherries would be trialled at the Kent Farm Institute at Borden,

---

[46] Chittenden, F. J., ed., *Apples and Pears, Varieties and Cultivation in 1934*, op. cit., p. 4.

[47] 'The Testing of Varieties of Hardy Fruit for Commercial Purposes', *JRHS*, vol. 48, 1922–23, pp. 65–67; *JRHS*, vol. 52, 1927, pp. 265–268.

[48] 'Trials of Varieties of Hardy Fruits for Commercial Purposes', *JRHS*, vol. 57, 1932, pp. 246–284; 'Apples from the Commercial Trials Wisley, at the Imperial Fruit Show, 1931', *JRHS*, vol. 57, 1932, pp. 285–286.

near Sittingbourne, opened in 1930, which continued to trial cherries up until the 1960s.[49]

Bunyard, who had been elected to the RHS Council in 1923, the year after the establishment of the Commercial Trials, had become essential to their management. Some idea of his involvement can be glimpsed from the Council minutes of 1931 and 1932, when the end of the initial ten-year Ministry grant was in sight and further funding had to be secured. The Society alone could not afford to fund them. At the meeting of 24 November 1931, Edward was charged with preparing the report and request for further support. Hall was very likely also involved, since he had joined the RHS Council that year. In May 1932, Hall was reporting on the trials and was president of the deputation 'appointed to wait' on the Ministry along with Bunyard and Lobjoit. The meeting, on 30 June, succeeded in obtaining funding of £750, but more negotiations were needed to secure the trials' future. On 20 September, Hall and Bunyard undertook to meet with Wisley staff to discuss estimates to put before the Ministry. It was also decided to stage a comprehensive exhibit from the trials for the Autumn Show in October. To oil the wheels, Chittenden suggested that 'the Departmental Committee of the Ministry be invited to see the exhibit and be entertained to lunch.' By the time of the Council meeting on 4 October, Hall and Bunyard reported that their submission to the Ministry was complete. It proved to be successful.[50]

The Commercial Trials fulfilled Edward's most ambitious specifications for undertaking fruit research. Each variety was assessed by planting a generous number of specimens – for example, 40 trees of each variety of apple and 100 plants of a strawberry. Records were compiled throughout the season, while every year more varieties were brought in for testing. By 1934 the area of the trials had extended from the initial two acres to 34 acres, and Bunyard was pressing for yet more to be allocated. At a Council meeting on 4 June 1935, he negotiated additional land for a 'standard collection of pears', and he gave the Society a collection of pear varieties. Standard pear

---

[49] RHS Lindley Library, RHS Council Minutes 23 Sept., 1932. My thanks to David Burd, former lecturer at the Kent Farm Institute.

[50] RHS Lindley Library, RHS Council Minutes, 24 Nov., 1931; 4 May, 1932; 30 June, 1932; 19 July, 1932; 20 Sept., 1932; 4 Oct., 1932.

trees can attain 20 or 30 feet in height, and although this is the best way to gauge the habit of a variety, they take up an enormous amount of space. With visions of Wisley becoming one great orchard, 'Mr Bunyard was asked to keep within limits'![51]

******

Another aspect of Bunyard's work of co-ordination was the organization of fruit conferences, which brought together the professionals and the amateurs – the research workers, fruit growers and gardeners. His efforts were recognized by the RHS by the award of its Gold Veitch Medal for contributions to pomology in 1934.

The idea of an event to publicize the work of the Trials was aired at a Council meeting in October 1932, when it was agreed to hold a conference on apples and pears the following autumn. A committee to make the arrangements was under Edward's chairmanship. He had taken over the Fruit and Vegetable Committee from Charles Nix and together they selected their forces from 'Fruit & Veg.' and the Commercial Trials Committees. He was also chairman of the organizing committee for a similar soft fruit conference in 1935.[52]

The intention of the Apple and Pear Conference was to bring 'before the apple-growing and the apple-eating public the results of our research at Wisley', declared the President in his opening speech.[53] Delegates heard lengthy reports by Hall and A. N. Rawes, who was in charge of running the trials; fundamental fruit research was aired by staff of the research institutes and there was a report on modern, long-term fruit-storage being undertaken at Cambridge by Drs F. Kidd and C. West. The new development allowed fruit to be kept in excellent condition past its natural season. Bunyard presented a long discussion on his classification system for apples and pears,

---

[51] Chittenden, F. J., ed., *Apples and Pears, Varieties and Cultivation in 1934*, op. cit., p 4; RHS Lindley Library, RHS Council Minutes, 4 June 1935.

[52] RHS Lindley Library, RHS Council Minutes, 4 Oct, 1932; 11 Oct., 1932; 11 April, 1933.

[53] Chittenden, F. J., ed., *Apples and Pears, Varieties and Cultivation in 1934*, op. cit., p. 6.

along with a talk by his old friend Herbert Durham. The conference was held in the Crystal Palace simultaneously with the RHS's Autumn Show. Here were mounted displays of new apples under trial at Wisley and of those varieties that had passed through the first stages of assessment and were being grown at the substations. The stars, which went on to be widely planted in commercial orchards after World War Two, were the Laxton varieties – Laxton's Superb and Lord Lambourne apples, Laxton's Superb and Beurré Bedford pears, Laxton's Delicious plum. The exception was Marjorie's Seedling plum, which was found growing at a farm in Beenham, Berkshire.

Both conferences were remarkable for the contribution made by the commercial growers whose interest and support for the trials was crucial. The county of Kent was well represented at each event. In 1933 [Sir] Thomas Neame, of Macknade Farms, Faversham (a member of the organizing committee) spoke of the secrets of his success with pears, and Talbot Edmonds, Bunyard's neighbour, and Spencer Mount of Canterbury were also involved. In 1935, Ronald Vincent spoke on large-scale strawberry growing and [Sir] Leslie Doubleday on cherries for market. EAB surveyed cherry varieties from the pomologist's viewpoint.[54] His sister Frances illustrated 11 cherry varieties, botanically complete with their stones. The paintings were published in the Proceedings and were likely used as lantern slides. In 1935, a dreadful frost in spring destroyed the blossom in many fruit plantations so there was no fruit from the trials. Instead there was a mouthwatering display of cherries and soft fruits staged by the Kent National Farmers' Union, organized by Bunyard.[55]

The eventual results of the Commercial Trials were not as satisfactory as everyone had hoped. The Wisley site proved frost-prone and the crops were often affected, making it difficult to achieve meaningful records. During the 1950s the whole operation was transferred to Brogdale Farm near Faversham in east Kent, an area long celebrated for its orchard crops, and reconstituted as the National Fruit Trials. The Ministry took sole charge. The

---

[54] For reports of conferences see Chittenden, F. J., ed., ibid.; Chittenden, F. J., ed., *Cherries and Soft Fruits Varieties and Cultivation in 1935* (Royal Horticultural Society, London 1935).

[55] See 'Edward Bunyard the Committee Man' in this volume.

reference collection also moved to Brogdale, and later the cherry collections at Borden and Swanley College were transferred to form the National Fruit Collections. It is now a unique resource, the largest collection in the world of temperate fruits growing on one site.

******

The first steps in the creation of this reference collection established alongside the Commercial Trials at Wisley were doubtless taken by Bunyard. The Bunyard Nursery provided many accessions, as did colleagues and competitors Edward Laxton, Joseph Cheal and John Allgrove. Fred Streeter, head gardener at Petworth House, supplied a number of old Sussex apples, and regional varieties came also from the research stations. Another rich source lay in the fruit sent in to the Fruit and Vegetable Committee for identification.

The Apple and Pear Conference of 1934 presented a singularly good opportunity to capture more rarities. A highlight of the Conference and the RHS Show was the exhibit of apples from all over the country which aspired to collect as many as possible of those grown, including local and uncommon varieties, so as to bring the entire population together in one place. The plan was hatched the previous autumn when Bunyard reported to Council that H. V. Taylor would collect local varieties through the regional Ministry Inspectors. By happy coincidence 1934 was more or less 50 years since the famous National Apple Congress of 1883, when over 1,500 apple varieties were brought from across Britain and abroad with the same objective.

The exhibit did not quite match the Victorians', but some 900 apples and 200 cider varieties (from Long Ashton) were on show. With £20 obtained from Council to cover the expenses, Bunyard organized contributions from six European countries.[56] Like the 1883 Congress, this was a unique opportunity to check identities, sort out synonyms, and clear up nomenclature. Bunyard must have felt that history was repeating itself when he laboured over the plates of apples, as his father had done in 1883. Any that were shown to be 'new' were accessed into the reference collection. This

---

[56] RHS Lindley Library, RHS Council Minutes, 28 Nov., 1933; 15 Aug., 1934.

formed the basis of H. V. Taylor's *The Apples of England* of 1936, illustrated with colour photographs in the style of the New York series. Taylor was then the Ministry's Horticultural Commissioner. Whether Bunyard was hurt that all his self-funded and meticulous work was apparently overtaken by that of a Ministry employee, we will never know. 'Taylor' replaced 'Bunyard' in many people's minds, but the book did not have Bunyard's precision and learning, nor his deep familiarity with the varieties.

A new impetus was given to this collecting with the appointment in 1936 of J. M. S. (Jock) Potter, a young scholarship student at Wisley whom Bunyard, together with Hall and Taylor, had selected for the post of 'pomologist to the Commercial Trials' following the retirement of Rawes. Potter became fired with the collector's acquisitive passion to track down as many as he could of the varieties described by Dr Hogg in his *Fruit Manual*. Apples were entering the conservation agenda and seen as the inheritance of the country-bred man, now threatened by an expanding urban population. The apple was in need of rescuing again. Potter came to regard Bunyard as his mentor, with an unrivalled knowledge of varieties and their identities. Together, by the time of Bunyard's death, they had further increased the number of named apples and of other fruits.

Potter was to raise the apple count to over 2,000 during and after the Second World War. Many new accessions were discovered in the parcels of fruit sent by home-owners curious about the identity of their own trees, a resource once more due to the exigencies of war. New varieties raised by fruit breeders in England, Canada, the USA and the Continent that were included in the commercial trials before the war continued to make the collections truly international.

Bunyard might have been gratified, if surprised, that the cause of fruit conservation and appreciation was taken up by Philip Morton Shand, author of books on wine and food. His *Book of Food* was on the Bunyard family's shelf of 'indispensables', although the two men did not meet, as far as anyone knows.[57] Shand was passionate about English apples. Like Edward, he was deeply concerned that their diversity should not disappear. He was inspired by his father's memories of the 1890s when affluent Victorians expected

---

[57] I thank the late Sir Leslie Martin for this and other information on Shand's fruit-collecting activities.

apples in a wonderful succession of qualities and flavours almost all year round. Shand was a linguist, scholar and ambassador for modern European architecture, but during the war with the Admiralty in Bath he had spent his spare time tracking down little-known varieties of apples. He was among the first members of the RHS Fruit Group founded in 1945, with Sir Ronald Hatton as chairman. One of its aims was to re-examine good, old varieties. Shand launched a campaign to prevent these treasures of the past slipping away. He made broadcasts and organized a network of friends, including (Sir) Leslie Martin, the architect, Gerald Finzi, the composer, and one Miss Holliday, in Yorkshire, to gather forgotten varieties. He raised public awareness, so that apples flooded in to be identified. Any that proved unusual and 'new' to the collection were pursued with missionary zeal – graftwood was obtained and passed on to Wisley. Shand recalled taking 'wood that was frequently not merely dishearteningly unpromising but to all appearances utterly sere and shrivelled' to Potter, who with 'a wizard's sleight of hand' grafted and propagated new trees.

When the collections and the trials moved to Brogdale in the 1950s, Potter became the first director of the Ministry's new horticulture station. At the same time a selection of varieties suitable for English gardens was planted at Wisley, which formed the RHS fruit collection. The Defra National Fruit Collections at Brogdale now contain over 4,500 varieties of apples, pears, plums, cherries, medlars, quinces, cobnuts, currants, gooseberries and grapes.

The collections are one of Bunyard's greatest legacies: a remarkable 'orchard' in which the fruits he documented, and very many more, are conserved for the use of everyone interested in fruit. Pomologists, nurserymen, breeders, students of history and lovers of fruit, myself included, can all be lastingly grateful for his ambition to create a comprehensive collection.[58] Bunyard would have heartily approved that records have been kept for over 50 years at Brogdale and that an *Apple Register*

---

[58] For a history of the Defra National Fruit Collections see Potter, J.M.S., 'National Fruit Trials: A Brief History 1922–1972' (Ministry of Agriculture Fisheries and Food, London, 1972); Morgan, J. and Richards, A., *The New Book of Apples* (London, 2002) pp. 100–104. *The New Book of Apples* contains a directory to all the apples, over 2,000 varieties, growing at Brogdale.

of all the varieties growing in the collection and the names of all those ever recorded in Britain, together with their hundreds of synonyms, was compiled by Potter's colleague, Muriel Smith. They remain a memorial to Bunyard's outstanding contribution. His and Potter's foresight and determination produced a gene-bank of fruit unrivalled in the world.

CHAPTER NINE

Edward Bunyard the Rosarian

JOAN MORGAN

Bunyard's achievements in pomology were outstanding but he also made a great contribution to the study of roses. His reputation rests on his book *Old Garden Roses*, published in 1936, and the remarkably large collection of roses formed at the Allington nursery. Bunyard's particular interest lay with old roses, the so-called 'European' roses cultivated for centuries in Britain and on the Continent as opposed to the much more popular modern roses of the 1920s and 1930s. His passion would fire the enthusiasm of some of the leading gardeners of the time, notably Vita Sackville-West, while he made sure the nursery could supply plants enough to fuel the revival. This interest gave Bunyard entry into another social group. Already mixing with the gardening aristocracy through the RHS, now he would make contact, in his search for roses, with the upper-crust English gardeners of the French Riviera. Here he could holiday in congenial company, enjoying fine food and wine.

Bunyard's research methods differed little from those he adopted in studying fruit save that he took far greater notice of the artistic record, visiting galleries all over the Continent. It was another side of the nursery trade for Edward: out of the kitchen garden into the pleasure ground. In Victorian years, the flower was at once the ladies' special preserve, the most prized cut-flower of the country house and the premier competition bloom. However, by the 1920s, it had reached a crisis point. For many years breeders had focussed on one group, the hybrid tea, and were now producing flowers with strong, harsh colours – oranges and fiery reds – often with no perfume. The hybrid teas were the exhibitor's favourite, the florist's most sought-after, and appeared *en masse* in the formal garden to replace Victorian bedding plants. The colours, the absence of perfume and the way they were grown as unnatural, stunted shrubs in rose gardens caused Bunyard and like-minded souls to shudder. But they were just one of many new groups pushing old roses into the background, so that they seemed almost lost for ever at the turn of the century.

The old groups were derived from species native to Europe or the Near East and long established as garden plants. The most ancient were the gallicas: short spreading bushes with large flowers of deep or bluish red, occasionally pink. The closely related damasks with a headier perfume, from which attar of roses was distilled, were larger shrubs with pale to deep pink and white flowers. Albas, which took their name from the white and blush-pink flowers and glaucous foliage, were tall and superbly scented. Finally, there were the centifolias with intensely perfumed, many-petalled flowers, ranging from palest to deepest pink, which opened into a cabbage shape; hence the popular name of cabbage rose. The moss rose, with its mossy, sweetly scented glands on the sepals of the flower and stalk, developed from the centifolias and was especially popular in England during the early 1800s. These roses were in their full glory in June but, except for the autumn damask or Quatre Saisons, did not flower again. Their failing was to be colourless for most of the year: one of the main reasons for their fall from grace.

Their eclipse was caused by four Chinese plants brought to Europe between 1791 and 1824. There were two China roses: Parson's Pink or Old Blush, and Slater's Crimson; and two tea roses: Hume's Blush and Park's Yellow.[1] They flowered in June and into July and again in August and beyond. This was seen as so remarkable that the poet Thomas Moore reputedly wrote the song that begins ''Tis the last rose of summer' straight after finding the Old Blush China in flower in September when at Powerscourt in Ireland. All four Chinese roses brought in the revolutionary feature of repeat flowering. The tea roses introduced a new shape of flower with a pointed bud and high-

---

[1] See Thomas, G. Stuart, *The Old Shrub Roses* (London, 1957, reprint 1986), 'Revolution', pp. 32–38.

centred bloom as well as a perfume said to be like a freshly-opened chest of China tea. Additional colours – yellow and a proper scarlet – also emerged in the new groups created by hybridizing these Chinese roses with the old 'European' roses. This proliferation of roses was both timely and convenient: they were more compatible with the country-house calendar and were ideal material for the increasingly popular flower shows.

Every rose garden was planted with the latest hybrids. These included rich pink Bourbons with the perfume of their damask parent and the colourful reds and crimsons of the hybrid perpetuals, which both flowered again in high summer after the family returned to the country from the London season. The climbing Noisettes, a marriage between the Old Blush China and the musk rose, that flowered pink, creamy yellow and white, garlanded its perimeter; and the bright pink and scarlet China roses, seedlings of the original introductions, flowered until the first frosts, during the shooting season. As cut flowers they lasted longer than the old roses, so through the summer their blooms were brought by the basketful to fill rose-bowls in the drawing-room and make centrepieces for the dining-table. The most desirable and decorative for indoor display were the tea roses, with colours from white through pink and yellow to deepest red. Their shapely form in bud made them first choice for the lady's bouquet and the gentleman's buttonhole. They were rather tender, however, and needed the protection of glass; but they could be brought on and into flower for Easter, a time the family was invariably at home, anticipating roses, peaches, figs and grapes from the early forcing-houses.

When tea roses were crossed with hybrid perpetuals, the resulting hybrid teas were hardy as well as beautifully formed. They set alight a passion for roses that knew no bounds, and contributed to the founding of the National Rose Society in 1876. The Society's shows provoked breeders to create ever more perfect exhibition blooms and seemed to confirm disdain for old roses. However, the enthusiasm got the better of itself. Hybrids raised from crosses with the so-called Austrian Briar, in fact a Persian species, added brilliant yellows and oranges into the spectrum but had no perfume at all. Furthermore, they suffered from an epidemic of the disease black spot. These began to appear in the 1900s and athough plenty of breeders carried on with this line through the 1920s and 1930s, a reaction set in. The RHS Clay Challenge Cup for 'a rose of good form and colour with a true old rose scent', introduced in 1913, might be thought a marker. (It was not always awarded, as on four occasions in the 1930s, when Bunyard was often one of the judges.)

******

Old roses had a romance modern sorts of the time lacked. Their names – Maiden's Blush, Apothecary's Rose and Rosa Mundi – evoked a different age. Edward expressed this well: he valued their 'softness of colouring, and their associations with the past, … their look of fitness in an old garden. … To have … the very rose of which Petrarch or Chaucer wrote or one which Botticelli or Crivelli painted so lovingly, will to most of us, lend an added glow to its beauty.' And their scent was unrivalled: 'the Damask and the Cabbage roses take first place in any scale of perfumes.'[2] To this could be added their practical virtues of hardiness, freedom from disease and tolerance of neglect and poor soil, which commended them to a wide range of gardening abilities – a bonus for nurseryman and customer.

Old roses were a minority taste when Bunyard published his book in 1936. The public needed a good deal of persuasion to buy the plants or even give them a second glance. The form of their flowers was supremely unfashionable while the 'long pointed bud of the Hybrid Tea reigns supreme' though this concealed 'the golden anthers … surely as beautiful in a rose as in a paeony.' Modern rose flowers, Edward thought, were unbalanced, and out of proportion to their leaves and the plant as a whole, a parody of the rose's native grace. In the wider rose world, in which the colours gold and flame were at their height of popularity, the purple stain in some gallicas was regarded as beyond the pale and treated with unspeakable disdain. Bunyard came eloquently to their defence: '[on the] rich crimsons of the Gallicas and the soft pinks of the Albas, there will be no two opinions the one rich without harshness, the other delicate without feebleness.'

Roses did not appear to be a central preoccupation of Edward Bunyard until the 1930s. Bunyard's nursery had always sold the plants and, as Victorian formality gave way to a stylized naturalism from the beginning of the century, had exploited any trend towards a revival of old roses. A leading advocate was Gertrude Jekyll. She commented at the RHS Rose Conference

---

[2] Bunyard, E. A., *Old Garden Roses* (London, 1936), pp. ix–xii.

in 1902 that although old roses had been neglected they 'are now valued as they should be, and, instead of merely existing in forgotten corners in some gardens only, they were being planted in fair quantity.' That every type of rose should be deployed – each in the manner best suited to it – was the theme of her *Roses for English Gardens* published in the same year.[3]

It was an approach closely followed by George Bunyard. In *England's National Flower*, an illustrated brochure intended as a 'drawing room book' issued by the nursery in 1904, he organized the varieties into their most suitable roles: roses for shrub borders at their peak in different months from June to November, roses for 'Arches, Pillars and Verandas', as well as 'Rampant Roses for Bowers and Pergolas', the latest garden feature as people took a greater delight in outdoor life. In line with 'the increasing desire to deck our gardens pictorially' that Miss Jekyll had observed, there were roses for decorating walls and covering buildings, clothing banks and planting as hedges. Nor were the necessities of elegant living forgotten: he presented varieties that were best for cut flowers, for buttonholes and bouquets, and were the sweetest scented. Exhibitors were told those blooms most likely to secure top prizes.[4] The nursery was, however, lessening its emphasis on the perfect competitive flower, the goal of the National Rose Society. Instead, it was promoting 'roses for the mansion, rectory, farm house, villa and suburban garden where owners prefer ... flowers of a natural growth rather than a limited number of well developed blossoms.' To silence any cavil at the presumption of a fruit-man writing of roses, George Bunyard declared that he had been amongst his roses since 1856 and 'for 20 years on the committee of the National Rose Society'. This did not, however, stop his questioning the direction rose-breeding was taking. The Bunyards were behind Miss Jekyll, offering 'heartiest congratulations' on her rose book in their catalogue of 1904–05.

Edward, too, was involved in his father's book. He provided the photographs of roses in bowls and baskets arranged to display their essential

---

[3] Jekyll, G., 'The Garden Roses', *Journal of the Royal Horticultural Society* (*JRHS*), vol. 27, 1902–03, pp. 503–504; Jekyll, G., *Roses for English Gardens* (London, 1902; reprint 1987).

[4] *England's National Flower* (George Bunyard & Co., Maidstone and London, 1904).

character – the shapely buds of the tea roses, the clusters of rambler flowers and the single, open flowers of the native sweet briars. Their style was in strong contrast to roses on the show-bench, jammed upright in the regulation boxes used to display prize-winning blooms. Perhaps Edward had a hand in the production too, helping in the choice of quotations (all relating to old roses) liberally scattered through the text. Comments on matters such as the beauty of single flowers, the necessity to take care with the colours in the placing of roses and the inclusion of recipes for rose *pots pourris*, might also be indications of his influence.

The demise of old roses was perhaps not so imminent as has been assumed. A number of nurseries and gardens still had collections. For example, G. N. Smith of Daisy Hill Nursery in Northern Ireland was a rich source and valuable contact, and the George Longley Nursery at Rainham had continously maintained a collection since the early part of the nineteenth century (it was still selling them in the 1970s).[5] The world's two largest collections were the Rosarium in Sangerhausen near Leipzig and the Rosaraie de l'Haÿ outside Paris. The Rosarium Sangerhausen, founded in 1903 by the Verein Deutscher Rosenfreunde (Society of German Friends of Roses), boasted 5,000 different roses in 1933 when it began to hold annual festivals. EAB certainly went to Dresden, but may not have visited Leipzig. Rosaraie de l'Haÿ was the creation of Jules Gravereaux who had retired in 1892 to a country house near Chatenay and the park of Sceaux to devote himself to roses. He was a partner in Bon Marché, the Paris department store founded by Aristide Bousicault and inspiration for Zola's novel *The Ladies' Paradise*. Gravereaux's garden was entirely filled with roses. By 1900 there were 3,000 varieties and increasing. Bunyard did make a trip to the Rosaraie de l'Haÿ although, it seems, not until 1939.

Although these nurseries and collectors, and others besides, had old roses to hand, few were advertising them. The Bunyard nursery was fundamental to the revival since it promoted them in catalogues, collected them, propagated them and introduced them as fast as possible. Roses had never been neglected by Bunyard's and by 1924–5 their 'Catalogue of Roses' was a beautiful, glossy production. Edward's photographs in the style of those in *England's National Flower*, together with paintings and

---

[5] My thanks to Tom La Dell for this information.

line-drawings presumably by his sister Frances, made it the most attractive of all the nursery's publications. From 1935, these were reinforced in prose by Marguerite Bunyard's precise colour descriptions.

Bunyard could see a market in the discerning gardener. He also appreciated that publicizing roses was good for the image of the rest of the stock. Roses, above all flowers, had a wide appeal. Moreover, roses had one advantage over fruit trees: they could be bulked up more quickly for sale. In two or three years a new rose could be worked up into hundreds of plants. Roses may have been seen as a quicker return in the economic depression of the early 1930s, although when purses are tight there is usually less demand for ornamental plants. Whatever the reason, the cause of old roses gave the name and reputation of Bunyard's a fresh appeal in another market sector.

As he had sold fruit and vegetables, so promotion of roses was geared to the self-image of the customer. Old roses had none of the vulgarity that tainted the modern hybrid teas; the vulgar and the unrefined were to be avoided at all costs by the aspiring and the established arbiters of good taste. National pride also flourished in the 1930s, when 'almost overnight the middle class rediscovered romantic patriotism' according to René Cutforth, who remembered that 'phrases like "Our English Heritage"... and "Pageant of History" took a firm hold in their hearts.'[6] Bunyard's marketing strategy promoted old roses as part of England's gardening heritage –'the roses of our grandparents to be planted in all old-world gardens' with visions of the Tudor roses of York and Lancaster. He extolled their tasteful luxuriance and their allusive refinement as the subjects of Old Master paintings. He sold a garden overflowing with the choicest blooms, perfumed, and redolent of gracious living.

******

The catalogue was one route to better sales, but the biggest promotional exercise was *Old Garden Roses* published in 1936. The book drew the reader into rediscovering their enduring charm and fascination. It proved inspirational to many gardeners, who found they could recreate this old-

---

[6] Cutforth, R., *Later Than We Thought* (Newton Abbot, Devon, 1976), pp. 25–6.

rose magic through Bunyard's Nursery. It placed roses in the wider context of literature and painting and, being a *Country Life* publication, it was executed with style. The layout was spacious with full-page plates and a watercolour by Frances Bunyard for its dust jacket. It was illustrated in part by photographs of roses arranged in the style of nineteenth-century still-lifes, but showing sufficient detail to gain a good idea of a variety's qualities. These were the work of P. Sweatman Hedgeland, whose business in the Broadway was close to Bunyard's shop. The incredibly-named photographer may have taken other pictures that one has presumed were Bunyard's, but this was the only time that Bunyard credited someone else.

The book's content was split between a directory and a history of the plant itself. Bunyard's definition of 'old' drew the line at 1840, so the listing included the old gallicas, damasks, albas, centifolias and moss roses, some of the earliest crosses such as the Bourbons, Noisettes and China roses, as well as native Scots or Burnet roses, dog roses, and species roses 'with a grace and charm which the gardener has lost in his selection of size and showiness.'

Bunyard's approach to the story of the rose combined, as always, his keen eye for plant detail with a close study of literature. An extra novel layer of evidence came from paintings. Many years of haunting galleries had convinced him that artists recorded the plants of their time and that these images provided valuable clues. Whenever on holiday in Italy, passing through Paris, or going to Germany, Holland or Belgium on horticultural matters, he seems to have made time for museums with Renaissance and Dutch still-life paintings.

The history of the rose posed many teasing questions which Edward approached with his usual brio. Not all of his answers were right, but his line of attack can be seen from what follows. Twelve different sorts of red and white roses were recorded in 100 AD by the Roman naturalist Pliny the Elder. Identifying these with any acknowledged group of roses was to an extent guesswork, although Bunyard's efforts were regarded as valiant.[7] Gallicas were believed to have been cultivated in Roman gardens, as well as the damask rose, a development from the gallicas, and probably also the alba, a cross between the native dog rose and a gallica or damask parent. The Paestum Rose, taking its name from a place near Naples and known all

---

[7] Darlington, H.R., 'Writings on the Rose – 1', *JRHS*, vol. 63, 1938, p. 122.

over Italy in Pliny's time, was thought to be the autumn damask. Bunyard's quest – following in the footsteps of previous travellers – to find it growing at Paestum proved fruitless: 'The tawny Doric temples still look over the uncultivated marshes towards the now distant sea and keep their secret. A few straggling plants of the [native] Ever-green Rose (*R. sempervirens*) were all that existed when I made my pilgrimage.'[8]

Some of the Roman roses may have disappeared with the fall of the Western Empire, but roses were sheltered in monastic gardens and became saintly emblems for the Christian Church. In the Middle East, Islam was the vector for the spread of the flower from its homes in Persia and Syria. The damask rose was said to have been reintroduced to Europe by the returning Crusaders, while gallicas were cultivated in thirteenth-century France and albas were found by the fifteenth century in Italy.

Bunyard weaves a scholarly narrative but some of his findings did not fit neatly into the story. He was reading widely, dipping into books untouched by previous rose historians. This led to his discovery that yellow as well as red and white roses were recorded in the estate manual of Ibn Al-'Awwâm, written in Muslim Spain during the twelfth century. Yellow roses could only have been a Persian species, but they were not recorded in Europe until much later. Ibn Al-'Awwâm revealed a Spanish horticulture centuries in advance of northern Europe, with a wealth of roses in palace gardens and botanic collections. The yellow rose must have come with the Umayyad dynasty from Persia, probably via Damascus. Bunyard identifies it as either the Persian Double Yellow, or the Yellow Austrian Briar, so-called because it entered Europe via Austria thanks to contacts with the Ottoman Empire.

Ibn Al-'Awwâm had also recorded roses 'the colour of zulite (celestial blue) and another which is blue outside and yellow within.' The 'blue rose' was an unresolved puzzle, but Bunyard offered a partial explanation in the use of colour terms – 'a subject of great complexity witness, the "purpurea" of the Romans as applied to human hair and also snow. The only link here seems to be the sheen which might be seen on both.' His candidate for the rose that was 'blue' without and yellow within was the Copper Austrian Briar, a form of the Austrian Briar with a coppery glow to the orange-yellow flowers.[9]

---

[8] Bunyard, E. A., *Old Garden Roses*, p. 19.
[9] Ibid. p. 24.

Although these were said to be late sixteenth-century introductions, somehow Edward had to explain away the apparently yellow blooms in the late fourteenth-century painting known as the Wilton Diptych acquired by the National Gallery in London in 1929. A portable altarpiece, it represents the English King Richard II being presented to the Virgin, who is surrounded by angels. As if falling from Heaven onto a meadow studded with violets and daisies are large double 'yellow' roses, causing Bunyard to propose the Persian Double Yellow as their identity. The colour in the painting itself is very pale, but Edward presumed it was originally deeper. If his identification was correct, how to explain that they were 'introduced' so much later and that the English climate was neither hot nor dry enough to support them easily, especially given the skills at the time? He suggested that the artist copied the images from a Persian drawing. When the Diptych was cleaned in the early 1990s, research showed a number of features suggesting the painter's techniques were Italian, thus one who was well travelled and who could have been influenced by a drawing that he had seen in northen Italy, which had many trade and cultural links with the Near East. This research, however, also revealed that the 'yellow' roses owed their colour to a yellow-tinged varnish, which would have been a paler yellow originally. This, of course, changes everything, making the bloom most likely an alba rose such as Alba maxima, which is often creamy white, and one that the artist could have seen with his own eyes in Europe, if not England.[10]

Evidence from paintings was more conclusive for the fifteenth-century, especially in works by Botticelli, Luini and Crivelli. These showed that albas were the most prominent roses of the Italian Renaissance. The work of Crivelli was well represented in the National Gallery, but a trip to the Uffizi in Florence was necessary for Bunyard to consolidate this piece of detective work. He confesses that 'my study of Italian pictures is but that of the ordinary visitor in Italy';[11] nevertheless, it was a quest for Italian paintings, especially those of Botticelli, that took him not only to the Brera

---

[10] Ibid., pp. 49–50; see also Gordon, D., *Making and Meaning, The Wilton Diptych* (National Gallery, 1993), pp. 80–81; my thanks to the National Gallery Information Services and also to Tom La Dell and Dr Alison Lean for their observations on the roses in the Wilton Diptych.

[11] Ibid., pp. 33–34.

in Milan, but to Paris and the Louvre, and Germany to the Kaiser Friedrich Museum in Berlin, and the Wallraf-Richartz Museum in Cologne.

The origin of the fourth old rose group, the centifolias or cabbage roses, was an enigma. Botanists had debated for many years whether centifolias were known to the ancients. Pliny had included the name 'centifolia' in his list, but no evidence of its existence was forthcoming from Roman murals or from fifteenth-century Italian paintings. Cabbage roses in all their splendour, however, were portrayed by the Dutch flower painters of the seventeenth century. They entered the English herbals a little earlier and were greeted in England as the Dutch rose, which gave support to the idea that they emerged first in that country. Bunyard nails the date of their appearance to between 1583 and 1589.[12] Cabbage roses, which would have needed some time to come to popular notice, were not painted by Jan Breughel who died in 1625: 'In those of his pictures I have seen at Antwerp and Berlin, and in those recently gathered together in the Exhibition of Flemish Art at the Brussels Exhibition (1935), there is no rose I should definitely like to identify as a Centifolia. ... It is thus probable that this rose was still a rarity in gardens.' Later paintings, however, frequently included cabbage roses. More galleries had been visited to prove this point: the *Bouquet of Flowers* of Jan Davidsz de Heem in the Royal Museum Brussels, shows 'an undoubted Centifolia ... [and] the Daniel Seeghers in the Dresden Gallery shows the same rose. When we come to Justus van Huysum (1659–1716), himself a great painter of flowers and father of his still more famous son Jan (1682–1749), undoubtedly Cabbage roses are frequently painted.' Appropriately, Bunyard chose the well-known *Vase with Flowers* of Jan van Huysum in the National Gallery as the colour frontispiece to his book. The trip to the Belgian galleries may have been undertaken during the Universal and International Exhibition at Brussels in April 1935 where a large display was staged by the RHS as part of the British trade exhibition; Bunyard was not part of the organizing committee but, as a Council member, there was good reason to cross the Channel. Bunyard's research on the cabbage rose supported the contemporary genetic work being undertaken by C. C. Hurst in Cambridge into the origins of the rose groups. Hurst wrote a paper in 1941 in the RHS *Journal* saying, 'thanks to the initial spade work of the late

---

[12] Ibid., pp. 39–40.

Edward Bunyard we are now in a position to trace the origin or rather the evolution of the *R. centifolia* ... commonly known as the Cabbage Rose' to a late sixteenth-century innovation;[13] now believed to be a cross between the autumn damask and an alba.

To trace the history of the roses of China was a more difficult task. Roses had been cultivated there since the earliest times, but only images in pictures, screens and fans were seen in the West until the first plant introductions to Europe at the end of the eighteenth century. A foray into the 'export' porcelain made during the reign of the Emperor Ch'ien Lung (1736–1795), however, revealed decorations that Bunyard concluded were a form of the China rose: an identification he substantiated after going to the little-known Musée Guimet in Paris to study 'a book of flowers said to have been drawn for the Emperor Chien Lung himself. One page shows the Blush China Rose exactly as we know it today.' A splendid opportunity to pursue this study further came at the 'recent Chinese Art Exhibition in London';[14] this was presumably the Chinese Exhibition of 1935 held at Burlington House. After close examination with a magnification glass of a very early drawing, he felt confident that the China rose in its double, that is cultivated, form was grown in gardens as early as 900 AD.

******

Bunyard had begun seriously collecting roses by 1929, when he wrote an article on 'Old World Roses'[15] that was a foretaste of his book. There was, however, always a good range of roses at the Allington nursery. Pre-war catalogues claim 500 varieties. Many varieties were mentioned in *England's National Flower*, but one cannot assume that all those quoted were grown by the firm. Stocks, too, may have diminished during the war. A number of listed varieties are later noted by Edward as new finds. In 1937 nearly 450 different roses were offered for sale and, although not the largest

---

[13] C. C. Hurst' 'Notes on the Origin and Evolution of our Garden Roses' published in *JRHS* in 1941 and reprinted in Thomas, G. Stuart *Old Shrub Roses*, as chapter IX; see pp. 70–71.

[14] Bunyard, ibid., pp. 55–58.

[15] Bunyard, E. A., 'Old World Roses', *New Flora and Silva*, vol. 2, 1929, pp. 3–10.

rose nursery, Bunyard's was probably one of the most diverse with 'The Best Roses' of every type from the hybrid teas to the more recent hybrid polyanthas (now floribunda), hybrid musks and rugosas for the wilder garden, ramblers and a range of climbers of all sorts, as well as old roses and species roses. It was a more comprehensive range than Laxton's or Rivers' (Laxton's raised new hybrid teas and Rivers' had long been famous for its roses). While specialist rose breeders like Dickson and McGredy were promoting their latest hybrid teas every year, Bunyard's 'striking novelties' were the old sorts, such as Fantin-Latour, 'for those who like the Rose as a garden flower, not Exhibition blooms' and the climber Jaune Desprez, noted for its scent, which was said to perfume a whole garden. These appealed to quite a different market: the customer who was selective, looking for old-world charm and the cachet that these forgotten roses were attracting. Between 1936 and 1939, Bunyard's main catalogue introduced a separate section, 'Old Garden Roses'. An increase in numbers in all the old groups was evident by 1939 with a selection of 18 different sorts of cabbage roses, 21 moss roses, 15 gallicas, and the number of species roses more than trebled to 74.

Bunyard's rose finds were very likely grown close to the Bungalow since he refers to the 'collection' as being in his garden. Here he budded up his latest acquisitions, brought home as a carefully wrapped bud-stick in his pocket.[16] Within a year or so he might have a flowering plant to study and bring into the nursery's stocks. Roses became a collecting passion that took him all over the country and to the Continent. Although the usefulness of a new 'discovery' as a garden plant was never far from his mind, his enthusiasm was never subverted by commerce. Witness his fascination for species roses, in many cases too vigorous and fleeting for all but the largest gardens. Bunyard's writings made it plain that his research went far beyond the remit of potentially marketable plants though some customers were now prepared to create whole gardens of old-fashioned roses themselves.

Bunyard's collection was naturally larger than the catalogue listings. A find would need identification and might take years before it could be introduced with certainty. He recounted in a broadcast made in July 1939 that there were 'some sixty Moss roses in my garden' but only 21 appear in

---

[16] Bunyard, E. A., 'Plant Hunting at Home', *The Listener*, 20 July 1939, pp. 138–9.

the catalogue. He was continually puzzling out the names of his discoveries: a China rose that had just flowered, Gloire des Rosomanes, he now believed to be true. The Banshee rose received from Canada as 'the hardiest Rose grown there but I have not so far been able to identify it', nevertheless appeared in the catalogue with the extra enticement of an eau-de-Cologne scent.[17] The pace of rose collecting quickened after his book was published, as people sent him information and plant material: the 'splendid free-masonry of gardening has made them anxious that others should share their treasures.' Inevitably many turned out not to be what they claimed and required 'time for comparison and study until I can recommend them as desirable and distinct.'[18]

Identifying a rose was much the same process as naming a fruit. It might be immediately recognizable, but it could take a number of seasons of observation before its correct name was discovered. Indications from a combination of flowers, hips, foliage, shoots and habit would allow the unknown rose to be placed in its correct group. 'Any gardener, whose eye is alert to note the difference between one plant and another, will recognize such a distinct group as the Albas, with their flat grey-green leaves and vigorous growth,' Bunyard encouragingly explained in his guide to the botany of roses.[19] 'So too, the Tea Roses whose smooth shoots and shining leaves do not require any long study.' The more difficult gallicas, damasks and centifolias demanded detailed examination, but Bunyard was on top of his subject and provided his readers with a clear understanding of the key features, with the help of Frances' drawings. Then it was a matter of careful but pleasurable observation and checking against the old rose books to track down which variety it might be.

The master reference work was Redouté's *Les Roses* (1817–1824) in which history's most famous botanic artist had recorded over 150 of the roses collected by the Empress Josephine in her Malmaison garden near Paris. Not only of unparalleled beauty, these paintings and their descriptions were an inventory of the old European groups at the height of their popularity and at the beginning of their hybridization with the new roses from China.

---

[17] Ibid.; Bunyard, E. A., *Old Garden Roses*, p. 99, p. 146.
[18] Bunyard, E. A., ' Old Garden Roses', *JRHS*, vol. 63, 1938, pp. 411–421.
[19] Bunyard, E. A., *Old Garden Roses*, p. 63.

Bunyard owned a 'fine' copy of the three-volume Redouté. A more recent record of old roses, early hybrids and rose species had been made by Ellen Willmott. Miss Willmott, an immensely wealthy and knowledgeable gardener, had built up a collection at Warley Place, her home in Essex. She also had over 1,000 roses at Château de Tresserve, in the Savoie at the foot of the Alps, which meant she could grow varieties that would only survive in England under glass. She had a third collection at Boccanegra, near Ventimiglia on the Italian Riveria. These gardens provided the material for her *Genus Rosa*, published in parts from 1910 to 1914, and illustrated by Alfred Parsons.[20] It may have been conceived as a modern Redouté. Miss Willmott's obsession almost matched the Empress's collecting fever. The project was not, however, a great success. The onset of war limited its sales; both the colour printing and the botany were criticized; and it all but bankrupted Miss Willmott. Nevertheless it was an invaluable record.

Searching for roses became an activity that clearly gave Bunyard enormous pleasure. It brought him in touch with owners of many private gardens as well as nurserymen. Mr Smith of Daisy Hill Nursery, Newry, Northern Ireland, who Bunyard complimented on his 'pioneering work in collecting old roses', provided a number of lost gems. These included the Boursault Blush rose, taking its name from a rich Parisian amateur breeder and 'probably the fruit of one of the first weddings of the China rose in Europe'.[21] It did not, however, graduate to the catalogue.

Some of Bunyard's roses 'even came from America where there is quite a cult for these old Roses which went over long ago and are found in the older states such as Virginia and Georgia.' Bunyard's counterpart in the States was Ethelyn Emery Keays, author of *Old Roses*, published in 1935. Mrs Keays lived in Long Island but had a holiday home in Calvert County in Maryland where she amassed a collection rescued from old colonial gardens. She fuelled American enthusiasm for the plants through many articles as well as her book. In 1936, she wrote Edward a congratulatory note:[22] 'Upon the announcement of the publication of your book about old garden roses

---

[20] See Thomas, G. Stuart, *A Garden of Roses* (London, 1987), pp.12–15.

[21] Bunyard, E. A., *Old Garden Roses*, op cit., p. 82.

[22] Bunyard, E. A., *The Listener*, op. cit.; Mrs Keay's letter is enclosed with Bunyard's own copy of his book in the RHS Lindley Library.

you have gathered in and recorded, I had my book seller send to England for it at once – and what a beautiful and scholarly book it is!' Mrs Keays also asked for advice over the identity of a rose, enclosing a picture for his comments. It may be that they exchanged plant material and there was a good deal more correspondence between Allington and Long Island.

Gifts of roses arrived through his RHS contacts. For example E. A. Bowles, a long-standing friend on the Library Committee and Council, sent flowers of the single white banksian rose and, no doubt, cuttings followed later. The banksian roses are glorious, vigorous climbers, introduced from China in the early nineteenth century. Usually the double or single yellow, or double white forms are grown. The single white, with small cupped flowers, was the first to be brought to England and the more interesting for Bunyard's historical studies, but it was a collector's item rather than nursery stock. Bowles was an avid plant collector, 'from whose garden anything may come'. Roses, however, did not do well on his soil at Myddelton in Enfield, but although the garden was poor in the latest introductions, it was rich in species. The 'various species and their forms and hybrids are the real Roses and I have managed to find nooks and corners for a goodly company of them.' He shared with Bunyard 'a very real affection for single Roses'.[23] After her death in 1934, Bunyard had secured from Miss Willmott's garden at Warley Place, a beautiful banksian hybrid climber, 'interesting albas', and a single moss rose.[24] A single-flowered moss rose was a rarity, since moss roses are usually many-petalled, but it was a parent of a number of the moss roses that were popular a century earlier and could have had potential for breeding. Further pertinent material came with some plants of the Persian Double Sulphur rose (*R. hemispherica*) from John Courtney Page, secretary of the National Rose Society, from their trial grounds in Haywards Heath, a source of many other specimens.[25]

A trip to Haywards Heath might also take in a diversion to Nymans where since the early part of the century the Messel family had been forming

---

[23] Bunyard, E. A., *Old Garden Roses* p. 79; Bowles, E. A., *My Garden in Summer* (London, 1914, reprint 1972), p. 141.

[24] Bunyard, E. A., op. cit., pp. 77, 125; Bunyard, E. A., 'Some Rose memories of 1937', *New Flora and Silva*, vol. X, no 2, 1938, pp. 116–121.

[25] Bunyard, E. A., *Old Garden Roses* p. 138–9.

plant collections. Many of these were of English 'firsts' raised from initial seed introductions. Leonard Messel was a prominent figure in the RHS and a member of the Library Committee; Bunyard knew him well. Edward often came to Nymans – motoring, one can imagine, from Maidstone with William Buss at the wheel. The Nymans visitors' book recorded 11 visits between July 1928 and June 1939. In July 1932, he was accompanied by his sister Lorna. An amusing recollection of one of these occasions is given by the gardening-writer, Edward Hyams and relates to *Lilium giganteum* (now *Cardiocrinum giganteum*) introduced from the Himalayas, which had proved at first extremely difficult to grow. Bunyard, who was remembered as a 'distinguished visitor' with a keen sensibility on matters concerning flowers, marched past the unique and spectacular display of giant lilies without a word. Asked to admire them, he replied: 'I cannot. I cannot bear to look at them, they are like very beautiful women utterly ruined by thick ankles' – referring, of course, to their substantial stems.[26]

Roses were the main attraction at Nymans. Leonard's wife Maud had collected them since at least the 1920s. They had come mainly as 'gifts from gardens in England, Scotland, Ireland, Italy and France'. They formed, Edward said in 1937, 'one of the most complete collections of species and old-time Roses that I know.'[27] Here, he saw a number of exquisite species such as *Rosa soulieana* from China: 'its small silvered leaves and ivory-white flowers made a picture the like of which would be difficult to repeat or even rival in any garden plant. Silver and ivory! The shoots are also silvered so that the whole effect is unique among Roses.' The tall shrub, *Rosa dupontii*, named after a famous rosarian of the Empress Josephine's era, was another 'very lovely single rose' growing in the wild garden along with a 'fine group of seedlings of *R. Moyesii*'. One of these caught his eye on account of its more compact habit, 'not the leggy stems we usually associate with Moyesii, which would be a great advantage to the garden and nursery trade.' The best known form, *R. moyesii, Highdownensis*, had arisen at Highdown, the chalk garden made by Sir Frederick Stern near Worthing. Bunyard's were

---

[26] My thanks to Rebecca Graham of the National Trust, Nymans, for information from the Nymans visitors' book; Hyams, E. *The English Garden* (London, 1964; second edition 1966), p. 160.

[27] Bunyard, E. A., 'Some Rose memories of 1937'.

already selling *Highdownensis*, which is a striking rose, vigorous with ferny foliage and single, scarlet flowers, rivalled in brilliance only by its sealing-wax-red hips that 'against a dark background makes a never-to-be-forgotten autumnal picture.'

Bunyard's visits to Nymans yielded a number of lost treasures that could be reintroduced through the nursery. Messel later recalled the discovery of 'one bright crimson China rose which was secured from cuttings from a plant growing behind the stem of an ancient Wisteria in this neighbourhood. The late Mr. E. A. Bunyard identified this as the true *Rosa indica* var. *semperflorens*', that is Slater's Crimson, the rose introduced to England in 1789, which began the rose revolution. Messel remembered also Edward's 'pleasure when he noticed a Rose which had been growing on the gardener's cottage for many years. It was certainly an old plant fifty years ago. He had been trying to find a specimen of this Rose for a long time, but although he had often passed the plant had somehow not noticed it before. It turned out to be one of the earliest Noisette Roses.' The thrill of this find formed one of Bunyard's outstanding memories of 1937: 'For many years I have looked at this Rose growing on Mr Comber's cottage and heard of it flowering continuously until Christmas, but could not put a name to it. Turning over Redouté in the library it suddenly jumped at me – why, of course – the original Noisette Rose! A bunch of flowers laid by the plate resolved all the doubts and so thanks to the owner of Nymans this charming old Rose comes back once more into "commerce" and thence, I hope, to many lovers of old Roses.' He had also discovered 'a charming single red-flowered variety' of the Scots or burnet rose, planted as a low hedge and here again 'Nymans turned up a trump.'[28]

By the late 1930s, Bunyard appeared to spend most of the month of June touring English rose gardens, lighting upon new plants and indulging his collector's fancy. June 1937 saw him at Nymans, the National Rose Society at Haywards Heath, Wisley, Kew, and travelling north to 'St Nicholas' at Richmond in Yorkshire to see the magnificent collection of the Hon. Robert (Bobbie) James – of the eponymous rose. Edward was almost speechless:

---

[28] Messel, L. C. R., 'Features of My Garden. – IV. Nymans.', *JRHS*, vol. 65, 1940, pp. 203–210; Bunyard, E. A., 'Some Rose memories of 1937'; Bunyard, E. A., *Old Garden Roses*, p. 90.

'entering into that enchanted Rose garden I could only say with the Queen of Sheba, "The half was not told to me". Moss Roses, old Damasks, Cabbage Roses and many others quite outside my acquaintance were here spread before me in astonishing profusion. One of the loveliest of all was of the Queen of Denmark group, not quite a Rosa alba but related, I imagine. This is an aristocrat in every part.' This and many other samples came home with him for budding. On the return trip (or perhaps part of another tour), he took in Saint Paul's Walden Bury in Hertfordshire, the garden of fellow RHS Council member Hon. David Bowes-Lyon and childhood home of the late Queen Mother. Here he found in bloom a rare double yellow rose known as the Glamis rose, which had presumably arisen on their Scottish estate. It was another one to acquire.[29]

He may have been at Wisley to check on the progress of the gift he made in the previous year of old roses and rose species. This complemented the collection given by the Cambridge geneticist C. C. Hurst. Bunyard and Hurst had probably first met at the Hybridization Conferences in 1899 and 1906 and their paths must have often crossed at various meetings, providing opportunities to discuss the finer details of rose genealogy as well as exchange a few cuttings. Hurst's collection of old roses was growing in 'interest and stature every year' with many fine specimens which, Bunyard was confident, 'will, I think, before long get out to everyone's delight.' One that did make it into the nursery catalogue, but only 'after many years of search and disappointment', was the Seven Sisters rose.[30] Introduced from China or Japan between 1815 and 1817, it took its name from the seven different colours displayed in a cluster at a single moment. The flowers open a deep cerise purple and fade to a spectrum from mauve to ivory-white before falling.

Rose-hunting was not confined to plants. There were books to read and chance discoveries among the written record. One such was a manuscript list of roses planted in Kent in 1844. I believe this was the result of Edward calling at Linton Park near Maidstone when gathering information for the RHS Conifer Conference of 1931. Linton was the home of the Cornwallis family, then one of Kent's largest landowners. Its garden was famed for its

---

[29] Bunyard, E. A., 'Some Rose memories of 1937'.
[30] Ibid.; Bunyard, E. A., *Old Garden Roses*, p 142.

conifer collection. The dates of planting and each tree's growth, height and girth were noted in a small, leather-bound book which Lord Cornwallis must have lent to Bunyard so that he could bring the records up to date. Linton's pinetum had featured as one of the country's finest at the first RHS Conifer Conference in 1891, so it was appropriate to record progress at the second Conference. The book contains Bunyard's handwritten notes of 'Measurements taken in Feb 1931'. It also contains a list of the roses – 556 in total – planted at Linton in 1844. They may all have come from the Canterbury nursery of William Masters, who was landscaping the grounds for the fifth and last Earl Cornwallis. This provided Edward with another window on the history of the rose especially the varieties grown by a local nurseryman at a time before the effects of the Chinese roses were widely apparent.[31] He never returned the book to Linton and it is now in the Lindley Library.

******

Bunyard's book and the nursery's catalogue were an inspiration to and a source for some of the most famous gardens made during the years between the wars, notably Lawrence Johnston's at Hidcote and Helen Muir's at Kiftsgate, both in Gloucestershire, and Vita Sackville-West's at Sissinghurst in Kent. Old roses here found sympathetic homes and their cause was given fresh impetus. In these now world-famous gardens, their owners planted a series of interconnecting 'rooms' with a finely tuned aesthetic sense for colours and form in which brash hybrid teas had no place, but old roses blended perfectly.

Bunyard was well-known at Kiftsgate Court through the head gardener, Ralph Arnold. Like Edward, he was a frequent contributor to the 'Fruit Register' column in the weekly *Gardeners' Chronicle* in the 1920s. He often referred to Bunyard's *Handbook* and was clearly an admirer. Kiftsgate had a large fruit and vegetable garden, which we might speculate included a number of those varieties promoted by Bunyard. In about 1938, Mrs Muir

---

[31] Bunyard, E.A., 'An Old Rose List', *Gardening Illustrated*, 28 May, 1938, pp. 333–334. For an account of Linton's gardens see Morgan, J., Richards, A., *Paradise out of a Common Field* (London, 1990); for the pinetum see pp. 166–168.

acquired from Bunyard a rose that came to be called Kiftsgate. It bears large clusters of perfumed, small white flowers and is the most rampant of all climbers. Some years later it had ascended 50 feet into a copper beech tree on the edge of the garden. It is a hybrid of the species *Rosa filipes*. The suggestion is that Edward obtained a specimen from the Rosaraie de l'Haÿ,[32] but he makes no mention of this and does not list it or the species, even in his last catalogue.

Kiftsgate is 'next door' to Hidcote and the Muir family and Lawrence Johnston were great friends. Johnston also had a large kitchen garden and was certainly ordering from Bunyard's in 1927 and 1929[33] – purchases which set in motion events which led to friendship between the two men – but he might well have been a customer long before that. Johnston had begun creating the gardens soon after his widowed mother bought the old Cotswold manor as their home in 1907. After his return from the war, he continued to develop its design – a complex of outdoor rooms, defined and protected by hedges and trees, which he lavishly planted, often with a themed colour scheme. A great friend and early influence was Norah Lindsay who had planted masses of old shrub roses at Sutton Courtenay near Abingdon before the war to create a garden in harmony with the medieval manor house.[34] Johnston was also captivated by old roses. He had a collection down the centre path of the walled kitchen garden. An enraptured Vita Sackville-West, writing in 1949 (the year after Hidcote gardens were given to the National Trust), recalled that Johnston 'grew these enchanting varieties long years before they became the fashion, and his collection includes many that are still hard to obtain. ... It would take pages to enumerate them all, so let me merely revive the memory of that June day and the loaded air, and the bushes weeping to the ground with the weight of their own bloom, a rumpus of colour, a drunkenness of scent.'[35] Old roses were massed in the 'Stream Garden' and roses were

---

[32] Thomas, G. Stuart, *Climbing Roses Old and New* (London, 1965, new edition 1983), p. 34.

[33] See *Country Life* 19 Feb, 2004, pp. 95–97, quoted in Wilson, E., 'Edward Bunyard by the Mediterranean', *The Mediterranean Garden*, no. 38, October 2004, pp. 5–14.

[34] Clarke, E., *Hidcote; The Making of a Garden* (London, 1989), pp. 68–71.

[35] Sackville-West, V., 'Hidcote Manor', *JRHS*, vol. 74, 1949, pp. 476–481.

included in the borders, contributing to 'the jungle of beauty ... always kept in bounds by a master hand.'

Johnston was a naturalized British citizen of wealthy American stock. He was an obsessive plant collector and 'a typical bachelor completely dedicated to his garden' opined Collingwood Ingram, the ornamental-cherry collector, who had accompanied him to South Africa. Johnston liked his creature-comforts and took along his Italian cook and chauffeur-butler on the safari, but he was a 'shy, modest man'. He painted, and he collected things such as Regency garden furniture, lead watering-cans and Anduze jars. He had a wide circle of gardening friends and he cultivated nurserymen. Bunyard's knowledge and expertise would have found a receptive ear and they were well-enough suited for Johnston to invite Bunyard to his place on the Riviera in 1937. It was possibly an introduction from Johnston that opened Robert James's rose collection in Yorkshire to Edward on his return from his French jaunt. Johnston and James were close friends and frequent guests at each other's houses. However, Edward's entrée may equally have been through the all-pervasive RHS network or down to the fact that James was the brother of Lord Northbourne, an east Kent landowner.[36]

Edward's introduction to Sissinghurst came after the appearance of his book, some six years since Vita Sackville-West and Harold Nicolson embarked on making the garden. The Tudor brick walls of the castle formed the structure for 'a succession of privacies', now familiar to us all. The great tower arch opens onto the lawn, and to the side through an open 'door' is the walled garden of old-fashioned roses. Roses are everywhere: on the walls, in sheltered nooks, growing in borders and in the orchard. The garden was 'drunk on roses', as Vita Sackville-West wrote in an *Observer* article in 1953. Soon after reading *Old Garden Roses*, she wrote inviting Edward for lunch. Thereafter, he was her constant mentor, as well as supplier of plants.[37] She began planting old-fashioned roses in 1936, and in 1937 the rose garden was commenced.

Vita Sackville-West's gardening notebooks, preserved at Sissinghurst, contain many references to Bunyard. In the autumn of 1937, there was

---

[36] Clarke, E., *Hidcote*, op. cit. p. 95.

[37] Lane-Fox, R., *V. Sackville-West, The Illustrated Garden Book; A New Anthology* (London, 1968), p. 14.

an order for roses which included the variety Queen of Denmark, and others that did not appear in the catalogue.[38] These may have been special favours, roses not yet bulked-up for general sale, but Queen of Denmark remained a favourite. She wrote in 1957 that 'sometimes I think that the alba celestial is one of the lovelist shrubs one could ever wish to contemplate ….. Then I look up into the tall bush of Queen of Denmark and think that she is possibly even more lovely, in a deeper pink than alba celestial, with a quartered flower looking as though someone had taken a spoon and stirred it round, as a child might stir a bowl of strawberries and cream.'[39]

Notes were made of questions to ask Bunyard: did he recommend the hybrid musk roses discussed in an article? What was his opinion on a rose advertised in the *Gardeners' Chronicle*? It may be that the rose which covers the gazebo in the 'White Garden', *Rosa longicuspis*, came from Bunyard; it was on offer in the catalogue. She particularly liked Bourbon roses, with 'all the rosy lavishness of the ladies of the Second Empire', like the cerise pink Zéphyrine Drouhin. Fantin-Latour was another 'must have', which was probably a cabbage rose, 'painted by, or honouring Fantin La Tour himself', but its origins did not matter 'so long as we can get this lovely thing in our gardens.' When she wrote this, more than twenty years after Bunyard's book had been published, she remarked on how large the increase had been in the numbers of Bourbons and other old roses over the intervening years. Needless to say, her column continued to refer to Bunyard's counsel.[40]

His advice on fruit was as valuable as that on roses. The notebook for 1937 has this list of queries: 'What fruit trees to plant on the garden wall? About the green fig, can it be bottled? How to prune peaches? What about fig suckers? What about Madresfield Court [grape]'? Her questions may have been prompted by articles she was preparing for the *New Statesman and Nation* in 1938 and 1939. There were pieces on figs, grapes, and one entitled 'Better not Bigger Fruit', with a special reference to the alpine strawberry that had a hint of Bunyard. Her article entitled 'Eternities of Kitchen Garden' revealed more than a passing glance at 'Vegetables for

---

[38] Ibid., p. 12; p. 15.
[39] Sackville-West, V., *Even More for Your Garden* (London, 1958), p. 126.
[40] Ibid. p. 128, p. 132, p. 127.

Epicures' in its references to red cabbage and pokeweed, whose young shoots resembled asparagus.[41]

With the special place that Persia held in her heart, she must have been charmed by Bunyard's careful analysis of Persian roses, their depiction in tiles and porcelain and westward movement across Europe. She was intrigued by the identity of the possibly Persian 'yellow' rose in the Wilton Diptych. Vita and Harold Nicolson had visited Iran in the course of his work as a diplomat in the 1920s. They had travelled on horseback with the Bakhtyari tribe from their winter quarters south of Shiraz, through the Chahar Mahals up to their summer pastures in the Zagros mountains. She never forgot the land carpeted with wild flowers, nor their woven images in the souks. In a letter to Edward, she recalled seeing growing in the wild near Tehran the yellow Persian species known in the West as the Yellow Austrian Briar.[42]

Bunyard's influence touched many other gardens being made in the 1920s and 1930s. The society florist Constance Spry formed her first collection of old-fashioned roses 'amongst the knarled veterans of an old cherry orchard' in Chelsfield near Orpington in Kent. She had been inspired by the example of her friend Norah Lindsay, and by reading *Old Garden Roses*, which 'revealed to her the diversity and scope of the hobby'. She was a customer of Bunyard's, recommending the nursery in her own books. In time her collection rivalled those at Nymans and Sissinghurst. Her biographer recalled 'the favourite picture that friends retain of Constance was her making an entry, on the lecture platform or in her own drawing room, on some day of high summer, her arms loaded with great fragrant sprays of moss or gallica or centifolia roses in all their rich colourings of crimson and purple, silvery pink and slaty grey.'[43]

******

---

[41] Sackville-West, V., *Country Notes* (London, 1939), pp. 41–44.

[42] Vita Sackville-West's letter to Bunyard is enclosed with his copy of *Old Garden Roses* in the RHS Lindley Library.

[43] Spry, C., *Favourite Flowers* (London, 1959), p. 70; Coxhead, E., *Constance Spry; a Biography* (London, 1975), p. 101.

As well as advancing the cause of old-fashioned roses, Bunyard was experimenting with the more exotic types, those that were not generally regarded as hardy in the English climate, but at their best beside the Mediterranean or in California. The Mediterranean climate was the answer to the northern gardener's prayers, a vast open-air greenhouse in which orange and lemon trees fruited. Even date palms grew and the most blissful flowers: strelitzias and agapanthus from South Africa, bougainvillaea and daturas from South America, and roses everywhere. In the mild winters and Riveria sunshine tender roses like the banksians were at their best, climbing into olive and cypress trees, cascading over walls and arches and attaining an abundance of flowers rarely seen in England. China roses flowered up to Christmas. Tea roses did so well that Lady Aberconway, one of the early English Riviera residents, set up a business at La Garoupe, on the south-east tip of Cap d'Antibes, growing tea roses and asparagus fern to dispatch in baskets by train to London for sale as gentlemen's buttonholes.

The English gardeners of the Riviera – around whose properties Edward would circle in pursuit of his rosarian studies – were inspired by the example of Sir Thomas Hanbury and his brother Daniel at La Mortola near Ventimiglia, which they bought in 1867.[44] The Hanbury wealth, derived from the pharmaceutical firm Allen & Hanbury and a second fortune made by Sir Thomas in Shanghai as a silk and tea merchant, allowed them to bring together an unrivalled collection of plants gathered from across the globe. Their garden also encouraged local growers to divert their energies from olive groves to raising flowers. This crop had almost supplanted the traditional one by the 1920s. From Ventimiglia, the 'Covent Garden of the South', roses, violets and carnations were exported northwards 'by the ton' on the 'Train des Fleurs'. Across the border in France, Cap d'Antibes was also famed for cut flowers and early vegetables. La Mortola garden had so excited Ellen Willmott of Warley Place that she bought the nearby Villa Boccanegra in 1903. The Hanburys, Miss Willmott, Lady Aberconway (the chatelaine of Bodnant Gardens in North Wales), and Norah Warre, a talented plantswoman who bought Roquebrune, close to Menton, in 1902, were the among the first of the

---

[44] Russell, V., *Gardens of the Riviera* (London, 1993), see chapter 1, 'English Gardens and Gardeners'.

rich and privileged to escape from British winters and spare no expense or effort on their gardens and their roses.

To La Mortola came a rich stream of specimens including many from China as well as Kazanlik roses from the Bulgarian valley of that name, used to make attar of roses, presented by King Ferdinand. The famous roses raised by Gilbert Nabonnand of Golfe Juan near Cannes were in everyone's garden: Norah Warre, wife of George Warre of Warre port wine fame, at Roquebrune, collected Nabonnand's roses. When the American novelist Edith Wharton first came to live at Castel Sainte-Claire above the old town of Hyères in 1919, Monsieur Nabonnand told her 'she could grow all the roses that ever were.'[45] Nabonnand had been employed by the second Lord Brougham to redesign the Château Éléonore near Cannes, built by his father, the founder of Cannes' reputation as a winter holiday resort and Queen Victoria's Lord Chancellor. Lord Brougham's gardens became renowned for roses which, when catalogued in 1898, were the envy of Europe and remained on the visiting-list for Riviera gardeners and their guests. Here banksians took 'possession of rows of trees', their long shoots covered with flowers like 'the "shower of gold" at a display of fireworks' and Nabonnand's best known tea rose, the carmine, Papa Gontier, so excelled that 'nothing in the rose-world can well be superior.'[46]

There was a wealth of roses, rose history and potential for English gardens to be experienced first-hand on the Riviera. Here was the justification, at least in part, for Bunyard's journeys in 1937 and 1939. Edward was now joining the upper classes on their playground as well as meeting them in their English gardens and on RHS occasions. The Riviera gardeners were an extension of the plant-loving fraternity that peopled the RHS Council and committees. Sir Thomas Hanbury had bought and gifted Wisley Gardens to the Society in 1904, shortly before he died. His son Sir Cecil was a trustee of Wisley and he had exhibited La Mortola's citrus collection at several Vincent Square shows. La Mortola, which was open to the public for one day a week, was a regular goal for travelling Fellows of the RHS. E. A. Bowles, for instance, had been to look it over. In 1925 the nurseryman Edward Laxton spent a day looking at the plants and was also shown the

---

[45] Ibid. p. 37, p.72, p. 101.
[46] Brougham & Vaux, *Catalogue of Roses, Château Éléonore, Cannes*, 1898, pp. 4, 27.

store of seeds collected every year for distribution to botanic gardens and plant enthusiasts across the world.[47] Lady Aberconway was the mother of the RHS president. Another Council member, Frederick Stern, named one of his paeony seedlings after Mrs Norah Warre who, like many of the Riviera residents, was collaborating with Wisley and Kew in nurturing the new plants in anticipation that they might be hardy enough for their English gardens. The ramifications of the RHS network were endless: Lady Alice Martineau, who had written the introduction to one of Bunyard's issues of 'Vegetables for Epicures' was a friend of Edith Wharton, who had contributed to Lady Martineau's *Gardens in Sunny Lands*. Bunyard was entering the holiday-world of the super-rich. The Riviera season from November to May was an endless succession of parties and picnics when Bentleys and Rolls Royces purred along the Corniche from one luxurious home to yet another stunning garden and glorious meal.

Bunyard's visit in 1937 was as guest of Lawrence Johnston at the Villa Serre de la Madone near Menton. Johnston had bought the Villa in 1924, for the benefit of his frail, elderly mother's health and his own – he had been badly injured in the war. Serre de la Madone was home to many plants collected from Mexico, South Africa and China which had no prospect of growing in the chillier clime of Hidcote. Here in France, like at Hidcote, he designed the gardens as a series of open air 'rooms', each on a different theme. Roses abounded. Edward's journey on board the Blue Train, the Englishman's Riviera express, took him to Nice and a final stage, perhaps, in Johnston's racy Lancia to enjoy good company, food and wine. It was, no doubt, here at lunch that he enjoyed the best French asparagus that he ever had eaten, freshly gathered that morning in Nice.[48]

The trip in late March was really a feast of roses. His room was decked with a welcoming bowl of the Riveria beauty La Follette, and he was to see it probably in every garden he called at. It is a climbing rose with large, fragrant, deep pink blooms and rich, dark green foliage. The Bunyard Nursery offered it for sale, suggesting that it could be grown 'Riviera style' up trees, although it is usually regarded as too tender for England. La

---

[47] Laxton. E. A .L., 'La Mortola', *The Gardeners' Chronicle*, 30 May, 1925, p. 377.

[48] Bunyard, E. A., 'A Few Meals in France', *Wine and Food*, vol. 23, 1939, pp. 223–229.

Follette was raised by Lord Brougham's gardener Mr Busby in about 1910 and probably introduced by Nabonnand. It was a hybrid of *Rosa gigantea*, which made it also of academic interest. *Rosa gigantea* was a proposed and now accepted species-parent of the tea rose. An idea that was substantiated in Bunyard's view by this vision of La Follette and other *Rosa gigantea* hybrids on the Riviera. Their distinctive and distinguished leaves resembled some of the best-known tea roses.[49]

The hardiness of these Riviera roses in England was a problem but, for some years, Bunyard had been suggesting, in letters to the gardening press, that they were more resilient than was suspected and encouraging people to plant them. *Rosa gigantea*, which is a climber with large, white, single flowers, was surviving at Allington, Nymans, Sissinghurst and he had heard of it 'doing well in a old garden in Gloucestershire [presumably Hidcote or Kiftsgate] where it flowered this year from early May despite many night frosts'. Edward had several hybrids under trial at Allington, of which Duchess of Portugal or Belle Portugaise and the Californian Susan Louise were 'new' entries in the 1938–39 catalogue; yet to appear was Château Éléonore.[50]

Bunyard's journey had turned into a succession of encounters with roses that offered tempting possibilities for warm nooks in English gardens. He called on Johnston's neighbour, Norah Warre at Roquebrune, where the sight of the Californian rose Ramona convinced him that 'everyone will want to try it on a warm wall as soon as they have seen it.' Ramona, a more highly-coloured form of the Anemone rose, is a vigorous climber with large, papery petals of deep pink, but tender. It was for sale at Bunyard's in 1938 and Vita Sackville-West was seduced; there used to be one on a wall at Sissinghurst, but it died one winter and has never been replaced.[51] Then he motored over to La Mortola to be entranced by the roses: 'I was fortunate to be south at the right moment to see *R. laevigata* at its best.

---

[49] Bunyard, E. A., 'Some Rose memories of 1937', op cit. p. 116.

[50] Bunyard, E. A., *Gardening Ilustrated*, 8 June 1935, p. 347; 25 April 1936, p. 244; 2 July 1938, p. 414; 'Garden Note', *JRHS*, vol. 63, 1938, p. 449; *New Flora and Silva*, 'Some Rose memories of 1937', op. cit.

[51] Bunyard, E. A., *New Flora and Silva*, ibid., p.117; my thanks to Tom La Dell for the information on the rose at Sissinghurst.

Both at Roquebrune and at La Mortola it clothed the balustrades and walls in a mass of pure white.' *Rosa laevigata*, a Chinese species, was a parent of the Anemone rose and Ramona, but in England its best-known seedling was Cooper's Burmese, a superb, evergreen climber, although rather tender as it blossoms very early, with large white flowers and the boss of golden stamens that Bunyard so admired. This, too, he was offering for sale.

Edward was always looking out for something unusual, for example, a rose variety that he had found mentioned in old lists or books, but not yet discovered growing anywhere, such as 'a buttercup yellow and pink' form of the banksian rose that had been recorded by Redouté. He was not blessed with luck in this instance, but he did see a splendid double white rose known on the Mediterranean as 'Banksia grandiflora', which he suspected was *Rosa x fortuniana* introduced from China in 1850 by the plant-hunter Robert Fortune. He had already collected a specimen from Ellen Willmott's garden.

Bunyard is credited by the rosarian the late Graham Stuart Thomas with bringing the La Mortola rose to England. This was subsequently introduced more generally by Thomas himself, drawing his initial material from the garden at Kiftsgate. He had been told by the owner Helen Muir that it had come from Bunyard. It appears in Bunyard's catalogue in 1938–39, but Bunyard was not the first to bring the La Mortola rose to England. Bunyard recounted that when at Kew in June 1937 he had seen 'the fine La Mortola rose at ... its best', presumably as a mature plant, and, since there was a reciprocal exchange of plants and gardeners between Kew and La Mortola, it is easy to imagine that it could have arrived at Kew some years previously. He went on to observe that 'I fancy this must also be known in California, as pictures which have been sent to me asking for a name exactly resemble this.'[52] La Mortola, now considered a sport of the Himalayan *Rosa brunonii*, rather than *R. moschata* as Bunyard noted, is a rampant climber, with attractive greyish-green, silvery, foliage and clusters of creamy white single flowers and, as he says, 'a fine thing'.

Bunyard's visit to Johnston in 1937 appeared to have been part of a longer trip which took him to Florence as well. Bunyard often went to stay with Norman Douglas and, perhaps, he was accompanied by his friend when he called at an 'old villa outside the city'. Here his attention was

---

[52] Thomas, G. Stuart, *Climbing Roses Old and New*, p. 33; Bunyard, ibid., p. 119.

caught by a 'veteran plant of the China Rose now called Tipo Ideale' or *Rosa mutabilis*. Its botanic name reflects the nature of the flowers which are single and range in colour from deep pink to buff and yellow. A bush in full bloom looks as if it is covered with exotic butterflies. It needs a good spot in England to perform as it does in Italy and, no doubt, the specimen at the 'old villa' was an exceptionally large bush such as one rarely sees. His Irish contact, Mr Smith of Daisy Hill Nursery, believed that it had been introduced to Ireland from Italy many years before, and in 1935 Bunyard had found a painting of it by Redouté in the library of the Jardin des Plantes in Paris. This would place its introduction to Europe early in the nineteenth century. In the summer of 1936 he had planned to see Tipo Ideale, in its climbing form, on 'a house in the Midlands where it has reached the top story.'[53]

Bunyard's next trip to the Riviera was to his friend Basil Leng's new home at Cap d'Antibes in May 1939. The two men had been introduced by Norman Douglas some time after December 1924 when he had suggested they might have a mutual interest in plants.[54] Edward had stayed with Leng at his previous home at Socoa near Biarritz in 1933 whence they had mounted an expedition to the Mediterranean coast. The trip is mentioned by Edward in an occasional piece on wine: with 'my good friend B. motoring across that gracious province of France, Béarn, en route for the Riviera.'[55] It is entirely possible that Bunyard's interest in the roses of the Riviera had arisen through his friendship with Leng.

Leng had made an appearance on the Riviera by 1926 and became 'one of the most knowledgeable gardeners on the coast' according to Edith Wharton, with whom he was a close friend.[56] He was a member of what was informally known as 'the gardening club' which, besides Wharton, included Norah Warre, Lawrence Johnston and the elegant Frenchman

---

[53] Bunyard, E. A., 'Rose Tipo Ideale', *Gardening Illustrated*, 2 May 1936, pp. 255–6; 30 May 1936, p. 329.

[54] See Wilson, E., 'Edward Bunyard by the Mediterranean', op. cit. and chapter 1 in this volume.

[55] Bunyard, E. A., 'A Visit to the Beaujolais', *Wine and Food*, vol. 5, 1938, pp. 362–364.

[56] Russel, V., op. cit., p. 94.

Vicomte Charles de Noailles whose Parc St Bernard was close to Edith Wharton's. The Vicomte also gardened at Villa Noailles in Grasse to the north of Cannes.

Bunyard had come to Cap d'Antibes in 1939 for a few weeks' holiday with Leng, although plant-hunting was also on the agenda. Together they called on a number of nurseries. EAB was more than a little scathing about the precision of some labelling and the conservatism of the local growers in their choice of varieties, but there were no problems with the accuracy of names or interest in the latest developments at Miraour's nursery at Mougins behind Cannes. Miraour was a disciple of Gilbert Nabonnand. The Englishmen were sure the great man's legacy was safe in the hands of an 'enthusiast for all Roses', and at his nursery 'one may see ... all the newest forms from all parts of the world and many old ones.'[57] The Macartney rose, *Rosa bracteata*, with large white single flowers (which gave rise to the well-known Mermaid) was one Riviera favourite they met with, but Bunyard was looking for older hybrids. M. Miraour had what he wanted in the form of Marie Leonida, 'a lovely, double pink' growing against a wall. But the rose that took his breath away was the Nabonnand tea rose hybrid Comtesse de Chaponay, 'tumbling 20 feet through an olive ... never have I seen any more beautiful contrast, the cream flowers among the silver-green Olive leaves.'

On this trip they met up with Norman Douglas, now living in the south of France. Together they enjoyed many memorable meals; tramping through the countryside finding little places to eat in out-of-the-way spots just as Bunyard must have done with Douglas on his journeys to Italy. Douglas was fanatical when it came to food, sparing no effort to find the best-quality, simple fare, prepared from the freshest, ripest ingredients. Always prepared for disappointment, he carried a chunk of good Parmesan in his pocket in case what was on offer failed to come up to his standard. They went to Grasse, the centre of the perfume industry, where Bunyard was smugly able to satisfy himself that the perfumers still used the ancient damask roses and had not found the new rugosa, Parfum de l'Haÿ, nearly as satisfactory. Parfum de l'Haÿ was raised by the great rosarian Jules Gravereaux as part

---

[57] Bunyard, E. A., 'Rose Hunting in 1939', *New Flora and Silva*, no 45, Nov 1939, pp. 11–17.

of a project to provide new robust varieties for the perfume industry. They found another collection at the home of Mrs Andrea at Peymeinade, seeing 'some of the old Roses famed in their day such as *Chromatella* [Cloth of Gold] known to me only in pictures up till then' and which was best under glass in England, but stupendous on the Riviera with abundant, large, intense yellow flowers.

Later in the holiday, after stopping at St-Tropez they roamed the Maures Mountains where by great good fortune Bunyard discovered an elusive, old damask rose in the garden of an inn. He had long pondered over the problem of the identity of the Tudor, heraldic rose, and 'often looked at pictures and carvings' to try to match the image to an existing variety. It had a peculiar feature in that 'the sepals – the little green structures which cover the bud before it opens – are always shown standing out beyond the flower when it is fully open. In all Roses I have so far met, the sepals do not project beyond the flower when it is open; they are either shorter … or fold down closely at the stem.' In the kitchen-garden of the inn, growing as a rose hedge, he found the pink flowered 'Heraldic Rose' in which the sepals protruded beyond the flower 'in the true heraldic fashion known as the "Rose Barbed"'. A plant was transferred to Leng's garden and from here it was planned to send cuttings to England to form, he believed, the most ancient damask in his collection.[58]

On the journey home, he paused in Paris to see yet more rose collections and he was so impressed that 'another visit in June was necessary.'[59] The Bagatelle Garden, on a corner of the Bois de Boulogne, was well known for its roses as well as paeonies, lilacs and clematis. It was an 'oasis of peace and delight for all gardeners' and contained trial grounds for new roses. He obtained bud-wood of two new German varieties which he hoped to stage at a future Chelsea Flower Show on the Bunyard exhibit, 'when they will first make their bow to an admiring public.' Another destination was the garden at Malmaison, formerly home to the Empress Josephine's famous collection of old roses, but now, alas, dominated by modern hybrid teas. A third was to the Roseraie de l'Haÿ, the renowned collection made by Jules Gravereaux (d. 1916), the largest collection of old-fashioned roses he

---

[58] Bunyard, ibid.; 'Plant Hunting at Home', pp. 138–139.
[59] Ibid.

had ever seen, which was not long in the hands of the local Département after some years of relative decline. The beds were still packed with old roses in 1939, especially of gallicas and Bourbons and also with species roses. Bunyard met the director, identified an unlabelled plant for him, and sympathized with his plight, now that an officious bureaucrat had removed Gravereaux's rose books to the Musée Carnavalet in Paris, commenting with some cause, 'Who, I wonder, will use them there?'

******

Bunyard's collecting and the demand that he was creating for old varieties encouraged the nursery to mount a special exhibit at the Chelsea Flower Show in 1937. It gained the firm a Banksian Medal, itself an extra boost to their promotion. The medal commemorated Sir Joseph Banks, a founder of the then London Horticultural Society, whose wife's name was honoured in the banksian rose. For roses to bloom on 26 May called for forward-planning: transferring the plants to pots the previous winter and taking them under glass some weeks before the Show to bring them into flower. It was a busy year for Bunyard. Late March and early April were spent on the Riviera, then Chelsea in May with three exhibits – apples and irises, which both received Gold Medals – and roses. That was immediately followed by tours of English rose collections in June, returning to more shows and committees. This was the year his *Epicure's Companion* was published and he still made time to prepare another issue of 'Vegetables for Epicures'.

The following year roses were publicized with increased energy. There was no trip to the Riviera, as far as we know, but at Chelsea the nursery received another Banksian Medal for 'Old Roses' and for herbaceous plants. Then in July 1938 he lectured on 'Old Roses' at a Westminster Show. Appropriately, the Hon. Robert James from Richmond in Yorkshire was in the chair. Bunyard's collection was brought alive in lantern slides although, he said, there were many more varieties at Allington awaiting investigation and identification before they could be introduced. The plant was even more heavily promoted in 1939 when, on his return from Cap d'Antibes, a rose exhibit was staged at Chelsea, followed by an exhibit of 'paeonies, delphiniums and old fashioned roses' at the Westminster Show on 20 June, with another exhibit of 'old fashioned Roses' at the 4 July Show. The last was followed by a BBC broadcast, 'Plant Hunting at Home', on 20 July, in which roses were again featured, with encouragement to gardeners to exchange plants and cuttings.

Bunyard had become the great champion of old-fashioned roses. By the time of his death in 1939 their revival was well under way. He had assembled 'one of the great collections of old roses' in the words of Graham Stuart Thomas, the eminent rosarian of recent times. It proved an inspiration to Thomas's own quest which resulted ultimately in the National Trust's collection of old roses at Mottisfont Abbey in Hampshire. Bunyard's book enthused some of the most influential gardeners and writers after the Second World War who carried his mission forward to achieve the complete rehabilitation of old-fashioned roses by the 1960s and 1970s. His contribution was profound and his book is now a precious collector's item.

CHAPTER TEN

Edward Bunyard the Committee Man

JOAN MORGAN

The Royal Horticultural Society's Council and its committees formed an exclusive gardening club to which Bunyard belonged for nearly 30 years. Election to Council, the Society's governing body, in 1923 brought him to the epicentre of the horticultural establishment, in touch with everyone of power and influence, involved in all major occasions and activities. He, in turn, gave the Society unstinting, loyal support. He initiated and organized conferences, shows, projects and publications to ensure the Society remained the leading body in its field. He was generous to a fault with time and devotion to the Society's affairs. He rose to a position of eminence within its Council, which made his fall from these influential heights and the tragic circumstances of his death all the more poignant.

Bunyard was elected to Council at a relatively young age, before he became chairman of any committee. He had shown himself to be excellent RHS material by the time he was forty years-old. An expert in his field, of good pedigree – the son of a former Council member – he was also clearly supportive of the Society's aims, witness his staging of Gold Medal-winning exhibits to boost the Society's image and please the public. Election required nomination by two Council members and endorsement at the annual general meeting. This latter was almost a formality: no Fellow was going to oppose Council's candidates. As recently as 1985, the general impression of Council was of 'a remote, elitist, self-perpetuating oligarchy'.[1] Once part of

---

[1] Elliott, B., *The Royal Horticultural Society* (London, 2004), p. 53.

the system, it was a rewarding, if at times arduous seat. Bunyard served on Council from 1923 until 1939, except for 1928 and 1934 when he stepped down to comply with the Society's rule that Council members should not let themselves be re-nominated after five years of office until at least twelve months had passed.

In its role as both a learned society and a force for promoting general horticultural excellence, the Society maintained its position through the combined expertise of special-interest committees. The membership of these usually provided the candidates for Council. Bunyard was welcomed for his expertise in fruit, as a practical fruit grower, pomologist, bibliophile, writer, compiler and publisher – the *Journal of Pomology* as well as the nursery catalogues were models of stylishly presented information – and as manager of a successful business. He proved an able and well-liked committee man. That he served so long on Council is testimony both to personal charm and utility. But it is hard to imagine that he could have retained his office without diplomatic skills to match. Many would be the occasions when his 'good manners', wisdom, tolerance and discrimination – qualities valued by his friend the barrister and bon viveur Maurice Healy – were called into play. He would press his points with confidence and revelled in debate: 'He was a grand controversialist, loving to give and even to receive hard blows; he hated compromise.'[2] Council ran the Society with few administrative staff; its membership then was less than a tenth of the number today. Council members each sat on several committees. In Bunyard's case, this was an astonishing number: Library; Fruit and Vegetable and its Show Schedule Committee and judging panels; Joint Commercial Fruit Trials; Publications; Paintings; Wisley Gardens Advisory Committee and its Scientific and Surplus Plant Distribution Subcommittees; and Finance and General.

******

Edward started his committee career in 1911 on the body governing the library. The Society's Lindley Library retains indeed his important legacy of fruit books. Books were, perhaps, his greatest delight, the Library Committee

---

[2] Healy, M., ' Edward Bunyard, In Memoriam', *Wine and Food,* vol. 6 no. 24 ,Winter 1939, pp. 324–26.

close to Heaven. A professional librarian was employed, but the purchase of books and drawings and the allocation of books for review was the committee's responsibility. Publishers sent in catalogues and consignments of their latest publications; antiquarian dealers submitted their rare volumes for the committee to peruse. Members decided which journals should be taken, attended book sales on behalf of the Society and kept their eyes open for potential accessions.

The Library Committee had only been formed in December 1910. Hitherto, books had been the responsibility of the Lindley Library Trust. This was set up some 50 years earlier in response to a catastrophic turn of events. In 1859 the Society had sold its original book collection as a way to resolve severe financial problems. The situation was partly recovered by using the profits from the International Horticultural Congress of 1866 to fund the purchase of the library of Dr John Lindley, botanist and former secretary of the Society. So that it might never again be sold, an independent trust was formed. Following the death of the last of the original trustees, the way was open for the library to come under the Society's control again. The remaining trustees, those appointed in more recent times, were reconstituted as the Library Committee.[3] One of those original trustees, and an instigator of the whole scheme, had been Robert Hogg, Bunyard's pomological predecessor (see chapter 9).

A place on any committee came through personal recommendation, and among the other members there were a number of points of contact with the Bunyard family. Sir Harry Veitch, the famous nurseryman, a former trustee and now chairman, would have been well known to Bunyard's father, if not also to Edward. There was also E. A. Bowles, who Bunyard would have met at the earlier conferences. But Edward's qualifications for the task spoke for themselves. His papers in the RHS *Journal* in early 1911 which indexed published illustrations of apple and pear varieties revealed a mastery of the subject, the skills of a meticulous bibliographer and an outstanding library. They were also a timely adjunct to research then in progress. In 1909 the Society had begun an index to published portraits of plants, the *Index Londinensis* (finally published 1929-31). This only covered plant species, not

---

[3] For the history of the RHS Lindley Library see Elliott, B., op. cit., pp. 165–175.

their cultivated varieties, thus excluding fruit, throwing Bunyard's valuable work into higher relief.

Pomology was an area of expertise not represented on the committee and probably hardly pursued at all since Hogg's active involvement in the early 1890s (he died in 1897). The purchase of 'missing' fruit books began in May 1911 but no sooner had Bunyard joined in the October, than he was tasked to look out for books on pomology. The following January, he submitted 'a list of books which he thought ought to be in the Library and an account of each'. By May 1913, the key pomonas of France, Italy, New York and Germany had been bought.[4]

The acquisition of books for himself or for the library was a continuing process, often marked by generosity on Edward's part. In 1914, he presented the very scarce *Gooseberry Growers Register* for 1852, 1859 and 1863 which list the prize-winning varieties at the northern gooseberry shows.[5] It seems likely that he had been lucky and found duplicates, since this coincided with his setting out on his own gooseberry studies and he would hardly have given away his only copies of these precious and essential volumes. Very few purchases occurred during the war years, but in June 1920 he attended the sale of the library of the rosarian, nurseryman and fellow committee member the late Arthur Paul, probably in the company of another colleague, Harman Payne, who had been authorized to buy books for the RHS. A 'good copy' of a rare book on citrus fruit was offered which Bunyard possibly bought for himself; but he, no doubt, arranged the library's purchase of a scarce work by the French pomologist Alphonse Mas.[6] EAB had 'only seen two copies in the course of 20 years of book hunting. These were discovered by the publishers, Messrs Levrault & Co., at Paris by a curious chance. The flooding of the Seine some years ago necessitated the sudden clearing out

---

[4] For Bunyard's admission to the Committee see: Royal Horticultural Society, Lindley Library; RHS Library Committee Minutes 10 Oct., 1911; 23 Jan., 1912. For book purchases see: 9 May 1911; 18 July, 1911; 2 April, 1912, 16 April, 1912; 12 July, 1912; 14 May, 1913.

[5] RHS Lindley Library, RHS Library Committe Minutes 24 Feb., 1914.

[6] 'News and Notes', 'Prices of Old Books', *Journal of Pomology*, vol. 1, 1920, pp. 207–208; 'News and Notes','Recent Book Prices', *Journal of Pomology*, vol. 1, 1920, pp. 261–2; both pieces written by the editor, Bunyard.

of their cellar stores and led to the discovery of two copies which they had lost. Both these copies found their way to England and one is now at the Library in Vincent Square', the other copy very likely making its way to Allington.

Bunyard had an eagle eye for treasures, spotting in a London shop in May 1920 a copy of the exceptionally rare '"The Orchard and the Garden" which was published anonymously in 1602. For many years only one copy was known to exist, that being in the University Library of Cambridge'. This *trouvaille* was 'very fortunately secured for the Lindley Library ... where it can be inspected by those interested'. These two copies remain the only ones known. Bunyard was always keen to share his discoveries with the wider world and this little 'bibliographic curiosity' and its glimpse of Elizabethan orchard culture was reprinted in the *Journal of Pomology*. Here he also threw down this challenge: 'those who are skilful at detecting plagiarism will be interested to run down the French and Dutch sources from which it is compiled'. He never revealed which they were.[7]

******

In 1925 Bunyard became chairman of the Library Committee with Bowles as vice-chairman, an arrangement that continued until 1939. They were both Council members and served together on other committees. Bowles was a much-admired gardener, author, painter and collector of plants, books, butterflies and stuffed birds, amongst many other things. At Myddelton House in Enfield, on the estate accrued through the entrepreneurial achievements of his ancestors, the 'squire' was known as a rich and lovable eccentric. Fine gardens and fine libraries were almost two-a-penny with the other members of the committee. Gerald Loder, who succeeded Veitch as chairman, owned Wakehurst Place in Kent, famed for rhododendrons, trees and shrubs, especially those native to New Zealand; Reginald Cory, the millionaire coal, oil and shipping magnate, had made Dyffryn in the Vale of Glamorgan

---

[7] '"The Orchard and the Garden". 1620', *Journal of Pomology*, vol. 2, 1921, p. 246. RHS Lindley Library, RHS Library Committee Minutes 11 May, 1920; 8 June, 1920. My thanks to Dr Brent Elliott, RHS librarian, for information on this accession.

renowned for its plant collections; and Leonard Messel, who lived in a plantsman's paradise at Nymans in Sussex, possessed a library of priceless early herbals and illustrated flora.

Soon after he became chairman, Bunyard and Reginald Cory were asked by Council to secure books from the sale of the late Harman Payne's library. Payne, who was the author of *The Florist's Bibliography*, had owned a collection that yielded 'a few books of great rarity and interest to students of Floriculture', and a rich haul of small pamphlets.[8] These were the ephemera of book sales, often discarded by the auctioneer but of great value to the historian. Into this category Bunyard also placed nurserymen's catalogues, which might be the only record of the date of introduction of a particular variety. Thinking ruefully, perhaps, of his own nursery's carefully crafted catalogues, he urged RHS Fellows to save them from 'an untimely death in the wastepaper basket' or leave them in their wills to the Lindley Library, where 'parcels of catalogues, old and new, will be very gratefully received.' Catalogues had been collected from the 1860s, since every nurseryman who exhibited at a show was meant to give the library a copy of his catalogue. How conscientiously this was followed is not known. Bunyard provided the extra stimulus that brought their purchase onto the committee's agenda. We have, in part, to thank his persistence during the 1920s and 1930s for the library's invaluable collection of catalogues today.

Valuable acquisitions and purchases continued at an increasing pace. In April 1930, for example, Edward was authorized to attend an important sale at Christie's with powers to spend up to £200. Two weeks later the committee bought £75-worth of books at a sale at Messrs Nijoffs, a Dutch publisher, who probably had offices in London, although Bunyard would not have turned down a trip to Holland. A work of Duhamel du Monceau, the father of systematic pomology, illustrated by Redouté, *Traité des Arbres et Arbustes*, 1801–1819, was bought for £72 in 1932 and the following year the enormous sum of £500 was spent on some 20 volumes of the exceptionally valuable Kerner's *Hortus Sempervirens*. There were over 70 slim volumes in the series as a whole, each with original drawings by the author.

---

[8] Bunyard, E. A., 'The Lindley Library', *Journal of the Royal Horticultural Society (JRHS)*, vol. 51, 1926, pp. 82–83.

The volume on grapes, later offered for £45, was inspected by Edward but found 'imperfect' and so declined.[9]

Special purchases of drawings as well as books were left to the committee's discretion, but EAB was often the instigator. In 1923, Council agreed to the purchase of 80 original drawings from Paris as a result of 'Mr Bunyard having recommended very strongly that the originals should be purchased by the Society as being excellent specimens of botanical drawings.' Then in 1926 there was the chance to buy '10 volumes of watercolours of drawings of fruit for £75 from Messrs Steedman'.[10] This was the once-in-a-lifetime opportunity to regain the most valuable of the library's treasures sold in 1859, the original paintings of fruits commissioned by the Society. The specimens had either been brought to the attention of members at its London meetings or had been grown in its Chiswick gardens. Six volumes were painted by William Hooker, one volume by John Lindley and the remainder by other artists during the period 1815–1824. There were portraits of over 200 fruits, spanning the whole range from apples, pears, plums and cherries to strawberries, raspberries, quinces, medlars, peaches, nectarines, nuts, grapes and pineapples. Some had been reproduced in the Society's early *Transactions*, but many were unique records of varieties captured by Hooker's rare talent that combined artistic skill with detailed knowledge. They were of inestimable value to the pomologist, as Bunyard's account and full catalogue in the RHS *Journal* revealed. They were also exquisite works of art and included some 30 rose and other flower paintings. In recent years Hooker's fruits have become familiar to everyone through their images on the Society's products.

A major contribution to the library's smooth running and efficient image was achieved with the publication of a catalogue. A card index had been started in 1907 by the librarian John Hutchinson, but the compilation of a printed catalogue proved more work than expected. In September 1926, Bunyard interviewed a suitable candidate to assist Hutchinson. The new

---

[9] RHS Lindley Library, RHS Council Minutes, 14 Jan., 1930; 8 April, 1930; 15 April, 1930; 24 Nov., 1931; 3 Feb., 1932; 23 Aug., 1932; 30 Aug., 1932. My thanks to Dr Brent Elliott for information concerning these volumes.

[10] RHS Lindley Library, RHS Council Minutes, 24 April, 1923; 30 Nov., 1926; Bunyard, E. A., 'The Hooker Lindley Drawings', *JRHS*, vol. 52, 1927, pp. 218–224.

recruit started work in October but by the following June Edward was requesting money for two further months to finish the job. *The Lindley Library Catalogue*, a substantial bound volume, was published in September 1927. There had been an earlier, although not totally satisfactory, catalogue published in 1897, but this one marked 'an epoch in the library's history'. It remains the only published catalogue until the library goes on-line in 2007.[11]

By the 1920s the library was outgrowing its space. With pressure from the Library Committee and the aid of a grant from the Carnegie Trust, a third floor was added to the Vincent Square building dedicated entirely to its accommodation in 1929. This allowed shelving for further acquisitions and a reading room for RHS members. A condition of the grant was that the library join what became the Inter-Library Loan system. Subsequently the library was opened to the public. This all added to the librarian's workload and the question of help was raised in January 1932. The job of finding someone was given to Bunyard, Bowles and F. J. Chittenden, who had moved from his position as director of Wisley Gardens to become keeper of the library in 1931. Some months passed, however, before Edward went up to see Bowles at Myddelton House on a Saturday in October to interview the prospective candidate that Bowles had found. He was the young William Stearn, soon appointed the new assistant librarian.[12] Later, during a career as a distinguished botanist, Stearn himself became chairman of the Library Committee.

Edward's finding and buying skills were not the only literary service he rendered Council. He also wrote on the Society's behalf. In 1930 it was given the 'Gardening Book' of John Wedgwood, of the pottery family. His initiative had led to the founding of the Society in 1804. At Council's behest Bunyard extracted the diary for a *Journal* article, in which he brought to life 'a garden essentially English in that the fancier's and collector's spirit

---

[11] Elliott, B., op. cit. p. 168; RHS Lindley Library, RHS Council Minutes, 21 Sept., 1926; 4 Oct., 1925; 8 June, 1927; 13 Sept., 1927; *Lindley Library Catalogue* (London, 1926), p. v.

[12] RHS Lindley Library, RHS Council Minutes 5 Jan., 1932; Allan, M., *E.A. Bowles & His Garden at Myddelton House 1865–1954* (London, 1973), p. 190; RHS Council Minutes 22 Nov., 1932.

predominates', a style that was also, of course, Edward's notion of a perfect garden.¹³ In 1932, Bunyard was in discussions with the magazine *Country Life*, which wished to publish 'articles on the historical and horticultural work of the Society and Library'. Again, encouraged by Council, he agreed to undertake the task. The following year 'his short history of the largest and most influential of all horticultural societies' provided an account of its fortunes and troubles, ending with a hymn of praise to its current achievements that 'following generous expenditure' made the Lindley Library 'unequalled as a Horticulture Library in this country, perhaps in the world'.¹⁴ Relations with *Country Life* must have been agreeable, since in 1936 it published Bunyard's book on roses. His library connections may also have led to Messrs Dulau's publication of *The Anatomy of Dessert*. Dulau was one of the most consistent suppliers of new books to the Lindley Library.

A continuing and pleasurable task for the Library Committee was the allocation of new books for review. This allowed Edward the opportunity to place his own volumes tactically, as well as to direct other titles towards friends and family. In 1937, for example, he suggested that John Nash review *Flower Portraits*; while his sister Lorna received a copy of a *Sussex Recipe Book with a few excursions into Kent*, by Margaret Samuelson, who had researched old manuscripts and travelled widely rescuing old recipes. Their own *Epicure's Companion* was sent to Lady Byng, wife of the First World War hero and owner of a celebrated rock garden, who presumably could be relied upon to appreciate its contents.¹⁵ Bunyard himself dealt with a Ministry publication on the cultivation of nuts, Agnes Arber's history of herbals and Tolkowsky's *Hesperides*. This latter was written in a style close to Edward's heart, drawing on diverse sources and languages. It 'surveyed all sides of life where Citrus fruit may enter; Literature, Painting, Cookery, Medicine and Horticulture are all brought in as evidence and

---

¹³ RHS Lindley Library, RHS Council Minutes, 8 April, 1930; Bunyard, E. A., 'John Wedgwood's Garden', *JRHS*, vol. 56, 1931, pp. 196–200.

¹⁴ RHS Lindley Library, RHS Council Minutes 24 May, 1932; Bunyard, E. A., 'The Royal Horticultural Society and its Work Past and Present', *Country Life*, 11 Feb., 1933, pp. 135–137.

¹⁵ RHS Lindley Library, RHS Library Committee Minutes, Dec. 14 1937; 4 Aug., 1937; 26 Oct., 1937.

indeed the work might well be entitled The Citrus Fruits in Human Life', Bunyard reflected. 'It stands alone as a model to all who propose to write on similar subjects, at once an encouragement and a discouragement.'[16] It was a manner of composition Edward had already explored with his book about the rose, and which he pursued again in his article on the peach and nectarine in 1938.

******

The years Bunyard and Bowles presided over the library were particularly rich in accessions and notable for the largest single donation ever made: the 'Cory Bequest' of over 400 titles and 24 collections of drawings. Many items lost in the 1859 sale were thereby returned to the Society's holdings. Reginald Cory had died in 1934 leaving his books to the Society and his plants to Cambridge Botanic Garden. As soon as the news was confirmed in January 1935, a subcommittee of Bunyard, Charles Musgrave, the Society's Treasurer, and Chittenden, with Stearn as secretary, began discussions with the executors. It was hoped that everything would be settled by Christmas. In the meantime, Edward was asked to prepare an article on the Cory library. Unfortunately, this never emerged. The collection had arrived and been catalogued by Stearn by June 1938, when the tricky question of the disposal of the duplicates was resolved by some being sent to Wisley for the use of staff, the remainder being sold at Sothebys in March 1939.[17]

Can it have been this bequest that prompted Bunyard to make a will on 19 July 1935 leaving his 'library of Pomological Books … to the Royal Horticultural Society … provided they are willing to preserve and maintain the library as a complete Collection with my name for the use of all students of Pomology'? In fact, following his death the library at Allington was broken up and sold. One of the saddest consequences of his financial plight was that the executors could not fulfil his greatest wish. The Society, however, had first choice in advance of the sale. On the advice and selection

---

[16] 'Book Reviews', *JRHS*, vol. 64, 1939; pp. 239–240.
[17] RHS Lindley Library, RHS Council Minutes, 8 Jan., 1935; 30 June, 1936; 18 Aug., 1936; 24 Nov., 1936; RHS Library Committee Minutes, 8 June, 1938; 12 March, 1939.

of William Stearn, it identified a total of 840 volumes for the library and 220 for Wisley at the bargain price of £365. Council, after a long discussion and persuasion by Sir Daniel Hall as to their unique value, decided to make the purchase but, with an ironic quirk of fate, using the funds realized at the sale of the duplicates from the Cory Bequest. Bunyard's books now account for much of the Lindley Library's 'outstanding collection of the literature of fruit, from the 16th to the 20th century in seven languages'.[18]

Bunyard's last service to the library had been to ensure its safe-keeping in the event of war, which was looking all too likely in 1938 when the committee, on 20 September, believed that 'in these critical times the Society ought to have arrangements for the preservation of its records and most valuable books.' He felt it 'wise to send duplicates to Wisley but was not happy about security.' He suggested a bomb-proof room be constructed in the basement of Vincent Square for the most valuable works, but the following week was in consultation with Chittenden over sending both 'unique [books] and duplicates to Wisley along with valuable pictures' and Messrs Bernard Quaritch had been employed to pack books. Then, at the Finance Committee in November there was the proposal to ask Fellows with 'large country houses to undertake to help with storing some of the [Society's] valuables in case of an international crisis.' The President, Lord Aberconway, offered the facilities of his home, Bodnant in North Wales, but suggested that the University of Aberystwyth was the safest place. After agreement was reached in August 1939, the cream of the library was sent to Aberystwyth and the pictures to Wisley.[19]

******

Closely allied to the work of the Library Committee and to the Society's finances were the activities of the Publications Committee, formed in 1917. Bunyard joined this body in the 1920s. He left his mark as the initiator

---

[18] RHS Lindley Library, RHS Library Committee Minutes, 19 March, 1940; 16 April, 1940; RHS Council Minutes 30 April, 1940; Elliott. B., op. cit., pp. 171–2.

[19] RHS Lindley Library, RHS Library Committee Minutes, 20 Sept., 1938; 27 Sept., 1938; Finance and General Committee Meeting included with Library Minutes 8 Nov., 1938; 29 Aug., 1939.

of the first cumulative index to the Society's *Journal*, published in 1936. Bunyard's bibliographic instincts are a quality for which all garden-writers and historians are lastingly grateful. The *Journal*, which had begun in 1866, was the Publications Committee's main on-going expenditure. While preparing an index was considered desirable, when Bunyard posed the question at a Council meeting in June 1927, the cost must have dominated their discussions. No resolution was achieved, but it was on the agenda again a month later when a report and costings were presented by EAB and passed by Council.[20] *The Cumulative Index up to 1935* was prepared by F. J. Chittenden, the *Journal*'s editor since 1908.

Bunyard also had a hand in the production of the RHS colour charts, the first volume of which was published in 1939. He had long been interested in the problem of accurately and unambiguously describing colour: words alone are often insufficient. A solution was provided by the introduction of colour charts – booklets or swatches of colour samples – which enabled the precise shade and tone of many natural objects, such as a flower petal, to be matched against the sample and given a specific name and value. Techniques for printing such charts were not perfect. Edward, commenting on one system in 1911, found 'the colours never approach to the conditions of natural pigment.'[21] The great improvements in colour printing in the years between the wars, however, led to the British Colour Council's decision in 1934 to publish a *Dictionary of Colours*. In consequence, the RHS initiated discussions on its application to plants. In November 1935, a committee was set up to work in collaboration with the Colour Council. Its members were George Leak, the Wisbech bulb producer, Bowles and Bunyard. Their long report setting out the way in which the format of the charts should be undertaken was approved, the collaboration went ahead and the Colour Council took charge of production.[22]

Bunyard's expertise in this area lay both with his knowledge of plants and botanic paintings and in the fact that he was already using existing colour charts in the nursery catalogues. The rose section of the Bunyard catalogue

---

[20] RHS Lindley Library, RHS Council Minutes 8 June, 1927; 5 July, 1927.

[21] Bunyard, E. A., 'Colour Charts', *Gardeners' Magazine*, vol. 54, 7 Jan., 1911, p. 15.

[22] Elliott, B. op. cit., pp. 222–223; RHS Lindley Library, RHS Council Minutes 24

of 1935–36 opens with the statement that, 'In this list we attempt for the first time in the history of the Rose a more exact definition of the colour terms.' Each rose variety's flower, which had been matched with Ridgeway's Colour Chart, was described in words and numbers. The list of varieties was prefaced by a spectrum of colours, with examples of specific roses. The introduction concluded with the information that the 'new Colour Chart now in preparation by the R.H.S. will, we hope, be available next year and it will then be substituted for Ridgeway's.'[23] The colour descriptions were his sister Marguerite's work, which went beyond roses to cover a wide range of flowers that she detailed in the RHS *Journal* in August 1935, a couple of months before the committee began its own report. Edward was not on Council in 1934 or early 1935 when the subject was first discussed, but was clearly aware of what was going on, and closely involved in the Council's decision to produce the colour charts, although never accorded credit for this. When the colour chart appeared, Marguerite's review concluded that 'this is a notable advance in every way.'[24] Standardized colours in flower descriptions, which brought a new level of precision to botanic records, have remained the botanist's preserve and never really penetrated to nurserymen's catalogues; this is one area in which Bunyard's pioneering enthusiasm did not set a new trend.

Another publishing venture to which Bunyard contributed was the RHS *Dictionary of Gardening* which was not published until 1951, although plans were set in motion in 1936. The Society had received a proposal from the Clarendon Press to undertake a revision of Nicholson's *Illustrated Dictionary of Gardening*, first published in 1885–88 and out of print since before the 1914–18 war. At a Publications Committee meeting in June 1936, the proposal was discussed and an advisory committee appointed consisting of Bowles, Bunyard, Sir Arthur Hill, the director of Kew, and John Barr Stevenson of rhododendron fame. The work of compilation fell

---

[23] 'Fruit Trees Roses Shrubs', George Bunyard & Co Ltd, Maidstone, p. 62.

[24] Bunyard, M. E., 'An Approach to Standardization in the Colour Descriptions of Flowers', *JRHS*, vol. 60, 1935, pp. 342–353; Bunyard, M. E., 'The Horticultural Colour Chart. Vol. 1', *JRHS*, vol. 64, 1939, pp. 314–317.

[25] Elliott, B., op. cit., pp. 187–8; RHS Lindley Library, RHS Council Minutes, 23 June, 1936.

to Chittenden who from 1939 devoted all his energies to the project.[25] Edward would, without doubt, have been a major contributor had not his death intervened; there were 43 contributors altogether and fruit and vegetables were made the subject of a separate volume.

The Society's Picture Committee was yet another arena in which our subject played a role. Its early years are not well documented and it is probable that two 'committees' were active during the 1920s and early 1930s: one that commissioned new paintings for the Society and one awarding medals for the paintings exhibited at its shows. In 1926, Bunyard, Bowles, Chittenden and Sir William Lawrence, the Society's treasurer, were appointed to check on the accuracy of paintings being undertaken for the Society; in 1929 he was a member of a 'new "Paintings Committee"'; and in 1935 when minutes began to be taken, a member of the 'Paintings (Exhibits) Committee'.[26] To this can be added the information that in 1929 Bunyard invited John Nash to join one or other of these 'committees'.[27] Nash was already known to him since he had illustrated both *Anatomy of Dessert* and the nursery's 'Vegetables for the Epicure' – which had brought him to Allington and an overnight stay in the Bungalow. The invitation to Nash 'to replace Sir William Lawrence on paintings' in March 1934, following Lawrence's death, could have come from Edward, although exactly where it fits into the complicated story of the Picture Committees is unclear. Nash was a member of the Paintings Committee until 1939.[28] Edward also figured on a special committee set up to arrange a week-long exhibit of paintings in the autumn of 1935, but his position was probably difficult as his sister Frances began successfully exhibiting her flower and fruit paintings in 1931.

******

[26] The Royal Horticultural Society, 'Report of Working Party on Committee Structure to RHS Council' May, 1991; Appendix V, History of Comittees by Dr Brent Elliott, Picture Committee, p. 87; RHS Lindley Library, RHS Council Minutes, 8 May, 1935.

[27] Wilson, E., see chapter 1 of this volume.

[28] RHS Council Minutes, 20 March, 1934; see also 'RHS Arrangements for 1939, Report for 1938'.

Bunyard's natural home within the RHS was the Fruit and Vegetable Committee. This was the Society's oldest and largest specialist body, with over 30 members. It was founded in 1860 in large measure through the efforts of the great fruit man, Robert Hogg, who was its backbone for most of the remainder of the nineteenth century. Edward's father became chairman from 1901 to 1913, in which year Edward himself was invited to join this eminent gathering of horticultural talent, now headed by Charles Nix (the Society's treasurer 1916–1921). Nix's family owned the Tilgate estate near Crawley in West Sussex, which he inherited on his brother's death in 1927. He also inherited the head gardener E. Neal, a colleague on the committee. Both Nix brothers were prize-winning exhibitors of fruit, especially apples and pears. Nix, then Edward, presided over the committee for many years. Bunyard became vice-chairman in 1925, and in 1929 chairman, when Nix finally relinquished the post.

In contrast to most RHS committees, few of its members were amateur gardeners or large landowners. More than half were head gardeners at country estates, who were also columnists in the gardening press as well as major prize-winners at shows everywhere. They included Edwin Beckett, gardener to the Hon. Vicary Gibbs at Aldenham House, Elstree, a legendary figure in vegetable exhibiting; T. Pateman, gardener to Sir Charles Nall Cain (Lord Brocket) in Hertfordshire, who regularly scooped prizes for fruit; and Fred Streeter, gardener to Lord Leconbury at Petworth, who became the well-known radio-gardener. Nurserymen were also well represented among the membership, as were market gardeners, wholesalers and, by the 1930s, some fruit farmers. The committee's role was to keep the Society abreast of developments, make awards for fruits and vegetables and provide judges for the exhibits and competitive classes at the shows.

The committee met on the first day of every fortnightly Westminster Show in the Horticultural Hall, and at the other major RHS shows of the season. We have already encountered Bunyard at these shows as an exhibitor, promoting his nursery's stocks, but as a committee member he was found too on the other side, judging the displays. Bunyard was an eminent judge, often also an adjudicator at fruit shows, acting as the final arbiter in tricky decisions. He was responsible for selecting the judges as well as being chairman of the Show Schedules Committee for Fruit and Vegetables, which drew up the criteria for judging the competitive classes.

'Fruit & Veg's' busiest times were in the autumn when the recommendations for medals and the awarding of some seven cups to the exhibits took hours of careful examination and deliberation. As the Bunyard Nursery was often exhibiting, Edward had to bow out of some of these duties, but he was eligible to join one of the panels for the more time-consuming task of judging the competitions. These could comprise up to 100 different classes, some with as many as 20 entries. At the Westminster Fruit Show in October 1926, for example, the hall was filled by tables of hundreds of competitive dishes.[29] A backdrop was provided by seven large exhibits staged mainly by nurseries, including Bunyard's, of hardy fruits, grapes and fruit trees in pots, and one of 'ornamental gourds, crabs and medlars' from the Earl of Dunraven in Ireland. Many of the competitive classes were themselves spectacular displays. For instance, the 'nine dishes of ripe dessert fruits of not less than six kinds' was a composition evocative of a Victorian dining-table. The prize-winning entry, staged by the Duke of Newcastle's gardener, comprised four bunches of grapes with 'enormous finely coloured berries' set on a platform with, in front, three raised stands of peaches, apples and a central melon, each set off with their own foliage, and four dishes of apples, peaches and pears in the foreground.

Equally magnificent were the grape classes, and even more demanding of the judges' total concentration. The class for 'twelve bunches in not fewer than four varieties' made a breathtaking display and competition between head gardeners (and between their employers) was fierce. Errors of judging were not an option. Classes for apples and pears ranged from collections of 30 dishes to single dishes of a specific variety. At this show, Allington Pippin proved the most popular apple, which must have given Bunyard a warm glow of satisfaction as he walked around the tables. There was a separate class for nurserymen, which Bunyard had won the previous year; market growers competed with boxes of apples and pears, packed and graded as for sale; and county societies from all four corners of Britain battled for prizes. It was a marathon for the committee.

Official duties at shows varied considerably through the year, but there was usually something to be examined. From January to May in 1929, for

---

[29] 'Societies', 'Royal Horticultural', 'Fruit Show', *The Gardeners' Chronicle*, Oct. 16, 1926, pp. 316–18; Oct., 23, 1926, p. 325.

example, at the fortnightly shows in the Horticultural Halls collections of late apples were interspersed with exhibits of root vegetables, potatoes, onions and salad vegetables. The late winter shows demanded the inspection of their highlight for a number of years, fruit from La Mortola, the garden of Sir Cecil Hanbury, in Ventimiglia on the Italian Riviera, which included groves of citrus plants brought from China. The first collection arrived in January 1925, when delays caused by the Christmas traffic meant the fruits were not at their best. Fruits were sent again in 1926, but in 1927 no chances were taken – 'They were brought direct from La Mortola on Sunday last by Mr Braggins', the head gardener and in 'splendid condition', including some with flowers attached. The collection of 51 varieties arranged 'very attractively on a black velvet ground' and decorated with vases of sprays of berries won a Gold Medal. That honour was repeated in 1931.[30] This was a pleasing outcome for everyone, since the Hanbury family was the Society's greatest benefactor not least by donating its Wisley garden. At spring shows, imported fruits were often exhibited – boxes of plums, peaches, apricots, apples and pears from South Africa – arranged by the Imperial Fruit Show Company. Apples from Australia, in particular Tasmania, the Apple Isle, and from Hawke's Bay, the 'Apple Bowl' of New Zealand, made an impressive appearance.

The RHS calendar really began with the Chelsea Flower Show in late May. As now, it was a sumptuous flower show, but offered only a modest judging-load for fruit and vegetables. It would have none the less been a demanding time for Edward as a Council member and exhibitor. He rarely joined the committee for the judging, but his colleagues often gave the Bunyard Nursery a Gold Medal or Silver Cup for its display of late apples. The star turn among his fellow-'Fruit & Veg' members, however – indeed of the entire Flower Show – was the vegetable exhibit staged year after year by Edwin Beckett. No Chelsea was complete without Beckett's display. He always won a Gold Medal for his spectacular vegetable montage, in which bouquets of radishes and carrots, sprays of parsnips, tall cones of peas and great columns of leeks and celery were interspersed with blue beans and scarlet chard arranged 'as an artist blends his colours in a picture.'[31]

---

[30] 'Societies', 'Royal Horticultural', *The Gardeners' Chronicle*, 17 Jan., 1925, p. 47; 29 Jan., 1927, p. 89; 7 Jan., 1931, pp. 58–59.
[31] 'Societies', 'Royal Horticultural', *The Gardeners' Chronicle*, 23 May, 1925, p. 362.

July and August again presented the committee with plenty of work judging soft fruits. In November 1922, Bunyard's Nursery offered an award to be given by Council for strawberries, cherries, gooseberries, peaches, nectarines, apricots and plums at the Society's summer shows. Although several medals were available for fruit, none was sponsored by a nursery. The Bunyard Medals, with an image of George Bunyard on one side, were cast in bronze, silver and silver gilt, accompanied by a prize of £2.00, £3.00 and £4.00 respectively. Staging soft fruit in the heat of the high summer was difficult and, no doubt, the reason that 'these fruits were comparatively seldom exhibited.' In 1923, the first year of the Bunyard Medals, the silver gilt was awarded to the Sittingbourne cherry-grower, [Sir] Leslie Doubleday and the silver to Lord Brocket's gardener.[32]

These prizes were part of Edward's larger plan to bring more fruit exhibits to the summer shows and establish fruit competitions like those of the autumn. He was determined from the outset to make this venture succeed. The unusual presence of fruit-farmers competing at the 1923 summer show might suggest that some persuasion took place in Kent to ensure a good turnout. Bunyard was closely connected with the Kent cherry-growers, who 'paid him the singularly graceful compliment of electing him yearly, for fifteen years as first choice judge of their own cherries at their own Show.'[33] The first such occasion was the inaugural Kent Cherry and Soft Fruit Competition, organized by the Kent Farmers' Union in 1924 at the County Show in Ashford. *The Gardeners' Chronicle* declared, 'never have we seen such a large number of exhibitors of cherries, gooseberries and currants'.[34] W. Talbot Edmonds, owner of Allington Farm next door to the Bunyard Nursery, was among the founders of the Kent Farmers' Union.

After a poor showing at Westminster, and still concerned to bolster the number of entrants in the RHS summer fruit classes, Bunyard asked Council in August 1924 if the Society would provide room for the Kent NFU Cherry Show in early July 1925.[35] Thus the second of these events

---

[32] RHS Lindley Library, RHS Council Minutes, 10 July, 1923.

[33] Hall, Sir Daniel, 'Edward A. Bunyard, F.L.S. An Appreciation', *Journal of Pomology and Horticultural Science*, vol. 17, 1939, p. 295.

[34] 'Societies', Kent County Show, *The Gardeners' Chronicle*, 1924, pp. 66–67.

[35] RHS Lindley Library, RHS Council Minutes 26 Aug., 1924.

came to London, when 'some idea of the keenness of the competition may be gathered from the fact that the entries varied from ten to thirty in each class.'[36] It proved excellent publicity for the fruit-growers as well as the Society, since their cherries in 'size and appearance left the Continental consignments in the markets far behind.' The more familiar exhibitors from the ranks of the RHS also played their part in the success of this year's displays: Bunyard's staged a collection of cherries, Laxton's of strawberries and currants, and there were further exhibits of raspberries and gooseberries. There was, however, only one entrant for the Bunyard Medal for cherries. Bunyard Medals continued to be awarded but, despite all Edward's efforts to increase the presence of fruit at these events, there was only one contestant for the award for gooseberries in 1926.

Initially, the Bunyard Medals had been offered at four Westminster shows but, following rationalization by Bunyard and Nix, this was reduced in 1927 to two, when the Cherry and Soft Fruit Competition in late July attracted 'a fair amount of interest', but the August show of 'peaches nectarines and other fruits was somewhat disappointing'. Similarly, in 1928 'the fruit competition could hardly be termed a success, for the number of entries in all the classes was very limited.' It was time for the Kent cherry-growers to come to the rescue once more and in 1929 the sixth Kent Cherry and Soft Fruit Show brought a 'grand display', filling the hall with entries competing for major challenge cups and attractive prize money. Bunyard's Nursery staged 'a magnificent representative collection of cherries embracing quite sixty varieties, including many continental sorts.'[37] The cherry-growers came again in 1935 to support Edward's Soft Fruit Conference, but in the following year the RHS itself was commenting on the waning of the summer fruit shows. Bunyard had eventually run out of energy. He had kept the impetus going for 12 years but now had another preoccupation: roses. His Bunyard Medal appears to have been terminated the previous year. The Doubleday family, who were among its first winners, still have theirs.[38]

---

[36] 'Societies', 'Royal Horticultural', 'Cherry and Soft Fruit Show', *The Gardeners' Chronicle*, 1 Aug., 1925, p. 97.

[37] *The Gardeners' Chronicle*, July 20, 1929, pp. 58–59.

[38] My thanks to Sir Garth Doubleday and Oliver Doubleday for showing me the Bunyard Medal.

At the Westminster shows, after the judging was completed and further discussions had taken place on the floor, members of the Fruit and Vegetable Committee assembled in an upstairs room to undertake another of their official duties. Like the other plant committees, they were responsible for making awards to specific plants. A First Class Certificate (FCC) bestowed great kudos on a variety and hence financial gain for the nursery that introduced it. As a nurseryman himself, Bunyard was as eager as any other to obtain this endorsement. While as a committee member he was involved in making these decisions, he absented himself when his own fruits or vegetables came up for discussion. Samples would be presented for tasting and the growing plants or trees could also be inspected *in situ*. The committee had two options. It might give an award or, after 1922, a promising variety could be recommended for the Commercial Fruit Trials at Wisley. The Laxton Nursery frequently received awards and recommendations for its new seedlings of every kind of fruit, but Bunyard often brought up samples of his own production for consideration. In 1921, for example, Claygate Pearmain, an old apple variety that the nursery was promoting, received an FCC at the same time as the recently introduced Laxton's Superb. In the same year, Maidstone Favourite was put forward, but although it went for trial, it never achieved an award. Orleans Reinette came up several times, yet only achieved the first step of an Award of Merit in 1921. In the case of vegetables, trials were held at Wisley, to which Bunyard's contributed seed of their best selections from time to time. Members would visit Wisley to comment on the plots and make recommendations, which were then finalized in committee.

Bunyard had added the Bunyard Silver Cup, 'value £21', to the various awards in the gift of the committee. It was first offered at the 'Autumn Fruit Shows in 1919 and 1920 for the most promising seedling Apple or Pear' as judged by a dish of six fruits for two consecutive years. The cup was retained by the prize-winner.[39] In 1926, to take a single year, there were five contenders, of which three were judged worthy of seeing the following year. The best-known recipient of the trophy was Laxton's Epicure apple, victor in 1929. By 1933, however, the cup appears to have been no longer offered. Perhaps, in a rare moment of financial prudence,

---

[39] 'Bunyard Cup' see *JRHS*, vol. 45, 1919–20, p lxxxviii.

Edward decided the cost was too much even for his generosity towards the Society.

******

The duties of 'Fruit & Veg' included, of course, vegetables. Members no doubt debated with great vigour that topical bone of contention, size versus quality, which we have seen influenced Edward's 'Vegetables for Epicures'. But, while it was permissible and desirable to taste a fruit or cook a vegetable submitted to the committee for an award or certificate of merit, it was another matter to eat the sample before awarding the prize in a competitive event. The arguments over vegetable competitions and whether giant vegetables were any good to eat have never gone away. However, in 1938 it was not epicurean treats that occupied the committee's thoughts but 'Vegetable and Fruit Growing in an Emergency', the title of a long and detailed paper that Bunyard delivered to Council on 25 October, but one month after the Munich crisis. Its conclusions became, in essence, the basis of government action. Advocating the need for a coherent policy in case of war, Edward proposed that for vegetables that might be scarce, increased quantities of seed should be obtained; as 'protein could be in short supply, beans suggest themselves' and the testing of different sorts of haricot beans should be undertaken; instructional pamphlets must be produced and 'vegetable trials arranged in various parts of the country'. For fruit, the most effective way to maximize production was to direct efforts towards reducing losses by spoilage, which could be achieved by good pruning and orchard hygiene.

Bunyard's ideas were swiftly taken up and planning began at a subcommittee held on 22 November. This was chaired by EAB and comprised F. A. Secrett, the Thames Valley commercial grower, John Cracknell, a wholesale seedsman, H. V. Taylor, the Ministry's Horticultural Commissioner, and Chittenden, the Society's indefatigable employee. Leaflets were needed to provide information to private gardeners and allotment-holders, and decisions had to be made on what was essential to their better performance. Brassicas, peas, onions and root vegetables were easy to grow and there would be no problems over seed supplies, but provision had to be made for extra quantities of, for example, carrot seed, which was largely imported. Trials of beans, including White Prédome, which Bunyard's Nursery seed lists had been promoting, were proposed in four regions across the country. The committee also advised consulting the Medical Research Council on the nutritional values of different vegetables, and proposed demonstration plots at Wisley and staging instructive exhibits at shows.[40]

This instructional drive was further supported by Edward in an article on the summer sowing of vegetables, drawing attention to the extra crop that could be obtained in this way and the beneficial effects of vitamins in green leafy vegetables such as kales – 'of greatest value in the late winter when green stuff and fruit are getting scarce'. Likewise he recommended spinach beet, 'not as good as true spinach' but very useful, and turnips, which 'will give us a good cutting' of '"Greens" in spring and are hardy and productive.' He followed it up with 'Simple Pruning for Beginners', which was a model of clarity for 'those who have never pruned their own fruit trees.'[41]

Bunyard did not see his ideas through to completion, for he had resigned from all his committees and Council some months before his death in October 1939. Nevertheless his plans were enacted by the combined forces of the RHS and the Ministry of Agriculture. On 12 September – Britain had declared war on Germany on 3 September – it was decided that vegetable growing should be encouraged through regional Garden Advice Centres and panels of lecturers. A series of pamphlets – 'The Growmore Bulletins' and 'Simple Vegetable Cookery' – were published by the RHS, and that same autumn, the phrase 'Dig for Victory' was coined and adopted as the name of the Ministry's campaign for the promotion of home and allotment gardening.[42]

******

The highest pinnacle of Bunyard's career at the RHS was his election to Council. Being a Council member was hugely demanding, requiring

---

[40] RHS Lindley Library, RHS Council Minutes, 25 Oct., 1938; 13 Dec., 1938 contains report to Council of meeting held 22 November, 1938.

[41] Bunyard, E. A. 'Vegetables for Summer Sowing ', *JRHS*, vol. 64, 1939, pp. 377–378; Bunyard, E. A., 'Simple Pruning for Beginners', *JRHS*, vol. 64, 1939, pp. 511–516.

[42] RHS Lindley Library, RHS Council Minutes, Sept. 12, 1939; Elliott, B,. op. cit., p. 260.

attendance at all the main shows, conferences, receptions and more, but there were compensations. Council met on the first day of the fortnightly shows when, after a morning spent with judging panels, chatting to exhibitors and committee engagements, it assembled in the oak-panelled Council Chamber, hung with portraits of past presidents, for a country-house-style luncheon, accompanied by good wine and brought to a close with fresh fruit brought up from Wisley Gardens that morning. Then Council turned to business.

The majority of members were wealthy amateurs – estate owners, industrialists, bankers and lawyers – brought together by a deep love of plants. In 1936, for example, the President was Henry Duncan McClaren, second Baron Aberconway, director of the John Brown shipyard in Glasgow and creator, with his mother, of Bodnant gardens in North Wales. His family also owned 100 acres on the Riviera. Other Council members at this time included Hon. David Bowes-Lyon, brother of the future Queen, who had a celebrated garden at St Paul's Walden Bury near Hitchin; Sir Frederick Stern, banker and owner of Highdown, the innovative chalk garden near Worthing; Gerald Loder of Wakehurst Place, chairman of Southern Railways and a former President; and E. A. Bowles, the plantsman of Myddelton House in Enfield. Commercial interests were represented by Bunyard, fellow-nurseryman W. R. Oldham of Windlesham, Surrey, seedsman L. Noel Sutton of Reading, and G. W. Leak, the Wisbech bulb- and market-grower. They all found time to travel to London for regular meetings, sometimes as often as every week.

Chelsea Flower Show was the most stylish of the Society's events. It opened the London social season and was attended by all Council and committee members. Meetings, lunches and dinners multiplied, with challenging judging decisions to be taken on the first day, the press to meet and royalty to entertain. Before the show was open to Fellows, the Royal party would be escorted around the exhibits by Council members and, while the President might do the honours to their Majesties, Edward or another Council member would be deputed to escort a lesser Royal Highness.

Council duties included out-of-town visits and trips abroad as the Society's representative to judge and award medals. Probably every year there were several such excursions, and Edward must have relished the travel and hospitality offered on these occasions, especially in the company of Sir

William Lawrence with whom he shared an interest in fine wines and good food. Sir William was the son of the Society's 'great' President, Sir Trevor Lawrence. Although he did not continue his father's interest in orchids, the glasshouses and gardens at Burford near Dorking continued to produce prize-winning grapes and vegetables. In September 1925 the two men travelled to Edinburgh to join William Cuthbertson, director of Dobbies' the local seed firm, to judge at the Royal Caledonian and International Flower Show. In the evening there was, no doubt, a triumphant banquet. In August that same year, EAB had been part of a deputation to the Stockport Summer Flower Show (the Chelsea of the North) – the nursery had also staged an exhibit. Bunyard and Charles Nix were often at the Imperial Fruit Shows staged at different cities around the country: in 1924 they were judging in Liverpool, in 1928 at Manchester and in 1930 at Leicester.

Prizes were also awarded by the Society at the shows of a number of major European horticultural organizations. This required Council members to present the awards, as well as to make sure standards were maintained. In 1926 Edward was again in the company of Sir William Lawrence at the fiftieth anniversary show of the Horticultural Society of the Nord region at Valenciennes, where they were 'received in a most cordial and hospitable manner.' In 1927, the centenary year of the French National Horticultural Society, Council sent two deputations to Paris, which for the summer show consisted of Bunyard, Dr A. W. Hill, director of Kew, and Surrey nurseryman W. R. Oldham.[43] He may also have attended the annual 'Ghent Florales' in Belgium, in particular their 125th anniversary in 1933, when the RHS staged an exhibit. From his accounts of his pursuit of roses, it seems likely that he went to the Universal and International Exhibition in Brussels in 1935, where the Society created an 'English garden'.

The most prestigious event staged by the Society during Bunyard's period on Council was the Ninth International Horticultural Congress, held from 7–15 August 1930, which formed one of three 'extremely important horticultural and botanic gatherings' that provided 'a severe test of physical and mental endurance' that summer.[44] The Congress, held in London for

---

[43] See 'RHS Arrangements 1927; Report 1926'; 'RHS Arrangements 1928; Report 1927'
[44] 'Ninth International Horticultural Congress', *The Gardeners' Chronicle*, 16 Aug., 1930, p. 125.

the first time, had brought a large cast of luminaries – 668 delegates and members of various plant committees, representing 51 countries. An RHS executive committee chaired by the President, Gerald Loder, and including Bunyard, organized an expansive programme covering propagation, pomology and tropical and subtropical horticulture with papers presented in three languages. To ensure no problems with comprehension, 'the sessions were presided over by an English-speaking chairman supported by a vice-chairman from abroad.' Edward was also chairman of one of the specialist conference committees – on nomenclature.

On the first day, he had the pleasure of listening to quotations from *The Anatomy of Dessert*, only then just published. They were used as evidence of British fruit preferences in the opening lecture of the pomology section given by W. T. Macoun, the fruit-breeder from Ottawa. He reported on a world-wide questionnaire aimed at discovering 'National Tastes in Apples', going on to say that British tastes had been described in 'a most appetising manner' by Edward's book, which also revealed his strong prejudice against American and Canadian apples. Canada's national fruit, the McIntosh, did not even merit a mention, 'despite the fact that [it] has on several occasions been voted the best dessert apple in the British Empire at the Imperial Fruit Shows held in England'.[45] This must have raised a few chuckles in the audience.

The session on the following Monday was chaired by Bunyard. It opened with one of the most influential papers on the origins of fruit yet given, its author the Russian botanist Nicolai Vavilov. He brought news of the pioneering work of the Institute of Plant Industry (now the Vavilov Institute) in Leningrad. Edward must have been enthralled, though no record survives of any comment that he might have made at the time. Vavilov's project formed part of the Soviet Union's search throughout its territories for new crops to grow. He had been exploring the wild fruit forests that stretched from the Caucasus to the Kopet Daghs north of Iran and across Central Asia to the foothills of the Tien Shan mountains in Kazakhstan on the borders of China. He described forests of wild pears and quinces entwined with grape vines, whole stands of wild apples and

---

45 Macoun, W. T., 'National Tastes in Apples' in *Ninth International Horticultural Congress Report. London 1930* (Royal Horticultural Society, 1930), pp. 219–244.

undergrowths of cherries and plums. 'In autumn,' he recounted, 'when the fruit is ripening, a traveller passing through the forests of Transcausia might think himself in the Garden of Paradise.' It was a similar picture further east, where the landscape was reflected in the name of Kazakhstan's capital, Alma Atar, which in Kazakh meant 'Father of Apples'. Vavilov proposed the idea of centres of diversity for different fruits, now the consensus view. It has been substantiated by recent work which suggests that Kazakhstan is probably the centre of origin of the domestic apple.[46]

Although the sessions were packed with lectures and discussions, the overall pace of the Congress was leisurely. Lecture days were interspersed with trips to gardens, research institutes and nurseries. Bunyard, who was part of the 'Reception and Entertainments Sub-Committee', laboured in the organization of these visits, and acted as host when delegates came to Allington. One can imagine the delight with which he showed off his fruit collections and the large range of varieties grown by the nursery; perhaps they also had a glimpse of his herbarium, records and even his library. That day's excursion took in Allington, East Malling Research Station and a fruit farm nearby at Paddock Wood.[47]

Delegates and guests were handsomely entertained. There was an official reception hosted by the government at Lancaster House on the first day, and a banquet given by the RHS two days later. Matters concluded at 'about 11.0 pm., but, at the invitation of the President, many of the delegates remained for another half an hour or so, making new acquaintances and cementing old friendships.' The Bunyard brothers presumably caught the last train home to Maidstone and were up betimes in the morning to receive the touring party just described.

Congress culminated in a flower show. Once more, Edward was occupied with the arrangements. Rather than the usual individual displays and competitive classes, nurserymen, seedsmen and private gardens had pooled

---

[46] Vavilov, N. I., 'Wild Progenitors of the Fruit Trees of Turkestan and the Caucasus and the Problem of the Origin of Fruit Trees' in *Ninth International Horticultural Congress Report*, op. cit., pp. 271–286. For recent work see Juniper, B. E., Mabberley, D. J., *The Story of the Apple* (Oregon, 2006); Morgan, J., Richards, A., *The New Book of Apples* (London, 2002), pp. 7–11.

[47] *Ninth International Horticultural Congress Report*, op. cit., p. 9.

their resources to fill the hall with a grand design of orchids, roses, carnations, sweet peas and masses of other flowers, to such effect that 'rarely in the annals of the Society has such a magnificent display of horticulture been staged.' Fruit was not forgotten: 'Mr. E. A. Bunyard arranged the display of fruit' contributed by 'Nix, Wisley Gardens, Allgrove's, Bunyard's, Laxton's and Rivers'. A glowing cornucopia in 'the form of an oval, with dishes of fruits arranged around a central mass of fruiting trees of Peaches, Plums, Apples and Pears, and at one end, cordon trained Gooseberries. Beneath the last named were baskets of Black Currant, … White Currant and Red Currants … with Gooseberries in variety. There were large baskets of Apples … Grapes were shown particularly well … Several well-grown Melons were included in the exhibit; there were boxes of peaches and dishes of Nectarines with baskets of Plums … and fruiting sprays of Blackberry.'[48]

******

Edward probably had to work hard to keep fruit at the centre of attention, since the interests of the majority of RHS Council members lay with flowers. Orchids had always been a favourite with Presidents and during the interwar years rhododendrons, lilies, irises and all kinds of herbaceous plants were immensely popular. Even so, Bunyard and Charles Nix were successful in making fruit the subject of two out of the seven RHS conferences staged in the 1930s. Bunyard and Sir Daniel Hall had nursed along the ambitious Commercial Fruit Trials, and he had valiantly made fruit a feature of the summer shows. All the while, he kept the subject of fruit and vegetables high on the list of lectures at the Westminster shows through many talks given by himself as well as by a number of his friends.

Bunyard was the fruit diplomat in the affairs of the RHS, bringing together the various sectors under the Society's umbrella – encouraging the exchange of information between the amateurs and professionals and keeping the Society at the forefront of developments. The 1920s and 1930s was a time of change within the horticultural hierarchy. The old guard, the head gardeners, the source of all wisdom where plants and gardens were

---

[48] 'Congress Exhibition', *The Gardeners' Chronicle*, 16 Aug., 1930, p125; 23 Aug., 1930, pp. 158–9.

concerned and in particular of fruit and vegetables, were being overtaken by the new scientific 'experts' from the research institutes. The emphasis was also moving towards the needs of the market grower, so that amateur interests were in danger of being marginalized. Bunyard made sure amateurs and all the professionals, be they market-growers, head gardeners, scientists or leisure-gardeners, were kept in touch; he had a foot in every camp.

Co-operation and good relations with the research institutes was an important element in the Society's encouragement of horticultural excellence and there were a number of close ties. For example, Sir Daniel Hall, the director of John Innes, was a Council member, while Edward was entrusted with the formal role of the Society's representative on the governing bodies of Long Ashton and East Malling Research Stations; Chittenden also served at Long Ashton. Bunyard's position also reflected well on his own place within the research community.

He was most involved with East Malling and its director Ronald Hatton. Here Bunyard's role as the 'man on the inside', helping his friends and the progress of fruit growing, was perfectly illustrated by the arrangements for the Walnut Competition of 1929. The walnut saga began in 1925, when, in a number of articles, Howard Spence contrasted the rather haphazard way that walnuts were cultivated in England with the amazing progress that had been made in the United States over the past twenty years through planting established varieties. Bunyard's earlier pieces on cobnut varieties and his call to establish fruiting plantations outside of Kent may have been an inspiration for Spence to embark on a survey of English walnut trees, undertaken with the help of H. V. Taylor and the Ministry of Agriculture's regional inspectors, and supported by Hatton, who began to build up a walnut collection at East Malling with scions taken from the best trees.[49]

A focus was needed, however, to awaken people's interest in home-grown walnut production and locate walnut trees that reliably produced good-quality nuts. A nationwide competition seemed the answer. The proposal was backed by the RHS in November 1928 and an organizing committee

---

[49] Spence, H. 'An Inquiry into the Quality of English Grown Walnuts', *Journal of Pomology and Horticultural Science*, vol. 5, 1925–6, pp. 223–240; Spence, H. 'English Grown Walnuts', *The Gardeners' Chronicle*, 10 Oct., 1925, pp. 290–91; Bunyard, E. A., Cobnuts and Filberts', *JRHS*, vol. 45, 1919–20, pp. 224–32.

chaired by Bunyard was formed. Howard Spence, who had undertaken to examine all the samples, donated a silver cup for the overall winner; the Ministry provided additional prize money; and the winners would be asked to supply East Malling with scions, in return receiving two new trees of their variety. An advertisement placed in August 1929 sought the co-operation of Fellows and others in sending samples to the Society from trees bearing good walnuts. Its prose has a Bunyard ring to it. Keen to set a high standard, Edward invited exhibits from firms in Los Angeles and in France (the major European walnut producer), and he extracted from Council the money for their expenses.[50] The Walnut Competition staged on 19 November at an RHS Vincent Square Show, accompanied by a lecture on walnuts given by Howard Spence, was 'an immense success'. There were 732 entries, from which 'Champion of Ixworth' in Suffolk emerged as the prize-winner and four other good varieties of English walnuts were discovered and propagated.[51] Trees of these and others were planted on several sites, including Wye College, where they continue to fruit every year.

Bunyard was a generous man, not only with his time and many gifts to the Society, but also to his colleagues. He seems never to have born any resentment towards his rivals, nor anyone else. 'Kindness was in his eyes the first of virtues,' wrote his friend Maurice Healy, 'and he was not a man who failed to practice what he preached.'[52] With Council membership came an opportunity for a little benevolent patronage. Friends and colleagues could be rewarded by suggesting and promoting their case for one of the Society's personal awards such as the Victoria Medal of Honour (VMH) and Veitch Award. Edward had received the latter in 1934 and later joined the Awards Panel. He would certainly have had a hand in the Veitch Award to Ronald Hatton, as well as the VMH to nurseryman Edward Laxton, who so often captured the glory with his new fruits, and that to his great friend and

---

[50] RHS Lindley Library, RHS Council Minutes 6 Dec., 1928, includes report from Fruit and Vegetable Committee of meeting on 19 Nov. on the 'Walnut Competition; see also RHS Council Minutes 9 July, 1929; 16 July, 1929; 13 Aug., 1929; 'Walnut Competition', *The Gardeners' Chronicle*, 31 Aug., 1929, p. 158.

[51] 'Societies', 'Royal Horticultural', 'The Walnut Competition', *The Gardeners' Chronicle*, 23 Nov., 1929, p. 413.

[52] Healy, M., op. cit., pp. 324–6.

colleague F. A. Secrett. Bunyard died before he could reap his own reward of the VMH, which he surely would have received. He was able, just in time, to secure an honour for the Bunyard Nursery foreman Frederick Buss, who was among the first to receive the Associate of Honour in 1930 but who died later that year.

******

By the 1930s Bunyard was living the life of a wealthy gentleman: enjoying good food and wine, and relishing the high life of those echelons of society with whom he mixed at the RHS and on his Riviera jaunts. He indulged these social pleasures to the full by joining London dining clubs and patronizing celebrated restaurants. He moved with ease and familiarity in these surroundings. Maurice Healy knew 'few men who possessed so many points of contact with their fellows, and who could be amusing upon so many subjects … Wit delighted him; he would turn an epigram upon his tongue as a gourmet might savour a particularly delicate morsel.'[53] Bunyard was 'always ready for the right kind of conversation' in congenial company around a dining table.

The RHS Council was itself upper-crust, its members accustomed to fine wine cellars and home-grown produce of the highest quality. Bunyard, too, had grown up in a family that lived well. His education in the refinements of dining had clearly not been neglected, with a father who confessed to collecting English china and a mother who owned rare linen damask tablecloths.[54] Nor were the pleasures of the table absent, with fresh fruit and vegetables all year round from their orchards and gardens, and game to shoot on their land. Maidstone was the county and market town, boasting a number of high-class food stores that drew on the riches of the Kent countryside and coastline such as Romney Marsh lambs fattened in the cherry orchards, and majestic turbots and Dover soles the size of dinner-plates caught off Folkestone. From Bunyard's accounts of meals, presumably cooked for him at the Bungalow, he dined in style. He loved French cooking

---

[53] Ibid.
[54] 'George Bunyard', *Journal of Horticulture and Cottage Gardening*, vol. 60, 1910, p. 197; Bunyard, L.Y., 'Letter to the Editor', *The Times*, 19 Sept., 1927, p. 8.

and had a favourite restaurant in Paris. For many years he had been visiting Italy and Norman Douglas, a man notorious for his love of food that, even when unpretentious, was always made from the finest local ingredients. Bunyard was an excellent and experienced judge of quality.

Kent was a county famed for its beer, with hop-gardens and breweries a-plenty. The East Malling Research Station, for instance, favoured Fremlins, invariably serving Gold Top at the annual lunch for the governors. But Edward's fancy seemed to lean more towards wine, and his first lessons may have been from the staff at Maidstone's George Prentice & Son, remembered as a first-class merchant. His extensive knowledge suggests many years of study although we learn elsewhere that his purchases were never dignified with proper cellar storage, being housed in anything from damp apple stores to a small but convenient cupboard.

Edward's first dining club was probably the Horticultural Club, founded in 1875 and still holding dinners and lectures today. In the 1920s it met in the Trocadero Restaurant near Piccadilly. It was a haven for RHS people – his father had been a member and its presidents included Lord Lambourne and Gerald Loder. The Trocadero was owned by J. Lyons & Co. whose buying-power led to one of the finest wine lists in town. From time to time, Edward frequented London's 'so many different and equally excellent restaurants … from the very large to the very small ones that there is no excuse for dining out to be monotonous,' as André Simon described in 1929.[55] Boulestin's in Covent Garden, for example, a mecca for lovers of French cooking and one of London's smartest and most expensive, almost certainly entertained him. (Marcel Boulestin himself provided the introduction to 'Vegetables for Epicures' in 1932.) Edward was also a member of the Royal Societies Club in St James's Street, perhaps to provide overnight accommodation for his expanding social life as well as for the sympathetic company it offered.

Since the early 1920s, a frequent dining companion was the bibulous barrister Maurice Healy. When reminiscing over a 'delightful red Graves, Château Smith Haut Laffitte', Healy recounted that he had shared a bottle in 1924 'in the company of my dear friend Edward Bunyard, who might have stood as a type of wine in his excellence and modesty.'[56] Many evenings

---

[55] Simon, A., *The Art of Good Living* (London, 1929, 2nd ed. 1930), p. 22.
[56] Healy, M., *Stay Me With Flagons* (London, 1940), p. 143.

were spent tasting apples, savouring wine and listening to Mozart. Healy was part of a group of bon viveurs which revolved around André Simon and other wine merchants and it may have been through his acquaintance that Edward too was drawn into the circle.

Simon, a Frenchman domiciled in England, held the sole agency for Pommery champagne. He was an old friend of Healy's uncle and had attended to Maurice's wine education when he began to practise in London in about 1920. Healy was a member of the old and distinguished club patronized by lawyers and writers, Ye Sette of Odd Volumes, to which A. J. A. Symons, another key player in London wine and food circles, also belonged. Here André Simon and Symons had met and, aside from their interest in wine, found they were both obsessive book collectors. Symons, who is remembered as the biographer of the eccentric baron Corvo, had inaugurated the First Edition Club in 1922. This published the *Book-Collector's Quarterly*. While the date when this coterie of epicures was first acquainted is not established, it existed by October 1929 when Simon recorded a lunch that brought himself, Bunyard, Symons, Healy and a number of other literary guests to meet members of the Empire Marketing Board at the Connaught Rooms.[57]

Edward's membership of the Saintsbury Club has been described by Alan Bell in a previous chapter. Edward fitted perfectly the criteria for the limited membership of the club – 'a love of wine and letters that is catholic and articulate'[58] – although he did take issue with Saintsbury's claim that 'medlars were the ideal fruit to join with wine'. His gift of apples and walnuts for the dessert – 'Pommes d'Allington' – served at the first dinner in 1931 has also been described.[59] André Simon and A. J. A. Symons together founded the more ambitious but less exclusive Wine and Food Society in 1933. Simon, after losing his contract with Pommery, planned to launch a wine and food quarterly, but had no publishing experience. He turned to Symons for help and they emulated his earlier creation the First Edition Club. The aim of the society was 'to overcome indifference to the

---

[57] Simon, A. L., *By Request: An Autobiography* (London, 1957), pp. 73–79; Simon, A. L., *Tables of Content: Leaves from My Diary* (London, 1933), pp. 42–43; my thanks to the late Julian Symons for information regarding his brother.

[58] Maxwell Campbell, I., *The Wayward Tendrils of the Vine* (London, 1947), p. 33;

[59] Simon, A. L., *By Request: An Autobiography*, op. cit. p. 85.

flavour, variety and cooking of food as well as ignorance of the merits and charm of wines.' While the times were not propitious in which to launch a magazine and dining club devoted to extravagance – England in the throws of depression with three million unemployed, and many not knowing where their next meal was coming from – the organizers neutralized any criticism by making a stand for excellence, not extravagance. Edward would have been familiar with arguments along these lines.

Professor William Stearn, who knew Bunyard well in the 1930s, thought he recalled him being closely involved with the founding of the Wine and Food Society, but Simon, writing many years later, does not accord him such prominence.[60] He was not on the initial Advisory Council, though circumstantial evidence places him in close association. Healy was a member, as were Boulestin and Lady Swaythling, 'a dear friend' of Simon and his wife, 'at whose hospitable board we had so often discussed how to make a start and choose the right name for our proposed Society.' Lord Swaythling was a prominent and successful exhibitor at the RHS shows, where his head gardener often carried off Gold Medals for fruit grown at Townhill Park near Southampton.

Edward was certainly among the first contributors to *Wine and Food* with articles in every issue of the magazine in its first year (see the Bibliography, below). Nor did he lose an opportunity to advertise as well as give support: the first issue had an announcement of the second edition of *The Anatomy of Dessert*, with its additional notes on wine, plus some flattering reviews by fellow club members. Reciprocal promotion of the Society followed in 'Vegetables for Epicures', but with probably no payment. Neither could Edward resist taking a hand in the organization: he devised a tasting of cider, and of apples in November 1938.

Friends from Bunyard's RHS circle had been drawn in: Sir Daniel Hall, who was a member of both the Saintsbury Club and the Wine and Food Society, entertained André Simon to a dinner at Merton Court, his home as director of the John Innes Institute.[61]

---

[60] My thanks to the late Professor W. Stearn for this and other information; Simon, A. L., *In the Twilight* (London, 1969), p. 56.

[61] Simon, A. L., *By Request: An Autobiography*, op. cit., p. 105.

Bunyard appears to have made an early impression on Simon who in his *Art of Good Living* published in 1929 makes a remarkable statement regarding the English apple.[62] At the end of his list of appropriate wines to drink with different fruits he adds, 'There is no fruit grown in England to greater perfection than the Apple ... there are so many excellent and distinctive varieties, that a great discrimination is needed to select the right sort of apple for the right type of wine.' For a patriotic Frenchman, born in Normandy, to state that England possessed this outstanding diversity, even given his anglophile inclinations, is quite astonishing, since the French never concede an inch on the quality of their apples! The debate on the perfect wine companion for each fruit was ongoing and Bunyard and Simon did not always share the same opinion. Nor did Bunyard find his RHS Council colleague Sir William Lawrence in agreement with him: 'He is too fond of a "rich Sauterne", an Yquem. Yquem to me is a sacrament, I drink it only at Christie's auction rooms, with a little bit of cheese, when some good fellow's cellar is put up for sale and he stands me lunch for the last time; wine before or after fruit, but rarely with fruit!'[63]

******

By the late 1930s, London dining-clubs and restaurants were claiming Bunyard's attention during winter months, the Riviera beckoned in the spring and roses were consuming much of his time during the summer. His friend Sir Daniel Hall thought that he should have been 'a gentleman of leisure living in his library and his garden, and cultivating by judicious travel a nice taste in matters of kitchen and cellar.'[64] But, of course, he had to make his living as a nurseryman and subsequent events suggest his personal circumstances were very far from comfortable. When Bunyard died in 1939, he left only £311.2s.3d: not technically bankrupt, but almost penniless. He had got himself into deep financial problems, although judging from his

---

[62] Simon, A. L., *The Art of Good Living*, op. cit., p. 107.

[63] Lawrence, Sir William, 'Notices of Books, Dessert Fruits', *The Gardeners' Chronicle* 26 Oct., 1929, p. 329.

[64] Hall, Sir Daniel, in 'Edward A. Bunyard, F.L.S.', op. cit.

activities earlier in the year he appeared to have been unaware of his position or ignoring it. Yet his family were well off – his father had left £19,268 in 1919; his mother, who died shortly after Edward, left £15,416; and his brother Norman died in 1969 leaving the princely sum of £58,177.

The explanation for Bunyard's suicide offered by Stearn, then assistant librarian at the RHS, was that Bunyard could not face the prospect of life without his accustomed luxuries once war was declared on 3 September 1939. This does not sit easily with his active preparation for that same war with respect to the securing of the RHS library or the improvement of the nation's diet during hostilities.

We may, however, be able to glean an insight into Edward's predicament from the fact that some months before his death he had been given a job by the RHS as the keeper of the library and editor of the Society's publications. The circumstances surrounding this appointment are not clear and all that survives of his meeting and correspondence with the President, Lord Aberconway, is contained in the 'Minutes of the Meeting of the Council held in camera on July 4th., 1939', reported in the minutes of 18 July, from which the following extract is taken:

> The President reported on his negotiations with Mr. Bunyard and read his letter addressed to Mr. Bunyard of June 21st and Mr. Bunyard's reply of July 7th.
>
> The President explained with regard to Mr. Bunyard's position with his firm, that he only desired to remain there as an advisor, he would take no part in the business arrangements, nor receive a fee. He would further like to assist in the naming of fruit. He further wished to keep his position as Commissioner of Income Tax and Chairman of the Library Committee of Maidstone. He also desired that his appointment should be one under the Council, it being understood that he would of course naturally work with the Secretary. He also agreed that his position on the Fruit and Vegetable Committee and Library Committee should be given up but he would be pleased to act in an advisory capacity on such Committees if desired.
>
> It was unanimously agreed to appoint Mr. Bunyard in the terms of the above quoted letters to the Position of Keeper of the Library and Editor of the Society's publications … It was understood that Mr Bunyard would be able to take up his appointment somewhere in mid-July. A date to

be definitely fixed, and would in the first place devote his time to the preparation of a Wisley Guide.[65]

If Bunyard had gone to the President to confess straightened finances, then Aberconway's response had been the offer of a job at Vincent Square, and the post of keeper of the library sounded prestigious when included in the 'RHS Announcements' in *The Times* of 31 July 1939. But Bunyard's RHS appointment was coupled with resignation from all his committees and Council. This must surely have been a mortal blow to his self-esteem. For someone of Bunyard's eminence and long service, the job of librarian and editor, no matter how dressed up, was hardly equivalent to being on Council. He had crossed the divide and become an employee. The post of keeper of the library had been created in 1931 as part of a reorganization within the Society, which had removed Chittenden as director of Wisley Gardens and transferred him to London. Chittenden now moved across to edit the new RHS *Dictionary of Gardening*. Bunyard was immediately replaced on Council by H. V. Taylor; as chairman of the Fruit and Vegetable Committee by F. A. Secrett; and of the Library Committee by E. A. Bowles.

Edward was also stepping down from the management of the nursery in Maidstone, but how he imagined that he could remain as Commissioner of Income Tax is a mystery. His obituaries stated that although he 'had retired as managing director of his firm he was still functioning in that capacity', and that his post with the RHS was part-time until September, when it became full-time. Even so, it could hardly have been very lucrative, since the Society was not known as a generous employer.

The money needed to sustain Bunyard's social and public life presumably exceeded the salary the nursery could afford to pay him. It is quite possible the nursery may not have been as prosperous as its glossy catalogues suggest. His pleasures – collecting rare books, fine wines, dining, and foreign travel – have never been cheap and royalties from books published or fees from writing could hardly have financed these. His public duties as a member of Council were undertaken at his own expense, which was the greater insofar as they removed him from his commercial functions at the nursery.

---

[65] RHS Lindley Library: RHS 'Minutes of the Meeting of Council held in camera on July 4th., 1939' is included with RHS Council Minutes 18 July 1939.

THE COMMITTEE MAN

Bunyard's situation in that summer of 1939 was painful. Stripped of his positions, with the prospect of commuting to an office in the very place where reminders of his former achievements would be the most piquant. We can only speculate as to what precipitated his taking his own life. War would mean reduced sales for the nursery and no prospect of a windfall from selling land to accommodate Maidstone's expansion. Perhaps a creditor was threatening to take him to court to force a sale of assets. The sale of his books or his wine collection, the reduction of his household, or doing without his manservant and housekeeper would certainly have aroused local gossip bringing damage to the business and shame on the Bunyard name. His father's words would haunt him – 'I have not made a fortune, but a reputation; which, I feel sure, my Sons will endeavour to maintain.'[66] And in his final hours, was he sparing his family, friends and colleagues by not choosing to deliver the mortal blow in the seclusion of his orchards or a deserted RHS committee room? Or was it a final statement of what he had become – a gentleman of letters in his own London club?

The RHS was publicly supportive. The obituary in the *Journal* ran to only two sentences, but a letter of condolence was sent by the President to the family. His sister Frances was offered employment as a botanic artist, but this could have only been for a couple of months since few paintings were commissioned during the war. The Library Committee recorded 'the sorrow of the members of the Committee at the death of the late Keeper, Mr Edward Ashdown Bunyard, and their recognition of the great services he had rendered to the Committee during his long period as Chairman.'[67]

After his death, Edward's library and rose collection were sold, but no one thought to preserve the invaluable records which he had accumulated over so many years. His executors could not have even met his bequest to 'his faithful servant' William Buss of £100 and £10 for every year of his employment since 1922, although perhaps he did receive 'my clothes and wearing apparel as he may select.'

---

[66] 'The History of the Bunyard Firm; from 1796 to 1911', privately printed and dated Maidstone, 1911; see p. 32.

[67] For Council's tribute to Bunyard see RHS Lindley Library, RHS Council Minutes 24 Oct., 1939; for Frances Bunyard's employment as a botanic artist see Council Minutes 28 Nov., 1939; for Library Committee tribute see Minutes Library Committee 28 Nov., 1939.

Very little trace remains of the Bunyard nursery. Of the land at Allington, about half is farmed under the name 'Bunyards Farm'. There survives a small block of pear trees and some cobnuts, and the area to the left of the London Road remains open fields. The rest of it, and the place where Edward's bungalow stood, is covered with houses. The sale of these acres may have been the source of some of his brother Norman's wealth. The lodge at the entrance to the nursery is still there, as are a few of the monkey puzzle trees that used to line its boundary on the London Road. The Bunyard shop premises in the centre of Maidstone remain, together with the cedar tree that reputedly marked the boundary of their adjoining nursery.

Because of the ignominious circumstances surrounding Edward's death, his peers drew a veil of silence over his many achievements in horticulture during the 1920s and 1930s. Yet he was Britain's leading pomologist and all-round fruit expert with an unequalled breadth of learning. His many contacts, his personal charm and his immense knowledge made him a key figure in the whole horticultural community.

Bunyard was an enthusiast with unflagging energy, prepared to give himself wholeheartedly to a task. That he was a dedicated collector as well as nurseryman, not always the most profitable combination, enabled him to provide and keep a great diversity of fruit varieties alive in people's gardens, and to revive the neglected but exquisitely beautiful old-fashioned roses. He was a marvellous communicator, able to convey his enthusiasm and love of a subject. He gave exceptionally generously to horticulture in its broadest sense, perhaps to his own personal detriment, but to the enjoyment of many still today.

The Apple War

The storm troops have landed,
The red and the green,
Their pips on their shoulders,
Their skin brilliantine.

Uniform, orderly,
Saleable, ambitious –
Gala and Granny
And Golden Delicious.

Quarter them, they're tasteless;
They've cotton-wool juice,
But battalions of thousands
Routinely seduce.

In shy hen-haunted orchards
Twigs faintly drum,
Patient as partisans
Whose time has almost come,

From Worcester and Somerset,
Sussex and Kent,
They'll ramble singing,
A fruity regiment.

Down with Cinderella's kind,
Perfect, toxic, scarlet;
Back comes the old guard
Costard, Crispin, Russet.

James Grieve, Ashmead Kernel,
Coppin, Kingston Black –
Someone has protected them.
They're coming back.

U. A. FANTHORPE

Bibliography of the Publications of Edward Ashdown Bunyard

compiled by
EDWARD WILSON

One difficulty in constructing this bibliography was knowing in which periodicals to look; there may well be omissions.

The following abbreviations for periodicals are used:

    G: *The Garden*
   GC: *The Gardeners' Chronicle*
   GI: *Gardening Illustrated*
   JP: *The Journal of Pomology*
 JRHS: *The Journal of the Royal Horticultural Society*

BOOKS

1. *A Handbook of Hardy Fruits More Commonly Grown in Great Britain*, I, *Apples and Pears* (London, 1920); II, *Stone and Bush Fruits, Nuts, Etc.* (London, 1925).
2. *The Anatomy of Dessert*, limited edition of 1000 numbered copies signed by the author (Dulau, London, 1929).
3. *The Anatomy of Dessert with a Few Notes on Wine* (Chatto & Windus, London, 1933, in a red binding); reprinted in 1936 by Chatto in its Phoenix Library of Food and Drink in a green binding. For the New York edition published by E. P. Dutton, 1934, Bunyard wrote a special

Preface (I am grateful to Mr David Karp of Los Angeles for sending me a copy).
4. *Old Garden Roses* (London and New York, 1936); note 'Photographs taken by Sweatman Hedgeland, Esq. Drawings and end-paper design [and, one suspects, the dustwrapper's painting of a rose, reproduced in colour] by Frances L. Bunyard' (EAB's sister, 1884–1982, p. [xvi]). See also *GI* no. 88, *JRHS* no. 26, and *The New Flora and Silva* no. 3.
5. *The Epicure's Companion* ed. by Edward and Lorna Bunyard (London, 1937); besides numerous contributions by EAB and his sister, Lorna (1876–1963), Marguerite Bunyard (EAB's sister, 1890–1959) wrote on spices and on 'A Dinner in India', and the drawings, doubtless including those on the dustwrapper, were by Frances Bunyard.

CONTRIBUTIONS TO BOOKS

1. George Bunyard (EAB's father, 1841–1919), *England's National Flower* [the rose] (Maidstone and London, [?1904]); the photographs of roses were by EAB (see chapter 1, Books above, no. 4, *JRHS* no. 26, and *The New Flora and Silva* no. 3).
2. 'On Xenia' in W. Wilks (ed.), *Report of the Third International Conference 1906 on Genetics…*, published for the Royal Horticultural Society (London, [1907]), 297–300; EAB, an invited guest (p. 22), delivered his paper on Wednesday, 1 August 1906 (p. 8).
3. 'Fruit' in Reginald Cory (ed.), *The Horticultural Record* [of the Royal International Horticultural Exhibition 1912] … *Accompanied by Contributions on the Progress of Horticulture Since the First Great International Horticultural Exhibition of 1866* (London, 1914), 153–62.
4. 'Apples and Pears', s.v. 'The Basis of Classification in Apples and Pears', in F. J. Chittenden (ed.), *Apples and Pears: Varieties and Cultivation in 1934: Report of the Conference Held by the Royal Horticultural Society at the Crystal Palace, Sept. 19–21, 1934* (London, 1935), 47–74; see also EAB's discussion of foreign apples at the exhibition, 209–11.
5. 'Gardening for Epicures', in Miles Hadfield (ed.), *The Gardener's Companion* (London, 1936), 13–37.

A BIBLIOGRAPHY

PAMPHLETS

I have excluded here the reprints in pamphlet-form of articles in journals.

1. a four-page pamphlet, *The House of Bunyard 1796–1919* (no place or date stated, but presumably Maidstone, 1919); it is anonymous but must be by EAB. It was published on 'the lamented death of our late principal, Mr. George Bunyard [on 22 January 1919]', and is addressed to 'our customers'. I know of 3 surviving copies: one in the Bunyard Family File in the Reference Library at Maidstone, and two in the Lindley Library of the Royal Horticultural Society: (a) in the main collection, indexed s.v. Bunyard, Edward A.; (b) in the collection of Bunyard catalogues in a box labelled 'BUNYARD 1914–1929 and undated', loosely inserted in *Catalogue of Fruit Trees 1919–20*, Geo. Bunyard & Co.

JOURNALS

Country Life
This weekly changed its volume numbers twice a year, in January and July.

1. Letter on 'The Judas Tree', XXXIX, no. 996, 5 February 1916, 190.
2. Letter on 'The Churchyard Yew', XLI, no. 1048, 3 February 1917, 118.
3. Letter on 'The Library at Rothamsted', [re. an article by E. J. Russell, 'The Agricultural Library at Rothamsted', 27 January 1917, 91–4], XLI, no. 1049, 10 February 1917, 142.
4. Letter on 'Vine, Moore's Early', XLII, no. 1086, 27 October 1917, 407.
5. Letter on 'Fruit Trees From Cuttings', XLIII, no. 1096, 5 January 1918, 23.
6. Letter on 'Ancient Trees in Gray's Inn Gardens', XLIII, no. 1102, 16 February 1918, 171; see others' letters of 12, 19, 26 January, and 2 February 1918.

7. Letter on 'Raleigh in Virginia', XLIII, no. 1109, 6 April 1918, 350.
8. Contribution (one of four) to 'Causes of Fruit Failure', XLIII, no. 1121, 29 June 1918, 591.
9. Letter on 'The Failure of the Fruit Crop', XLIV, no. 1122, 6 July 1918, 19.
10. Letter on 'The Mistletoe and the Pear', XLIX, no. 1253, 8 January 1921, 54.
11. 'Springtide in the Fruit Garden', LIII, no. 1375, 12 May 1923, 642–3.
12. 'Spur-Pruning of Apples & Pears', LV, no 1409, 5 January 1924, 28–9.
13. 'Fruit Blossom in Kent', LV, no. 1425, 26 April 1924, 659–60.
14. Letter on 'Fruit-Growing in this Country', LVI, no 1458, 13 December 1924, 969, answering a letter from 'Fruit-Grower', 29 November 1924, 854–5; 'Fruit Grower' replied on 27 December 1924, 1045. An article, 'Fruit-Growing at Home', by 'Kent', 3 January 1925, 30–1, commented on all the correspondence.
15. Letter on 'Gold Fish in England', LIX, no 1522, 6 March 1926, 362.
16. 'Pears for Every District', LXII, no. 1601, 24 September 1927, lxxiii–lxxiv.
17. 'Ornamental Crab Apples', LXIV, no. 1656, 13 October 1928, cxxxviii, cxl.
18. 'The Gourmet's Fruit Garden', LXVI, no. 1709, 19 October 1929, cxliv, cxlvi.
19. 'The Gadding Vine', LXVI, no. 1719, 28 December 1929, xxxii.
20. 'A Seaside Garden', LXVIII, no. 1763, 1 November 1930, 563–4.
21. Letter on 'Horticultural Catalogues', LXIX, no. 1782, 14 March 1931, 328; identical with letter in *GI*, no. 30. In this appeal as Chairman of the Lindley Library of the Royal Horticultural Society for the gift of catalogues, EAB practised what he preached: there is an extensive collection of Bunyard catalogues in the Lindley Library.
22. 'The Royal Horticultural Society and its Work Past and Present', LXXIII, no. 1882, 11 February 1933, 135–7.
23. Letter on 'Roses of Olden Days', LXXV, no. 1942, 7 April 1934; xxvi; cf. the reply on 21 April 1934, 415.
24. 'Roses of Olden Days', LXXVIII, no. 2018, 21 September 1935, 308–9.
25. 'Wild Roses for Garden and Woodland: A Descriptive List of Vigorous

Growing Kinds', LXXXIII, no. 2147, 12 March 1938, 287–8, with 3 drawings by Frances Bunyard (1884–1982).

The Countryman

This journal first appeared in April 1927; vols. I–VI contain 4 issues each, and vol. VII onwards has 2.

1. 'Malthus in the Fruit Garden', IV (April 1930), 15–16.
2. 'The Gardener's Eye', IV (July 1930), 215–16.
3. 'How to Store Fruit Successfully', IV (October 1930), 457–9.
4. 'Fruit Trees and Grass', IV (January 1931), 679–81.
5. 'Waste Not Want Not', V (April 1931), 52.
6. 'Rural France as It Really Is', V (July 1931), 305–7.
7. 'Strawberry Troubles', ibid., 319.
8. 'Dead Wood', V (October 1931), 542–3.
9. 'The Cooking Apples to Choose', V (January 1932), 823–5.
10. 'Off Years in Apples', ibid., 825.
11. 'Clean Fruit', VI (April 1932), 73–5.
12. 'Really Fresh Vegetables', VI (July 1932), 417–19.
13. 'Some Plants for Dry Soils', VI (October 1932), 725–7.
14. 'Cob Nuts and Filberts', VI (January 1933), 939–41. Cf. *G* no. 6; *JRHS* no. 10.
15. 'Hints on Fruits for Bottling', VII (April 1933), 153–5.
16. 'Virus in Strawberries', VIII (October 1933), 151–3.
17. 'The Seed Catalogue', VIII (January 1934), 451–3.
18. 'Old Roses', IX (April 1934), 187–9.
19. 'Plants for Dry Shade', X (January 1935), 583–5.
20. 'Vegetable Adventures', ibid., 585–7.
21. 'Dry Weather Plants', XVIII (October 1938), 193.

The Garden

This weekly does not list contributors' names in any list of contents or index; I may have missed some contributions. It ceased independent publication with the issue of 17 December 1927 (XCI, no. 2924) when it was incorporated by *Homes and Gardens*, but EAB made no contribution to this combined journal.

1. s.v. *The Fruit Garden*: 'The Packing of Apples and Pears for Market', LXXVI, no. 2128, 31 August 1912, 440.
2. s.v. *The Fruit Garden*: 'The Best Apples and How to Grow Them', LXXVI, no. 2131, 21 September 1912, 479–80; Part 2: LXXVI, no. 2132, 28 September 1912, 491–2.
3. s.v. *The Fruit Garden*: 'The Best Pears and Their Cultivation', LXXVI, no. 2136, 26 October 1912, 543–4.
4. Letter on 'Reinette Apples', LXXVI, no. 2137, 2 November 1912, 550.
5. s.v. *The Fruit Garden*: 'The Best Plums and Their Cultivation', LXXVII, no. 2148, 18 January 1913, 35–6.
6. 'The Cultivation of Cob Nuts and Filberts', LXXVIII, no. 2206, 28 February 1914, 105–6, cf. *The Countryman* no. 14, and *JRHS* no. 10.
7. 'The Japanese or Cape Plums. Can They Be Grown in This Country?', LXXVIII, no. 2208, 14 March 1914, 135.
8. 'Making New Strawberry-Beds', LXXVIII, no. 2229, 8 August 1914, 403–4. Cf. no. 50.
9. 'Storing the Apple Crop', LXXVIII, no. 2232, 29 August 1914, 438; cf. *GC* nos. 65, 81.
10. 'Apples and Pears: Flavour and Pedigree', LXXIX, no. 2252, 16 January 1915, 29.
11. ? 'How to Increase Supplies of Vegetables' by A.E.B. [*sic*], LXXIX, no. 2256, 13 February 1915, 81. This metathesis of initials does sometimes occur (e.g. no. 1 above was attributed to 'A. E. Bunyard'); for the topic cf. s.v. *JRHS* no. 9.
12. 'The Origin of the Loganberry', LXXIX, no. 2298, 4 December 1915, 589–90.
13. 'Flavour in Apples', LXXX, no. 2306, 29 January 1916, 57, and a follow-up letter in no. 2311, 4 March 1916, 110.
14. 'A Selection of Flag Irises', LXXX, no. 2330, 15 July 1916, 346–7.
15. 'Figs in Pots', LXXX, no. 2332, 29 July 1916, 374. Cf. *JRHS* no. 17.
16. Letter on 'Pear Comte de Lamy', LXXX, 2346, 4 November 1916, 534.

17. 'The Nonpareils', LXXX, no. 2354, 30 December 1916, 622.
18. Letter on 'Apple Allington Pippin', LXXXI, no. 2355, 6 January 1917, 2.
19. 'Apple Orleans Reinette', LXXXI, no. 2358, 27 January 1917, 35; cf. *GC* no. 22.
20. Letter on 'The Spraying of Fruit Trees', LXXXI, no. 2366, 24 March 1917, 96.
21. Letter on 'Variation in Apple Cox's Orange Pippin', LXXXI, no. 2369, 14 April 1917, 121.
22. Letter on 'Père d'Ardène', LXXXI, no. 2391, 15 September 1917, 382.
23. 'The Culture of Fruit Trees', LXXXI, no. 2393, 29 September 1917, 406–7. The following articles all, except no. 11, in vol. LXXXI, belong as a series under this heading: (2) 'Gathering and Storing Fruit', no. 2394, 6 October 1917, 422; (3) 'The Apple. A Utility List and a Quality List', no 2395, 13 October 1917, 432; (4) 'Pears: Selections for Utility and Quality', no. 2396, 20 October 1917, 448; (5) 'Plums: Selections for Utility and Quality', no. 2398, 3 November 1917, 476; reprinted as no. 36; (6) 'Cherries', no 2399, 10 November 1917, 481; (7) 'Gooseberries: A Selection for Flavour', no. 2400, 17 November 1917, 492; (8) 'Nuts', no. 2402, 1 December 1917, 517–18; (9) 'Of Berries in Their Kinds', no 2403, 8 December 1917, 529–30; (10) 'On Manuring', no 2405, 22 December 1917, 556; (11) 'Currants: Red, White, and Black', LXXXII, no. 2408, 12 January 1918, 23–4.
24. Letter on 'The Golden Pippins', LXXXI, no. 2398, 3 November 1917, 466.
25. Letter on 'L'Année Champêtre', LXXXI, no. 2399, 10 November 1917, 478 (referring to no. 22).
26. Letter on 'Greek Colour Perception', ibid., 478.
27. 'Codlins, Pippins, & Other Matters', LXXXI, no. 2401, 24 November 1917, 506.
28. Letter on 'Apple Scotch Bridget', LXXXII, no. 2412, 9 February 1918, 64.
29. 'On Eating Fruit', LXXXII, no. 2418, 23 March 1918, 131–2.
30. Letter on 'Some Plant Names', LXXXII, no. 2421, 13 April 1918, 156–7.

31. Letter on 'Plant Names', LXXXII, no. 2424, 4 May 1918, 182.
32. Letter on 'A Fruit Bottling "Tip"', LXXXII, no. 2433, 6 July 1918, 256.
33. Letter on 'The Raspberry Beetle', LXXXII, no. 2435, 20 July 1918, 277.
34. 'The Pollination Question', LXXXII, no. 2446, 5 October 1918, 374.
35. 'Apples at Wisley', LXXXII, no. 2452, 16 November 1918, 430.
36. 'The Culture of Plum Trees: The Doctrine of Freedom – Selections for Utility and Quality', LXXXIII, no. 2461, 18 January 1919, 24; an unacknowledged, almost verbatim, reprint of no. 23 (5).
37. s.v. *Columns for the Curious*: 'An Early Record of Tulips', LXXXIII, no. 2476, 3 May 1919, 207.
38. s.v. *Columns for the Curious*: 'Witch Hazel', ibid.
39. Letter on 'Mr. Charles Ross' Seedling Apples', LXXXIII, no. 2497, 27 September 1919, 458. Cf. *GC* no. 47.
40. 'Apples at Allington', LXXXIII, no. 2500, 18 October 1919, 497–9.
41. 'Apple May Queen', LXXXIV, no. 2516, 7 February 1920, 73.
42. Letter on 'Foxes and Grapes', LXXXIV, no. 2539, 17 July 1920, 357.
43. Letter on 'Gladiolus primulinus', LXXXIV, no. 2543, 14 August 1920, 404. Cf. *GC* no. 51.
44. 'Scraps from a Notebook', LXXXIV, no. 2556, 13 November 1920, 559–60.
45. 'The Value of Shelter for Fruit Trees', ibid., 561.
46. 'The Alleged Washington Gage', LXXXIV, no. 2557, 20 November 1920, 570.
47. Letter on 'Kant Apples', LXXXIV, no. 2558, 27 November 1920, 582.
48. Letter on 'Cherry Culture in Kent', LXXXV, no. 2583, 21 May 1921, 256–7.
49. 'A Sequence of Dessert Cherries', LXXXV, no. 2610, 26 November 1921, 592–3, with 2 drawings by Frances Bunyard. Cf. *JRHS* no. 11.
50. 'The Strawberry Bed', LXXXVIII, no. 2733, 5 April 1924, 227–8. Cf. no. 8.
51. 'The Duke Cherries', XC, no. 2829, 6 February 1926, 88–9.
52. Letter on 'Codlin Moth', XCI, no. 2898, 18 June 1927, 406. Cf. *GC* no. 50, and *GI* no. 4.

A BIBLIOGRAPHY

The Gardeners' Chronicle
This weekly periodical does not list contributors' names either on its contents pages or in its volumes' indexes; I may have missed some of EAB's contributions. All volumes are those of the Third Series; their numbers change in January and July.

1. Letter on 'The Effect of Salts upon Pigments', XLVI, no. 1180, 7 August 1909, 97–8.
2. 'The Use of Arsenic in Horticulture', XLVII, no. 1204, 22 January 1910, 60.
3. Letter on 'Columella and Graft Hybrids', XLIX, no. 1266, 1 April 1911, 203.
4. s.v. *Fruit Register:* 'Cherry Fruheste der Mark', L, no. 1285, 12 August 1911, 116.
5. Letter on 'Seedling Apples', L, no. 1295, 21 October 1911, 293–4.
6. Letter on 'Hogg's "Fruit Manual"', L, no. 1298, 11 November 1911, 341.
7. Letter on 'Hogg's "Fruit Manual"', L, no. 1305, 30 December 1911, 477.
8. Letter on 'The History of the Jargonelle Pear', LII, no. 1343, 21 September 1912, 234.
9. Letter on 'Juvenile Characters [of plants]', LIII, no. 1374, 26 April 1913, 272–3; the contents make it probable that its author, 'E.A.B.', is Bunyard and not E. A. Bowles.
10. 'The History of Cultivated Fruits as Told in the Lives of Great Pomologists' [the first was 'J. B. van Mons (1765–1842)'], LIII, no. 1381, 14 June 1913, 395–6. For the rest of this series [henceforth 'Lives'] see nos. 11, 12, 16, 17, 18, 20, 21, and 30.
11. 'Lives', 'Antoine Nicholas Duchesne', LIV, no. 1387, 26 July 1913, 61–2.
12. 'Lives', 'Olivier de Serres', LIV, no. 1392, 30 August 1913, 149–50.
13. Letter on 'London and Wise', LIV, no 1395, 20 September 1913, 207.
14. Letter on 'Parmentier and the Potato', LV, no. 1410, 3 January 1914, 13. Cf. nos. 15, 88, 89, and *GI* no. 68.
15. Letter on 'The Parmentier Myth', LV, no. 1418, 28 February 1914, 151.

16. 'Lives', 'Duhamel du Monceau', LV, no. 1427, 2 May 1914, 293–4.
17. 'Lives', 'Alexandre Bivort. A Great Belgian Pomologist', LVI, no. 1458, 5 December 1914, 363–4.
18. 'Lives', 'A. J. Downing', LVI, no. 1461, 26 December 1914, 409.
19. Letter on 'Colour Charts', LVII, no. 1474, 27 March 1915, 171; cf. *Gardeners' Magazine* no. 1. The topic was one on which his sister Marguerite E. Bunyard (1890–1959) later wrote: see her articles and letters – 'Colour Description of Flowers', *GI*, LVII, no. 2945, 17 August 1935, 501; 'Colour and Climate', ibid., LVIII, no. 2990, 27 June 1936, 385–6; 'Colour Description in Roses', ibid., LVIII, no. 2998, 22 August 1936, 498; 'A Consideration of the Colours Required in the Colour Description of Flowers', *GC*, XCIX, no. 2569, 21 March 1936, 182; 'An Approach to Standardization in the Colour Descriptions of Flowers', *JRHS*, LX (1935), 342–53; 'The Horticultural Colour Chart vol. I', ibid., LXIV (1939), 314–17.
20. 'Lives', 'Alphonse Mas', LVII, no. 1485, 12 June 1915, 321.
21. 'Lives', 'Thomas Andrew Knight', LVIII, no. 1497, 4 September 1915, 145–6.
22. s.v. *Fruit Register:* 'Apple Orleans Reinette', LIX, no. 1517, 22 January 1916, 52; see below nos. 40, 43, 68, 73. Cf. *G*, no. 19.
23. Letter on 'Nomenclature of Apples', LIX, no. 1522, 26 February 1916, 120.
24. s.v. *Fruit Register:* 'Apple Reinette Rouge Etoilée', LIX, no. 1536, 3 June 1916, 295.
25. s.v. *Fruit Register:* 'Plum Jaune Hative', LX, no. 1543, 22 July 1916, 39.
26. Letter on 'A Rare Pomological Work' [Mathieu van Noort, *Pomologia Batavia* (Leiden, 1830)], LXI, no. 1569, 20 January 1917, 30.
27. Letter on 'The White Wood Strawberry' (answering a query in the issue of 24 February 1917, 88, on this plant in Jane Austen's *Emma*, chap. xlii), LXI, no. 1575, 3 March 1917, 101; EAB offered to send the correspondent, A.N., a few plants 'in honour of the Immortal Jane', and was thanked by A.N. on 21 April 1917, 166.
28. 'A Revision of the Red Currants', LXII, no. 1613, 24 November 1917, 205–6, with 7 illustrations over the parts by Frances Bunyard (1884–1982); continued in nos. 1614, 1 December 1917, 217; 1615, 8 December 1917, 232; 1616, 15 December 1917, 237. The article was

reprinted in the *Journal of Pomology*, but with only 5 of the illustrations; see s.v. *JP* no. 10. In its obituary of EAB the *GC* (CVI, no. 2757, 28 October 1939, 274) said that the article was 'published in book form in 1917', but I have not seen a copy. Bunyard published other articles on the red currant: see *GI* no. 40, *JRHS* no. 8, and *Proc. of the Linnean Society*.

29. 'The Winter Aspect of the Buds of Plums', LXIII, no. 1621, 19 January 1918, 23.
30. 'Robert Thompson' [in the 'Lives of Great Pomologists' series' see above no. 10], LXIII, no. 1630, 23 March 1918, 121–2.
31. 'Cotton's "Planter's Manual"', LXIII, no. 1635, 27 April 1918, 174–5. See further E. Wilson, 'Charles Cotton's *The Planters Manual* (1675): A Discovery Rediscovered', *Notes and Queries* n.s. L (2003), 189–90.
32. s.v. *Fruit Register*: 'The "Himalaya" Berry', LXIV, no. 1665, 23 November 1918, 205. See also below nos. 34. 46.
33. Letter on 'The Origin of the Apple, Pear, and Other Fruits', LXIV, no. 1666, 30 November 1918, 220.
34. s.v. *Fruit Register*: 'The "Himalaya" Berry', LXV, no. 1673, 18 January 1919, 27.
35. Letter on 'Apple Queen Caroline', LXVI, no. 1721, 20 December 1919, 316.
36. Letter on 'The Flowering of the Kent Filbert', LXIX, no. 1780, 5 February 1921, 69.
37. s.v. *Fruit Register*: 'Apple Claygate Pearmain', LXIX, no. 1783, 26 February 1921, 105.
38. 'An Early Vilmorin Catalogue' [1771], LXXI, no. 1834, 18 February 1922, 78.
39. s.v. *Fruit Register*: 'The Origin of the Pine Strawberry', LXXI, no. 1835, 25 February 1922, 94.
40. s.v. *Fruit Register*: 'Apple Orleans Reinette', ibid.
41. 'Some Dessert Cherries', LXXII, no. 1863, 9 September 1922, 152–3.
42. 'Variegated Fruits', LXXII, no. 1864, 16 September 1922, 168–9.
43. s.v. *Fruit Register*: 'Apple Orleans Reinette', LXXII, no. 1879, 30 December 1922, 381.
44. s.v. *Fruit Register*: 'Pear Admiral Gervais', LXXVII, no. 1984, 3 January 1925, 13.

45. s.v. *Fruit Register:* 'Pear Comte de Paris', LXXVII, no. 1998, 11 April 1925, 257–8. Cf. *GI* no. 27.
46. s.v. *Fruit Register:* 'The Himalaya Berry', LXXX, no. 2072, 11 September 1926, 215.
47. s.v. *Fruit Register:* 'Apples Raised by Mr. Charles Ross', LXXX, no. 2082, 20 November 1926, 415. Cf. *G* no. 39.
48. s.v. *Fruit Register:* 'Pear Glou Morceau', LXXXI, no. 2090, 15 January 1927, 55.
49. 'Fruit Growing in the Western Cape Province [South Africa]', LXXXI, no. 2107, 14 May 1927, 338–40; LXXXI, no. 2108, 21 May 1927, 357–8.
50. Letter on 'High Price for a Cherry Orchard', LXXXI, no. 2108, 21 May 1927, 360.
51. Letter on 'The Codlin Moth', LXXXI, no. 2112, 18 June 1927, 439–40. Cf. *G* no. 52, and *GI* no. 4. The three letters are practically verbatim identical.
52. 'Two Valleys in the Western Cape Province', LXXXII, no. 2119, 6 August 1927, 110–11.
53. Letter on 'The Hooded Gladiolus primulinus', LXXXII, no. 2119, 6 August 1927, 117. Cf. *G* no. 43.
54. s.v. *Fruit Register:* 'The Cambridge Gage', LXXXII, no. 2124, 10 September 1927, 214.
55. 'Fruits in 1927', LXXXII, no. 2139, 24 December 1927, 513.
56. s.v. *Fruit Garden:* 'The Mirabelle', ibid.
57. 'Apples on Metz Paradise Stock', LXXXVI, no. 2237, 9 November 1929, 367–8.
58. s.v. *Fruit Garden:* 'Strawberries in 1930', LXXXVIII, no. 2275, 2 August 1930, 95.
59. s.v. *Fruit Garden:* 'Alpine Strawberries', LXXXVIII, no. 2279, 30 August 1930, 179.
60. s.v. *Fruit Garden:* 'Apples and Pears in 1930', LXXXVIII, no. 2293, 6 December 1930, 477.
61. s.v. *Fruit Register:* 'Pear Charles Ernest', LXXXVIII, no. 2296, 27 December 1930, 535.
62. ' "The Floral Calendar" ' [by James Mangles (London, 1839)], LXXXIX, no. 2303, 14 February 1931, 133.

63. Letter on 'Primitive Potatoes [sic]', XC, no. 2324, 11 July 1931, 36; 'In the course of wanderings through the valleys of the West Pyrenees…'.
64. s.v. *Fruit Register:* 'Apple White Astrachan', XC, no. 2334, 19 September 1931, 239.
65. Letter on 'Apple White Astrachan', XC, no. 2337, 10 October 1931, 299.
66. Letter on 'Apple Cox's Orange Pippin in a Wet Season', XC, no. 2344, 28 November 1931, 416.
67. Letter on the storage of 'English Apples', XC, no. 2345, 5 December 1931, 432; the letter is signed 'George Bunyard and Co., Ltd.'. Cf. no. 81.
68. s.v. *Fruit Garden:* 'Pears and Shelter', XCII, no. 2384, 3 September 1932, 181.
69. 'The Early History of the Sweet Pea', XCII, no. 2390, 15 October 1932, 284–5.
70. s.v. *Fruit Register:* 'Apple Orleans Reinette', XCII, no. 2401, 31 December 1932, 486.
71. Letter on 'Adam in the Garden', XCIII, no. 2408, 18 February 1933, 123; cf. *GI* no. 29.
72. 'Apples in April', XCV, no. 2469, 21 April 1934, 265–6.
73. Letter on 'Apple Bushey Grove', XCV, no. 2471, 5 May 1934, 297.
74. Letter on 'Naming Fruits', XCVI, no. 2489, 8 September 1934, 179.
75. s.v. *Fruit Garden:* 'Apple Orleans Reinette', XCVII, no. 2508, 19 January 1935, 52.
76. 'Pre-Robinsonian Gardening', XCVII, no. 2521, 20 April 1935, 258–9.
77. Letter on 'Pears on Hawthorn', XCVII, no. 2525, 18 May 1935, 327.
78. s.v. *Hardy Fruit Garden:* 'Pear Josephine de Malines', XCVIII, no 2555, 14 December 1935, 429.
79. Letter on 'Virus Diseases', XCIX, no. 2573, 18 April 1936, 253.
80. Letter on 'Figs', XCIX, no. 2583, 27 June 1936, 423.
81. Letter on 'Outdoor Figs', C, no. 2591, 22 August 1936, 147.
82. s.v. *Fruit Garden:* 'Sugar and Sun', C, no. 2592, 29 August 1936, 168.

83. Letter on 'Storing Apples', C, no. 2600, 24 October 1936, 308. Cf. no. 65; and *G* no. 9.
84. 'A Test of Dessert Apples' [by the Wine and Food Society at the Restaurant of the Horticultural Hall], C, no. 2605, 28 November 1936, 395–6; see also 366.
85. Letter on 'Perowskia atriplicifolia', C, no. 2607, 12 December 1936, 430.
86. Letter on 'Effect of Salt Spray on Plants', CI, no. 2610, 2 January 1937, 14; cf. no. 96.
87. 'Apple Api Etoilée', CI, no. 2622, 27 March 1937, 208.
88. Letter on 'Rose Caroline Testout', CI, no. 2631, 29 May 1937, 376.
89. s.v. *Fruit Garden:* 'Apple Gravenstein', ibid., 377.
90. Letter on 'The Parmentier Legend', CII, no. 2647, 18 September 1937, 219; cf. nos. 14, 15, and *GI* no. 68.
91. Letter on 'The Legend of Parmentier', CII, no. 2652, 23 October 1937, 308.
92. Letter on 'Planting Rhododendrons', CIII, no. 2672, 12 March 1938, 185.
93. Letter on 'Apples from Seeds', CIII, no. 2675, 2 April 1938, 241.
94. Letter on 'Plant Hormones', CIV, no. 2697, 3 September 1938, 183.
95. Letter on 'Redouté's Rose Album', CIV, no. 2705, 29 October 1938, 326.
96. s.v. *Fruit Garden:* 'Plum Denniston's Superb Gage', CIV, no. 2712, 17 December 1938, 444.
97. s.v. *Fruit Garden:* 'Late Pears', CV, no. 2715, 7 January 1939, 15.
98. Letter on 'Storm Damage and Salt Winds', CV, no. 2717, 21 January 1939, 46; cf. no. 84.
99. Letter on 'Pear Doyenné d'Hiver', CV, no. 2722, 25 February 1939, 125.
100. Letter on 'Pears', CV, no. 2723, 4 March 1939, 142.
101. 'The Strawberry and its History', CV, no. 2724, 11 March 1939, 154; cf. *JRHS* no. 5.
102. Letter on 'Prunus incisa', CV, no. 2730, 22 April 1939, 251.
103. s.v. *Fruit Register:* 'Pear Packham's Triumph', CV, no. 2732, 6 May 1939, 283.

A BIBLIOGRAPHY

The Gardeners' Magazine
Once again, contributors' names are given neither on contents pages nor in annual indexes. This weekly ceased publication at the end of 1916. From no. 2 below the numbers of the issues are those of the New Series.

1. 'Colour Charts', LIV, no. 2984, 7 January 1911, 15; cf. *GC* no. 19.
2. 'Some Belgian Pears', LVIII, no. 54, 9 January 1915, 19; Part 2: LVIII, no. 55, 16 January 1915, 30; Part 3: LVIII, no. 56, 23 January 1915, 39.
3. Letter on 'Mirabelle and Myrobalan Plums', LVIII, no. 85, 14 August 1915, 401.
4. 'Apple Beauty of Hants', LVIII, no. 101, 4 December 1915, 557.
5. The magazine's note on 'Pear Bergamotte de Coloma' quotes EAB: LVIII, no. 102, 11 December 1915, 568.
6. Letter on 'Pear Bergamotte de Coloma', LVIII, no. 104, 25 December 1915, 591.

The Gardener's Year Book
This annual appeared only from 1927–31.

1. 'Fruit for Cooking and Dessert', divided into 'The Epicure's List' and 'The Amateur's List', I (1927), 270–3; the same listings appeared again in II (1928), 240–1, and III (1929), 239–40.

Gardening Illustrated
This weekly has no index, and contributors' names are not listed in the Contents.

1. Letter on 'Sowing Mistletoe Seed', XLVI, no. 2352, 5 April 1924, 196.
2. Letter on 'Does Fruit Growing Pay?', XLIX, no. 2499, 29 January 1927, 61 (EAB thought basically that it did). The letter arose out of the leading article in XLIX, no. 2498, 22 January 1927, 45, and a letter in the same issue from 'A Disillusioned Apple Grower' (46–7); the correspondence continued until 2 April 1927.

3. Letter on 'Prunus triloba', XLIX, no. 2514, 14 May 1927, 284; I have not included a letter from 'E.A.B.' (284) as I think this was from E. A. Bowles.
4. Letter on 'Codlin Moth', XLIX, no. 2518, 11 June 1927, 357; cf. *G* no 52 and *GC* no. 50. The three practically verbatim identical letters were an appeal to amateur fruit growers to burn any infected apples.
5. Letter on 'March Spraying for Aphis on Fruit Trees', L, no. 2557, 10 March 1928, 143.
6. Letter on 'The Curse of Cornwall' [on planting plants which grow well in Cornwall elsewhere, where they do not], L, no. 2560, 31 March 1928, 195.
7. Letter on 'Apple Delicious', L, no. 2569, 2 June 1928, 346.
8. Letter on 'The Old White Pine Strawberry', L, no. 2576, 21 July 1928, 457.
9. Letter on 'The "best" Peach', LI, no. 2602, 19 January 1929, 36.
10. Letter on 'Regelio-Cyclus Iris', LI, no. 2617, 4 May 1929, 294.
11. 'Thinning Fruit Blossom', ibid., 300.
12. 'Studley Royal and a Forgotten Poet' [Peter Aram, 'Studley-Park. A Poem', pp. 1–28 of Thomas Gent, *The Antient and Modern History of the Loyal Town of Rippon* (York, 1733)], LI, no. 2620, 25 May 1929, 355–6.
13. Letter on 'The Hardest Helianthemums', LI, no. 2630, 3 August 1929, 529.
14. 'Some Second Thoughts on Pears', LI, no. 2648, 7 December 1929, 815.
15. Letter on 'Twelve Best Pears', LI, no. 2651, 28 December 1929, 862.
16. 'A Few Garden Notes', LII, no. 2661, 8 March 1930, 154.
17. 'Peaches without Walls', ibid.
18. Letter on 'Pioneer Fruit Growing' [in Newfoundland], LII, no. 2668, 26 April 1930, 267.
19. Letter on 'Hemerocallis Baroni', LII, no. 2683, 9 August 1930, 514.
20. 'Late Gooseberries', LII, no. 2685, 23 August 1930, 550.
21. Letter on 'Autumn Colour in Japanese Cherries', LII, no. 2697, 15 November 1930, 738.
22. Letter on 'The Conference Pear', ibid., 738.
23. Letter on 'The Season of Apples', ibid., 740.

24. Letter on 'Birds and Berries', LII, no. 2701, 13 December 1930, 805.
25. Letter on 'Cooking Pears', LIII, no. 2705, 10 January 1931, 18.
26. Letter on 'Winter Flowers', LIII, no. 2710, 14 February 1931, 99.
27. Letter on 'Pear Comte de Paris', LIII, no. 2711, 21 February 1931, 112; cf. *GC* no. 45.
28. 'Late Planting', LIII, no. 2712, 28 February 1931, 127–8.
29. Letter on 'The First Gardener' [Adam], ibid., 131; cf. *GC* no. 69.
30. Letter on 'Horticultural Catalogues', LIII, no. 2713, 7 March 1931, 146; identical with letter in *Country Life* no. 21.
31. Letter on 'Summer Pruning', LIII, no. 2737, 22 August 1931, 516.
32. 'The Novelist in the Garden', LIII, no. 2738, 29 August 1931, 533.
33. Letter on 'Pear Emile d'Heyst', LIII, no. 2750, 21 November 1931, 707.
34. Letter on 'Vegetables for Cooking', LIV, no. 2762, 13 February 1932, 89–90.
35. 'Globe Artichokes', LIV, no. 2771, 16 April 1932, 228.
36. Letter on 'Iris Stylosa', LIV, no. 2772, 23 April 1932, 244.
37. Letter on 'Globe Artichokes and Cardoons' [in reply to Sir William Lawrence's letter, LIV, no. 2772, 23 April 1932, 242, commenting on EAB's article, no. 35 above], LIV, no. 2773, 30 April 1932, 260.
38. Letter on 'Grease-banding Quinces', LIV, no. 2774, 7 May 1932, 275.
39. Letter on 'The Poulsen Roses', LIV, no. 2788, 13 August 1932, 484.
40. 'A Selection of Red Currants', LIV, no. 2791, 3 September 1932, 541; cf. *GC* no. 28, *JRHS* no. 8, and *Proc. of the Linnean Society*.
41. Letter on 'A Good-flavoured Runner Bean', LIV, no. 2801, 12 November 1932, 676.
42. Letter on 'November Roses', LIV, no. 2803, 26 November 1932, 704.
43. Letter on 'Fruit Tree Stocks', LIV, no. 2806, 17 December 1932, 746.
44. Letter on 'Cold Feet' [in the pruning season, recommending wooden-soled Lancashire clogs], LIV, no. 2807, 24 December 1932, 766.
45. 'Folk Lore in the Garden', LV, no. 2814, 11 February 1933, 71.
46. 'Some By-way Roses', LV, no. 2817, 4 March 1933, 118–19.
47. Letter on 'Morello Cherries and Fertilisation', LV, no. 2826, 6 May 1933, 254.
48. Letter on 'Apple Thomas Rivers', LV, no. 2852, 4 November 1933, 642.

49. Letter on 'Winter Green', LV, no. 2857, 9 December 1933, 712–13.
50. Letter on 'Pompon Chrysanthemums', LV, no. 2858, 16 December 1933, 724.
51. Letter on 'Winter Drought', LVI, no. 2861, 6 January 1934, 4.
52. Letter on 'The Winter Rosebud Cherry' [*Prunus subhirtella* var. *Autumnalis* for which EAB proposed the name 'Winter Rosebud Cherry'], LVI, no. 2866, 10 February 1934, 75.
53. Letter on 'The Best Evergreen Shrub?' [*Berberis aquifolium*], LVI, no. 2867, 17 February 1934, 88.
54. Letter on 'Galanthus byzantinus', LVI, no. 2872, 24 March 1934, 169.
55. Letter on 'Viola Moonlight', ibid., 170.
56. 'Prunus Davidiana', ibid., 174–5.
57. 'Naming Fruit', LVI, no. 2894, 25 August 1934, 510.
58. Letter on 'Rosa Gigantea', LVII, no. 2935, 8 June 1935, 347; cf. nos. 63 and 77 below.
59. Letter on 'Apple Ellison's Orange', LVII, no. 2946, 24 August 1935, 515.
60. Letter on 'Apple Maltster', LVII, no. 2954, 19 October 1935, 629.
61. Letter on 'Salvia farinacea', ibid., 629–30.
62. Letter on 'Lilium Sulphureum', LVII, no. 2957, 9 November 1935, 672.
63. Letter on 'Rosa Gigantea', LVIII, no. 2981, 25 April 1936, 244; cf. nos. 58 and 77.
64. Letter on 'Rose Tipo Ideale', LVIII, no. 2982, 2 May 1936, 255–6; cf. no. 65.
65. Letter on 'Rose Tipo Ideale', LVIII, no. 2986, 30 May 1936, 329; cf. no. 64.
66. Letter on 'Figs and Water', LVIII, no. 2990, 27 June 1936, 386–7.
67. Letter on 'Ostrowskia Magnifica', LIX, no. 3046, 24 July 1937, 438.
68. Letter on 'The Potato in France' [re. Parmentier], LIX, no. 3052, 4 September 1937, 523; cf. *GC* nos. 14, 15, 88, 89.
69. 'Rose Boule de Neige', ibid., 525.
70. Letter on 'Rosa microphylla fl.-pl.', LIX, no. 3061, 6 November 1937, 650; cf. no. 71.
71. Letter on 'Rosa microphylla fl.-pl.', LIX, no. 3068, 25 December 1937, 748; cf. no. 70.

72. Letter on 'The Best Gooseberry', LX, no. 3072, 22 January 1938, 47.
73. Letter on 'The Double Alpine Rose', LX, no. 3073, 29 January 1938, 60.
74. Letter on 'Local Names' [for plants], LX, no. 3081, 26 March 1938, 188.
75. Letter on 'Leaf Hoppers' [pests of roses and fruit trees], LX, no. 3089, 21 May 1938, 311.
76. Letter on 'An Old Rose List' [from Linton Park, near Maidstone, then in the possession of Earl Cornwallis, 1844], LX, no. 3090, 28 May 1938, 333–4.
77. Letter on 'Rosa Gigantea', LX, no. 3095, 2 July 1938, 414; cf. nos. 58 and 63.
78. Letter on 'A Rose "S.O.S."', LX, no. 3101, 13 August 1938, 498.
79. 'A Selection of Pears for English Gardens', LX, no. 3107, 24 September 1938, 586.
80. Letter on 'Rose Glory of Steinforth', LX, no. 3114, 12 November 1938, 696.
81. Letter on 'Autumn Colour', LX, no. 3120, 24 December 1938, 795.
82. s.v. *A Plantsman's Notebook*, 'The De Meaux Roses', LXI, no. 3123, 14 January 1939, 22–3.
83. Letter on 'After the Snow', ibid., 25.
84. s.v. *A Plantsman's Notebook*, 'Rose Lady Curzon', LXI, no. 3125, 28 January 1939, 54.
85. Letter on 'The Narrow Leaved Sage', LXI, no. 3131, 11 March 1939, 156.
86. Letter on 'Rose Species', LXI, no. 3135, 8 April 1939, 221.
87. Letter on 'Names in the Garden' [re. pronunciation], LXI, no. 3139, 6 May 1939, 282.
88. 'Roses of Olden Days', LXI, no. 3147, 1 July 1939, 415–16. Three of the five photographs are identical with Plates 17, 23, and 31 by Sweatman Hedgeland in *Old Garden Roses* (1936; s.v. Books, no. 4).
89. 'Wild Flowers of the Riviera: A Walk in the Maures Mountains', LXI, no. 3151, 29 July 1939, 488.

The Journal of Pomology
This journal was founded in 1919 by EAB, its first editor. In November 1922 (III.i) it changed its title to *The Journal of Pomology and Horticultural Science* [*JPHS*] and its publisher from George Bunyard and Co. Ltd., Royal Nurseries, Maidstone, to Headley Brothers of London. In a foreword to that issue Sir A. Daniel Hall said that the *Journal of Pomology* was 'started and maintained by the sole energies of Mr. E. A. Bunyard' (p. 4), but that financial responsibility for the new title was now taken over by the Fruit and Cider Institute at Long Ashton, the Horticultural Research Station at East Malling, and the Horticultural Institute attached to Cambridge University, the *Journal* now being in effect the official organ of those bodies. Bunyard continued as its editor for a year or so, last being so designated in July 1924 (IV.i); he remained 'an active member' ('Edward A. Bunyard, F.L.S.: An Appreciation', *JPHS* XVII. iv (January 1940), 294–6, p. 294) of its Publication Committee until his death. His articles are all found in the first three volumes, though he published a few reviews in it thereafter.

I have listed only those articles of which Bunyard's authorship is stated (or where anonymous ones are attributed to him in the *Index of First 10 Volumes* (1933): see nos. 3 and 12 below); there are several unsigned pieces.

1. 'The Length of Stem in Pears and Apples', I (1919–20), 20–22.
2. 'Henry van Oosten and the "Dutch Gardener"', ibid., 37–40, and see p. 144.
3. 'The Patenting of New Fruits', ibid., 50–53 (anon., but attributed in *Index*).
4. 'Seedling Apples – A Record of Some Raisers' Experiences', ibid., 110–15.
5. 'The "New Orchard and Garden" of William Lawson', ibid., 125–34.
6. 'Fruit Notes', ibid., 140–3.
7. 'The History of the Paradise Stocks', ibid., 166–76.
8. 'John Tradescant, Senior', ibid., 188–96.
9. 'The Prices of Old Books', ibid., 207–8.
10. 'A Revision of the Red Currants', II (1920–1), 38–55; reprinted from *The Gardeners' Chronicle*; see no. 28 for that journal.
11. 'A Pomological Pilgrimage', ibid., 56–63.

12. '"The Orchard and the Garden." 1620', ibid., 246–61 (anon., but attributed in *Index*).
13. 'An Introductory Note on the History and Development of the Raspberry', III (1922–4), 5–6.
14. 'Notes on a Trial of Gooseberries', ibid., 148–52.
15. review of *Horticultural Abstracts* (1931), X (1932), 216.
16. review of *The Horticultural Education Association's Year Book*, i (1932), XI (1933), 175–6.
17. review of *The Horticultural Education Association Year Book*, ii (1933), XII (1934), 80.

The Journal of the Royal Horticultural Society
It should be noted that, with the odd exception, book reviews were anonymous until volume LIX (1934) when some, but by no means all, began to appear signed with either initials or names.

1. 'The Physiology of Pruning', XXXV (1909–10), 330–4; reprinted in *The Journal of Horticulture*, LX (3rd series), no. 3215, 12 May 1910, 416–18; cf. no. 29 below.
2. 'An Index to Illustrations of Apples', XXXVII (1911–12), 152–74; reprinted as a pamphlet, London, 1911 (copy in British Library).
3. 'An Index to Illustrations of Pears', ibid., 321–49; reprinted as a pamphlet, London, 1912 (copy in British Library).
4. 'The Flowers of Apples as an Aid in Identifying Varieties', XXXVIII (1912–13), 234–7.
5. 'The History and Development of the Strawberry', XXXIX (1913–14), 541–52; cf. EAB's briefer article in the *Gardeners' Chronicle*' (*GC*), no. 99, and *New Flora and Silva*, no. 5.
6. 'A Guide to the Literature of Pomology', XL (1914–15), 414–49; reprinted as a pamphlet, London, 1915 (copy in British Library).
7. 'The History of the Classification of Apples', XLI (1915–16), 445–64.
8. 'The History and Development of the Red Currant', XLII (1916–17), 260–70; see also EAB's articles in *GC* no. 28, *GI* no. 40, and *Proc. of the Linnean Society*.

9. 'Increasing the Home Fruit Supply', XLIII (1918–19), 23–7; cf. *G* no. 11.
10. 'Cob-Nuts and Filberts', XLV (1919–20), 224–32; cf. *The Countryman*, no. 14, and *G* no. 6.
11. 'The Winter Study of Fruit Trees', XLVII (1922), 18–25; drawings by F[rances] Bunyard (1884–1982) face p. 25. EAB's sister illustrated a number of his works: see Books, nos. 4, 5; *GC* no. 28; *G* no. 49.
12. 'Some Early Italian Gardening Books', XLVIII (1923), 177–87.
13. 'The Lindley Library', LI (1926), 82–3.
14. 'The Hooker and Lindley Drawings', LII (1927), 218–24.
15. 'Some Recent Accessions to the Lindley Library', LIII (1928), 103–5.
16. 'John Wedgwood's Garden', LVI (1931), 196–200.
17. 'The Cultivation of the Fig', LIX (1934), 61–6; cf. *G* no. 15.
18. review of V. Markham, *Paxton and the Bachelor Duke* (London, 1935), LX (1935), 330–1.
19. 'The Tree Heath, Erica arborea' (s.v. 'Garden Notes'), LXII (1937), 326.
20. 'The York and Lancaster Rose' (s.v. 'Garden Notes'), ibid., 420.
21. review of F. Kobel, *Die Kirschensorten der Deutschen Schweig* (Bern, 1937), ibid., 177.
22. review of D. Bois, *Les Plantes Alimentaires* IV, *Plantes à Boisson* (Paris, 1937), ibid., 469.
23. review of 'Nuts', *Bulletin* 106 of the Ministry of Agriculture (London, 1937), ibid., 546.
24. 'Books on Fruit and Vegetables for the Amateur', LXIII (1938), 74–6.
25. 'The History and Cultivation of the Peach and Nectarine. – I', ibid., 114–21; Part II, 170–7.
26. 'Old Roses', ibid., 411–21; one of the photographs, facing p. 413, of the rose 'Village Maid', is, as is acknowledged on p. 421, the same as one attributed in EAB's *Old Garden Roses* (London and New York, 1936) to Sweatman Hedgeland, Esq. (p. xvi; see Plate 26, facing p. 110).
27. 'The Hardiness of Rosa gigantea and its Hybrids' (s.v. 'Garden Note'), ibid., 449.
28. 'Vegetables for August Sowing', LXIV (1939), 377–8.
29. 'Simple Pruning for Beginners', ibid., (November 1939), 511–16; as

EAB died on 19 October 1939 this article thus appeared posthumously. Cf. no. 1 above.
30. review of A. Arber, *Herbals, Their Origin and Evolution* (Cambridge, 1938), ibid., 99.
31. review of S. Tolkowsky, *Hesperides: A History of the Culture and Use of Citrus Fruits* (London, 1939), ibid., 239–40. EAB also wrote a different review of this book in *Wine and Food* no. 18.

My Garden
This monthly journal, edited and owned by Theo. A. Stephens, first appeared in January 1934. The issue numbers are consecutive across volumes (whose numbers change every four months).

1. 'Fruit Growing in Small Gardens: Cordon Apples and Pears', XV, no. 58, October 1938, 233–7.
2. 'Stone Fruit for Small Gardens', XV, no. 59, November 1938, 387–90.

The New Flora and Silva
This quarterly journal, whose founding editor was E. H. M. Cox, first appeared in October 1928, and was published by Dulau who published the first edn. of *The Anatomy of Dessert* (1929).

1. 'The Anatomy of Dessert: I. The Cherry Succession', I.i (October 1928), 47–51. This appeared as the chapter on 'Cherries' in *The Anatomy of Dessert*, 35–43.
2. 'The Anatomy of Dessert: II. Melons', I.ii (January 1929), 109–11. This appeared as the chapter on 'Melons' in *The Anatomy of Dessert*, 65–70.
3. 'Old World Roses', II.i (October 1929), 3–10. The photographs, Bunyardian in style, are not found in his other works on roses.
4. 'The Problem of the Dry Border', II.iii (April 1930), 187–9.
5. 'The Strawberry: Its History and Culture', III.iv (July 1931), 256–64; cf. *JRHS* no 5.
6. 'Second Thoughts on Pears', IV.i (October 1931), 23–24.

7. 'The Violet: Its History and Development', IV.iii (April 1932), 187–94.
8. 'The Camellia in Europe: Its Introduction and Development', V.ii (January 1933), 123–9. This article was co-authored with Basil Leng (see above, 'Bunyard and Norman Douglas', Letter A.8, n. 3).
9. 'Alpine Strawberries', V.iii (April 1933), 161–3.
10. 'Berries – Black and Red', VI.ii (January 1934), 133–5.
11. 'The Newer Dessert Apples', IX.i (October 1936), 31–4.
12. 'More Plants of Good Intent', IX.iii (April 1937), 191–2.
13. 'Some Rose Memories of 1937', X.ii (January 1938), 116–21.
14. 'Quality in Fruit', XI.iii (April 1939), 146–50.
15. 'Rose Hunting in 1939', XII.i (November 1939), 11–17. This article appeared posthumously.

Night and Day

This weekly journal appeared only from July to December 1937, and EAB contributed two articles. Selections, including both Bunyard's contributions, were edited by C. Hawtree, *Night and Day* (London, 1985). I owe knowledge of Bunyard's articles to Mr Ian Jackson of Berkeley, California.

1. 'The Decay of Carving', 21 October 1937, 34 (Hawtree edition, 187).
2. 'The Christmas Dinner', 18 November 1937, 26 (Hawtree edition, 233).

Proceedings of the Linnean Society of London

1. Brief report of a paper by EAB delivered to the Society on 'The Origin of the Garden Red Currant' on 4 May 1916: 128th session November 1915 to June 1916 (October 1916), p. 13. Cf. *GC* no. 28, *GI* no. 40, and *JRHS* no. 8.

A BIBLIOGRAPHY

Reports of Papers delivered to the Horticultural Club
The Club met in London.

1. 'Recent Advances in Plant Breeding', on Mendelian experiments on peas, delivered to the Club on 14 January 1908: *Gardeners' Chronicle*, XLIII (3rd series), no. 1100, 25 January 1908, 62; see also *Gardeners' Magazine*, LI, no. 2830, 25 January 1908, 75.
2. 'The Colours of Plants', on 'the underlying causes of colour and change of colour in plants', delivered to the Club on 20 April 1909: *GC*, XLV, no. 1166, 1 May 1909, 285.
3. 'The Introduction and Development of Some of Our Hardy Fruits', delivered to the Club on 4 March 1913: *GC*, LIII, no. 1368, 15 March 1913, 173.
4. In *Gardening Illustrated*, LVI, no. 2861, 6 January 1934, 5, it was reported that EAB would 'deliver a lecture on "Vegetables Considered Historically and Prophetically"' at the A.G.M. of the Club on 9 January 1934; there is a brief reference to the event in LVI, no. 2863, 20 January 1934, 44. A lengthy abstract, 'The Introduction of Vegetables', of 'a lecture given at the Horticultural Club' by EAB is in *GC*, XCV, no. 2462, 3 March 1934, 148–9 (cf. *GC*, XCV, no. 2457, 27 January 1934, 70).

The Rose Annual of the National Rose Society

1. 'Some Early Rose Catalogues', 1930, 224–6.
2. 'Roses for Shrubbery and Woodland', 1935, 65–73.
3. 'A Border of Rose Species', 1936, 150–1.
4. 'The Earliest Illustration of the Rose in Europe', 1937, 160–1.
5. 'Who's Who in the Rose Garden', ibid., 162–5.
6. 'The Rose in Art', 1938, 39–47.
7. 'Some Old Roses Worth Growing', 1939, 220–4 (n.b. the Bodleian Library's copy is date-stamped 6 April 1939, and so the article was not published posthumously).

The School Science Review
This quarterly was published by the Science Masters' Association and the Association of Women Science Teachers. Its publisher, John Murray, reprinted Bunyard's article as a pamphlet (London; n.d.; the only copy I know is in the Lindley Library of the Royal Horticultural Society).

1. 'The History and Development of the Apple', XX, no. 77, October 1938, 69–76.

Wine and Food
A gastronomical quarterly edited by André L. Simon. Note that the numbering of parts is continuous through the volumes, e.g. the first part of volume II is numbered 5, not 1; each no. has its own pagination.

1. 'The Spring Dessert', I.1 (1934), 40–2.
2. 'The Summer Dessert', I.2 (1934), 41–4.
3. 'The Autumn Dessert', I.3 (1934), 58–62.
4. 'The Winter Dessert', I.4 (1934), 26–9.
5. 'Vegetable Adventures', II.5 (1935), 51–3.
6. 'The Onion in Human Life', II.6 (1935), 42–6.
7. 'Fine Fare', review of L. Tendret, *La Table au Pays du Brillat-Savarin* (Chambéry, 1934), ibid., 52–3.
8. 'Christmas Dessert', II.8 (1935), 50–3.
9. 'The Pea Across the Ages', III.9 (1936), 41–4.
10. 'The Saga of Coffee', review of H. E. Jacob, *The Saga of Coffee* (London, 1935), III.10 (1936), 48–9.
11. 'Apple Pie', III.11 (1936), 29–31.
12. 'The Wine List', III.12 (1936), 32–4.
13. 'Chez La Mère Fillioux', V.18 (1938), 167–9.
14. 'A Visit to the Beaujolais', V.20 (1938), 362–4.
15. 'A Guide to Publand', review of T. E. B. Clarke, *What's Yours?* (London, 1938), ibid., 409–10.
16. 'Bordeaux Labels', VI.21 (1939), 27–9.
17. 'Lancashire Cheese' (s.v. 'Members' Own Recipes and Others'), VI.22 (1939), 162–3.

18. 'Hesperides', review of S. Tolkowsky, *A History of the Culture and Use of Citrus Fruits* (London, 1939), ibid., 165–7. EAB also wrote a different review of this book in *JRHS* no. 31.
19. 'A Few Meals in France', VI.23 (1939), 223–9; this was the Autumn Number.

Wireless Broadcasts (and *The Listener*)

At the British Broadcasting Corporation, Written Archives Centre, Caversham Park, Reading, are the scripts of four broadcasts. Nos. 1–3 below were in the series 'In Your Garden' whose host was the Radio Gardener, C. H. Middleton; no. 4 was under the heading 'In Other Gardens', and involved Bunyard alone. The versions printed in *The Listener* are somewhat edited, and nos. 1–3 omit the dialogue format with Middleton, appearing as solo talks.

1. No special title on the typescript; Sunday, 17 October 1937, 2.0 – 2.20 p.m.; printed in *The Listener*, XVIII, no. 459, 27 October 1937, 917, as 'Apples for the Epicure'.
2. 'The Meaning of Plant Names'; Sunday, 11 December 1938, 2.0 – 2.20 p.m.; printed under the same title in *The Listener*, XX, no. 518, 15 December 1938, 1313–14.
3. 'Novelties from the Kitchen Garden'; Sunday, 2 April 1939, 2.0 – 2.20 p.m.; printed in *The Listener*, XXI, no. 534, 6 April 1939, 749, as 'Unusual Vegetables'.
4. 'Plant Hunting at Home'; Sunday, 16 July 1939, 2.0 – 2.15 p.m.; printed under the same title in *The Listener*, XXII, no. 549, 20 July 1939, 138–9.

APPENDIX

(i) *Publications under the pseudonym 'Rosine Rosat'*
Bunyard used this pseudonym twice; for the evidence that it is a pseudonym see my first chapter and its discussion of *Old Garden Roses*.

1. Appendix, 'The Rose in the Still Room' in EAB's *Old Garden Roses* (1936), 150–5.
2. 'Recipes and Reflexions' in Bunyard's annual catalogue, 'Vegetables for Epicures', 1937 edn., 1–4; there is a copy in the Lindley Library of the Royal Horticultural Society; I discuss these Reflexions in my first chapter.

(ii) *Letters to* The Times
Quotations from the letters are included when they are judged to be of particular interest. Bunyard's letters are frequently contributions to a lengthy correspondence, but I have given this context only when it is necessary for clarity. My annotation 'Hodgson' refers to the two-day sale of books at Hodgson's, 13–14 June 1940, at which Bunyard's library was sold (see Chapter 1).

1. Monday, 6 December 1926, p. 10 e: On plants which incorporate the name of Tradescant. Bunyard concluded:
   'It is a graceful custom of botanists to give a new genus or species the name of a famous colleague, past or present. They do not, however, name plants after themselves, as a recent article by a well-known writer would suggest.'
   The letter arose out of an article, 'A Botanist and Collector. The Tradescant Window at Oxford', Friday, 26 November 1926, p. 17 f. I do not know the article to which Bunyard refers.
2. Saturday, 8 September 1928, p. 6 c: On when to gather apples, warning especially against 'gathering late apples before they are ready'.
   Cf. no. 5 below.
3. Thursday, 3 October 1929, p. 10 e: On the first steamer (in the naval sense). Bunyard notes:
   'The inventor was Blasco de Garay, who lived in 1543, and who appears

in Balzac's "Ressources de Quinola." Edouard Fournier, in his "Le Vieux Neuf," discusses and dismisses this evidence in favour of Denis Papin …'

The work cited is Édouard Fournier, *Le Vieux-Neuf: Histoire Ancienne des Inventions et découvertes modernes* 2nd edn. (Paris, 1877), i, chaps. xxviii–xxix, pp. 204–20; Hodgson, lot 386. The letter arose out of a query by Mr A. G. Grenfell, Tuesday, 17 September 1929, p. 10 e.

Cf. no. 14 below.

4. Saturday, 7 June 1930, p. 8 d: On oranges not being a commercial proposition in England.

5. Tuesday, 16 September 1930, p. 13 d: 'a word of advice to amateurs' on when to gather apples and pears, emphasizing that it should not be too early.

Cf. no. 2 above.

6. Monday, 16 February 1931, p. 8 d: On *Homard à l'Américaine*. Bunyard observed:

'The conjunction of lobster and tomato known as Homard à l'Américaine was invented somewhere between 1853 and 1870 and probably by Constant Guillot, of the Restaurant Bonnefoy, Paris. It was known then, as now, in Parisian restaurants, and also in cookery books, as l'Américaine.'

Part of a controversy on the subject (see Wednesday, 11 February 1931, p. 8 e; Friday, 13 February 1931, p. 10 e; Saturday, 14 February 1931, p. 8 d). Oddly, precisely the same topic (and especially on 'l'Américaine/l'Armoricaine') arose again seven years later, though Bunyard took no part. André L. Simon said the dish was introduced at the Restaurant Noel Peters in Paris in the 1850s or 1860s (Tuesday, 13 September 1938, p. 8 f; see also his letter on Tuesday, 4 October 1938, p. 10 d). In *A Concise Encyclopædia of Gastronomy* (London, 1952), p. 346, Simon has a fuller account.

7. Friday, 20 February 1931, p. 10 e: On the planting of London squares. Bunyard believed that the owners of London squares should dig up the evergreens and plant:

'such deciduous flowering trees and shrubs as have been proved to support our London climate. We owe a great debt to John Claudius

Loudon, who planted the pink almond so freely in London (did it not inspire Mr. George Moore to one of his most eloquent passages?); ... Let us have a tracery of bare twigs and coloured stems rather than the grimy laurel and privet which form the main winter colour in London's squares.'

J. C. Loudon (1783–1843) is also referred to in no. 26 below. The reference to George Moore (1852–1933) is to his *Memoirs of My Dead Life* (London, 1906, with a number of subsequent impressions and editions), chap. i, 'Spring in London', p. 2.

8. Monday, 4 April 1932, p. 8 c: On birds attacking fruit buds. Bunyard reported that an 'old Belgian paper' suggested that birds which pick out fruit buds are seeking their moisture, and that 'an ample supply of water in winter and spring protected ... trees from damage'.

9. Wednesday, 31 August 1932, p. 6 d: On Empire wines and why their label should state their vintage. Bunyard said:
'Young wine is to myself and many others little less than poison, ... One can buy Bordeaux wine of 1924 at 2s. 6d. a bottle, which, while lacking the higher virtues, has no vices. I have never yet met a Colonial wine of similar age, ... I hope that Colonial growers will see their way to assure purchasers on this point.'
Cf. no. 10 below.

10. Tuesday, 6 September 1932, p. 8 e: On the maturity of Dominion wines (cf. no. 9 above). Mr Cuthbert Burgoyne had replied to no. 9 above on Thursday, 1 September 1932, p. 6 d, saying that Dominion wine merchants were concerned not with a particular year but 'maturity' more widely. Bunyard found that Burgoyne's reply:
'smacks rather of the Treasury Bench in its loftier moments, "the matter has not been lost sight of." In other words, the distributors of Dominion wines give you wine of the maturity they consider suitable for you. Now I am quite willing to be told how much taxation is good for me, or what mixture of air and petrol will be best for my car, but in the case of my own internal combustion engine I claim to be the greatest authority. ... I repeat, "ripeness is all."'

11. Monday, 28 November 1932, p. 10 e: On November raspberries, noting some fruitful varieties.

12. Wednesday, 28 December 1932, p. 6 e: Replying to a letter by G. D.

Lake (Monday, 19 December 1932, p. 18 f), attacking the quality of English dessert apples, though not cookers, Bunyard defended the quality and length of season of dessert apples.

13. Friday, 24 February 1933, p. 10 d: Signed 'George Bunyard and Co., Limited, Maidstone', the letter reports in the aftermath of the Ottawa Conference that a customer in Nova Scotia had on grounds of cost cancelled an order for fruit trees from the United States and was buying from Bunyard's.

14. Saturday, 6 May 1933, p. 8 a: On the origins of the omnibus. Bunyard said that in celebrating the centenary of the English omnibus we should remember the inventor of the omnibus, Blaise Pascal. He said: 'While it can hardly be accounted one of his deepest *Pensées*, it is instructive to see that metaphysics and physics may combine for practical ends.'

    The source is almost certainly Fournier, *Le Vieux-Neuf* (see edition cited no. 3 above), ii, chap. lvi, pp. 37–47.

15. Wednesday, 1 November 1933, p. 8 e: In reply to a letter by Mr J. M. K. Lupton, Saturday, 28 October 1933, p. 8 d, arguing for Bramleys as dessert apples which, along with Blenheim Oranges, are superior to Cox's Orange Pippins. Bunyard said that happily both Bramleys and Cox's Orange Pippins are in plentiful supply.

16. Monday, 6 November 1933, p. 15 e: In answer to an article on 'Evelyn's Apples' by 'A Correspondent' (Wednesday, 1 November 1933, p. 15 e) Bunyard said that a number of Evelyn's varieties do survive, some in 'my collection'.

17. Tuesday, 12 December 1933, p. 10 b: On a proposal for a motor-racing track on the South Downs; Bunyard wrote:
'When the two gods of the day, Speed and Profit, conspire to rob us of our ancient peace, can we hope for any successful opposition? Had we not best accept the fact of their domination and adjust, as soon as may be, our ideas to the spirit of the times? Our poetry must be revised at once; its parade of quietude is out of date. May I lead the way?

> Here through the new cemented ways
> The barking motor thrills,
> And track promoters praise the Lord,
> Who made these useful hills.

> So here the new gods lead us on
> To profitable ends,
> The heathen Kingdom Wilfred found
> Now pays us dividends.

And so on.'

Brighton Corporation had revived an earlier scheme, dropped in 1928, for a 'Super Motor-Racing Track' south-west of the Devil's Dyke: see *The Times*, Monday, 27 November 1933, p. 15 c and e. In *The Times* of Wednesday, 29 November 1933, p. 10 e, Mr J. B. A. Parish published a letter of opposition in which he quoted from Kipling's 'Sussex':

> Here through the strong unhampered days
> The tinkling silence thrills;
> Or little, lost, Down churches praise
> The Lord who made the hills:
> But here the Old Gods guard their round,
> And, in her secret heart,
> The heathen kingdom Wilfrid found
> Dreams, as she dwells, apart.
>
> [st. 7, ll. 49–56]

Bunyard's version is nicely mock-heroic; Wilfred is the patron saint of Sussex.

18. Friday, 19 January 1934, p. 10 e: A plea for there to be books of postal orders.
19. Friday, 16 March 1934, p. 15 e: On filming the *Odyssey*:
'If the filming of Homer should come to pass may I enter a plea for horticultural accuracy? We thankfully acknowledge the great pains our film producers take to attain archaeological exactitude in such matters as the correct disposition of halberds and javelins. But once in the garden, or the wild, historical niceties are thrown to the winds and we endure such anachronisms as seeing the walls of Paris in Villon's day mantled with the lush growth of Virginian creeper. Medieval knights offer enamoured ladies American Beauty roses of a prodigious length of stem. We have lately seen Anne of Cleves in a garden of sunflowers, a flower which Europe did not know until 60 years after her arrival in England.

'We gardeners are a growing body, and our influence in Filmland may be almost as great as that of the archaeologists. Let us not be outraged in any coming Homeric film by Nausicaa appearing in a forest of Australian eucalyptus or "mimosa," or Eumaeus proffering the returned Ulysses a dish – I should say a cylix – of bananas.'

The *Times*, Friday 9 March 1934, p. 15 d, had published a 4th Leader headed 'Why not film the Odyssey?'

20. Monday, 29 October 1934, p. 10 e: 'Here are a few reasons why herrings are not more popular … '

    Herring consumption was a current topic; see the letter by Sir Arnold Wilson, Friday, 26 October 1934, p. 10 d.

21. Monday, 5 November 1934, p. 8 d: On identifying a Cox's Orange Pippin.

    Bunyard was answering a letter by Mr Iolo A. Williams, Friday, 2 November 1934, p. 10 e, as to whether shaking a Cox to hear its seeds rattle is a means of identifying it. Bunyard said that other apples besides a Cox rattle, and that 'The easiest way to identify a Cox is to taste it.'

22. Saturday, 30 March 1935, p. 10 d: Quotes 'several nut-shell curiosities' from the *Musæum Tradescantianum: or, A Collection of Rarities Preserved at South-Lambeth neer London by John Tradescant* (London, 1656), including 'A set of Chesse-men in a pepper-corn turned in ivory' (sig. D4, p. 39).

    Part of a correspondence, begun by Miss Catherine Cotton on Wednesday, 20 March 1935, p. 10 d, on the objects people in the past had placed in nutshells. Hodgson, lot 452.

23. Monday, 24 June 1935, p. 10 d: On frost damage to plants; part of a long-running correspondence.

24. Tuesday, 19 November 1935, p. 10 e: On how to look after figs in winter.

25. Tuesday, 26 November 1935, p. 10 e: On the expression 'bottle of (the) boy'.

    The correspondence had begun with a letter by Sir Harry Preston, Wednesday, 13 November 1935, p. 8 b, in which he had used the expression 'a bottle of the boy'.

    Bunyard cites Dekker, *English Villanies Seven Severall Times Prest to Death* … (London, 1638), chap. xvi, 'The abuses of Ale-houses';

'little leather Jacks [vessels for liquor], … called the Gyngle-Boyes' (sig. K3^v). He concludes: 'Thus the "Boye" might have been called for in Shakespeare's day'.

26. Wednesday, 4 March 1936, p. 10 e: On the gingko tree.

    The correspondence had begun with a letter from Sir Herbert Maxwell, Wednesday, 26 February 1936, p. 13 e, and there was a 4th Leader on 'The Gingko' on Wednesday, 11 March 1936, p. 17 d.

    Bunyard cites J. C. Loudon, *Arboretum et Fruticetum Brittanicum* (London, 1838), wondering if any of the gingkos mentioned there are still alive; Loudon was Hodgson, lot 525. Cf. no. 7 above.

27. Monday, 21 September 1936, p. 18 e: On storing apples. Bunyard recommended the damp air of a cellar, the less well ventilated the better. He observed 'Life would indeed be dull for the layman if experts did not occasionally differ'.

    The letter arose out of an article from 'a correspondent', Monday, 14 September 1936, p. 17 d, on the storage of apples for small gardeners.

28. Wednesday, 14 September 1938, p. 6 e: On Roman horseshoes. Bunyard said there was no literary evidence for horseshoes before the 8th century, citing J. Beckmann, *A History of Inventions, Discoveries, and Origins* translated from the German by W. Johnston (probably the 4th edn., London, 1846), i, pp. 442–54, and C. Daremberg and E. Saglio, *Dictionnaire* … (See chapter 3 above, I.1; Hodgson, lot 279).

    The correspondence arose out of an article by 'a correspondent', Monday, 15 August 1938, p. 13 f, 'Horse-shoes: From Gloucester into Antiquity'.

29. Friday, 30 September 1938, p. 8 e: On flowers and fruit appearing simultaneously on apple trees.

    The letter was in reply to one from Mr Robert E. Aske, Monday, 26 September 1938, p. 8 c.

30. Monday, 3 October 1938, p. 8 d: On flageolets and beans.

    In reply to Mr Ambrose Heath, Monday 26 September 1938, p. 8 c.

31. Wednesday, 2 November 1938, p. 10 e: On plums fruiting in October.

(iii) *Letters to the* Times Literary Supplement

1. 'Cotton's "Planter's Manual"'; 4 April 1918, p. 162.
   Cf. *GC* no. 31.
2. 'Canary Wine in England'; 24 June 1926, p. 432.
3. 'Medieval Gardens'; 16 August 1928, p. 593.
4. '"Pleris cum Musco"'; 19 September 1936, p. 748. On the Muscat Pear in relation to John Skelton's 'Speke Parott', 185; following up a letter in *TLS*, 12 September 1936, p. 729. Modern scholarship has preferred another explanation.

Bibliography of Articles and Obituaries on Edward Ashdown Bunyard

compiled by
EDWARD WILSON

1. [anon.], 'Leaders in the Fruit World', s.v. 'Mr. E.A. Bunyard', *The Journal of Horticulture and Home Farmer*, 3rd series, LXI, no. 3238, 20 October 1910, 369–70; has a photograph on p. 370.
2. [anon.], 'Mr. Edward A. Bunyard', *The Gardeners' Magazine*, LV, no. 3036, 6 January 1912, 2; has a photograph (different from that in no. 1 above) on p. 1.
3. Anne Amateur, 'Apples at Allington', *The Garden*, LXXXIV, no. 2562, 25 December 1920, 639.
4. [anon.], 'An Afternoon with a Pomologist', *The Gardeners' Chronicle*, 3rd series, LXXXII, no. 2124, 10 September 1927, 213–14.
5. P[oeticus], 'Potted Plantsmen', no. II, 'E.A. Bunyard, F.L.S.', a seven-line poem, *Gardening Illustrated*, LII, no. 2671, 17 May 1930, 316.
6. [anon.], 'An Expert Pomologist: Mr. E.A. Bunyard', *Amateur Gardening*, XLIX, no. 2513, 2 July 1932, 188; has a photograph (different from nos. 1 and 2 above, but the same as no. 12 below).
7. [anon.], 'Head of Famous Maidstone Firm Found Shot: Mr. A.E. [*sic*] Bunyard dies at his club in the West End', *Kent Messenger*, 21 October 1939, 4.
8. [anon.], 'Mr. E.A. Bunyard', *The Times*, 21 October 1939, 9.
9. [anon.], 'Edward Ashdown Bunyard, F.L.S.', *The Gardeners' Chronicle*, 3rd series, CVI, no. 2757, 28 October 1939, 274.

10. [anon.], 'The late Mr. E.A. Bunyard: Fruit Grower and Rosarian', *Gardening Illustrated*, LXI, no. 3164, 28 October 1939, 694; in issue no. 3166, 11 November 1939, 715, was a letter in tribute from 'Oriflamme'.
11. Maurice Healy, 'Edward Bunyard: In Memoriam', *Wine and Food*, VI.24, Winter 1939, 324–6.
12. [anon.], 'Edward A. Bunyard, F.L.S.: An Appreciation', *The Journal of Pomology and Horticultural Science*, XVII, no. 4, January 1940, 294–6; has the same photograph as in no. 6 above.
13. [anon.], a brief tribute in the *Journal of the Royal Horticultural Society*, LXV, no. 2, February 1940, ii; see also the words of Lord Aberconway, Chairman of the RHS, ibid., no. 4, April 1940, xxvii.
14. Fred Stoker, untitled obituary, *Proceedings of the Linnean Society of London*, 152nd session (1939–40), part 4, May 1940, 362.
15. [anon.], 'Personalia', s.v. 'E.A. Bunyard', *Chronica Botanica*, VI.2, 21 October 1940, 43.
16. Silvio Martini, *Geschichte der Pomologie in Europa* (Bern, 1988), 110, 112; the photograph on p. 107 is that found in nos. 6 and 12 above.
17. Alan Major, 'The Bunyards of Kent'; the article is in 3 parts in *Bygone Kent*; EAB is in Part Three, XII, no. 5, May 1991, 275–80; Parts One and Two are in the issues for March and April 1991, 176–81, 229–32. There is a family photograph, c. 1898, including EAB, on p. 276.
18. Brent Elliott, 'The gastronomic works of Edward Ashdown Bunyard', *The Garden* (as *The Journal of the Royal Horticultural Society* became), CXVI, 1991, 320–1.
19. Ray Desmond, with the assistance of Christine Ellwood, *Dictionary of British and Irish Botanists and Horticulturists* ... (London, 1994), 117–18.
20. Edward Wilson, ' "If on Fragrance We Might Thrive ..." ', *Food and Wine*, XXIV, 1999, 66–9; has the same photograph as in no. 17 above.
21. Joan Morgan, 'Bunyard, Edward Ashdown': entry in the *Oxford Dictionary of National Biography* VIII (Oxford, 2004), 711–12.
22. Edward Wilson, 'Edward Bunyard by the Mediterranean', *The Mediterranean Garden*, no. 38, October 2004, 5–14.
23. Edward Wilson, 'E.A. Bunyard and Norman Douglas', *Norman*

Douglas 3. Symposium, ed. Wilhelm Meusburger and Helmut Swozilek (Bregenz, 2005), 73–9.

24. David Karp, '*The Anatomy of Dessert* Reissued', *Fruit Gardener* (published by California Rare Fruit Growers), XXXVIII, July & August 2006, 26, a version, here with bibliography, of Mr Karp's preface to the reissue of the American edition (1934, with EAB's special preface) of *The Anatomy of Dessert with a Few Notes on Wine* in the Modern Library Food Series (New York, 2006), xxi–xxiii; this reissue also has an introduction (xv–xix) by Michael Pollan.

25. Edward Wilson, 'Edward Bunyard, F.L.S. 1878–1939', the Brogdale Lecture 2006 delivered at the Linnean Society, London, 25 November 2006, *The Linnean*, forthcoming.

APPENDIX

Edward Bunyard in Memoriam

MAURICE HEALY

The following obituary is reprinted from *Wine and Food*, VI.24, Winter 1939, 324–6.

MAURICE HEALY
EDWARD BUNYARD
IN MEMORIAM

The death of Edward Bunyard came as a major shock to all (and they were many) who cherished his friendship. The roses that he loved and preached so charmingly did not seem more remote from sudden death. In the last number of this Journal he wrote, lightly and, as always, amusingly, upon a recent holiday in the South of France; and no reader can have detected in those graceful pages any lurking premonition of the tragedy that was almost upon him. He seemed destined to saunter through a quiet life, drinking a glass here, dipping into a book there, making some botanical discovery to-day, to-morrow instructing us how to get some new and delightful variety into our daily menu by using fruits and vegetables of which he possessed the secret. And always ready for the right kind of conversation. For he had that great and rare gift: his silences were as companionable as his speech, and it was friendly and pleasant to have him sitting at the other side of the hearth, whether he happened to be browsing in a casual book, or listening to the gramophone, or talking.

When he talked, the talk was good. Of his own professional subjects I am myself so pathetically ignorant as not to be able to contribute anything beyond intelligent questioning and interested listening; but I know few men who possessed so many points of contact with their fellows, and could be amusing upon so many subjects. He read as much French as English; and in neither tongue did he care much for anything later than the eighteenth century. He was an apostle of quiet and of melody, with simple harmony. Mozart was to him, as to me, the quintessence of music; and many are the works of the master to which he first opened my ears. The G Minor Quintet was his idea of perfection; and perhaps I ought to have recognized in his affection for its pathos an omen: a confession that he too knew what it was to sorrow, without Mozart's gift 'to ease his breast of melodies', and throw away sadness as a thing, beautiful but melancholy, capable of being stripped off and cast abroad, to be shared like another Saint Martin's cloak with those whose souls might need such a covering. Many a night did we sit here and listen together; and I never guessed the secret.

For his talk was always cheerful and robust. He was a grand controversialist, loving to give and even to receive hard, honest blows; he hated compromise. Wit delighted him; he would turn an epigram upon his tongue as a gourmet might savour a particularly delicate morsel. The more sonorous passages of poetry or prose did not so much appeal to him; here again quiet possessed him, and it was sometimes to remote fountains that he went for his refreshment. Herrick pleased him more than Herbert; perhaps it was the formal religion of Herbert that made a handicap, for Bunyard always seemed to me to be ethical rather than religious. His principles were firm and excellent; but I cannot recall any occasion when they were expressed in the language of any formal creed. Kindness was in his eyes the first of virtues; and he was not a man who failed to practise what he preached.

His mind was so vital that it seemed ready to interest itself in every subject; I can remember an occasion when a visit of his to me coincided with that of a small boy, whose amusement became Bunny's one object for that afternoon. And I suspected that he was leading up to it; yes, out it came. 'I can only perform one parlour trick; but would you like to see me balance an egg on its end?' And, to the delight of the youngster (and, I confess, to my incredulous amazement), he so manipulated the unruly egg that in a very few minutes it was standing on its end on the back of an overturned plate as though that were the natural and ordinary way for eggs to behave! No deception; no preparation of the egg or of the plate; and, he assured me, no trick at all, beyond the patience necessary in the case of every beginner. But I don't think the small boy will ever forget that marvellous afternoon, although I do not suppose he enjoyed it as much as Bunny did.

For his mind was much younger than his body, not that he had yet reached years that in these days would be reckoned burdensome. His intimate friends were generally younger than himself; some of them a generation younger. To these he never condescended: they were his equals, to be treated as equals, not pupils to be instructed. You see, they never suspected the instruction. But I cannot imagine a more valuable course of education for a young man than the companionship of Edward Bunyard. Wise, tolerant, full of knowledge, with a mind that not only discriminated but taught discrimination, his gentle guidance lost nothing through the lightness of the rein. I suppose there were subjects upon which we differed; but to me he appeared always to be on the side of the angels. And he was one of those rare persons who do appreciate the important part that good manners play in life; and to take careful note of the artless art with which he took pains to be agreeable was in itself a valuable education.

Into the last shadows let us not follow him; we know not what they concealed, or in what secret temple his soul may have found its peace. But I hope to meet him again, as I hope for my own salvation. I feel that there is another garden, the secrets of which are delighting his newly-opened eyes; there are books he never heard of that now are beckoning him from one to another in eager and excited exploration. Mozart may not be conducting the G Minor, but the Kleine Nacht-Musik or some other gay piece is surely in his ears. But all the time he is searching, seeking. He is looking for the nurseries of Heaven. And may a divine welcome await him there.

Index

With the exception of books written by E. A. Bunyard, George Bunyard and Norman Douglas, works of literature are indexed by their author's name. The titles of articles in journals and magazines have not been indexed separately, although the name of the journal or other publication by which they were published is indexed. The botanical names of fruits, flowers and vegetables have not been indexed save when they occur in the text. Plants are otherwise indexed under their English or common names.

Aberconway, 2nd Baron, 66, 315, 327, 339-340
Aberconway, Lady, 295, 297
Aberystwyth, University of, 315
Ackerley, J.R., 145
Acton, Harold, 141
Admiral Gervais pear, 245
Alba rose, 280
Aldington, Richard, 100, 144
Algeria, 257-258
Allen, H. Warner, 180
Allgrove, John, 266
Allgrove's Nursery, 202, 206
Allhusen, Dorothy, 186
Allington Pippin, 22, 48, 76, 193, 202, 320
Allington, Kent, 33, 38, 47, 55, 194-195, 199-200, 245, 283, 298, 322, 330, 341
Alma Atar, Kazakhstan, 330
Alone, 110, 129, 137, 139, 144
Amateur Gardening, 381
Ananas strawberry, 248
Anatomy of Dessert, The, 44-45, 47, 49, 119, 140, 146, 148, 153, 171, 216-217, 219, 313, 329, 337, 345
Andrea, Mrs, 53, 302
Anemone rose, 298-299
Angers, Maine-et-Loire, 235
Antagonist gooseberry, 248
Antwerp, Belgium, 281
Apple and Pear Conference 1933, 264-265
Apple and Pear Conference 1934, 266
apple pie, 227
Apple Register, 268
Apples and Pears: Varieties and Cultivation in 1934…, 346
Apples of New York, The, 250

apricot, white, 257
Arabian Nights, 75, 81
Arber, Agnes, 313
Archer-Straw, P., 84
Aristophanes, 89
Armstrong, Martin, 45
Arnold, Ralph, 290
Art of Cookery, The, 48
Art of Good Living, 338
artichoke, Japanese, 223
Ashdown, Charles, 27
Ashford, Kent, 24
Ashford County Show, 322
Athenaeus, 89
Ausone, Château, 91
Austen, Jane, 99, 101
Austrian Briar rose, 273, 279
Bacon, Francis, 77
Baglione Hotel, Florence, 113, 116
Baker, Josephine, 83-84
bananas, 83-85
Banksia grandiflora rose, 286, 299
Banksian Medal, 303
Banshee rose, 284
Barbellion, W.N.P., 106
Barming, Kent, 72, 194
Bateson, William, 40, 77, 157-158, 232, 262
Bath, Avon, 268
Beaulieu, Alpes Maritimes, 59
Beckett, Edwin, 223, 319, 321
Beech, Spencer A., 241
Beerbohm, Max, 80, 100
Beeton, Isabella, 176
Bell, Clive, 84
Belle de Boskoop apple, 207
Belle Portugaise rose, 298

Belloc, Hilaire, 76, 171
Bennett, Arnold, 100
Ben's Red apple, 202
Benson, A.C., 97
Benson, E.F., 76
Berg Collection, New York, 129
Berlin, 281
Bertorelli, Joe, 178-179
Bethel, David, 182
Beurré Bedford pear, 206, 265
Beurré Six pear, 245
Biarnez, Pierre, 94
Bigarreau Gros Noir cherry, 246
Biot, Alpes Maritimes, 59
Birds and Beasts of the Greek Anthology, 136, 139
Blackmore, R.D., 78-79, 245
Blunden, Edmund, 185
Blush China rose, 282
Bodnant, North Wales, 295, 315
Boisson, Marius, 70
Bon Marché, Paris, 276
'Bon Viveur', 182
Book-Collector's Quarterly, The, 170, 336
Borrow, George, 99
Bossuet, Jacques-Bénigne, 94
Botticelli, Sandro, 280
Boulestin, X. Marcel, 46, 152-153, 178, 180, 224, 337
Boulestin's restaurant, 178, 335
Bourbon rose, 273
Boursault Blush rose, 285
Bowdich, Mrs E.W., 176
Bowes-Lyon, Hon. David, 53, 289, 327
Bowles, E.A., 54, 66, 233, 286, 296, 306, 309, 312, 316-318, 327, 340
Braggins, Mr, 321
Bramley's Seedling apple, 227-228
Breughel, Jan, 281
Brinkman's Nursery, 202
British Colour Council, 316
British Empire Board, 201
British Institute, Florence, 113, 155
Brocket, 1st Baron, 319, 322
Brogdale Farm, Kent, 265
Brompton Park Nursery, 235
Brooks, Samuel, 41
Brougham, 2nd Baron, 296, 298

Browne, E.G., 123, 126
Browne, Sir Thomas, 99
Browning, Robert, 104
Brussels, 281
Bunyard Medal, 210, 322-323
Bunyard Silver Cup, 199, 324
Bunyard, Charles, 23, 25-26
Bunyard, E.A., see also 'Rosine Rosat',
Bunyard, Frances Lucy Butler, 27, 34, 47, 56, 216, 227, 239, 250-251, 265, 277-278, 318, 341
Bunyard, Frederick, 24-25
Bunyard, George, 17, 20-21, 24-25, 27, 33-35, 37-38, 40, 68, 105, 191, 193-195, 197, 199, 239, 275, 319, 339
Bunyard, George Norman (Norman), 26-27, 36-40, 55, 68, 72, 197, 199, 211, 216, 256, 339, 341
Bunyard, George Pearson, 27
Bunyard, Harry, 24-26
Bunyard, James (d. 1844), 17
Bunyard, James (Jim), 23, 26
Bunyard, Janet, 27, 37
Bunyard, John Butler (Jack), 24-25
Bunyard, Miss Katharine, 36, 72, 73
Bunyard, Katherine Mary, 27, 37
Bunyard, Katherine Sophia (née Ashdown), 27, 72, 339
Bunyard, Lorna Frances, 27, 36, 56, 72, 79, 186, 227, 287, 313
Bunyard, Marguerite Eveline, 27, 37, 56, 216, 227, 277, 317
Bunyard, Mary Ann, 24
Bunyard, Norman Philip, 27
Bunyard, Richard Geoffrey, 27, 37
Bunyard, Thomas, 20, 23, 26-27
Bunyard, Mrs Thomas, 24
Bunyard, Thomas (Tom), 20, 24-26
Bunyards and Laxtons Ltd., 72
Bunyard's Nursery, 17ff., 191ff.
Burbank, Luther, 207
Burdett, Osbert, 185
Burford, Surrey, 328
Busby, Mr, 298
Buss, Ada, 200
Buss, Frederick, 200, 334
Buss, William, 200, 287, 341
Butler, Samuel, 86, 94, 99, 103-104, 125

INDEX

Bygone Kent, 382
Byng of Vimy, Viscountess, 57, 313
Byron, Alfred Lord, 99
cabbage rose, 281-282
cabbage, Chinese, 223
Cahen, Edward, 56
Calderon, George, 124
Calvert County, Maryland, USA, 285
Cannes, Alpes Maritimes, 31, 296
Cap d'Antibes, Alpes Maritimes, 59-60, 295, 300-301
Cap Ferrat, Alpes Maritimes, 59
Cape plums, 259
Capri, Italy, 32
Carnegie Trust, 312
Casanova, Giacomo, 70, 93
Catalogue of Fruit Trees of Le Lectier, 256-257
Cato, 91
Ceres, South Africa, 259
Cerio, Edwin, 32, 99, 132
Chadwick, Sir George, 47
Chahar Mahal, Iran, 294
Chamberlain, Sir Austen, 221
Champin, Pierre and Nicole, 59
Champion of Ixworth walnut, 333
Chasset, L., 256
Château Éléonore rose, 298
Chatto & Windus, 61, 147ff.
Chaucer, Geoffrey, 97
Cheal, Joseph, 266
Cheal's Nursery, 202
Chelsea Flower Show, 43, 321, 327
Chelsfield, Kent, 294
Cheng, S.K., 182
cherries, 41, 43, 73, 246, 257, 265
Ch'ien Lung, Emperor, 282
Chilean strawberry, 248
China, 282
Chinese cherry, 207
Chinese Exhibition 1935, 282
Chinese fruiting cherry, 41
Chiswick botanic garden, 233-234
Chittenden, Frederick J., 64, 66, 262-263, 312, 314, 317-318, 325, 340
Christie's, auctioneers, 310
Chronica Botanica, 382
Cibber, Colley, 82
Clarendon Press, 317

Clarke, Mrs Gladys, 60
Clay Challenge Cup, 273
Claygate Pearmain apple, 215, 324
Cloth of Gold rose, 302
Cobbett, William, 99
Colchester-Wemyss, Sir Francis, 178
Collobrières, Var, 31
Colmar d'Été pear, 245
Cologne, Germany, 281
Colt cherry, 258
Colvin, Clare, 46
Comber, James, 52
Commercial Fruit Trials, 260-263, 265, 324, 331
Comte de Paris pear, 245
Comtesse de Chaponay rose, 301
Conference pear, 206
Conifer Conference 1891, 290
Conifer Conference 1931, 289-290
Connaught Rooms, 47, 171
Connolly, Cyril, 60
Conrad, Joseph, 100
Constable's Wine Library, 180
Constantia, South Africa, 259
cooking apple, 227
Coole Park, Co. Galway, 81
Cooper's Burmese rose, 299
Copper Austrian Briar rose, 279
Corday, Michel, 93
Cornwallis, 5th Earl, 290
Cornwallis, Lord, 290
Correns, Carl, 158, 161-162
Corvine Society, 183
Cory, Reginald, 309-310, 314
Coryate, Thomas, 105
Cos d'Estournel, Château, 94
Cottington Taylor, D.D., 177
Cotton, Charles, 238
Country Life, 35, 45, 47, 50, 64, 177-178, 278, 313, 347-349
Countryman, The, 50, 217, 349
Coward, Noël, 87
Cox's Orange Pippin apple, 215
Cracknell, John, 325
Craig, Elizabeth, 177, 180-181
Crane, M.B., 254
Cranston's Nursery, 202
Crescenzi, Pietro de, 236

Crivelli, Carlo, 280
cucumber, Russian, 225
Cummings, B.F., 106
currants, 247
Cutforth, René, 277
Cuthbertson, William, 328
Czar plum, 206
D.H. Lawrence and Maurice Magnus: A Plea for Better Manners, 134
Daily Mail, 126
Daily Mail Cookery Book, 177
Daily Telegraph, The, 67, 178
Daisy Hill Nursery, 276, 285, 300
damask rose, 279, 302
Dane, Clemence, 81
Daremburg C., and Saglio, E., 136
Darwin, Charles, 160-162
Darwin, Frank, 161
Davos, 60
Dawson's Book Shop, Los Angeles, 130ff.
de la Bretonne, Restif, 70
de Vries, Hugo, 158, 161-162
Deeley, Lilla, 182
Delicious apple, 207
Dent & Co., publishers, 114
Desmond, Ray, 382
Dickens, Charles, 100
Dickson and McGredy, rose-breeders, 283
Dictionary of British and Irish Botanists and Horticulturalists, 382
Dictionary of Gardening, 317, 340
Disraeli, Benjamin, 93, 99
Doubleday, Sir Leslie, 265, 322
Douglas, Archie, 118, 120, 121, 129, 140, 155
Douglas, Lord Alfred, 96, 99
Douglas, Norman, 31-32, 40, 44, 58-59, 61, 64, 86, 99, 109ff., 216, 237, 299-301
Doyenné du Comice pear, 87
Dr Hogg strawberry, 248
Drayton, Michael, 105
Dryden, John, 82
Du Maurier, Sir Gerald, 48
Duchess of Portugal rose, 298
Duchess's Favourite apple, 213
Dufy, Raoul, 178
Duhamel du Monceau, Henri-Louis, 310
Dulau of Bond Street, Messrs, 44, 313
Dumelow's Seedling apple, 228

Dunraven, Earl of, 320
Durham, Herbert E., 46, 225, 256, 260, 265
Durham, Lt. Col. F.R., 67
Dyffryn, Glamorganshire, 309
Early Rivers cherry, 206
Early Rivers plum, 206
Early Sulphure gooseberry, 215
East Malling Research Station, 234, 254, 258, 330, 332-333, 335
'Eat More Fruit' campaign, 201-202
Eckermann, J.P., 92
Edden, Helen, 177
Edinburgh, Royal Botanic Garden, 42
Edmonds, W. Talbot, 265, 322
Egremont Russet apple, 205
Eliot, T.S., 185
Elliott, Dr Brent, 66, 382
Ellis, Havelock, 67, 70, 146
Ellwood, Christine, 382
Elstree, Hertfordshire, 319
Émile d'Hyest pear, 205, 245
Empire Marketing Board, 48, 336
England's National Flower, 34, 36, 43, 50, 275, 276, 282, 346
English Folk Cookery Association, 186
Epicure's Companion, The, 35, 37, 45, 56-58, 137, 148-152, 177, 184-187, 227, 313, 346
Erfurt, Germany, 31
Europe, 121, 131
Evans, Joan, 71
Evelyn, John, 81
Evening Standard, 68, 178
Evergreen rose, 279
Experiments, 117, 119-120, 130, 134, 139
Fabio Giordano's Relation of Capri, 133, 138
Fantin-Latour rose, 283, 293
Ferdinand, King of Bulgaria, 296
Fertility pear, 206
Fielden, G. St Clair, 69
Fielding, Henry, 81, 99
Filbert Pine strawberry, 248
Finzi, Gerald, 268
First Edition and Book Collector, The, 119
First Edition Club, 170, 183-184, 336
Fisher, H.A.L., 123
Fitzgerald, Edward, 102
Flora and Sylva, 213
Florence, Italy, 113, 280, 299

INDEX

Focke, W.O., 160, 162
Food and Wine, 382
Forbes, Ellert, 180
Fortnum & Mason, 178
Fortune, Robert, 299
Fountains in the Sand, 114, 129
France, Anatole, 93
Frank Matthews' Nursery, 203
Frazer, Sir James, 102, 103
Fremlins Gold Top beer, 335
French National Horticultural Society, 257, 328
French Pomological Society, 254-255
Fruit Experimental Station, Wye, 234, 254
Fruit Garden, The, 34, 239
Fruit Gardener, 383
Fruit Group, RHS, 268
Fruit Manual, 233-234
fruit records, 249ff.
Fruit Room, 211
Fruiterers, Worshipful Company of, 18, 197
Garden Advice Centres, 326
Garden, The, 19, 35, 39, 64, 137, 138, 349-352, 381, 382
Gardeners' Chronicle, The, 28, 31-32, 34-35, 40-41, 45, 49, 57, 200, 213, 237, 253, 290, 293, 322, 353-358, 381
Gardener's Companion, The, 49, 55-56, 82, 226, 346
Gardeners' Magazine, The, 18, 22, 359, 381
Gardener's Year Book, The, 359
Gardening Illustrated, 43, 46, 50, 54, 55, 67, 73, 77-78, 86, 359-363, 381, 382
garlic, 126
Garnett, David, 142
Gascoyne's Scarlet apple, 193, 202
Gaselee, Sir Stephen, 172
Gaskell, Elizabeth, 104
Gathorne-Hardy, Robert, 60
George Bunyard & Co., 72
George Longley Nursery, 276
Geschichte der Pomologie in Europa, 382
Ghent Florales, Belgium, 328
Gibbons, Stella, 86
Gibbs, Hon. Vicary, 319
Giordano, Fabio, 133
Gloire des Rosomanes rose, 284
Goethe, Johann Wolfgang, 92

Gogarty, Oliver St John, 185
Golden Delicious apple, 208, 213
Golden Noble apple, 228
Golding, Louis, 129
Gomme, Alice Bertha, Lady, 186
Good Housekeeping, 177, 181
gooseberries, 247-248
Gooseberry Growers Register, 308
Granny Smith apple, 208
Grasse, Alpes Maritimes, 31, 59, 301
Gravenstein apple, 245
Gravereaux, Jules, 276, 301-303
Graves, Richard, 99
Gregory, Augusta, Lady, 81
Gregory, Maundy, 183
Grenadier apple, 202
Grenfell Medal, 47, 250
Grosse Schwarze Knorpelkirsche cherry, 246
'Growmore Bulletins, The', 326
Grubb, Norman, 254
Guignard, Jean-Louis-Léon, 161
Gunnersbury Park, Middlesex, 93
Gwynn, Stephen, 180
Hadfield, Miles, 49, 55, 82
Half Hundred Club, 182
Hall, Sir Daniel, 261-264, 315, 331-332, 337-338
Hamburg, Germany, 195
Hampton, Dr Frank, 224
Hanbury, Daniel, 295
Hanbury, Sir Cecil, 296, 321
Hanbury, Sir Thomas, 295-296
Handbook of Hardy Fruits More Commonly Grown in Great Britain, 40, 199, 231ff., 241ff., 345
Handbook of Hardy Trees and Shrubs, 34
Hanley, James, 99
Harben, Philip, 183
Harper's Bazaar, 178
Hatfield, Herts, 246
Hatton, Rev. Edmund Christopher, 254
Hatton, Sir Ronald, 254, 256, 332-333
Haywards Heath, Sussex, 286, 288
Healy, Maurice, 48, 62-63, 72, 88, 92, 103, 146, 170, 181, 216-217, 333-337, 382, 385-387
Heath, Ambrose, 31, 181, 185, 221
Hedgeland, P. Sweatman, 34, 278
Hedrick, Prof. Ulysses, 255-256
Heem, Jan Davidsz de, 281

Hehn, V., 111
Herbert, A.P., 76
Herm, Channel Islands, 59
Herrick, Robert, 105
Herstmonceux, Sussex, 154
Hex Valley, South Africa, 259
Hickey, William, 121
Hidcote, Gloucestershire, 290-291, 297-298
Hill, Sir Arthur W., 317, 328
Himalaya berry, 247
Hind's Head, Bray, 181
Hit or Miss gooseberry, 248
Hodgson's, auctioneers, 69-70, 138ff.
Hogg, Robert, 78-79, 233-236, 243-245, 306-307, 319
Holland, Vyvyan, 183, 185
Holliday, Miss, 268
'Home Grown Produce' exhibitions, 221
Home, Health and Garden, 177
Homer, 88, 111
Hooker, William, 311
Horace, 90, 91
Horticultural Club, 35, 225, 258, 335
Horticultural Record, The, 346
House of Bunyard 1796–1919, The, 347
How About Europe?, 130, 135
Humble, Nicola, 217
Hume, Rosemary, 186
Hume's Blush rose, 272
Hurst, C.C., 233, 281, 289
Hutchinson, John, 311
Hutton, Edward, 116, 121, 145, 155
Huxley, Aldous, 100, 125, 141, 144
Huysmans, Joris-Karl, 95-96
Huysum, Jan van, 281
Huysum, Justus van, 281
Hyams, Edward, 287
hybrid tea roses, 271ff.
Hyères, Var, Castel Sainte-Claire, 296
Hyères, Var, Parc St Bernard, 301
Ibn Al-'Awwâm, 279
Illustrated Dictionary of Gardening, 317
Imperial Fruit Show Company, 321
Imperial Fruit Show 1931, 262
Imperial Fruit Shows, 328
Imperial Preference, 201
In the Beginning, 139
Index Londinensis, 306

Ingram, Collingwood, 41, 257, 292
Institute of Plant Industry, Leningrad, 329-331
International Conference on Genetics 1906, 35, 93, 157ff., 232
International Conference on Hybridization 1899, 232
International Federation of Professional Horticulturalists, 255
International Horticultural Congress 1866, 306
Iran, 294
Italy, Bunyard and, 32
Jack, Florence, 176-177
Jackson, Dr Benjamin Daydon, 233, 236
Jackson, Ian, 105, 109
Jackson, Sir Herbert, 47
James, G.P.R., 88
James, Henry, 86, 125
James, Hon. Robert, 50, 52, 288, 292, 303
'Jason Hill', 224
Jaune Desprez rose, 283
Jekyll, Gertrude, 193, 275
Jekyll, Lady, 177
Jethou, Channel Islands, 59
Johannsen, Wilhelm, 158
John Innes Research Institute, 234, 332
John, Augustus, 185
Johnson, Samuel, 82
Johnston, Lawrence, 52, 59, 61, 290-292, 297, 299-300
Jonathan apple, 202, 259
Jonson, Ben, 90
Josephine, Empress, 284
Journal of Horticulture and Home Farmer, The, 21, 32, 37, 39, 40, 381
Journal of Pomology and Horticultural Science, The, 40, 199, 247, 255-257, 260, 309, 364-365, 382
Journal of the Royal Horticultural Society, The, 32, 35-36, 39, 45, 50, 57, 59, 64, 281, 312, 315ff., 326, 365-367, 382
Joyce, James, 70, 100, 185
Juvenal, 90
kale, Labrador, 223
Karp, David, 383
Kazakhstan, 330
Kazanlik rose, 296

INDEX

Keats, John, 99, 102
Keays, Ethelyn Emery, 51, 285, 286
Keen's Seedling strawberry, 248
Kelly, Prof. John, 80
Kelsey plum, 259
Kent Cherry and Soft Fruit Competition, 322-323
Kent Farm Institute, Borden, 262, 266
Kent Messenger, 18, 28, 68, 71, 381
Kent National Farmers' Union, 265, 322
Kerner, Johann Simon, 310
Keswick Codlin apple, 228
Kew, Royal Botanic Gardens, 53, 299
Keyzer, Frances, 177, 179
Kidd, Dr F., 264
Kiftsgate Court, Gloucestershire, 53, 290-291, 298-299
Kiftsgate rose, 291
King of Trumps gooseberry, 248
King, William, 48
Kinninmont, K., 227
Kirke's Blue plum, 215
Knight, Thomas Andrew, 235
Knowles, Guy, 170
La Follette rose, 297-298
La Garoupe, Alpes Maritimes, 295
La Mortola rose, 299
La Mortola, Italy, 52-53, 295-296, 298-299, 321
Laboureur, Jean-Emile, 178
Lady Sudely apple, 193
Lake, Nancy, 176
Lamb, Charles, 82, 104
Lambourne, Lord, 335
Laurencin, Marie, 178
Lausanne, Switzerland, 255
Lawrence, D.H., 100, 134, 141, 144-145
Lawrence, Sir Trevor, 160, 163-164, 328
Lawrence, Sir William, 45, 219, 225-226, 318, 328, 338
Lawrence, T.E., 100
Laxton, Edward, 256, 266, 296, 333
Laxton, William, 232
Laxton Brothers' Nursery, 72, 202, 204, 206
Laxton's Delicious plum, 206, 265
Laxton's Epicure apple, 324
Laxton's Fortune apple, 206
Laxton's Nursery, 283, 323-324

Laxton's Superb apple, 206, 265, 324
Laxton's Superb pear, 265
Leak, George W., 316, 327
Leconbury, Lord, 319
Leng, Basil, 28, 53, 58-61, 64, 120, 123, 300-302
Leng, Kyrle, 60
Leroy, André, 235, 257
Leslie, Shane, 183
Levrault & Co., Paris, 308
Lewis, Wyndham, 100, 183
Leyel, Mrs Hilda, 220
Licht, Hans, 70
Life and Letters, 45
Lileum giganteum, 287
Lily of Valley gooseberry, 248
lima bean, 223, 225
Lindley, John, 306, 311
Lindley Library, Royal Horticultural Society, 54, 64, 69, 306ff., 339-340
Lindley Library Catalogue, The, 312
Lindley Library Trust, 306
Lindsay, Norah, 291, 294
Linnean Society, 38, 53, 233, 247
Linnean, The, 383
Linton Park, Kent, 289-290
Listener, The, 50, 371
Lobjoit, Sir William, 262-263
Loder, Gerald, 309, 327, 329, 335
Lodge, Sir Oliver, 142
London gooseberry, 248
London Horticultural Society, 233
London Mercury, The, 44, 184
London Street Games, 129, 139
Long Ashton Research Station, 332
Long Island, USA, 285
Looking Back, 131, 136
Lord Lambourne apple, 265
Lorette, Louis, 260
Lorne Doone, 79
Lotus, boot and shoe makers, 129
Louise Bonne of Jersey pear, 215
Low, David and Heather, 61, 150
Lucas, Dione, 186
Lucas, E.V., 45, 219
Luini, Bernadino, 280
Luxemburg, 31, 255
Lyons, J., & Co., 335

Macartney rose, 301
McClaren, Henry Duncan, 327
MacColl, D.S., 171
McIntosh apple, 208, 329
Mackenzie, Compton, 48, 59, 76, 80
McNeill, F. Marian, 187
Macoun, Dr W.T., 255, 329
Magnus, Maurice, 134, 145
Maidstone, Kent, 17-19, 195, 200
Maidstone, Kent, Bower Mount Road, 195
Maidstone Choral Union, 22
Maidstone Favourite apple, 206, 324
Major, Alan, 39, 382
Malmaison, Hauts-de-Seine, 284, 302
Malory, Sir Thomas, 99
Manchester Guardian, 67
Manning Foster, A.E., 179
Margil apple, 215
Mari, René, 145
Marie Leonida rose, 301
Marjorie's Seedling plum, 265
Marnier-Lapostolle, Julien, 59
marrow, African, 223
Martial, 91, 126
Martin, Sir Leslie, 268
Martineau, Lady Alice M., 46, 220, 224, 297
Martini, Silvio, 382
Mas, Alphonse, 252, 308
Masters, William, nurseryman, 290
Maures Mountains, France, 302
Mavrogordato, J.N., 121
Mediterranean Garden, The, 382
Meier, H.E., 70
Melville, Herman, 98-99
Menton, Alpes Maritimes, 31, 59, 297
Mereworth, Kent, 27, 72-73
Mermaid rose, 301
Merryweather's Nursery, 202
Messel, Leonard, 52, 287-288, 310
Meusberger, Dr Wilhelm, 109, 139
Meynell, Francis, 183
Middleton, C.H., 28, 181, 228, 371
Milan, Italy, 281
Miles, Eustace Hamilton, 176
Miraour, nurseryman, 301
M'Laren, Moray, 185
Moby Dick, 115
Modern Salads, 36

Moinaux, Jules, 70
Monarch apple, 206
Monte Carlo restaurant, 179
Moore, George, 80-81, 100
Moore, Thomas, 272
Morgan, Joan, 382
Mottisfont Abbey, Hampshire, 304
Mougins, Alpes Maritimes, 301
Mount, Spencer, 265
Mrs Phillimore apple, 213
Muffett, Thomas, 101
Muir, Heather, 53
Muir, Helen, 290-291, 299
Munich crisis, 325
Munro, H.H., 99
Musée Guimet, Paris, 282
Musgrave, Charles, 314
My Garden, 367
Myddleton House, Enfield, 286, 309
Nabonnand, Gilbert, 296, 298, 301
Napoleon pear, 245
Nardini Hotel, Florence, 113
Nash, John, 44, 46-47, 184, 220, 313, 318
Nation Mark scheme, 1928, 201
National Apple Congress 1883, 192, 239, 266
National Fruit Collections, Brogdale, 268
National Fruit Trials, 265
National Institute for Cider Research, 234
National Rose Society, 273, 275, 286, 288
National Rose Society Trial Ground, 53
Nawaschin, Sergei, 161
Neal, E., 319
Neame, Barry, 223
Neame, J. Armstrong, 69
Neame, Sir Thomas, 265
Nerinda, 135, 139
Nessel, Maud, 287
New Flora and Silva, 36, 43, 47-48, 50, 52, 59-60, 64, 74, 86, 367-368
New Statesman and Nation, 293
New York Agricultural Station, Geneva, 240
New Zealand, 321
Newcastle, Duke of, 320
Newdigate, Bernard H., 105
Newfoundland, 211
Nicolson, Harold, 51, 292, 294
Night and Day, 56-57, 61, 148, 154, 368
Ninth International Horticultural Congress,

INDEX

1930, 328ff.
Nioffs, Mssrs, publishers, 310
Nix, Charles, 262, 264, 319, 323, 328, 331
Noailles, Vicomte Charles de, 59, 301
Noble cherry, 246
Noisette rose, 273, 288
Norberg, Inga, 182
Norman Douglas 3. Symposium, 383
Northbourne, Lord, 292
Notes on the Medical History of Cider, 46
Nova Scotia, 211
Nymans, Sussex, 52, 286-288, 298, 310
Observer, The, 292
okra, 225
Old Blush China rose, 272-273
Old Calabria, 129, 138
Old Garden Roses, 34-35, 50, 51, 271ff., 346, 372
Oldham, W.R., 327-328
Oldmeadow, Ernest, 185
Olschki, Leo, 236-237
On the Herpetology of the Grand Duchy of Baden, 133, 138
'On Xenia', 35, 157ff.
onions, 126
orache blonde, 225
Orchard and the Garden, The, 309
Orioli, Guiseppe (Pino), 61, 99, 135, 140, 144-145, 154, 237
Orleans Reinette apple, 205, 217, 324
Ovid, 90
Oxenford, John, 92
Oxford Dictionary of National Biography, 382
Paddock Wood, Kent, 330
Paestum, Italy, 279
Paestum rose, 278
Page, John Courtney, 286
Page, T.E., 180
Palmer, Godfrey, 221
Paneros, 135, 139
Papa Gontier rose, 296
Parfum de l'Haÿ rose, 301
Paris, 31, 281-282
Paris, Bagatelle garden, 302
Paris, Jardin des Plantes, 300
Paris, Musée Carnavalet, 303
Park's Yellow rose, 272
Parson's Pink rose, 272

Parsons, Alfred, 285
Parsons, Ian, 61, 147ff.
Pateman, T., 319
Paul, St, 98
Paul, Arthur, 308
Payne, C. Harman, 238, 308, 310
peach, Chinese flat, 257
Peacock, Thomas Love, 99
Pearl, R.T., 251-252, 257
Pearson's Nursery, 202
Peel, Mrs C.S., 176
Penenden Heath, Kent, 195
Perceval, Deane, 113
Persian Double Sulphur rose, 286
Persian Double Yellow rose, 279, 280
Petworth, Sussex, 319
Peymeinade, Alpes Maritimes, 53, 302
Phillpotts, Eden, 79, 97, 202
Pickering, Marie, 182
Pickstone, H.E.V., 258
Pinsent, Cecil, 125
Pitmaston Pineapple apple, 205
Plea, 145
Plesch, Arpad, 59
Pliny the Elder, 111, 278-279, 281
Plutarch, 99
Pollard, Major Hugh, 177
Pomologia Batavia, 236
'Pomona', 213
Pope, Alexander, 82
Postgate, Raymond, 183
potato, Kipfler, 225
Potter, J.M.S., 267-268
Powerscourt, Co. Wicklow, 272
Powys, John Cowper, 100
Prentice, Charles, 61, 123, 126, 154
Prentice, George, & Sons, 335
Proceedings of the Linnean Society of London, 368, 382
Proust, Marcel, 93, 152-153
Prunus cerasus, var. *Bunyardii*, 42
Quaritch, Messrs Bernard, 315
Quatre Saisons rose, 272
Queen of Denmark rose, 293
Quintal d'Alsace cabbage, 223
Quintynie, Jean-Baptiste de la, 238
Rabelais, 70, 93
Racine, Jean, 93

Rackham, Arthur, 79
Ramona rose, 298-299
Rawes, A.N., 264, 267
Red Champagne gooseberry, 248
Redgrove, H.S., 49
Redouté, Pierre-Joseph, 284-285, 288, 299-300, 310
Reeves, Frere, 126
Reinette Rouge Étoilée apple, 207
Report of Papers delivered to the Horticultural Club, 369
Report of the Third International Conference 1906 on Genetics, 346
Rev. W. Wilks apple, 206
Ribston Pippin apple, 49
Richardson, Samuel, 101
Ridgeway's Colour Chart, 317
Rivers, H. Somers, 232
Rivers, Thomas, 206
Rivers' Nursery, 202, 204, 206, 283
Rochester, Lord, 99
Rolfe, Frederick William, 'Baron Corvo', 100, 183, 336
Rollit, Sir Albert, 93
Ronsard, Pierre, 93-94
Roquebrune, Alpes Maritimes, 52, 59, 295-296, 298-299
Rosa bracteata, 301
Rosa brunonii, 299
Rosa brunonii, La Mortola, 32, 53
Rosa dupontii, 287
Rosa filipes, 291
Rosa filipes, Kiftsgate, 53
Rosa gigantea, 298
Rosa laevigata, 298-299
Rosa longicuspis, 293
Rosa moschata, 299
Rosa Moyesii, Highdownensis, 287-288
Rosa mutabilis, 300
Rosa soulieana, 287
Rosarium Sangerhausen, 276
Rose Annual of the National Rose Society, The, 50, 369
Rose Conference 1902, 275
Roseraie de l'Haÿ, 53, 276, 291, 302
roses, 271ff.
'Rosine Rosat', 46, 52, 224, 372
Ross, Janet, 176

Rothschild, Leopold de, 93
Royal Caledonian and International Flower Show, 328
Royal Horticultural Society, 36, 40, 53-54, 64, 66, 305ff.
    Council, 326ff.
    Fruit and Vegetable Committee, 319ff.
    Library Committee, 309ff.
    Picture Committee, 318
    Publications Committee, 315ff.
    shows, 209ff., 320ff.
Royal International Horticulture Exhibition 1912, 197
Royal Societies Club, 54, 67, 170, 335
Royal Sovereign strawberry, 206
Roy-Chevrier, J., 136
Rudd, Hugh, 181
Ruskin, John, 101-102
'Ruslin Lieves', 55
Sackville-West, Eddie, 60
Sackville-West, Vita, 51, 290-294, 298
Sadleir, Michael, 48
Saintsbury Club, 45, 48, 49, 76, 169ff., 180, 183, 184, 336, 337
Saintsbury, Prof. George, 48, 169ff.
'salicina' plum, 206-207
Salisbury, Lord, 246
Samuelson, Margaret, 313
Sand, George, 93
Saturday Review, 45
School Science Review, The, 370
Scots rose, 288
Scotson-Clark, G.F., 177
Scott, George Forrester, 45
Scott, Sir Walter, 104
Scott-Moncrieff, Charles, 93, 120, 141, 144-145
Scott's Nursery, 202
Seabrook's Nursery, 202, 206
Seawright, ---, 123
Secker, Martin, 114, 134
Secrett, F.A., 221, 325, 334
Seeghers, Daniel, 281
Senn, C. Hermann, 176
Seven Sisters rose, 289
Sfax, Tunisia, 258
Shakespeare, William, 98-99
Shand, Philip Morton, 177, 267-268

INDEX

Shanghai restaurant, 182
Shaw, George Bernard, 100
Sheffield Daily Telegraph, 59
Shepard, E.H., 185
Sidney, Sir Philip, 105
Simon Louis Frères, nursery, 254
Simon, André, 46-47, 49, 64-65, 76, 170, 172, 175, 179-181, 183-185, 221, 225-226, 335-338
'Simple Vegetable Cookery', 326
Siren Land, 114, 129
Sissinghurst, Kent, 51, 290, 292-293, 298
Sitwell, Edith, 185
Slater's Crimson rose, 272, 288
Smeed, George, 25
Smith, G.N., 276
Smith, Muriel, 269
Smith, Sydney, 97
Smollett, Tobias, 99
Snowdrop gooseberry, 248
Société Nationale d'Horticulture de France, 242
Socoa, Landes, 59, 300
Some Limericks, 127-128
sorrel, 225
Souter, John B., 84
South Africa, 31, 211, 258-259, 292, 321
South Wind, 129, 137, 139
Spectator, The, 82
Spence, Howard, 332-333
Sprenger, Carl Ludwig, 111
Spry, Constance, 294
Squire, Sir John Collings, 48, 76, 170, 184
St Nicholas, Richmond, Yorkshire, 53, 288
St Paul's Walden Bury, Hertfordshire, 53, 289
St-Tropez, Var, 31, 302
Stanley-Wrench, Mrs Molly, 181
Stearn, William T., 54, 65, 66-67, 69, 72, 146, 312, 314, 337, 339
Steedman, Mssrs., 311
Steele, Richard, 82
Stellenbosch, South Africa, 259
Stern, Sir Frederick, 287, 297, 327
Sterne, Lawrence, 106
Stevens, Henry, 185
Stevenson, John Barr, 317
Stockport Summer Flower Show, 328
Stoker, Fred, 26, 57-58, 211, 382

Strachey, Peggy, 60
Strauss, Ralph, 183
strawberries, 248-249
Street, Julian, 179
Streeter, Fred, 266, 319
Studio and Vista Books Ltd., 46
Sunday Times, 45, 219
Surtees, Robert Smith, 101
Susan Louise rose, 298
Sutton Courtenay, Oxfordshire, 291
Sutton, L. Noel, 327
Swanley Agricultural College, 266
Swaythling, Lady, 337
Swift, Jonathan, 82, 106
Swinnerton, Frank, 126
Switzerland, 31
Symons, A.J.A., 48, 65, 76, 170, 175, 179, 183, 185, 336
Symons, Julian, 182
Synge, J.M., 100
Synge, Patrick M., 59
Tallents, Stephen, 48
Talleyrand, Charles Maurice de, 94, 103
Tasmania, 321
Taylor, G.C., 45
Taylor, H.V., 262, 266, 267, 325, 332, 340
Teddington, Middlesex, 78, 245
Tehran, 294
Temple, Reginald, 125
Temple, Sir William, 105
Tennyson, Alfred Lord, 104
Thackeray, W.M., 88
Thérèse, cook to Basil Leng, 60
Thesing, Curt, 70
They Went, 129, 139
Thomas Rivers apple, 215
Thomas, Graham Stuart, 32, 50, 53, 299, 304
Thomas, Owen, 193, 256
Thorpe Hall, Essex, 57
Tilgate, Sussex, 319
Times, The, 67, 84, 176-177, 372-379, 381
Times Literary Supplement, The, 45, 57, 379
Tipo Ideale rose, 300
Toddington, Gloucestershire, 193
Together, 129, 139
Tolkowsky, S., 313
tomatoes, American, 225
Townhill Park, Hampshire, 337

Tradescant, John, 246, 256-257
Tradescant's Heart cherry, 246
Transparent Gage plum, 259
Transparente de Croncels apple, 207
Tresserve, Château de, Savoie, 285
Trier, Germany, 31
Trocadero restaurant, 335
Tschermak, Eric von, 158, 159, 160, 162
Turner, Reggie, 142-144
Twain, Mark, 98
Universal and International Exhibition, Brussels 1935, 281, 328
Urmston, Edward, 69
Vachell, Horace Annesley, 185
Valenciennes, Nord, 328
van Mons, J.B., 237
van Oosten, Henry, 238
Vautier, François, 238
Vavilov, Nicolai, 329-330
vegetable seeds, 222ff.
vegetables, 325-326
'Vegetables for Epicures', 46, 48, 52, 184, 220ff., 293-294, 337, 372
Veitch Memorial Gold Medal, 54, 264, 333
Veitch, Sir Harry, 233, 306, 309
Venette, Nicholas, 238
Ventimiglia, Italy, 295
Verein Deutsche Rosenfreunde, 276
Victoria Medal of Honour, 333
Victoria Wine Company, 180
Villa Boccanegra, Italy, 285, 295
Vincent, Ronald, 265
Vintners' Hall, 171
Virginian strawberry, 248
Vivish & Baker, printers, 215, 257
Vorarlberger Landesbibliothek, 109ff.
Wagonville Horticultural School, 260
Wakehurst Place, Kent, 309
Walnut Competition 1929, 332-333
Walpole, Horace, 81, 96, 99
Walton, William, 60
Ward, Ned, 99
Warley Place, Essex, 53, 285-286
Warre, George, 52, 296
Warre, Norah, 52, 59, 295-298, 300
Waters, Mrs W.G., 179
Webb, Mrs Arthur, 187
Wedgwood, John, 312
Weintraub, Stanley, 142-143
Welby, T. Earle, 183
Wellington, South Africa, 259
Wells, H.G., 99-100
Wensinger, Prof. Arthur S., 124, 129, 132
West, Dr C., 264
West, Rebecca, 185
Wharton, Edith, 296-297, 300
White, Florence, 186
White Alpine strawberry, 248
White Pine strawberry, 248
Whitman, Walt, 98
wild strawberries, 248
Wilde, Oscar, 70, 96, 99, 143
Wilks, Rev. W., 158, 164
Willesborough, Kent, 25
Williams, John, of Pitmaston, 205
Willmott, Ellen, 53, 285-286, 295, 299
Wilson, Edward, 382-383
Wilson, Harriette, 121
Wilson, John, 104
Wilton Diptych, 51, 280, 294
Wine and Food, 28, 49, 60, 62, 64-65, 75-76, 180, 225, 227, 337, 370-371, 382
Wine and Food Society, 49, 56, 62, 65, 178, 179, 180, 182-185, 336ff.
Wine Trade Club, 49
Winter Ribston apple, 205
Wisley gardens, 53, 69, 234, 253, 262, 265, 289, 296
Wittmack, Prof., 164
Wodehouse, P.G., 87
Women's Institute, 187
Wood, Ean, 83
Woolf, Virginia, 81
Worcester, South Africa, 258-259
Wright, John, 21
Wye College of Agriculture, 196, 234, 254, 257, 333
xenia, 157ff.
Ye Sette of Odd Volumes, 336
Yeats, W.B., 100, 185
Yellow Austrian Briar rose, 279, 294
Yellow Warrington gooseberry, 248
Yqem, Château d', 338
Zagros Mountains, Iran, 294
Zéphyrine Drouhin rose, 293
Zoologist, The, 133